Shake It Up Baby!

Shake It Up Baby!

Notes from a pop music reporter
1961-1972

Norman Jopling

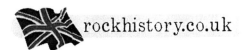
rockhistory.co.uk

Shake it Up Baby!
A RockHistory Book

www.RockHistory.co.uk

1

Published and printed in the United Kingdom and the
United States of America by RockHistory Ltd.

RockHistory Ltd
PO Box 509A, Surrey KT7 0WQ

Cover Design: Raven Design
Book Design: Velin@Perseus-Design.com

PAPERBACK ISBN   978-0-9576881-3-1
EBOOK ISBN   978-0-9576881-4-8

CONTENTS

ACKNOWLEDGEMENTS

SPECIAL thanks to: Mark Rye, Terry Chappell, Mazy Burns, Alan Robertson, Lee Simmonds, Glen Marks, Lucy Jopling, Iker Spozio, Cécile Schott, Peter Burns, Alan Stinton, John Beecher, and everyone else involved for their encouragement, contribution and support.

INTRODUCTION

It's a May morning in 1965 and I'm standing rigid at the edge of a vast indoor soundstage on the set of the Beatles' movie "Help!" – paralysed with indecision and nervousness. With me are two equally immobile colleagues, photographer Feri Lukas and girl reporter Gail Forsythe. Accompanying us are our charges, readers Wendy and Marian, winners of our recent "Meet The Beatles!" competition, here to receive their enviable prize. Wendy and Marian don't seem at all nervous, simply excited, fondly and possibly naively believing all will be well on this their day of days.

I work in London as a young reporter on the weekly pop music newspaper Record Mirror, and what should have been a juicy journalistic assignment is rapidly turning to ashes in my mouth. Earlier this morning I collected Gail and the girls in my battered Mini Cooper and drove like crazy to Twickenham, eventually finding a place to park, bumping into Feri almost by accident, then managing to hassle our way through the studio gates, past the uncomprehending security staff and across the no-go zones; a desperado with four people in tow. But no-one anywhere seems to be aware of any "Meet The Beatles!" competition, and – disturbingly – there's no sign of anyone on the set from the Beatles' management or co-sponsors Radio Luxembourg who could help effect the necessary introductions.

I'm feeling uncharacteristically out of my depth here in big-time movieland, any superficial bravado long evaporated. This huge cavernous space is a-buzz with executives, technicians, cameramen, cast members, money men, several important-looking Americans being loud, all focussing intently on the Fab Four. I feel invisible. The busy Beatles are filming so far in the distance you'd need binoculars to see them distinctly. Every time they break from filming, which is often, they're instantly surrounded by swarms of people. It doesn't look much like fun.

What I must do, I sternly tell myself, is march my troupe on to the set and confront the Beatles. Gulp! But each time I marshal my slender inner resources for this act of boldness, they start filming again. As I dither, various scenarios of humiliation begin to play themselves out in my overheated brain. I foresee visions of their henchmen chucking us off the set, out of the studio and on to the street, from whence I will have to slink away in shame.

The four Beatles are currently the most popular people on the planet, the only planet we know for sure has life, therefore the most popular people in the universe. We, on the other hand, are just a motley bunch of unknowns from a sixpenny pop weekly the Beatles left behind years ago. That was when I'd met Paul McCartney. He'd visited Record Mirror's grubby little West End office with manager Brian Epstein back in October 1962, shortly after their first record "Love Me Do" came out. We sat around joking and talking about rhythm and blues, and afterwards I wrote an article about them, one of the first. That was it. Since then they'd conquered the world while I was still working in the same grubby little office.

Now, at the edge of the "Help!" soundstage, the seconds tick agonisingly by. I become progressively disconsolate. The others are getting impatient, looking to me, the 21-year old 'senior' reporter, for guidance, unaware how frozen I am with trepidation. It's like a bad dream...except here there'll be no waking up.

Then a miracle occurs.

Shooting stops and again the Beatles break off, looking bored. All five of us are watching them intently. Paul steps out of the ring of people surrounding him, takes a breather, looks around. He starts staring in our direction and I could swear he's looking straight at me... but it can't be. Suddenly he breaks away from the crowd, strides over towards us – still looking at me – and when he's twenty yards away calls my name: "Norman!"

This is my cue – and I take it.

I bound on to the set to greet him but he speaks first,

"Norman, great to see you man, what you doing here?"

Leading him over to my little party I explain in broken English: "Record Mirror and Radio Luxembourg…'Meet The Beatles'… competition… the winners…here"

He understands immediately, flashing me a look that puts me completely at ease.

"Leave it to me," he says.

Night instantly becomes day. He can tell who the winners are. He goes straight up to them, grabs their hands.

"Hello, I'm Paul…"

The girls' faces are a joy to behold.

I introduce Paul to Gail and to Feri.

"Come on," he says, escorting Wendy and Marian, taking them by the arm, "I'll introduce you to the others".

My relief is overwhelming.

It feels like a scene from a play…a real-life play. But then it would. Because for the past four years, ever since working at Record Mirror, I've been experiencing the curiously satisfying sensation that I'm a character in a play which is being acted out in the real world, that I've somehow been plucked from my dreary working-class suburban origins and deposited in the middle of pop music heaven and allocated a small but groovy part writing for Record Mirror during the '60s pop music revolution.

It subsequently occurred to me this was a strange thing to happen, particularly as I was no trained writer. I can only surmise my enthusiasm was more important than my dodgy writing skills: a Swedish reader once wrote to us saying she loved Record Mirror because "it was written by men who feel their articles". Or maybe the whole thing, my career in pop music journalism, was simply luck, being in the right place at the right time – although, I guess, that's a kind of a skill in itself.

Writing this now, over forty years later, it would be easy to attribute Paul's bonhomie to the reputation he endured at the time as "the PR man of the Beatles". But that wasn't it at all. That day in 1965, three years after a single conversation, he recognised and remembered me

– a person not in the public eye – after three of the most intense years anyone has ever experienced in the music business or, for that matter, probably any business. You can't fake remembering somebody – recognising their face, knowing their name. How many people did the Beatles meet between October '62 and May '65? From "Love Me Do" to "Help"? From the Cavern to Shea Stadium? Thanks Paul, thanks for remembering, thanks for rescuing me.

Yet even though this felt like a play, I was no student of drama and fondly assumed the play would only get better and better. But drama, onstage or off, requires dramatic elements – up and down and sideways – and these I was destined to experience. Yet those ups and downs were a small price to pay for the satisfaction of my infatuation with pop music. As the character Amanda Prynne famously says in Noel Coward's *Private Lives*, doubtless echoing the sentiments of Coward himself, "Strange how potent cheap music is…"

Potent indeed, and from 1961-1972 I was privileged to observe at first hand the potency and the power – and the strangeness – close-up. For those like me, lucky enough to grow up with the unfolding soundtrack of the seemingly evergreen pop music of the '60s – and for anyone else fascinated by that era – here in comprehensive detail is what it was like to work as a pop music reporter during that golden decade, month by month and year by year. Not just the big-name interviews, but the arcane details: the esoteric R&B columns, the week-in-week-out lists of who was interviewed and profiled, the stories behind the stories, the forgotten and the famous, the passions of the readers, and the day-to-day nuts and bolts of producing a weekly pop newspaper forty-odd years ago. And of course my own youthful thoughts and feelings, and how the job affected every aspect of my life – because for twelve years it was my life. Sounds like a dream job? You bet it was.

4

1944-1960

Pop music. Earliest recollection, sometime in the late 1940s: looking up at my mother ironing as she sings a song –"Buttons & Bows". Later, when I was nine or ten, I was given a wind-up gramophone with a tin of steel needles and a pile of shellac 78s, big ones and little ones, all from the '30s and '40s. The only two I liked were the Latin-American instrumental "Tico Tico" by the organist Ethel Smith which I played over and over, and a funny frantic song about a guy who yodels in Yiddish – long-forgotten music from an era now taught as history yet transmitting a decade-spanning comic vitality…and I can still sing that song today.

A year or so later, when I was eleven, a classmate said: "You've got to come over and hear these records!" That evening in his little living room he took some Bill Haley 78s from a drawer – and he had a proper electric gramophone to play them on. He told me it was called "rock'n'roll". It was an epiphany. All the pop music I'd ever heard was what was broadcast on the the BBC radio's Light Programme. I'd never heard rock'n'roll, never heard country & western, blues, jazz, rhythm & blues. It was akin to the Second Coming. It's all in Haley's music – country, R&B, blues, a few jazz licks.

Early in 1956 newspaper articles began to appear about an American singer with the unearthly name of Elvis Presley. It turned out Haley hadn't been the Second Coming: he'd been John The Baptist to Presley, who even looked like a god. "Obviously not his real name," said another classmate, "no-one could have a real name as great as that". We all agreed – what a name. And we hadn't even heard the record.

Like most great pop records Presley's UK debut "Heartbreak Hotel" didn't grab you straightaway. It wasn't like a better sort of Bill Haley. It wasn't fast or frantic, didn't have that Haley swing. It was moody, bluesy, doomy, with a stabbing rock guitar and jazzy piano solo and a voice that went with the looks and went with the name and mumbled words so incoherently to English ears so that they slid into each other in an exciting sexy way. Not that I knew what "sexy" was, having only just learned the 'facts of life' in the same playground.

Rock'n'roll began to trickle in to Britain despite sparse encouragement from the media establishment which regarded it as a gimmick – but good for mockery. Soon, Little Richard emerged – exploded, more like – revealing the awesome power of black R&B, while "Why Do Fools Fall In Love" by Frankie Lymon and the Teenagers, a huge hit, sounded to me, with that squawking instrumentation, Frankie's golden, heavenly, passionate, unbroken voice and his group's strange thrilling vocal harmonies, like something the Martians had brought down with them as a gift, something new and wonderful for the human race to enjoy. How could anyone not be happy with this music happening?

We didn't have a record player, but the rock'n'roll and skiffle kept on coming: another friend one day insisted I hear a record titled "That'll Be The Day" by the Crickets. It opened up something in my head that recognised this was on another level somehow: the mixture of country and black music and blues, and the beat was a little different. The voice transfixed me

I sold my Triang train set, my prized layout with sidings, bridges, three locos, turntable, signals, that filled our front room still almost a parlour, and bought a little single-play record player, two LPs, "The Chirping Crickets", "Elvis's Golden Records", and some 45s: oldies "Diana", "Be-Bop-A-Lula", and newies "All I Have To Do Is Dream", "Endless Sleep" and hit the record trail for myself.

My family – mother Dorothy, father Ernest, and me – had moved to Wood Green in North London from Edmonton in late 1953 when I was nine. It was "a step up", and probably still is, as Wood Green was considered 'better' than Edmonton. Nowadays it's still a bit dearer – but not much 'better'. My dad worked as a machine operator all his life in a factory, the wire-weaving 'shop' at Sparklets Siphons, part of British Oxygen in Edmonton, and he was one of the self-educated working class who didn't expect any more from life for himself, but held hopes for his child. All those siphons with all that wire wrapped round them and he never drank a whiskey-and-soda in his life. My mum did various jobs; shops, factories, piece-work, whatever was available, to subsidise my dad's paltry wage. They had it hard, and their parents, my grandparents, from what I heard had it even harder.

I didn't know about the weekly music papers till I started cutting out the Top Ten list every week from my dad's weekly Sunday newspaper the News Of The World with the credit "Chart compiled by Record Mirror". I enquired about this Record Mirror at the local newsagent and found out about Record Mirror, New Musical Express and Melody Maker – which was of no interest to me then because it was all about jazz. New Musical Express was the best of the bunch, but Record Mirror was also interesting; too much show-business, but with good record reviews. I began buying them both but gave up on Record Mirror when, after the long printers' strike in 1959, it re-emerged even quainter as Record And Show Mirror. By that time there was a new contender, Disc, which was very good and seemed more modern. All the music papers were tabloid format, though Melody Maker was a bit smaller, but most other newspapers were broadsheet, including the News Of The World which was Britain's biggest-selling newspaper, mainly on the strength of its in-depth reportage of the week's most salacious sex scandals...and its excellent sports reportage.

Now I needed money. The quid a week from my parents, generous, really, couldn't buy me enough clothes or records. So I left school at 16 and took a bog standard junior clerk job at the Cambridge University Press's Education Department in Euston Road. After giving my parents a quid, I had three pounds weekly left after tax. In quick succession I bought a peach of a small transistor radio in a red leather case, plenty of records, and a new outfit: a bespoke double-breasted bumfreezer jacket in a subtle green Harris Tweed, dark brown trousers, loafers. I'd ditch the look in a year, but loved it for a few months. Took the tube to work, and every lunchtime when the weather wasn't terrible walked up Tottenham Court Road and explored Soho.

That winter I discovered alcohol. None of us, me or my friends, drank, yet. It was at a party one Saturday evening in a big house in a private road off Muswell Hill. Very middle-class – the hostess was a fellow student at Hornsey College Of Arts and Crafts, where I attended part-time (in the hope of soon being offered a full-time course). I started drinking: gin. It was wonderful. They kept playing Johnny & The Hurricanes' "Rocking Goose" and Ray Charles' "Georgia On My Mind". Staggering back down the hill to the gates at Alexandra Palace, the magic lights of the cars weaving by, falling down painlessly, finally arriving home, the lock constantly avoiding the key, the world transformed. What a discovery!

1961

I decided I wanted to work in Soho. Didn't much care what I did, as long as I could do it there. This was early January 1961, and the deadly tedium of six months at the Cambridge University Press had provoked this ambition in me – my first real ambition. It was a bit vague, to be sure, but for someone utterly clueless about personal advancement it was to prove of momentous import.

As luck – or destiny – would have it, I was mooching around the West End during my lunch break when I spotted a sign next to a doorway in Oxford Street – "Soho Youth Employment Bureau". I resolved to investigate, assuming that there must be legions of dissatisfied teenagers like me, all with vague semi-romantic yearnings to work in tawdry yet glamorous Soho and that these misfits were being specifically catered for by this minor branch – a twig, even – of the Ministry Of Social Security.

The next day I ventured up the rickety stairs and into a bare anteroom with just a couple of chairs and a few Social Security posters on the wall. I sat down. After a minute or so I realised I was experiencing a most uncommon feeling: that I was a character in a play which was being acted out in the real world.

There was only one other door in the room and it was shut so I moved my chair around a bit to make a noise. This other door then opened and out came a nondescript middle-aged man who indicated for me to follow him into an inner office.

There was a desk and two chairs, we sat down and he asked me what I wanted to do. I told him I wanted to work in Soho, which seemed to satisfy him.

"How old are you?"

"Sixteen."

"Are you working now?"

"Cambridge University Press, Euston Road."

"Yes I know the place. How many GCEs?"

"Three." I had English Language, English Literature, and English Economic History.

He began sifting through a card index file, telling me about the available jobs in Soho and the West End that required three GCEs. They all sounded terrible. So we went through the two GCE jobs. They all sounded terrible too. The last category was the one GCE jobs (that one GCE always had to be English Language) and there were a lot of these not-so-fussy jobs. Once again nothing grabbed me.

"Well," he said mildly, "you are hard to please".

He paused, looked through the index file again, then, with almost stage-y surprise, noticed some barrel scrapings, a couple of lonely cards at the end of the box.

"There's a couple here don't care if you've got any GCEs or not. Don't s'pose you're interested?"

I thought his surprise was strange because the card index box was the very nub of his job and he should have known the cards intimately, like a book or stamp dealer would know his stock. Still, maybe previous applicants had always snatched jobs from the upper echelons and he'd never ventured down this far. Nevertheless I had a suspicious feeling he was playing a game with me.

"Yes please," I said brightly. I wanted to check out the lot.

The first job was as a factotum at a glossy-sounding marketing company in Savile Row owned by a prominent MP. It was easily the best job so far.

"Sounds all right," said I.

"Good," he said, "that's that then." He wanted to get rid of me. I guess I was becoming tiresome.

"What about the last job," I asked, "then I've seen them all."

10

"Oh, this one," he said offhandedly, "they want an office boy at the Record & Show Mirror in Shaftesbury Avenue".

I actually felt the words coming out of his mouth and into my ears and into my brain, which then pounded like I'd won the Pools.

"Yes, that's the one I want!" I was emphatic.

"Excellent," he said, almost smirking, "I knew we'd find you a job." He seemed as relieved as me.

He made a call to a number on the card, spoke a bit, put down the phone and told me to be there at 4.30pm the next day. I was to see a Mr Isadore Green. He noted down the details, gave them to me, wished me luck. I thanked him and floated away. The possibility I might not get the job never entered my mind.

Human nature appears to magnify the importance of matters of personal interest and so next day I went goofing like a rube along Shaftesbury Avenue looking for the Record & Show Mirror HQ, figuring it to be some impressive edifice. Nearing the magic number I found merely a row of shops. 116 – Egmont House – was simply a large doorway with a polished granite portico in the Egyptian style sandwiched between an expensive (though flashy) men's outfitters called Gaylord, and Drum City, the percussionists' paradise. There were four brass push-bells and several brass plates, including a nicely polished one for Zahar the dentist, another simply for Record Mirror, not even updated to Record & Show Mirror, which it became in 1959. This was nothing more than converted apartment premises above shops.

I had no time to ponder on my misconceptions and went straight in, through a gloomy hall and up a curved flight of stone stairs that wound around to face the first floor entrance, the doorway to Record & Show Mirror. How many times have I subsequently visited surreal variations of this hall and this staircase in my dreams.

It was indeed a converted apartment, and not a big one either. The front door opened to a short corridor with a door on the left two yards down which I would discover was a toilet, the dingiest I ever encountered before or since, a room opposite on the right, used for accounts, advertising and circulation personnel (sometimes all in the same person), and a further door on the right – a green door – which was closed. The corridor opened out into a small reception area with a room off it to the left, and contained, among much else, a desk supporting an ancient switchboard that seemed far too big and complex for such a small organisation, occupied by a classy blonde in a tailored suit who looked like the actress Jill Bennett, and who had the trick of being both cool and friendly at the same time. When I explained my purpose she spoke to somebody on yet another telephonic device, a complicated-looking intercom, and following a short response, informed me that Mr. Green would see me shortly. She invited me to take a seat in a chair by the desk, so I sat down, relaxed, and began soaking up the atmosphere.

And what atmosphere. It was dingy, grubby, show-bizzy, bundles of newspapers everywhere. I waited and waited and people came in and out, up and down the stairs, glamorous people. To my suburban gaze they looked like film stars. The women, cosmopolitan, sophisticated, fresh; the men, the journalists, in rumpled velvet jackets or tonic suits, exuding a jazzy aura – a parade of superbeings who without exception were extremely nice to me, not to mention gracious, especially when learning of my mission.

As I waited I fell in love. A deep and profound desire to become part of this place enveloped me. I felt like I'd arrived home.

I waited half an hour then Mr Isadore Green summoned me: "Behind the green door," said the receptionist.

I entered with trepidation and justly so. Nothing could have prepared me for the Aladdin's cave within. Mr Green's office was the biggest room in the apartment, much of it occupied by a huge table creaking under the weight of papers, books of all description, assorted cups, saucers, pens, pencils, photographs, records, typewriters, several telephones and much, much else, a huge haphazard mass, or mess, of show-business debris that must have taken years to accumulate. I was so flabbergasted at the sight of this formidable array of stuff that my first thought – because, I suppose, I was still partly in that state I'd fallen into yesterday where I felt like a character in a real-life play – was that no movie set could ever possibly duplicate the sheer authenticity of this fantastic scene.

Isadore Green sat in a comfily battered old chair at the long side of the table facing a large window overlooking Shaftesbury Avenue and Frith Street. He gestured to me to sit in a chair on the opposite side of the desk and before saying anything paused briefly to size me up, while I, in my turn, took in the rest of his incredible office.

The walls were plastered with posters, bits of paper, notes, memos and photographs. Records – LPs mostly – were heaped on the floor and under the desk, some intact, some sleeveless. A naturally tidy person, I nevertheless nurture a secret admiration for those who can blithely live and work in the midst of chaos, disdaining the prissiness of order. Isadore Green's office was the epitome of chaos – and show business chaos too – and I was utterly awestruck.

"The Green Man" himself, for that was the title of his editorial column in Record & Show Mirror, was short and stocky, indeterminate middle-age, evidently Jewish, several chins but not a soft-looking man, in fact slightly pugnacious with a couple of chipped teeth on view. Crinkly greying hair greased back on a round head with narrow eyes and wearing a well-worn buttoned-up grey double-breasted suit with a white handkerchief and pen sticking out of the top pocket, white shirt and broad-striped tie.

He came to the point straightaway, spreading his hands in a forlorn gesture.

"I should have taken that advertisement out months ago my boy, the position was filled, our photographer's son, he took the job on, I'm very sorry."

Upon hearing this worse-than-bad news, I can only assume some profoundly woeful expression must have passed across my face indicating my utter desolation and communicating to him my heart's desire to work in this place.

Struck dumb with disappointment I just sat staring at him, presumably slack-jawed and hollow-eyed, or some such dismal expression. A black void of panic started welling up inside me and I thought, No, I can't have been brought this close and then for it not to happen, it isn't right, what will I do, how will I live with it? I felt seriously bad. I couldn't move. Issy stared at me, looked down, then looked up again, then came out with it. He knew.

"I tell you what," he offered, "Douglas'll be here for a few months more, then he'll be going to work for his father. I don't know when he's going, but that's when we'll need an office boy."

I anticipated he was about to palm me off with a "We'll call you then" sop to spare himself the discomfort of outright rejection. I was wrong. He was either a quick thinker or maybe the whole routine was a test.

"Look, my boy," he went on, "if you really want the job then come up here every week on Thursday after your work and when the time comes we'll tell you when Douglas'll leave. Then you give your present employer notice on the Friday and start the job the following week after you've served out your notice. How does that sound?"

It sounded good. Lost in admiration at this happy solution and with hope restored, I nodded acknowledgement, thanked him, and was dismissed. So I was to be part of the club after all. No, I was already part of the club – he'd made that clear. He could have shooed me away but he saw something in me, knew this was where I belonged... well, that's what I've always told myself. Yet that's what it felt like at the time, at that crucial crossroads.

"How did it go?" asked the receptionist. Light-headed with joy, I gushed the whole story to her. Now I could really talk to her, I could gabble and babble to her now that I too was part of all this: we were in it together. I told everybody there, and everybody was happy for me.

I began my weekly pilgrimages to R&SM, generating much gentle mockery of me by the staff, and 'regulars'. I became a fixture, hanging around for an hour or so every Thursday evening, staking my claim and chatting to all and sundry including cocky Douglas who assured me he was moving to a far better job than this one, a job working as an apprentice lensman for his photographer father Bill Williams, who, somewhat mysteriously as I was later to learn, was also head of catering at New Scotland Yard. Flash but friendly, Douglas regularly updated me on his own prospects and therefore mine, passed me various tips about the job, none of which I can now remember except the advice not to bother to wash my hands as they'd always straightaway get filthy again from handling all the newsprint.

Fascinating people came and went including, most memorably, the celebrated midget Wee Georgie Wood, delivering his Record & Show Mirror column on a Thursday evening, a tiny brown wizened creature looking like a little old elf wearing a flat cap and a boy's overcoat trudging up the stairs straight into Issy's office.

The Great Day came sooner than expected. One Thursday evening about five weeks after the interview, Issy summoned me. Though brusque, he was nevertheless complacent at his ability to fulfil his promise.

"Douglas is leaving next week. You can give them your notice tomorrow and start Monday week. How much are they paying you?"

"Four pounds fifteen a week," I said, adding quickly, "but as it's my birthday next week, I'd get another pound a week."

"Then you can start here at six pounds a week," beamed Issy, the soul of generosity. Five bob extra wasn't much, but it was something. I'd be earning more than my mates, but I would have worked there for nothing. It was 1961. I'd be seventeen. I would be office boy at Record & Show Mirror. I would be in heaven.

At the luxuriously late starting time of 9.30am on my firstMonday morning at Record & Show Mirror I raced up the stairs – but the door was locked. This was baffling. Did I get the date wrong, shouldn't somebody be here by now? Had they gone bust and nobody told me? Had it all been a joke, a dream?

I decided to stay calm, wait, and sit down on the stairs. Sure enough, ten minutes later someone appeared. Six foot three, two-button midnight blue tonic suit, white shirt, thin blue silk tie, suede shoes, broad shoulders, handsome as anything – matinee idol looks. It was the famous Peter Jones, the paper's top free-lance journalist. Monday was one of his two days a week at Record & Show Mirror – that's why I'd never seen him before. Amiable and charming, he introduced himself, opened up the office, suggested I make some tea. He showed me the tea and coffee stuff in the back room off the reception area, gas ring on the floor, together with piles of the unsold back issues known as returns. Like the rest of the apartment it was an organised mess, seedy, and dingy too, with a single window looking out over nothing really, just a sort of a well comprised of the backs of nearby buildings.

I put on the kettle and went to chat with Peter in Issy's office. He told me he was usually the earliest to arrive: nobody bothered to get in much before ten. Then he wandered out the room for something.

15

"Fire!"

At first I thought he was joking, but rushed out anyway and to my horror saw that smoke was billowing through the office. In the back room flames were everywhere, bundles of returns ablaze – I'd managed to set fire to the office in my first five minutes on the job.

Racing in and out of the toilet-washroom with various receptacles, Peter and I managed to dump enough water to put out the fire, but one entire wall of the back office was badly singed, most of the paint on the door was flaking, and the floor was a sodden mess, bits of burnt newspaper everywhere. And it smelled. It didn't help that the other employees were by now trooping in, every one of them highly amused in his or her own sardonic manner by this unexpected diversion, the saga of which had rapidly reached dramatic proportions of embroidery as told by the delighted Peter Jones.

I spent the next hour frantically trying to clear up the mess till Issy arrived, who took a perfunctory look at the damage, told me to fix it, and demanded tea.

"He likes his tea hot," they all sniggered.

I had no idea why they were sniggering till I presented a cup of tea to Issy, who took one sip and started shouting at me that the tea was stone-cold and I was a useless tea maker – what good was I if I couldn't make a decent cup of tea?

Undeterred I made a fresh pot. It was an old metal tea pot, a green one, and Issy's cup and saucer was also green. His tea had to be served in the green cup and saucer. My second attempt brought even more invective than the first. I retreated to consider my tactics.

There was little time to think because he kept shouting for his 'decent cup of tea', to great amusement from all present. My next plan, which I thought was a brilliant strategy, was to make the tea, then when it was brewed re-boil it in the metal tea pot over the gas ring, have the milk next to Issy's office so the tea had as little time to cool as possible. I arranged this with military precision, closely observed by the sniggering staffers.

I made the third pot of tea, checked it was brewed – or stewed – thoroughly, re-boiled it, poured it into a heated cup, dashed through the reception area, gave it a splash of milk and ran into Issy's office and thrust it in front of him. It was so hot I couldn't touch the cup. Defiantly I stayed to watch. He picked it up and drained it in one gulp.

"Luke warm," he said, "is this the best you can do? Try harder next time."

The making of copious amounts of tea and coffee for everyone gave me some sort of focus that first day. There was also the damage to repair: for most of the rest of the week I was scraping burnt paint off the door and clearing up the mess. Issy couldn't have cared less about it, never gave it a second glance – but there was a reason for his unconcern.

For all his journalistic ability, popularity among London's show-business fraternity, personal charisma and enviable reputation, Isadore Green was yesterday's man. Changing the name and format of Record Mirror two years earlier to Record & Show Mirror had been a disaster. I didn't know till later but the circulation had fallen to a pathetic seventeen thousand copies weekly. NME was selling several times that.

And Issy didn't own the paper. At some juncture Issy and his various shareholders, mostly show-biz cronies like Norman Wisdom and Eddie Calvert, had sold out to the mighty Decca Record Company. Every week Decca would send a company accountant to check the books, but with gentlemanly forbearance did not attempt to influence the editorial content of the paper. It was supposed to be a secret but all the industry knew, which is why Decca's rival EMI seldom advertised. Enough, however, was evidently enough, even for Decca's brilliant and benign boss, Sir Edward Lewis.

One day, later that first week, I was on my hands and knees scraping some final flecks of burnt paint off the woodwork when I heard an unfamiliar voice.

"If you didn't want to work here Norman, you just should have said so, not tried to burn the bloody place down."

I looked up and saw a tall lanky man, small black goatee, Scots accent, blazer and flannels.

"I'm Jim Watson," he said, "I'm your new editor from next month."

My duties at Record & Show Mirror were thus: Teamaking, which included coffee, Horlicks, Ovaltine. Delivering the new edition of the paper on foot to Denmark Street ("Tin Pan Alley"), Shaftesbury Avenue & environs, and on the van to the West End and the City. Printing addresses on the subscription wrappers. Sticking stamps on said wrappers. Wrapping the subscriptions. Dragging the sacks full of subscriptions to the Post Office in Gerrard Street. Compiling the charts. General dogsbody.

The most important member of the editorial team was corduroy-jacketed Ian Dove, of wry expression, crooked nose, and sharp intelligence. Not only was Ian a fine journalist, but also a talented cartoonist – and he designed the paper's lay-outs: he was the sub-editor. It was Ian who put the paper to bed on Tuesday at the Merritt & Hatcher printing press in High Wycombe. The printing process was letterpress – hot metal, linotype, closer to Gutenburg than to today's digital technology…and this only 50-odd years ago. Size of the tabloid Record & Show Mirror would depend on the amount of advertising – anywhere from twelve to twenty four pages. Ian calculated it after a weekly staff meeting when he would be told how much advertising was scheduled for the next issue and thus could work out how many pages we could afford. He would allocate the forthcoming advertisements, features, reviews, news stories, letters, photographs and charts to each page, then throughout the week design the individual pages to a five-column format, write the headlines, and give them to the printer's messenger who called late each afternoon to deliver the latest galley proofs and collect the layouts. And that's how it went, week after week, month after month, year after year.

The first issue I delivered to the local newsagents and music publishers was No.336, week ending March 4th 1961. The front cover summed it up: a shorts-clad Marty Wilde beaming during his South Africa tour triumph; a shot from *King Kong*, an all-African jazz musical opening at the Princes Theatre; a little news photo of '50s hitmaker Eddie Calvert headed "Still the man with the Golden Trumpet" – Eddie had entertained at the Variety Club Of Great Britain Annual Dinner at the Dorchester the previous week. Inside the twenty pages were such attractions as Marty being mobbed by an audience of all-white all-female teenagers in Johannesburg, Beryl Reid readying for the West End revue *Pied Piper Of Hamelin*, a featurette on Nero & The Gladiators, a UK instrumental outfit dressed in ancient Roman togs – and togas – who scored an instrumental hit with a rocked-up Grieg's "In The Hall Of The Mountain King". There was a terrific jazz page from Benny Green, two or three pages on *King Kong*: "King Kong – It Can't Go Wrong!" (it did), bits on Russ Conway, Shirley Bassey, Shirley Abicair ("Zither Girl's Biggest Test"), the Green Man page, which was Issy schmoozing his show-biz cronies, the *Pepe* movie premiere, two pages of singles reviews by David Gell and Don Player (the same person), loads of little show-biz news stories, plus dozens of small ads including a page crammed with single-column contact ads for individual artists with their photos and agent's addresses and phone numbers, or, for the agent-less artists, their personal addresses and/or phone numbers – oh, innocent days. It was the newspaper equivalent of Issy's desk. Anyone over fifty reading it now would most likely find it addictively fascinating. But back then, man, it was square.

The column of charts on page 19 comprised *Britain's Top Ten, the 'Second Ten', Best Sellers By British Artists,* and *Best Selling Long-Players First Five*. There was a curious section next to them: nearly two pages devoted to "Record Dealers' Best Sellers". These were little top tens from individual record shops all over the country – Bobby's Records from Welling, Kent, Leading Lighting in Chapel Market, Imhofs in New Oxford Street, Sonic Studios in Weymouth, The Turntable in Erith Kent, The Music Salon in Wembley, Al's Records, E17, Gamages, Holborn, and dozens more, all returning similar yet slightly different top tens. They were the sales returns the main charts were compiled from, and, I guess, tiny free advertisements to encourage the shops to submit those returns.

Our advertising manager was also our circulation manager, Roy Burden, a gruff yet genial charmer for whom Record & Show Mirror's proximity to Ronnie Scott's Jazz Club, just round the corner in Gerrard Street, then almost Oriental-less, was a distinct bonus. Roy loved the jazz milieu, as did Ian Dove: Peter Jones' tastes veered more towards show-biz and pop.

On the Friday after I joined, the classy blonde receptionist left. There had been a thing with one of the guys, something unresolved. On the Monday we had a new receptionist – Pamela Blee. Elegant, good-looking, a West London super-modernist, Pam was the same age as me but immediately copped an attitude of imperceptible superiority, like a slightly older sister. All the blokes – Peter, Roy, Jimmy, and particularly Ian – adored her. Her boyfriend Peter rode a Vespa GS, and I wanted one of those machines so badly I carried on and on about it. To my surprise Roy offered to lend me £50, to be paid back at a pound a week. A brand-new metallic silver-grey Italian-styled ultra-flash GS was ninety-something quid then, and I already had £40 saved. Suddenly I had wheels.

Climax of the working week was when the hot-off-the-press papers were delivered to the office by van man Fred on Wednesday morning. Everyone was excited: no-one had yet seen a finished version of the new edition, not even Ian. We'd rip open the first bundle – thirteen quire, twenty four papers in a quire, the quires one way up then the other so you could check the folded side and grab the right number of papers. We'd all snatch a paper, race through it, oohs and ahhs, curses at overlooked literals, and then suddenly it was history: everyone was already working on the next issue. Fred, our part-time driver, hung around and drank coffee while I grabbed as many papers as I could carry to do my first round on foot – back through Newport Court to Solossy's, along Charing Cross Road to Dobells Jazz, then Apollo Music on the corner of Cambridge Circus, in and out the instrument shops, down Denmark Street and up and down all the rickety stairs to deliver half a quire each to the music publishers, who'd instantly start flipping frantically through the pages. I'd detour back to the office, grab another batch and race round to finish the job, dropping the last few off at Imhofs, dash back with the returns and cash, drop them off at the office. Then Fred and I would jump in the van – a battered Bedford Dormobile with an unpredictable sliding door – and career off round the West End, Bloomsbury, the City and Mile End. After a few weeks I knew all the stops and all the orders and all the proprietors. In a jiffy I could grab the right amount of papers from the bundles in the back, jump off the van and deliver them, figure out what was owed after deducting the returns, race back to the van. Fred drove while I'd sit with the door jammed open, leg braced on the inside wheel arch, no belt of course, sorting the papers for the next drop, reading the new paper, clocking the scene. Tea from a

Thermos and sandwiches on the move. We were on the ball, the first music paper out there. Thrilling!

The thrill wore off with the Wednesday afternoon task: subscriptions. I'd fold the papers, wrap them, stick them down (with a strip of sticky brown paper that had been damped), make sure they stayed stuck, and load up the sacks for the Post Office. Messy, sticky, dirty, newsprint everywhere. Mr Frankham, the Decca accountant, took an accountant's interest in this procedure, quizzing me whether cancelled subscriptions had been cancelled and new subscriptions were being sent out immediately. The addresses of the subscriptions were printed on to the wrappers by a noisy heavy little hand-operated device which needed constant loading with metal plates, each plate embossed with the address of the subscriber. It had to be bashed in a certain way to get the address printed properly. If the plates hadn't arrived for the new subs then the addresses would be hand-written. Frankham once asked if I'd "had any new plates lately" which prompted suppressed guffaws from Ian and Peter who were hovering over the nearby gas ring: "plates" (and "plating") being a possibly now redundant term for fellatio, a fact then unknown to myself and apparently Mr Frankham. Final job of the day would be staggering with the sackfuls of subscriptions to the Post Office round the corner in Gerrard Street, dumping them off, then home on the tube, Piccadilly Line from Leicester Square to Wood Green.

The second issue of Record & Show Mirror that I delivered was the last under that title. More of the same editorially, with the biggest spread given to the Bristol opening of "The Music Man", and the back page devoted entirely to George Formby, who'd died that week. Appropriate that George and Record & Show Mirror crossed over together. And then Issy vanished. Whatever goodbyes he said to the others, he never said a word to me. One day he was just gone. No more scalding cups of tea. The Green Door sign was taken down and Jimmy Watson took over his office and the Herculean task of clearing it up.

Later that year Issy launched Show Pictorial, which ran for a few issues then flopped. Not long after that he died. I have no idea what Issy did for anyone else – much, I suspect – but what he did for me was beyond gratitude. Nevertheless, thank you Issy, thank you so much.

Record & Show Mirror metamorphosed into New Record Mirror, a leaner and cleaner looking paper, almost no show-biz, and a number of interesting innovations. Expert jazzer Benny Green's Modern Jazz column became a regular weekly feature, as did the expert James Asman, who wrote about Country & Western and Traditional Jazz. Asman was a died-in-the-wool traditionalist, a bearded giant who ran a quirky record shop in New Row off St Martin's Lane, and by "traditional jazz" did not mean Barber, Ball & Bilk. Countrypolitan wasn't his thing either – Don Gibson, Patsy Cline, Floyd Cramer – to him they were pop stars. Reading Asman's and Benny's columns week after week was an education. Readers' letters, news spreads and singles reviews stayed pretty much the same, but with the non-existent Don Player dispensed with. Jimmy took over the LP reviews, a job considered the editor's perk as he could flog the albums, or at least the ones he managed to hide from the rest of the staff who were not shy with their requests. Unfortunately Jimmy was no great shakes as a writer, and during his considerable absences I occasionally found Ian and Peter in fits of laughter reading out his reviews to each other.

All the same, Jimmy started moving the paper ahead quickly: one of his best innovations was to print *The Cash Box Top 30*, "air mailed from New York", and beneath it a list of five "Likely Entries". For hard-core fans of US pop – and there were plenty of them – this was a must. Circulation improved immediately. The "air mailed from New York" bit ensured we published the American Top 30 a few days before the imported US music trade weekly Cash Box was available at Solossy's in Charing Cross Road, the best newsagent in London. Not only were we ahead of the NME, who used the Billboard chart, but we published ten more entries plus the five likely entries. Hot stuff!

Mondays I'd start working on compiling the UK Top Twenty. We dropped the individual retailers' top tens and soon there were so few returns that by the time I'd calculated the top fifteen or sixteen singles, the bottom four or five could have been any one of a dozen. So I'd pick what I thought was likeliest...or what I liked best. We quickly dropped *Best Sellers By British Artists* and expanded the five *LP Hits* into a Top Ten LPs. Once the charts were calculated I'd phone them through to Ian at the printers and give them to Pam so she could recite them, dozens of times, to the publishers, agents, record companies and assorted music business others who wanted the info pre-publication

Ever since the mechanical syndication of popular music – printed sheet music, cylinder rolls, records (78s, LPs, 45s, cassettes, CDs) – there've been lists of best-sellers. Sometimes these hit lists – the charts – are brim-full of goodies, in other eras mediocrity reigns. After the US payola scandal in 1959, the US charts reflected the cleaned-up state of American radio and became a lot more "adult". For "adult" read "dreary". In Record & Show Mirror, week ending January 28th 1961, NY's top five in descending order was "Exodus" – Ferrante & Teicher, "Wonderland By Night" – Bert Kaempfert, "Will You Love Me Tomorrow" – Shirelles, "Calcutta" – Lawrence Welk, "Are You Lonesome Tonight" – Elvis. Thank goodness for the Shirelles!

But as 1961 progressed, the US chart started to get better. Maybe it was the doo-wop revival, maybe the advent of the Twist, maybe a new generation of rock'n'rollers, maybe the sheer commercial appeal of R&R-oriented pan-American rhythm & blues, maybe the rise of the girl groups, maybe the Brill Building hit factory. By April the US top five looked like this: "Blue Moon" – Marcels, "Runaway" – Del Shannon, "Mother In Law" – Ernie K-Doe, "But I Do" – Clarence 'Frogman' Henry, "100 Pounds Of Clay" – Gene McDaniels. The Gene McDaniels record may be pure kitsch, but can anyone hear the line "...then he rolled his big sleeves up" without cracking a grin?

I studied all this closely. One of my office boy tasks was to get "the papers" from Solossy's, and "the papers" included Billboard, Variety and Cash Box. I read them cover to cover every week, as well as our rivals NME, Melody Maker and Disc.

One day Ian asked me if I could write. I told him I'd been good at essays at school, which was why I'd passed English Economic History when I didn't even know what the word "economic" meant. He gave me a press release and asked me to re-write it. I couldn't. It was beyond me. I couldn't make any sense of it in the first place.

Our circulation began to pick up and all the staff were gung-ho in the cause. Sometimes on Sundays, Jimmy, Roy and me would meet and go out in the Dormabile, stick up posters around North London, then head for the queues outside cinemas for the evening's live music performances. We'd hand out free New Record Mirrors (the previous week's returns) to the kids. I was a kid too, but now I was an insider.

When no-one else wanted to go to pop concerts, I got the tickets. One Sunday in April I went to a show at the Albert Hall, and on Monday Ian asked me how it went. Great, I said, especially because the Adam Faith fans had been so noisy and impatient during the other acts. Ian asked me to write a review, which I did, and pretty terrible it must have been because he completely re-wrote the whole thing and made it much more journalistic, taking an indignant line to the effect that these fans were spoiling it for the well-behaved majority. It wasn't true: everybody loved the mad fans, but I got the picture – it was a good hook for a story. I guess it was a bit like acting a part – it was a lot easier to write something around an attitude. The pompous piece started out with the sentence "I say that a small minority of the audience at the second BBC 'Beat Show' put on the worst display of ill-manners since last year's Beaulieu Jazz Festival fiasco" and went on – and on – in much the same vein. It was published in the next edition and Ian put my first by-line on it (though the 'g' was left off my surname, not for the last time). That was nice but I had that slightly shameful feeling that I'd been given the credit for something I hadn't done.

As the year progressed New Record Mirror improved even more. The format bedded down and felt right. It was tight and looked good. To reflect the current trad craze, which was huge in the clubs – even my local Fishmongers Arms in Wood Green was regularly crammed – Ian started a newsy Trad Scene column. I never discovered what James Asman thought about it, but I can guess. Kenny Ball was becoming a massive hitmaker, the other trad bands, especially Acker Bilk, were pulling big crowds even at pop festivals, and the related '20s syncopation pastiche of the Temperance Seven was a chart-topping phenomenon.

One day I idly penned a collection of snippets from items culled from the US trade mags which I entitled *A Look At The US Charts*, commenting on the mutually successful splits of certain singers and their former vocal backing groups: Dion and The Belmonts, Rosie and The Originals, Cathy Jean and The Roomates, and Ben E. King and The Drifters. It was published, proved popular and soon metamorphosed into a regular item which appeared under Ian's Top Twenty Comment on the Charts Page.

A Look At The US Charts soon crystallised into three short paragraphs. The first paragraph began with "Fast rising US hits include" and listed half a dozen hits 'with a bullet' that hadn't yet reached our Likely Entries chart. The second paragraph began with "New US releases include" and listed half a dozen or so new releases I considered interesting. The third paragraph was a collection of snippets of fairly esoteric chart facts culled from either Cash Box or Billboard. I figured I'd be pleased to know this information if I was buying a pop paper. The formula worked: *A Look At The US Charts* would run for years. I was right – it was what our readers wanted. And I wasn't ashamed of the little 'NJ' after it.

I continued to obsessively pore over Cash Box and Billboard, musing especially on the crazy names of the groups thrown up by the US doo-wop revival. Inspired by their lunacy, I scrawled a light-hearted piece categorising and gently sending up this plethora of zaniness. I showed it to Ian who took it from me without a word. In the next issue it was published in the prime feature spot at the top of page three with my correctly-spelled by-line and a photo of the Coasters, which I guessed was the closest picture Ian could find of a doo-wop group. He must have typed it up, did a brief editing job as it was published more-or-less as I'd originally written it, and told everyone to keep quiet that he was running it:

w/e 29th July 1961
ALL THOSE WEIRD, WILD AND WONDERFUL
NAMES, NAMES, NAMES, NAMES, NAMES, NAMES,
NAMES, NAMES, NAMES,

For a record to be a hit in the States nowadays, it needs just one of three things: either a good song, a good singer, or a group with a crazy name singing on it. And just lately, records in the last category have been appearing in gay profusion all over the best-sellers.

25

The first spate came with such teams as Kathy Young and the Innocents, Rochelle and the Candles, and Rosie and the Originals.

Then Shep and the Limelites, Cathy Jean and the Roomates (all boys), and B.Bumble and the Stingers.

Now we have such groups as Rose's Baby Dolls, T.P. and the Turnpikes, and Mad Mike and Maniacs rearing their heads in the vicinity of the charts.

But it was certainly no overnight phenomenon which made the rock groups pluck up courage enough to invent names for themselves as mad as these.

It seems to have been a gradual process, stemming from the birth of Rock'n'Roll music, for even then, there were groups with names which then seemed most outlandish.

Yet compared with some of today's monstrosities they pale into insignificance.

For instance, what have the Clovers, the Chordettes, or the Teenagers got on Gabriel and the Angels, Randy and the Holidays, or Rick and the Keens?

Some of the efforts after 1956 became a little more imaginative though, with the accent on nature's creatures as the main theme.

We had the Crickets, the Impalas, the Penguins, the Teddy Bears, the Flamingoes, ad infinitum.

Others persisted in telling their audiences the noise they made on record. There were the Wailers, the Shouters, the Ravers, the Coasters and the Chanters. Akin to these were the combos which told all and sundry the number of personnel in their outfit. Like the Two-Timers, the Three Friends, the Four Sportsmen, the Jive Five and the Six-Teens.

The majority took the easy way out and used the suffix "tones". This led to the Truetones, the Timetones, the Bosstones, the Jivetones, the Rocktones, the Larktones, the Temptones, the Youngtones, the Softones, and the Cleftones.

The amazing thing is that only a tiny percentage of old Rock groups still make records; after their initial hit (or flop) they seem to fade away. Or maybe they change their name and start all over again.

Anyway, so many groups are popping up that various muddles have occurred. Apart from the British and American Drifters mix-up, a more recent example has been pushed into the charts via the athletic-sounding Marathons.

Now the "Cash Box" top hundred, which not only lists all the hit records but also all the artists who've covered it, reads something like this: "Peanut Butter." The Marathons. Also by the Vibrations (recorded as the Marathons).

Both records are on different labels!

But surely the names just can't get any crazier than Francis X and the Bushmen, Nino and the Ebb Tides or Little Caesar and the Romans.

What monsters the American disc scene will launch upon the world in the next few months is anybody's guess.

Here in Britain though, this commercial tomfoolery is almost non-existent. Apart from Nero and the Gladiators and the Flee-Rekkers, we seem to be sadly lacking in Rock groups with zany names. And as comedy records are so few and far between these days, we could do with a few laughs to brighten up our own hit parade.

I flipped when I saw it. Suddenly I was a journalist!

But I was also an office boy and a very busy one too. It took me hours and hours to write and research *Names Names Names*, but now I'd seen it in print I was determined not to let another issue go by without penning a piece. I quickly planned a follow-up: a chart analysis from August '58 to August '61, based on the little Top Ten charts compiled by Record Mirror and published in the News Of The World, which I'd been religiously clipping out and keeping for the past three years. To be a proper journalist I needed to write quicker so I learned to type, fast, in a couple of days – with six fingers (and still do). This next article *Survey: The Big Discs Since August 1958* became another Page 3 special, cementing my self-esteem considerably. The following week I penned a lesser offering bemoaning the lack of rock'n'roll instrumentals in the chart, and it only made the back page. But it made my hat-trick.

The following week I was on holiday, in a caravan in Hastings. When I returned to pen my next opus *The Shirelles Need A Hit*, I found Ian had instigated a new and exciting column titled *Rhythm'n'Blues Disc Round-Up* that kicked off stating ex-skiffler Chas McDevitt, with singing wife Shirley Douglas, had "embarked on an R&B policy" and was wondering what had happened to Screaming Jay Hawkins, who Chas had toured with in '57 on the back of his USA "Freight Train" hit. Ian then quoted reader David Godin (more of him later) who reported that Chuck Berry's "Memphis Tennessee" had been played on the BBC radio Light Programme's Saturday Club. "Nothing strange, you say", wrote Ian, "except that this was in the Country And Western part of the show!" The column then listed new US R&B releases, and reviewed, in a few sentences some recent UK R&B releases. Ian, a hip connoisseur, appreciated jazz, country, pop, R&B and more, and had recently slated Elvis's "His Hand In Mine" gospel LP, dissecting it cruelly, which brought a juicy post-bag the following week. He was ahead of everybody with his R&B column. I became fascinated with the subject, not least because it was just beginning to dawn on me that rhythm & blues was the true direction for we rock'n'roll-starved beat addicts to follow. I resolved to investigate.

Then *Rhythm'n'Blues Disc Round-Up* vanished, to reappear the following week simply as *Rhythm'n'Blues* by James Craig, one of RM's several house pen-names, its derivation from James Craig Watson, our beloved editor. Luckily it was Ian who wrote it, not Jim. It was another great column, opening with news that the Pye Records group, one of the Big Four majors – and which had wrested the legendary Chess label away from Decca's London-American outlet – would be issuing the LP "Bo Diddley Is A Gunslinger". Ian then reviewed all sorts of new R&B items on Pye International by such diverse talents as Howlin' Wolf, the Ideals, Tiny Topsy, the Vibrations and Slim Harpo. There were also informative news paragraphs on Ray Charles and Chubby Checker. This was August 1961 and the New Record Mirror was the first music paper to focus on rhythm & blues, the music of Black America, that in a few eventful years would sweep the British Isles, Europe, and via its white British devotees would musically conquer the world, giving birth to the phenomenon of rock music.

For over a year I had been a fully paid-up member of the Buddy Holly Appreciation Society and in this capacity was invited to an event at the legendary studio of the legendary Joe Meek, who wasn't legendary as yet. But he was hot, and getting hotter: the singing actor John Leyton with the big hair was currently topping the charts with his weirdly thrilling death disc "Johnny Remember Me", produced by Joe and penned by his cohort Geoff Goddard. The event was held to "gain the opinion of members of the Buddy Holly Appreciation Society" on Joe's latest production, another Geoff Goddard composition titled "A Tribute To Buddy Holly", by Mike Berry & the Outlaws. The record was possibly a "thank you" to Buddy, as Geoff claimed his highly-successful compositions were being sent to him from "the other side" by the spirit of the late much-lamented bespectacled one, a fact frequently reported in *Psychic News*.

Together with my friend Terry Chappell, another Holly devotee who even wore the specs, we scootered to Holloway Road, parked, and made our way to Joe's studio. I'd already decided this event would make a good piece for NRM, and so it did, beginning thus:

> *THERE is nothing from the outside to tell where Joe Meek's flat is. There is actually a door between two shops with no plate which leads into five medium-sized rooms.*
>
> *This is Joe Meek's office and recording studio, where Joe claims to be able to produce "the sound". He seems to be right.*

The article continued in this laconic manner neglecting, out of politeness or fear of libel, to mention that Joe was obviously gay, and shaking hands with him was like shaking hands with a fish. These details can now safely be revealed. But it was fun, Joe's tiny up-and-down-stairs studio packed with Holly-ites, with Mike and the Outlaws – one of London's premier beat groups – delivering an exciting show in the tiny studio. Couples jived, Mike "proved that his vocal similarity [to Buddy Holly] was no myth", and I met affable Holly Appreciation Society president John Beecher, scrawled some notes, and on the following Monday penned my first roving report.

Thinking about it years later, I have no clear idea why the staff of New Record Mirror let me have my head when it came to writing. Peter Jones and Ian Dove were properly-trained professional journalists who had risen in the local newspaper ranks before joining Record Mirror. I had no training at all. I can only assume they considered me some sort of "primitive" whose scribbles would be good for the paper because my tastes effectively coincided with that of millions of other teenagers.

But on one occasion – just one – they did offer me a few words of journalistic savvy.

"Make sure your features have a beginning, a middle and an end", advised Peter, "grab them at the beginning."

"And keep your sentences short and don't use old-fashioned words like 'whilst'", added Ian.

That was all they ever taught me about my trade. Maybe that was all I needed to know in order to write for New Record Mirror. After all, it wasn't the New Yorker.

Jimmy Watson, listening to this basic tutorial, then brought me down a peg or two, "…and don't go thinking you'll be doing any proper interviews yet because you're not ready". I guessed he'd sooner have me making pots of tea all day, delivering papers, compiling the Top Twenty, stamping out subscriptions and running errands than taxi-ing all over London interviewing exciting and glamorous pop stars in posh hotels and record company HQs, which I confess I was straining at the leash to do, though still a mere youth of 17. Well, at least I'd met Joe Meek, and Joe did become a bona-fide pop legend (though as much for the manner of his death as for his life and career accomplishments). And I knew I was already a better writer than Jimmy.

Better writer or not, my next slew of articles were decidedly mediocre. They ranged from *Presley's Most Talked-About Disc* ("Wild In The Country" / "Feel So Bad" – the moot talking point being that the A-side and B-side were different in the USA and UK), *Duane's New Disc Has Less Twang* ("Drivin' Home" – anyone remember that?), *He Records In This Front Room* ('technical' report plus pix on Joe Meek's studio), *The Crickets – New Charts Bid* (label manager Tony Hall "inundated", "bombarded", "beseeched" by requests from fans to release "A Sweet Love" b/w "I Fought The Law"), *Is This The Year's Best Rock Disc?*

30

("The Mountain's High" by Dick & Deedee – well, it sounded pretty sensational to me), *The Inconsistent Drifters* (21 hits in USA, 3 in UK), *Meet Dion – Late Of The Belmonts* (those Belmont-less teen ballads Dion was churning out were about to get buried by "Runaround Sue"), *Has Helen Really Eclipsed Brenda?* (yet more stirrings of the evergreen Brenda v. Helen controversy), *And An 'Ace Of Hearts' Hit Too* (Buddy Holly's ancient US "That'll Be The Day" LP finally gets a budget UK release). I also penned a review of the autumn "Pop Prom" featuring – on the same bill – Adam Faith, Cliff Richard, and Billy Fury. All three were cleaned-up rock'n'rollers who'd become UK teen idols and "polished performers". 'Twas a funny old bill though – other acts included Chas McDevitt & Shirley Douglas, Robin Hall and Jimmy McGregor, The Allisons, Dave Sampson & the Hunters, Bert Weedon, the John Barry Seven, Peter Elliott, the Monty Sunshine Combo with Beryl Bryden, and Helen Shapiro. Something for everyone, except R&B fans, and all sponsored by the triple-threat romance magazines Marilyn, Valentine, and Roxy.

While I was churning out all these teenbeat fillers, Ian's *Rhythm'n'Blues* column was going from strength to strength, James Asman's country, folk and traditional jazz columns were as riveting as ever in their stern purity, and Benny Green's insider takes on modern jazz were passionate, forthright and supremely self-confident. Peter Jones covered every genre with his usual immensely-readable professional aplomb, and Jimmy Watson still reviewed the LPs in his inimitably dire manner. Dion DiMucci himself came to the tatty New Record Mirror office and was interviewed by Peter. To the best of my knowledge Dion was the only artist with a current American chart-topper to have taken a dump in the tawdry New Record Mirror lavatory-cum-washroom. He was reported to be "sniffly" with a cold, but in light of future revelations was possibly suffering withdrawal symptoms. In those days it was assumed only jazzers used heroin: RM staffer knowledge of other Class A's in 1961 was equally vague. Peter and Ian once returned from an interview with a bona fide US superstar singer, sniggering that a sore beneath his nostrils was probably due to some disease caught from his then-illegal and known-only-to-the-in-crowd gay sex antics. The singer later confessed to being a heavy cocaine user at that point in his career, a far more likely explanation.

Speaking of drugs, another visitor to the office was Billy Fury, great-looking, moody – actually shy – and charismatic. He was also about the only UK rocker at that time heavily into smoking grass. I knew nothing about drugs except for their names, but unknown to me I was in close proximity to them. Roy Burden would retire several times daily to the lavatory-cum-washroom ("The Record Mirror bog") and emerge smiling and glaze-eyed, while the bog itself would be thick with smoke of a peculiar odour now known to millions. It must have been fun for Roy to have gone through the Sixties at Record Mirror stoned on grass. And maybe the rest of us staffers were frequently, yet in my case, unknowingly contact-high too.

I did drink a bit, but not much. Booze and scooters didn't mix. But I got drunk at the Record Mirror party in November 1961. Leaning back and sliding slowly down the wall in the editorial office, I watched Peter Jones flirt with his new girlfriend, the actress Carol White, who exuded a magnetic sexiness apparent even to callow me. But I had little time to enjoy the spectacle because one of our guests, a million-selling disc artiste (as we used to call them), started haranguing me over a recent piece I'd penned.

The offending article was titled The Sad Scene and began like this:

OVER three years how many stars have made one big hit disc and then faded into obscurity?
Hundreds?
Wrong!
From January 1st 1958 to January 1st 1961 there have been precisely ten.
Ten artists or groups whose records shot into the top three, and whose follow-up recordings just haven't made the grade. Ten ships in the night whose passing has been forgotten by many and remembered by only the faithful few.
Let's take a close look at these one-shot hitmakers and try to analyse the reasons why they failed and failed again.

This was a typical NJ article of the time, which might well be described as "flannel", but which nevertheless (hopefully) sucked in the unsuspecting reader. The ten artists in questions were Johnny Tillotson, Ricky Valence, Jerry Keller, the Teddy Bears, Vic Damone, Tommy Edwards, the Kalin Twins, the Four Preps, and Marvin Rainwater. Everyone of a certain age will be able to name their only major hit. Chart aficionados will note that only Tillotson ever again came close to big UK chart success after the article was written, hitting (if that's the word) No.21 with "Send Me The Pillow You Dream On". After the promised "analysis" of each "sad" one-shot hitmaker, the article ended ominously:

> *These are the ten artists who cover the period between 1958 and 1960. And of 1961?*
>
> *Already there are the Allisons, the Shirelles, and, of course, the Marcels. Going by the past three years one of these groups will make no more hits. Which one it will be is anybody's guess, but one thing is certain, there will be yet another addition to the sad scene of pop music – the one-shot hitmakers.*

In fact none of those three groups ever scored another UK Top 20 hit, although the superb Shirelles achieved considerable US success. The million-selling hitmaker giving me a hard time was John Allison of the fraternal duo the Allisons, whose self-penned "Are You Sure" was Britain's entry in the 1961 Eurovision Song Contest. It didn't win (it came second) but was a massive smash all over Europe and in the UK. I couldn't quite figure what John's gripe was, but he was evidently offended by the Allison's inclusion in the article – or maybe he thought I'd jinxed them.

"No offence meant," I gurgled, as John held me up to keep me from sliding to the floor, and before collapsing I promised to write a fulsome piece on the "brothers", who were not related, though John and Bob certainly looked like siblings.

Dutifully, an article titled *The Allisons – What Happened?* appeared at the beginning of December, bemoaning their lack of follow-up success and urging RM readers to suggest what kind of material they should be recording. All to no avail. The Allisons scored one more minor hit then quit the business. But this was not the last time I would hear from John Allison.

That month Mike Berry's "Tribute To Buddy Holly" climbed to No. 18 in the Record Mirror charts, higher than in any other paper, surprise surprise. My little autumn features included a preview of Cliff's "The Young Ones" flick, yet another piece on Buddy Holly headlined *We Aim To Keep Buddy Alive For Two Years* – the press release from Coral Records from which I'd cribbed the headline in fact read "We aim to keep Buddy's name alive for two years" – plus anodyne articles on Bill Haley, Doo-Wop, Fats Domino, the Tokens and the Ventures.

In our year-end chart survey, the top ten record artists in the UK charts for the year of 1961– according to the charts point system – were:

UK	USA
Elvis Presley	Chubby Checker
Helen Shapiro,	The Shirelles
The Shadows	Del Shannon
Cliff Richard	Brenda Lee
The Everly Brothers	Elvis Presley
Bobby Vee	Roy Orbison
Billy Fury	Bobby Vee
Del Shannon	U.S. Bonds
John Leyton	Connie Francis
Petula Clark	Ricky Nelson

Del Shannon's "Runaway" was top disc in the UK and the USA.

Jimmy Watson's Scottish heritage graced our December 30th issue: a front page full-page photo of kilt-clad Andy "Donald, Where's Your Troosers" Stewart toasting RM readers with a hefty tumbler of scotch accompanied by the headline *A Guid New Year Tae Ane And A'*, much to the disgust of Ian and Peter. More pertinently, the page three article in this final issue of 1961 pointed presciently to the next Big Thing lumbering towards us from America: titled *The Battle Of The Twist Has Started*, it was an in-depth survey of the revolutionary dance craze currently huge in the USA and about to hit Britain. Chubby Checker had arrived in the UK, the movie "Twist Around The Clock" was being released, everyone was jumping on the bandwagon. The sound of rhythm & blues, disguised as dance music, was about to hit the UK mainstream. Partner dancing would never be the same again.

1962

I got my provisional driving license back in December following a three-month ban for getting caught driving without L-plates. In January I took the scooter/motorbike test.

"It's easy", explained my modernist pal Ray Gaunt, "he asks you a few questions, you drive round the block and he's supposed to jump out in front of you so you do the emergency stop. But they're all scared you'll run 'em down so they come out in the road miles away and hold their hand up. You can hardly see 'em. All you have to do is make sure you put your front brake on first so the front of the bike goes down a bit. Then you pass the test".

His words were uncannily prophetic. It happened as he predicted. After the test I tore off the L-plates, stuffed them in the side bubble and drove back with a swagger, because you can do that on a GS. Arriving home I was elated almost to the point of apoplexy and rushed to my record player where an HMV test pressing, white label, big red A, of Dion's next release "The Wanderer" sat on the deck. I played it over and over. Yes, I would now be The Wanderer, the ultimate hip scooterist, giving lifts to girls, giving them free copies of New Record Mirror bearing my by-line, breaking their hearts, roaming around and round and round.

I still wore casual gear for work because I was still the office boy doing the dirty jobs: formal attire was aired mostly for trips to the big Mecca ballrooms I started to frequent – the local Tottenham Royal or the in-town Lyceum in Wellington Street off the Aldwych. Hanging

37

around the local coffee bars was fun but the real style action was at these dance palaces. Not that I danced, just jigged around on the spot. Pam Blee would sometimes go to the Lyceum at lunchtimes where she would learn and practise the latest moves.

Checking the action at these ballrooms became de rigeur. They were built to impress and impress they did. You got to hear great records played loud in a huge space. That impressed straightway. Tottenham Royal was ten minutes by scooter from Wood Green. The dance floor was on ground level, vast and 'modern'. Record night was Tuesday and didn't get too crowded so there was plenty of space to mooch around, wander upstairs, dig the scene, the chicks, the groups of guys, what everyone was wearing. And dig the music. The DJs were hip, but anonymous.

The most baroque of the Mecca ballrooms was the Lyceum, built as an Edwardian theatre, not the biggest ballroom but the most gorgeous. Sunday was the obligatory night at "the Ly", the music alternating between records and Cyril Stapleton's Orchestra. Stapleton looked a bit like King George VI, ran a tight swinging ensemble and played modern big band arrangements of contemporary pop hits using his own vocalists, whereas the record selection tended more towards R&B and hard beat. When the orchestra played one of the new dance fads – mostly variations on the Twist – a very sharp blond kid called Jeff Dexter would demonstrate the moves. He was tiny but awesomely confident, and later became a DJ with impeccable tastes.

Many people say the same thing about their first trip to the Lyceum: that they are awestruck. You enter the pillared portals and climb up and up admiring the ornate Edwardian décor, past the vast cloakrooms, then suddenly emerge at the top with the whole interior spread out below. The first time I went there I found myself looking down on the dance floor at dozens and dozens of girls wearing similar clothes (in fashion that season were long tight-ish skirts – sometimes with Spanish pleats at the bottom – worn with gold tops) and all doing the Fly, which was more or less the Twist but waving both arms and hands around in the air and making buzzing sounds. Dozens of girls all doing this silly dance, all dressed in the latest street fashion, with different coloured lights playing on them. It took my breath away.

The Twist craze got bigger and bigger. By the beginning of February Chubby Checker was charting with "Let's Twist Again" and "The Twist", Bobby Darin was top three with "Multiplication (Twist)", and Joey Dee's frenetic "The Peppermint Twist" was in the Top 20. Amazingly Checker had returned to the top of the US charts with "The Twist", which had occupied pole position two years earlier – America was even more twist-crazy than the UK.

New Record Mirror dropped David Gell, the DJ who'd been reviewing singles for years. It was a matter of saving money. He was replaced by the 'New Record Mirror Disc Jury' – Ian Dove, Peter Jones, me. We sat around the big editorial desk, one of us would put on a 45 and we'd scatter-gun our various comments while Peter, the fastest typist, would cut-and-paste in his head and bang out the review. This was fun. When something was particularly in someone's favourite bag then they'd write it alone. But occasionally, after reviewing dozens of discs, it would descend into farce:

DEE DEE SHARP Gravy (For My Mashed Potatoes); Baby Cakes (Columbia DB 4874)
NO NO, Dee Dee Sharp doesn't want some flavour on her Saturday dinner. Gravy is the term for kisses while dancing, the dance being the Mashed Potatoes. The disc should really be called "Mashed Potato Time Part 2".

Nevertheless it's a good dance song and one of those that can really grow on you. That is if you can stand listening to it about twenty three thousand times. At the first play it sounds good if you don't listen hard, and the medium-tempo number will bring alive any dull party. It did ours.

More food on the flip, this time some gooey baby cakes which seems to be Dee Dee's pet name for her feller. Fast-ish bluesy number but we'd really like to see this guy. Perhaps he's pasty-faced.
THREE BELLS

The bell system had temporarily replaced the star-rating system, chiefly, we suspected, so Ian Dove could award his "No-bell" prize of the week for the new release which offended him the most, the

Lettermen's yawn-inducing "When I Fall In Love" targeted for his initial sally. Jimmy Watson then diplomatically forbade this booby prize, fearing offence to record companies and thus possible loss of our pathetically meagre advertising. This was partly the fault of New Record Mirror being owned by Decca, partly our circulation, and partly our advertising manager Roy Burden smoking pot in the bog.

We were also in a crowded market where there was little difference between the various pop papers. There was nothing sophisticated or intellectual about any of them. Melody Maker apart, they dealt with the pop scene overall. Their format was similar – news stories, features, articles, plenty of black-and-white photographs, specialist columnists, nostalgia, charts, readers letters, LP and singles reviews. The brief was broad – a record in the charts was presumed interesting, no matter who the artist. What went on in the States was deemed crucial, what went on anywhere else outside the UK barely worthy of comment. Yet they gave a weekly snapshot of the pop scene that was evidently fascinating enough to have a combined circulation of maybe half a million. That's a lot of hard-core pop music lovers, all with their fierce loyalties, their favourite columns, their lists that they'd send in, their love-and-hate mail. They also sent in written pieces of their own, usually concert reviews, and if they were good they'd be printed – but not paid for. Especially at New Record Mirror.

In March 1962, encouraged by the response to his earlier Cash Box Top 30 initiative, Jimmy instigated a deal with the fledgling British music trade weekly Record Retailer to print their Top 50 chart, plus their Top 20 LPs and Top 20 EPs. He also arranged with Cash Box to extend the Top 30 to a Top 50. In a stroke this made New Record Mirror the best of the music papers for charts and began to establish the legitimacy of the Record Retailer chart against the NME chart, generally considered the market standard and the most accurate. Of course none of them were, the NME chart later revealed as the most fixable. Years afterwards I learned that of all the charts, the Melody Maker chart was probably the most accurate and the Record Retailer chart – at least at that time – probably just as inaccurate around its lower reaches as the New Record Mirror chart that I thankfully no longer had to compile.

The trad boom, which had been filling clubs and concert halls for years, was still thriving. Only Kenny Ball was scoring hit records in that genre, but hit records weren't really the point. Doing the 'Trad Stomp' in the clubs was the point, raving to a bunch of guys enthusiastically reviving twenties Dixieland jazz. Trad even had its own movie that spring, the Dick Lester-directed "It's Trad, Dad!", featuring the bands of not only the ubiquitous "three B's" of Trad – Kenny Ball, Chris Barber and Acker Bilk, whose decidedly un-trad "accidental" hit "Stranger On The Shore" was currently selling millions globally – but also the bands of Terry Lightfoot, Bob Wallis and, barely in the trad corner, the Temperance Seven. Wisely, the movie hedged its musical bets: lined up in the opposite corner were popsters Helen Shapiro and Craig Douglas, both with starring roles, plus cameos from John Leyton, Gary U.S. Bonds, Gene Vincent, the Brook Brothers, Gene McDaniels, Del Shannon and, to make sure all bases were covered, Chubby Checker, whose own movie "Twist Around The Clock" was currently on release.

Jimmy still wouldn't let me do interviews so I kept churning out my little articles which seemed to fall into several distinct categories: chart analysis – *Elvis Around The World* (El's weird worldwide singles hits including film songs, album tracks, etc), *The Answer Game* ("answer" records through the years, inspired by the Chantels' current hit "Well I Told You" answer to Ray Charles' "Hit The Road Jack"), *And Now It's Twist International* (twistin' hits around the world), *We Don't Follow America* (not much we don't), *Elvis and Lonnie Are The Most Consistent* (5-year survey of regular hitmakers), *Singer As Composer* (in those days it was unusual), *The Classics And All That Jazz* (a list of classical tunes stolen by popsters, inspired by the No.1 smash "Nut Rocker"), the predictable *6 Month Chart Survey* and *The Rise, Decline And Fall Of The Instrumental*. Then there were the lamentations for the UK chart failure of an established hitmaker's most recent 'waxing' with features on Ben E. King, Del Shannon, Johnny Burnette, and Bobby Vee, the latter whose classy flop "Please Don't Ask About Barbara" then inspired the spin-off *Girls' Names And Hit Records* piece. There were also straight biographies of artists I liked with current releases: Sam Cooke, Linda Scott, Jan & Dean, Ritchie Valens, Bruce Channel. And there were the news features: Little Richard (emerging from a three-year gospel sabbatical – the big question: will he rock or not?), *The*

41

Everlys – A Rumour Scotched (no, they weren't about to retire, despite Don's highly-publicised UK breakdown), *The Gold Disc Mystery* (US record companies claiming big sales on certain singles but the RIAA refusing to award them a Gold Disc). And finally the odds & sods: *The Twenties Are Still Roaring* (the cult of the syncopation revival with reference to a camp middle-aged hairdresser attempting a Temperance Seven), *Funny, Peculiar and Non-Comic Comedy* (different types of comedy records making the rounds in the UK and USA), *All-Time Top Ten* (analysis of the recent Readers' Letters theme 'Your Personal Top Ten', an idea so simple and successful it threatened to completely take over our correspondence) and, harking back to my very first feature *Names Names Names* nearly a year previously – *Beat Group Names From America and Liverpool*.

As for Liverpool, something was evidently happening up there, wherever exactly it was. No-one in London as yet seemed to have noticed. I was intrigued:

NRM w/e 4th August 1962
BEAT GROUP NAMES FROM AMERICA AND
LIVERPOOL

IS the Liverpool area the rockingest part of the great British Isles? A publication, "Mersey Beat", just arrived, makes me think this is the case.

"Mersey Beat" is designed for beat groups, artists and singers. And they are in apparently great demand…but the supply is there too.

For example, groups mentioned include The Tremors, Fabulous Fourtones, the Deltas, the Skyliners, the Tremolos, Rick Shaw & The Dolphins, Ken Tracey and the Beat Squad.

The Cyclones, the Dakotas, the Zodiacs, the Midnighters, the Four Jays, Group One, the Bluegenes, Gerry and the Pacemakers, the Solohettes, the Mersey Beats, the Dennisons, the Searchers.

Names that intrigue are the Beatles (who were billed as big as Bruce Channel in Liverpool), the Spidermen, the Morockans.

I feel sorry for Carl Vincent. Carl, says "Mersey Beat",
"a first class vocalist in the Elvis Presley vein whose group
the Counts disbanded last year when Carl broke his leg
ON STAGE."

The emphasis is mine because I feel no singer can
suffer more for his art. Was it all that feverish Presley leg
twitching that caused his tibia to crack...everyone always
thought it would happen to someone!

The article concluded with still more names of these raffish Liverpool groups, then listed a competitive bunch of zany American names. Mersey Beat was edited by Bill Harry, who'd studied art with John Lennon, and was a glimpse into an alternative rock universe. I felt I was getting a sniff of something interesting but wasn't sure what. Who were these 'Beatles' and why, as a supporting act, did they merit billing as big as Bruce Channel, currently touring the UK just off his global chart-topper with the harmonica-drenched "Hey Baby"?

Then I saw a picture of the Beatles and knew immediately that they would be huge. They had something no-one else had...they looked like a cross between art students and modernists. They weren't trying to look like Elvis Presley – they actually looked hip. That was enough. All the beat groups in London (at least the ones making records) and all the pretty-boy and not so pretty-boy singers were still quiffed-up, be-greased or just plain ordinary. It was truly uncanny how stylistically unfashionable and out-of-touch the London pop scene was at that point in time.

What I didn't know was that earlier in the year the Beatles had been taken on by Brian Epstein, trekked around London, and a couple of weeks before I wrote my article, signed with EMI. In August, the month the article was published, they sacked Pete Best, hired Ringo, and John wed Cynthia. Busy month. And no-one on the London scene had a clue.

It was a silly article but for New Record Mirror it was the first mention of the 'new thing' in pop music. It was also the first mention of the Beatles in any of the London music press. The Sixties had already taken off with fashion, with art, with attitude, but not with music. Later that very same month our folk critic James Asman reviewed the debut Bob Dylan album, released on the new CBS label. He was far from dismissive, reserving his normally stern judgement.

However, the approach of the monster from Liverpool paled besides my more immediate prospects: I had been promoted. The ball began to roll when Jimmy Watson had the bright idea of asking Decca if he could print a mini four-page New Record Mirror and insert it into the sleeve of a dead-cert hit 45. OK, said Decca – if you do the inserting.

So we designed a dinky little New Record Mirror and awaited delivery of the dead-cert hit single. Decca then delivered us a large quantity of "She's Not You", the next Presley 45, which they figured would sell close on a million units.

I can't pretend to remember how many mini-NRMs we printed but it was in the tens of thousands. It took time to unpack the singles, insert the mini-NRMs and repack them. Nobody on the staff could face doing this tedious work so we hired temps, and rather than pay an agency we found our own. Ian brought along a moody beatnik girl of his acquaintance, and I brought along my genial school buddy Bob Bedford. The temps each worked for £1 a day, tax-free – not bad money – and the back room of the New Record Mirror office was a congenial, if dowdy environment.

Jimmy decided that as I'd been writing now for a year and gagging to do more, I should be promoted. So after the mini-NRM gig was over, Bob was offered the office boy job and accepted. But being a full-time pop journalist at the precocious age of 18 didn't stop the senior writers still treating me like a dogsbody.

"Go get my telly so Peter and I can watch the Test Match" ordered Ian, lobbing me his bunch of keys. Bob and I zoomed off to Holland Park on my GS and returned sitting back-to-back, the scooter wobbling somewhat, and Bob steadying Ian's huge bulky television on the Vespa's chromium luggage rack. Amazingly it worked perfectly. Benny Green also made use of my scooter services on occasion, instructing me to collect unwanted review LPs (of which he had an extraordinary amount) from his flat in Marylebone and ferrying them to Dobells for cash.

In 1962 the four major British record companies, Decca, EMI, Pye, and Philips, and the one serious independent, Oriole, all released records under several labels. Decca released American material on its RCA-Victor, Coral, Brunswick, Vogue and London-American labels. Its Decca label was reserved for UK releases. EMI released material on HMV, Capitol, Columbia, Parlophone, Liberty, Stateside, Verve and MGM – most of which released both UK and US material. Pye released its material on Pye, Piccadilly, Pye International, and Reprise, while Philips released the Philips, Fontana, Mercury, and CBS labels. Little Oriole also exclusively supplied Woolworth's with the copycat budget Embassy label.

These five companies, as well as several major music publishers, loved to throw press receptions for new releases and now I was a roving reporter I could attend them. This was a mixed blessing. It was fine if I was with someone else from Record Mirror, but lonely if not: I was the youngest reporter by a mile and didn't know anybody. In early 1962 nobody of my generation was doing what I was doing. Everybody at these press receptions was older and, to my teenage sensibilities, mostly square. It wasn't as simple as just going in, grabbing a drink, quizzing the artist, then split. These were social occasions, canapés, plenty of booze, usually some sort of announcement by some bigwig executive and then the artist being wheeled on. I was self-conscious and socially inept in the extreme.

The first reception I attended was at Decca's West End office in Great Marlborough Street where RCA-Victor was throwing a bash for Nashville stalwarts Floyd Cramer and Chet Atkins. Peter Jones and I chatted to the charming country twosome, made some notes, wrote the piece and shared a by-line. But I went alone to EMI's Chubby Checker reception, and with some other game journalists clambered up on to the little stage to be personally taught by the King Of Twist himself how to do the biggest dance craze since the Charleston: "You're stubbing out a cigarette with your foot while drying your back with a bath towel". In the midst of this twist-fest Chubby complained that Little Eva's current smash "The Locomotion" was a hit record, not a dance. Posterity proved him wrong. I got an article out of that.

My next bright journalistic idea was for an ongoing series titled *Fallen Idols*. This would enable me to write about my rock'n'roll heroes and I kicked off with a piece on the mysteriously magnificent Jack Scott. The series would prove popular, but later got me into trouble. Then, exactly a year after I started writing articles, Jimmy finally declared I was now allowed to do interviews, and the big break came in the October 13th 1962 issue where I had two interviews published. The small one was with Roger Greenaway of the Kestrels, fully two years before his massive successes as a performer and writer with Roger Cooke. The Kestrels were a vocal group who'd captured the US vocal group sound on "Chapel In The Moonlight", then made a great hully-gully record with "All These Things", the hully-gully being a dance beat that was a much-hyped big-thing-that-never-was, staggering along for a few months during the previous year and best epitomised by teen idol Eden Kane's chart-topping "Well I Ask You".

But my first proper interview – the major interview in that issue – was with none other than Little Richard. Wow! This was beyond my imagination. For a teenage beat addict like me to be sent to talk to the wildest man in rock'n'roll, just arrived in the UK…well, dreams can come true.

Mr Richard Penniman was staying in an extremely modest hotel in Bayswater, on the top floor, in a small double room. I was immediately struck by the fact that Little Richard wasn't little at all but quite a big man. I was also struck by the fact that Richard's young accompanist, organist Billy Preston, was lying on the other bed. I sat on Richard's bed and we chatted, during which time he moved over to me and fondled my cheeks and told me that although they were wonderfully soft, no-one had cheeks as soft as Elvis's, whose cheeks were like ripe peaches. The penny swiftly dropped as regards to Richard's sexual orientation.

Little Richard spoke about his retirement into gospel music and religious studies, about the flight fright over Australia which caused his 'conversion', how he would only sing gospel on this tour – which resolve would swiftly be abandoned once he realised how popular his rock'n'roll still was – and mostly lots of fantastic boasting which impressed me mightily. He said there was going to be a film in Technicolour and Cinemascope about his life, with Little Richard playing himself and Sidney Poitier in a lesser role. He named his favourite artists as Ray Charles, Elvis, Fats Domino and Jackie Wilson.

46

I floated away from the hotel on cloud nine, couldn't believe my luck. When that, for me, very special edition of NRM was published, Jimmy Watson got stingy and said I could have my by-line on only one of my interviews that week. He put it on the Kestrels piece.

The next two *Fallen Idols* were Lloyd Price and the Platters. For someone so young I was peculiarly nostalgic. But I made up for my disappointment in not getting a Little Richard by-line when I was sent to interview Ketty Lester the following week. Again, I had to pinch myself in disbelief that this was really happening. Everybody loved, and still loves, her definitive version of the oldie "Love Letters" and though her subsequent records never matched its popularity, everything she recorded was special.

But if the Little Richard interview was slightly bizarre, the Ketty Lester interview was unsettling. She was ensconced, not in a cheap room, but in a tasteful hotel suite. When I saw Little Richard I was dressed casually because the interview was a spur-of-the-moment job. The Ketty interview had been pre-arranged with the Decca press office, and so I was besuited, beshirted, the lot, wearing my gear. Ketty was dressed in a tasteful sleeveless dress, typical early-Sixties style. And she was really nice. Gracious, warm, friendly. We got on well, she made tea. She was twenty-eight years old, ten years older than me, a tall, big-boned very elegant black woman with a palpable sexuality.

Whatever subtext I then started to feel I was picking up, I told myself it was probably in my own imagination. What did I know? I was completely inexperienced. And besides, she was the star, the artist, the talent, and I a mere scribe. Yet I couldn't shake the feeling that she was curious about me. How that curiosity would, or could, ever manifest itself was almost beyond the realms of fantasy…and I was there to work, not daydream. The interview itself went well, if a bit girlie.

"MARRIED? Before they're twenty?" KETTY LESTER showed signs of amazement as a well-known statistic was revealed to her – that most girls in Britain are wed before their twenty-first birthday.

"My sister was wed at twenty-three," she revealed. "And the rest of the family thought she was too young!

*Of course everything's all right now. But when you come
from a family of twelve children like me you tend to get
very family-minded."*

*Before "Love Letters" made it, Ketty's career had been
varied and uncertain. Aspects of it ranged from nursing
to a Ziegfeld Follies girl.*

*"I don't think I was cut out for nursing though," she
confessed, "and parading around in the near-nude didn't
exactly leave me career-minded"*

Ketty then spoke about how she'd been turned down by several record labels, didn't think "Love Letters" would make it so big, and how she figured that the spiritual beat of Gospel music was behind the current sound in the American charts. Then she started discussing her current tour.

*"Most performers have someone travelling along with
them. I haven't on this tour. Having no companion means
you can get awful lonely sometimes – especially so far
away from home."*

This confession of vulnerability seemed to confirm my imaginings and I strongly felt that I was expected to respond in some way but had absolutely no idea how. Head down, I scribbled her words on my pad, wondering frantically that if she was indeed hinting at something tremendous, what should I do now? What could I do? Or did my naivety and attraction towards her simply mean I was reading into an innocent remark something that didn't exist.

I even sensed, or imagined I sensed, that she was thinking it would be inappropriate for her, an older woman, to make a move on me and therefore it was up to me to make a pass. And, of course, I then wondered again if this was my fantasy and that making a pass, something I didn't even know how to do, would be a ghastly and embarrassing mistake. These were strange and complicated feelings for me.

Anyway, I didn't take the chance. I did nothing.

Had I been older I might have known how to handle the situation, steer the occasion confidently, take it forward diplomatically. But I didn't, so I thanked her for the interview, said goodbye and left.

Many years later I learned, gratifyingly, that Ketty had been consoled
in her loneliness on that tour by Aussie hunk Frank Ifield, then enjoying
a run of three consecutive UK chart-toppers. Good on yer, cobber!

Another reason why I told myself I shouldn't get closer to Ketty was
that in the past week I had acquired a girl-friend, a real live girl-friend
called Jill. And, not to put too fine a point on it, there had been an element
of not wanting to jeopardise or test my new relationship so drastically,
so quickly, by having a fling with a hot black star hitmaker. Winter was
now approaching, the notoriously long and bitterly cold winter of '62-
'63, and a warm and devoted girlfriend was to prove most serendipitous.

Still churning out *Fallen Idols*, my next victim was Johnny Otis who
I described, with amazing disdain for facts and courtesy, as *"a renegade
jazzman...who turned to beat because of the extra loot he thought he could make."*
In that same October 27th issue I celebrated the release of "Love Me
Do" with a piece titled *Meet The Beatles*, a patchy but reasonably detailed
introduction to the Fab Four using info garnered from an EMI press
hand-out, Bill Harry's Merseybeat, and finishing with a super quote
from Cavern DJ and compere Bob Wooler:

> **"The biggest thing to hit Liverpool for years...the hottest
> property any promoter could hope to encounter. Musically
> authoritative and physically magnetic, the Beatles are
> rhythmic revolutionaries with an act which is a succession
> of climaxes."**

Personally, I wasn't much impressed with "Love Me Do" but
then I didn't dislike it either – and now they had a record out I could
write about them. I was determined to do my bit for the group as I
was more than ever convinced they'd be huge, though my evidence
still rested on the way they looked rather than the way they sounded.
Heavily featuring the then-fashionable harmonica (as did recent chart-
toppers "I Remember You" by Frank Ifield and Bruce Channel's "Hey
Baby", as well as James Ray's US smash "If You Gotta Make A Fool
Of Somebody"), "Love Me Do" seemed a bit cautious. I preferred
the B-side, "PS I Love You".

But "Love Me Do" grew on me, like every subsequent Beatles' single. Yet who did like their singles immediately? New Beatles' singles throughout the Sixties were invariably strange, if not downright disappointing – then after a couple or three plays – wow! All the influences you could already spot in those first two sides – Buddy Holly, R&B, the Everly Brothers, blues, R&R – were ingredients to make a dish that was brand new: their own recipe.

In November I boasted three articles on one page – profiles on new hitmakers Chris Montez and the Four Seasons, plus an interview with Sonny Curtis, now a member of the Crickets touring the UK and hot with Carole King and Gerry Goffin's teen song "Don't Ever Change". Sonny, a fine musician and songwriter who'd already written "Walk Right Back" and "I Fought The Law", had worked with Buddy Holly before "That'll Be The Day", clashed egos with him and left the group, and was now masterminding the Crickets' renaissance. Opposite those three articles was the latest *Fallen Idols* victim Fabian, including a line which still gets me scratching my head, *"But in England he meant nothing. And he means even less now"*. I guess I was overdoing starting sentences with "And" and "But" to spite my old English teachers. But unfortunately there was a reason why I had so many articles in one issue. My journalistic mentor, Ian Dove, had announced he was leaving New Record Mirror. I was stunned – he was breaking up the team and Jimmy was left in a fix. Ian was moving onward and hopefully upward to become Features Editor at NME, which doubly irked us. In the best of possible worlds, Ian should have been editor of New Record Mirror, but Jimmy was Decca's choice and Decca called the shots. Jimmy was a good editor but Ian was the better journalist. Perhaps that was one of the reasons he quit.

Jimmy now had two problems. The first was lack of by-lines. He couldn't have most of the articles seen to be written by only two writers – Peter Jones and me. Secondly, Ian wasn't just a writer – he was our sub-editor, did the layouts, put the paper to bed. Jimmy's solutions were reasonably ingenious. He recruited some freelancers from New Record Mirror's more literate correspondents, among them Ray Northrop, Alan Stinton, and Graeme Andrews, all fine writers (and all better than me). He didn't pay them much, if anything. Jimmy also recruited his friend David Griffiths to handle the news page. Griffiths was a

trained and experienced entertainment journalist who'd graduated on
TV Times and was now working for Radio Times and various other
high-profile publications. He was also a BBC broadcaster. Before long,
David would be given special assignments including page three lead
interviews. Jimmy's strategy also included Peter and me writing some
of our features under pen-names: I moonlighted as Wesley Laine, and
Peter as Langley Johnson.

I made the decision that my special features, my rock'n'roll, my
best interviews, and, increasingly importantly, my rhythm & blues
articles, would bear the name of Norman Jopling, whilst the mere
pop pap which I churned out would be written by that hack Wesley
Laine.

It didn't quite work out like that. Under my various by-lines were
published such gems of pop journalism as *Elvis And That Royal Command*
(Presley snubs Queen's charity bash but Col. Tom sends a donation),
The (Rather Unnecessary) Brackets (a "list" feature of recent hits with bits
of the title in parenthesis), *Can You Can-Can?* (Wesley's debut feature, a
biog of Peter Jay and the Jaywalkers, a minor Joe Meek triumph), *The
Unbilled Million Sellers* (chart-topping Tornados – with a major Meek
triumph – contractually obliged to anonymously back Billy Fury for
the most crucial weeks in their career), *Jazz Jamboree Review* (trad-fest),
That Twangy 'Men Only' Sound (Duane Eddy's new sound – with girl
vocalists – and why he sells only to blokes), *It's Madison Time* (children
of the Twist – Madison, Bossa Nova, Limbo, Popeye), more *Fallen
Idols* (Conway Twitty, Johnny Duncan), *Brenda's Years-Old Hit* ("Rockin'
Around The Christmas Tree", first Yule hit that year and first time
around in the UK), *Paul Fell For The Babysitter* (retrospective on Paul
Anka), *Atmosphere & Mutiny* (Neil Christian wants to see "Mutiny On
The Bounty" because it features his ancestor).

You might think that for someone as callow, shy, and naive as I was,
interviewing celebrities would be an ordeal. Not at all. The gleeful
feeling that I was playing a part in a real-life play enabled me, like any
actor, to be as confident and forthright as the situation demanded.
If I could have bottled that feeling and sold it, wow! Later, I found
that's why people take uppers.

One morning in November I was lounging around the reception desk chatting to Pam when Jimmy yelled from the editorial office, "Sid Gillingham wants to know if anyone wants to talk to one of the Beatles, they're down from Liverpool with their manager, not much interest apparently." Sid was EMI's chief Press Officer.

"Yes, I'll interview one of 'em," I shouted back. I was intrigued. Would they just be yobbos who looked good, or something more?

That afternoon Brian Epstein arrived with Paul McCartney and we all sat drinking tea in the editorial office. Brian was a smooth sweet man, thoughtful and well spoken, not at all like a London music manager, and blushed regularly throughout the interview. I thought it curious that the Beatles' manager was gay, but he was evidently extremely protective and his attitude seemed paternal. Paul and I hit it off because we were part of the rhythm & blues fraternity and instantly began talking about Tamla, Arthur Alexander, the Shirelles, James Ray, Little Richard (himself reciprocally a big Beatles fan) and all the rest of the current greats. Paul did ask me if I'd heard "Love Me Do" and of course I said I liked it a lot. He replied that a lot of people didn't like it. He was well-dressed, easy-going, confident, and after they left I wondered if his records would get as good as his looks, his attitude, his clothes. Their music had to get better, surely. I was still convinced they were special, even more now I'd met Paul. Could anyone then have known just how special? Even they didn't know that. Only God knew.

I wrote up the interview for the next issue: *"We Made Sure Of Applause – We Took Our Fans With Us" reveal the Beatles.*

> **"WHEN we played outside Liverpool, as often as not we would hire a couple of coaches and take an audience with us," said a Beatle.**
>
> **He was not black and shiny nor did he have six legs. His name is Paul McCartney and he is the bass player of the Beatles.**

The article continued with Paul talking about the fans, the massive Liverpool beat scene, the Cavern, rhythm & blues, "Twenty Flight Rock", their own way of playing original American R&B songs in their stage act, and the title of their probable next single – "Please Please Me".

We ran a photograph with the article picturing the foursome leaning against a rail on a boat. It was supplied by EMI. What I didn't know was that New Record Mirror already had its own very good photographs of the Beatles. Normally, if I used a record company freebie photo or bought a snap from an agency when our studio already had pictures of the artist, our chief photographer Dezo Hoffmann would come storming up to the office: "Why you using zese peectures when I have exclusives from zee studio for months now?" he would demand.

His gripe was about money. When we used a picture from our studio we marked it "NRM picture" and readers could write in for a print. A half-plate (6"x8") was 3/6d, a 10"x8" was 5/-, and a 12"x10" was 7/6d. Not cheap, but they were original black-and-white prints with the studio's stamp on the back. Nowadays you could auction any one of those original Beatles prints for a useful sum. The income from the prints went to the studio, then in Wardour Street, soon to move to even larger premises on three floors above a restaurant in Gerrard Street, pre-Chinatown, and far larger than our Shaftesbury Avenue office.

But Dezo never mentioned to us that he had already been to Abbey Road and turned in a wonderful session, later published in *With The Beatles – The Historic Photographs Of Dezo Hoffman*. In these photos – taken at the session when the single version of "Love Me Do" was recorded, George Harrison was still sporting the black eye from a punch purportedly thrown by an angry Pete Best fan after the ex-drummer's sacking. And Ringo's bass drum features not the name of the group, but the name RINGO, crudely hand-lettered. They look young and they look great.

So why didn't Dezo tell us he had those early Beatles photographs? No-one knows. But everyone does know that Dezo went on to become the finest visual chronicler of the Beatles' rise to fame in '63 and '64. Yet even Dezo himself believed that the first photographs he took of them were much later – in spring '63. The story, as he tells it, describes how a Liverpool Beatles fan, a girl, had written to NRM in May 1962 complaining bitterly at our neglect of Liverpool groups in general and the "Fab" (new word then) Four in particular, enclosing a clipping of a photo of the Beatles. Roy Burden showed the letter to Dezo, mentioning it might be good for circulation to feature the group. Curious at the writer's passion, Dezo suggested to Jimmy that they should all go up to Liverpool and do a photo spread. Jimmy laughed and said he shouldn't take every reader's letter to heart. Dezo would have to wait almost a year before making that trip.

Dezo Hoffmann was a Slovakian émigré in his early fifties, stocky and handsome, a master photographer who also trained apprentices. The deal was that he ran the studio for Record Mirror but was allowed to freelance. Profits were split, the system worked. Although much of the work was posed sessions in the big downstairs studio, Dezo himself was best at candids – unposed news stills, shot on the hoof. He had an East European eye for an image, developed from his university studies as a photojournalist and cinematographer in Prague in the '30s. He'd graduated with honours, and as a prize was sent to the famed UFA movie studios where he met the guest of honour that weekend – Adolf Hitler. Ironically, Dezo was one-eighth Jewish and would recount to us stories his own grandparents had told him about the 19th century Ukrainian pogroms. He began his career working for the 20th Century Fox newsreel teams out of Paris in the 1930s; he covered Mussolini in Abyssinia, the Spanish Civil War, then joined the expatriate Czech army in the UK as a World War II cameraman, worked with the UK Crown Film Unit, freelanced post-war in Fleet Street. His pivotal role in '60s pop photography was little more than a postscript to the central aspect of his life and career – his photographic reportage and involvement in several of the dominant political events of the 20th century. His archive from that period is now housed in the Imperial War Museum.

Dezo was to grow enviably close to the Beatles, closer than any journalist, and the images of them he was to make would come to visually define them during the next two years of their ascent to global domination.

Ian's imminent departure still worried Jimmy. Who would do the layouts? Who would supervise the production? Who would put the paper to bed? Who, in a word, would be the sub-editor? Bringing in an experienced journalist and sub-editor would be expensive and New Record Mirror couldn't afford it. Circulation was rising slowly, but advertising revenue was terrible. Jimmy himself would never take on the work, even assuming he could develop the skills. He never arrived in the office till mid-afternoon. Ian and Peter theorised it was because he liked spending so much time in bed with his new wife Pam.

The solution arrived when Ian suggested to Jimmy that I should do it and Jimmy reluctantly agreed, reluctantly because he considered I already had enough responsibility for someone so young. For the two weeks before he departed, Ian showed me the ropes – how to produce a weekly newspaper. I was amazed at his artistic eye. He'd draw the new layouts on top of a page from a previous issue. This really impressed me. But I couldn't do it. So I dispensed with his method and drew my layouts on large plain sheets of drawing paper with the columns ruled out on a grid.

The method was to take the twelve or sixteen pages, allocate the pitiful amount of advertising, and then design each page using the features, letters, news stories, record and concert reviews as they became deposited into the in-tray during the week. Lots of the photos came from our studio, some from the record companies, some from our own photo-files. I learned to sub-edit the copy, size-up the pictures. Writing headlines was the hard part – the idea was to grab the reader. Jimmy was completely useless at this. In fact, his background wasn't in journalism but PR. He'd worked in the press office of several major record companies and been particularly active in artist liaison. One of his great stories concerned Frankie Lymon and the Teenagers. Jimmy escorted them during their UK tour in '57 and observed a steady supply of prostitutes coming and going to and from their hotel rooms. Jimmy said that one of the girls who'd been with Frankie himself after the Newcastle concert had commented, "He fooks like a little steam engine".

As the layout and headline for each page was finalised, typed copy and photos would be attached and the completed page put in a tray to be collected late every afternoon by the printers' messenger who would put them on the train from Marylebone to High Wycombe. When we arrived at High Wycombe to put the paper to bed on Tuesday morning through to Tuesday evening, roughs would be ready for most pages. Printing was a skilled job requiring apprenticeship, and print meant hot metal. This was letterpress. The copy was set into words, lines and columns of metal type by a compositor. The photographs were electronically engraved by the process department into half-tone metal plates which were 'screened' (made up of graded dots, like pixels) allowing subtleties of shading. It was a complex process. The metal type and the plates and the headlines were mounted on pieces of wood, then arranged on a page-size wooden base with columns to follow the layout. Everything was back-to-front. The wood-and-metal page was then hand-inked, a sheet of paper put on it and pressed down with a roller and the result would be a proof page. That page would be brought to me and I'd work on it, indicating where copy should be cut, where and how pictures should be trimmed and – more difficult – figuring out what to do with any gaps.

The men we worked with were highly skilled. They allowed for my inexpertise and taught me much. Our "main men" were George and Dan, and once I knew the layout of the factory I would frequently wander around by myself to gaze at the huge rotary printing machines in noisy operation, the compositors with their clickety-clacking like organists playing some huge and intricate instrument, the racks full of metal typefaces, the vats of hot metal, the stacks of picture blocks everywhere. It was grimy and you had to wear overalls.

For the first couple of weeks Jimmy met me at the printers on Tuesday morning, worked alongside me, and drove me back in the evening. When he realised I was a quick study, he arrived Tuesday afternoon, checked out the final proofs and drove us back, stopping for food on the way. The first week I put the paper to bed we went to a little restaurant outside High Wycombe and Jimmy bought me my first steak. I was eighteen, never eaten a steak. It came with crinkly chips, tomatoes and mushrooms. I couldn't believe meat could be so delicious. But returning from High Wycombe wasn't always fun. The last of the great smogs descended in '62 and headlights and tail-lights were still feeble, making the journey long, arduous, and dangerous. Heavy rain was another problem: the windscreen wipers on Jimmy's Ford Anglia were vacuum-driven, taking their power from the engine manifold (a crazy system) resulting in dead-slow wipers whilst hurtling, insofar as an Anglia could hurtle, along the A40 in the belting rain.

I picked up the production process quickly, which was unusual because normally I was a slow learner. It was because I enjoyed it all so much. The whole process of producing a newspaper week after week was extremely satisfying. Whereas the journalistic side of New Record Mirror didn't much feel connected to "real" journalism, the production side did have that connection with something real, something solid, a skill, a trade that young men were still being apprenticed to, allied to a staggeringly complex tried-and-tested technology – a technology that in less than thirty years would be completely superseded.

My new infatuation with sub-editing didn't stop me churning out articles. Timeless gems such as *Superstitious Johnny Sings Better With His Shirt Out!* (Tillotson gets casual whilst rehearsing), *Protest For Pitney* (fans bemoan lack of UK hits for Gene, despite huge US success), *Those Forgotten Originals* ("list" feature mildly condemning cover versions), *Fallen Idols* (Bill Haley, Chuck Berry – got that one wrong!), and various seasonal bits and pieces including *The Christmas Hits…or just how many of the Yuletide discs have made the Top 20 grade* (Xmas list), *The Year's Biggest Hits – Survey Of The Year* (end of year chart commentary), *Back In The Good Old Days – The Best-Sellers 1956-1961* (nostalgia lists and commentary) and, in the regular seasonal feature *Our Pick Of The Pops*, both Norman Jopling and Wesley Laine named their fave discs of the year. NJ's threesome were Sam Cooke's back-to-back biggie (as we used to call them) "Havin' A Party" / "Bring It On Home To Me", The Shirelles' "Baby It's You", and The Showmen's "It Will Stand". Who could argue? Wesley went for Buddy Holly's "Reminiscing" / "Wait Till The Sun Shines Nellie", Peter Paul & Mary's "If I Had A Hammer", and the Quotations' doo-wop slaughter of the standard "Imagination". Always a bit of a lightweight character, that Wesley Laine.

But I did nail my colours to the mast with *The Wildest Men In The World – The Story Of The British Rhythm And Blues Riot-Raisers*, profiling Alexis Korner, Chris Farlowe, Jimmy Powell, Mel Turner and Davy Jones. The Cliffs, Adams, and Billys were already explaining they'd always been rhythm & blues fans, and their next disc was "R&B". I resented this, as only an opinionated teenager can: these guys had already had their shot. I knew in my soul that the UK beat boom was about to explode and I knew it would be fuelled by real rhythm

& blues and would ignore the Presley imitators no matter how clever or talented or successful. The pretty boy popsters would simply not register on the wavelength of the future, or so I reasoned.

Our year-end chart survey would be the last before the onslaught of Merseybeat ushered in the UK beat boom and forever changed the course of pop music. The top ten record artists in the UK charts for the year of 1962 – according to the charts point system – were:

UK	USA
Acker Bilk	Chubby Checker
Elvis Presley	Elvis Presley
Cliff Richard	Ray Charles
Billy Fury	Brenda Lee
Kenny Ball	Connie Francis
Chubby Checker	Dion
Frank Ifield	Dee Dee Sharp
The Shadows	Sam Cooke
Karl Denver	Gene Pitney
Pat Boone.	Joey Dee & The Starliters

Acker did that well on the strength of one single, "Stranger On The Shore".

One dark weeknight evening that December I happened to bump into Andrew Oldham on the way to EMI House in Manchester Square. We knew each other slightly, and at that period he was unfailingly polite and politely curious, commenting, as one young dandy to another (or so I assumed), that he very much liked my suit and he supposed that I must have, what, about ten or a dozen suits? What could I say? I said Yes, I did. In fact I had two.

As we approached EMI we saw to our amazement it was swarming with ecstatic semi-hysterical girls. It seemed that the Beatles were there that evening. Neither Andrew nor I were visiting EMI in connection with the Beatles but there was something slightly awesome about this spectacle. I'd seen plenty of crazy fans before but this lot were different. There was a radiance about them. We stood and stared at the girls, then looked at each other. We knew instantly something magic was happening. A week or so later I heard Andrew was working as PR for Brian Epstein. He was that on the ball.

Andrew had become an established presence during '62 among the music-business publicity agents, that fraternity of professionally-amiable hustlers who enjoyed a symbiotic relationship, usually over a glass, with any journalist able to deliver column inches devoted to their respective clients. Ex-journalists frequently gravitated to PR as it paid more money, but Andrew was not from a journalistic background. Nevertheless he, and many of his friends and contemporaries, tell his story very well in his autobiographies *Stoned* and *2Stoned*, both of which are veritable bibles of the UK music scene in the crucial years of the Sixties, albeit reflecting Andrew's precociously razor-sharp sensibilities and filtered through his somewhat idiosyncratic spectrum. He was the same age as me – twenty-one days older actually – but a lot more worldly. He dressed with great style and originality without excess, was extremely self-aware, and seemed hugely driven, though towards what I'd no idea and probably neither did he. But in a few months time Peter Jones and to a certain extent myself would help him find a vehicle for his visions.

1963

Nineteen sixty-three was to prove a good year for meeting like-minded music fiends – similar age, similar wavelength – who'd started hanging around the music business. This was to be the year British music finally began reflecting the Sixties instead of the Fifties. And it was the year my personal taste proved, briefly, enough in tune with the zeitgeist – which you'd think was a obligatory requirement for a pop music reporter, but plenty get by without it – that I would score a major scoop. Well, I should qualify the bit about being in tune with the zeitgeist. I appreciated the phenomenon of the Beatles and everything that followed, or wallowed, in their wake, but the sounds of the Beatles and Merseybeat and the beat boom were never on my record player and were seldom played at the clubs and dives where I hung out. And all the UK groups and solo artists I interviewed or socialised with in '63 knew they weren't as good as the Americans. It wouldn't be for another year till British pop music would evolve sufficiently to stand in the same artistic arena as the Americans.

The New Record Mirror office was always accessible to anyone who wanted to see us – 116 Shaftesbury Avenue was a convenient and central location. Our friends would pop in, musicians, managers, agents, promotion people, the occasional fan trying his or her luck. At lunchtimes Peter Jones held court at DeHems Oyster Bar, a pub with a U-shaped bar, just round the corner in Macclesfield Street.

Peter always sat on the same stool in the same spot at the bar. The same sorts of people congregated there during the extended lunch hour between 12.30am and 3.15pm. Jimmy rarely went to the pub, mainly because he was rarely in the office that early. Roy preferred to drink at his jazz clubs, and Ian would drop in regularly from his new job at NME. But it was Peter most people wanted to see: genial, good company, and, importantly, an easy touch for those precious column inches.

A new and friendly face who came up and introduced himself to me at the beginning of 1963 was Guy Stevens, intrigued by a music journalist writing about rhythm & blues. Guy was about to become an influential person: Ivy League-styled, moon-faced with short curly hair already thinning, Guy was THE rhythm & blues fan par excellence. A year older than me and already married, his tastes were eclectic, his knowledge awesome, his record collection unmatched, and his enthusiasm overwhelming. We hit it off, our tastes mutually veering towards a hard, rock'n'roll-flavoured rhythm & blues, and Guy's erudition made my own knowledge seem patchy. He was the expert, the guru, someone to learn from, and was happy to share his knowledge of the music he loved. This gave him credence with everyone on the scene from musicians to managers to record company executives to fellow fans to friendly journalists. He worked in insurance in the City when I met him, but never spoke about it. Anyway, he soon blagged his way into the music business.

I kicked off my '63 scribblings with a list of the previous year's million-sellers; then a couple of pieces about the rise of the Phil Spector and the Cameo-Parkway groups; various *Fallen Idols* (Fats Domino, Emile Ford, Jackie Wilson, The Marcels); *The Neglected Shirelles* (more plugs for my favourite girl group); *Hits & Hurricanes* (Johnny & The Hurricanes finally tour the UK – but it should have been a *Fallen Idols* column as they'd been hitless for almost two years); *The Off-Beat Teen-Beat* (the long-forgotten Federals); *The Love Or Hate Sound* (the falsetto than "annoys or appeals" – Frankie Valli / The Four Seasons / Vee-Jay Records); *"I Dared Not Hold My Head Up"* (Mel Turner, "the wildest man in the world"); *"Give Me The Flamenco"* (that's what Chris Montez told me); *Beatles Beatles* (Fab Four update as "Please Please Me" rockets up the charts, "Love Me Do" slowly descends, John Lennon talks to Wesley Laine on the phone); *Elvis – Or Pelvis!* (summing up bags of letters from fans of the post-Army Elvis vs. fans of the pre-Army "Pelvis"); *Is Elvis Becoming A Hermit?* (Wesley Laine realises Elvis doesn't tour anywhere anymore); *Don't Call Us 'Paddy' Begged The Bachelors* (likeable Irish trio plugging debut hit "Charmaine") *The Beatles – New Album & Single* (more Beatles updates – we'd put them on the front and sold more papers – and this time John Lennon speaks to Norman Jopling on the phone instead of Wesley Laine. Does he notice it's the same person? No...)

In the third week of February I was sitting in a large bright chilly room at Merritt & Hatcher in High Wycombe, checking and correcting proofs, when I started getting terrible stomach pains. Jimmy arrived, took one look at me, and drove me to the station, sent me home on the train and finished the paper alone. Back home the pains were worse. I couldn't move, so the doctor came to see me. It was appendicitis and I was off work for three weeks.

While I was absent from NRM Jimmy had to sub-edit the paper. The headlines were awful. But he did fill in as a substitute on my *Fallen Idols* column and penned a fine piece on Frankie Lymon. One of the best things he wrote, it included his on-the-spot memories of Frankie's UK tour, omitting to mention the queues of prostitutes and the "little steam engine" story. Peter Jones got in on the act too, writing about his old buddy Johnnie Ray for the next *Fallen Idols*. Ray even wrote to Peter thanking him for the article, the only Fallen Idol ever to so do.

I staggered back to the office in some pain, and after reclaiming my *Fallen Idols* column with a piece on the String-A-Longs (not quite in the same class as Frankie Lymon or Johnnie Ray), I decided that the column's popularity, which we tended to judge on the amount of feedback from readers, was sufficient to launch yet another regular NJ column. This time I slyly decided on a column which would give me an excuse to feature all the rhythm & blues greats who would normally merit only a line in *A Look At The US Charts*. With breathtaking originality I christened it *The Great Unknowns* and launched with a piece on Tamla's Miracles. How I loved Tamla Motown! Not yet the Hit Factory (certainly not in the UK), in early '63 records from the Berry Gordy stable of labels were rare and mostly unreleased here. Berry's Anna and Tamla labels had first been distributed by Decca via

London American: then Fontana (part of the Philips group) released a handful of 45s from the Tamla, Motown and Gordy labels by the Miracles, Eddie Holland and the Marvelettes, and now the little UK independent Oriole had acquired the licensing rights and was embarking on a more ambitious release programme which included LPs. By the time the first *The Great Unknowns* appeared, Oriole had already issued several Mary Wells sides – "You Beat Me To The Punch" and "Two Lovers", plus the Contours' "Do You Love Me" and the Marvelettes' "Beechwood 45789". One of the aims of the article was to persuade Oriole to release "You Really Got A Hold On Me" by the Miracles, which they soon did, and *The Great Unknowns* went on to become the most popular thing I'd ever write. Decades later, enthusiasts would contact me who'd cut them all out and lovingly pasted them in scrapbooks. Amazing! But it wasn't easy collating the info on these obscure artists. I had to scour the US music mags, garner bits from the backs of EPs and LPs, pick up a bit of gossip here and there. Maybe make something up. Nowadays an incredible amount of detailed information is available about rhythm & blues, soul music, black music in general. Back in '63, little of that had been revealed. I was a pioneer and proud of it.

One day Jimmy hired some men to dismantle and remove Issy's huge table which dominated the editorial office. It was appropriate that it should go. Issy had gone, now it was his table's turn. It was replaced by three desks, one for Jimmy, one for Peter, one for me. Mr Frankham persuaded Decca we needed a full-time accountant and so they hired Pat Farnham for us. Jimmy's editorial decisions seemed to be steering us along the right course because the circulation was now rising rapidly. Pat, a warm attractive brunette, moved in with Roy Burden into the advertising, circulation, and now accounts and finance room next door to the editorial office. Everyone also got a new telephone, the swish new plastic 700 series in various colours replacing our battered black bakelite 332s.

We all used manual typewriters: Peter's, the newest, was all in upper-case but with the capital letters a size up, which was sometimes confusing when subbing his copy. Peter was always first in the office.

His routine rarely changed. He would arrive early and hammer out his freelance columns for other publications. He always had several on the go, not to mention books, ghost-writings, and much else I never knew about. He'd then concentrate on his Record Mirror features and reviews, typing like a machine-gun and flipping through his shorthand notes.

Not being a trained journalist I knew no shorthand but nevertheless took my notebook to interviews and scribbled down what I considered to be the key quotes as fast as possible, missing out obvious words which I could fill in later. I discovered it was possible to develop my memory prodigiously, and fortunately no-one ever complained about being misquoted.

Peter would finish most of his writing by twelve-thirty, then walk to DeHems to hold court. Many were the artists who trotted obediently along to be interviewed by him there, so congenial was the environment. Peter did also attend receptions, go to hotels, parties, record companies, wherever necessary, for interviews – but not unless he had to. He was far happier at his "office" at DeHems, his home-from-home. Unfortunately he tended to be slightly irascible on his return to the office mid-afternoon, around the time Jimmy would usually roll into the office after, presumably, lying a-bed all morning with his lovely blonde wife Pam. Roy Burden was another of the gang whose drinking – and furtive pot-smoking – often put him in a surly mood later in the day...but then, at five-thirty pm, the doors of the pubs would open, off they'd trot, and all would be well again. Roy suffered from what David Griffiths would later, sympathetically, describe as "Burden-itis": "When I have a drink it makes me want a smoke, and when I have a smoke it makes me want a drink".

Peter was now coming into the office daily, and newshound David Griffiths arrived each Monday to finish off his news page and get assigned, or assign himself, an interview feature for the following week's edition. We still used a wide range of reliable out-of-town freelance writers: Alan Stinton, in Birmingham, would soon contribute a regular "Brum Beat" column in addition to his reviews or features; Graeme Andrews and Ray Nortrop still contributed many fine leading articles and interviews; Jeff Bayliss supplied our "Provincial Round Up"; Merseybeat's pioneering editor Bill Harry was recruited for a "Northern Beat Scene" column; Graham Knight specialised in vintage rock'n'roll stories and interviews; and Leslie Gaylor, who ran the Bing Crosby Appreciation Society, specialised in all things Bing. There were other fans whose enthusiastic scribblings often proved so useful and interesting as well as perceptive and often well-written that we would run them, payment-less, for the "glory" of a by-line. We could also cram more in: early in '63 Jimmy changed the format from five columns to six columns and cut the size of the headlines proportionately. It worked. And it looked tighter.

My own enthusiastic scribblings continued. When Maureen Evans' "Like I Do" and the Cougars' "Saturday Night At The Duck Pond" charted the same week, my hoary old pop-hits-with-classical-tunes article got wheeled out again and rewritten as *Those Musical Mutilations* (the above mutilatees being "Waltz Of The Hours" and "Swan Lake" respectively); *The Great Unknowns* continued with Buddy Knox and Roy Hamilton; *A Year Of R&B* (survey of US chart activity); The Springfields popped into the office, Dusty truly groovy (and funny), a memorable 'compliment' from Cliff providing the headline *The White Negress – That's What They Call Me*; Del Shannon was *The Biggest Star For Five Years*; on the transatlantic phone (an expensive luxury then) 'The Big O' denied that art mirrored life, declaring: *"I'm A Very Jolly Person" said Roy Orbison, the Saddest Singer On Record* – though his life, tragically, would soon mirror his art. *"You Sound Too Much Like Elvis"* profiled Ral Donner; *Fallen Idols* limped on with the Fleetwoods and Gene Vincent, the latter penned, strangely, by Wesley Laine; I reviewed two important LPs in depth – Buddy Holly's "Reminiscing" and, crucially, the Beatles' "Please Please Me". I also suggested most of Chubby Checker's hits were somewhat less than original creations, but Jimmy, fearing the wrath of Pye Records, changed my headline *The Unoriginal Dance King* to *He's The Commercial Dance King*, and toned down my invective.

That April I managed to monopolise pages 6 and 7, generally the middle pages of our slender newspaper, with the *Rhythm & Blues Centre Spread* featuring *The Man With A Hundred Guitars – Diddley The Great*; (profile on my hero Bo Diddley); *The Soul-Beat revival* (interview with Cyril Davies who'd formed a breakaway group from the Korner ensemble); *When Chuck Shocked Jazz Fans* (biog on Mr Berry); and *The*

Great Unknowns – Ben E. King. The spread was my clarion call, tying in with Pye Records' Pye International label's R&B Series which had just released a batch of singles by Bo Diddley, Sonny Boy Williamson, Cyril Davies and Howlin' Wolf, and LPs by Diddley and Chuck Berry. Rhythm & blues was exploding in the UK and the shock waves would soon be heard around the world.

Two years ago I'd landed my dream job and now I'd found my mission: to write about rhythm & blues, spread the word in print. Fortunately I didn't need to be any great shakes as a writer in order to fulfil this self-appointed destiny – all I needed to do was a lot of raving and shouting about the artists and music I liked. I was just nineteen, opinionated, with the arrogance of youth. One of my opinions, never reflected in print but which I certainly didn't keep quiet about, was that the British so-called rhythm & blues movement was useless. The previous year I regularly checked out Alexis Korner's Blues Incorporated at Ealing Jazz Club and at the Marquee, followed the comings and goings of the various vocalists and musicians who wandered in and out of his troupe, kept checking them out, and after a while even stopped being disappointed as one contender after another just didn't hit the spot – and not for lack of trying. The purist expectations I'd brought along, fuelled as much by my own wishful thinking as by the underground whisperings that so-and-so or such-and-such was the great white hope of UK rhythm and blues, were regularly dashed. I became resigned to the fact that British rhythm & blues, in my closeted opinion, was even more useless than British rock'n'roll, which had at least produced a handful of good records. But in fairness, Cyril Davies did manage a scintillating single with "Country Line Special" in the Pye R&B series – the man could seriously blow harp.

One afternoon in April Peter Jones returned again slightly irascible from DeHems and, like a recurring nightmare, yet again began subjecting me to a haranguing on the subject of Giorgio Gomelsky's constant pestering. Gomeslky, a Russian émigré, had been an important figure on the '50s UK jazz scene. He'd worked extensively for Chris Barber where his contacts with American blues artists brought by

Barber to the UK had given him a keen appreciation of their music. Giorgio was also a film-maker, an actor, concert promoter and club manager. His latest in a series of mostly short-lived club ventures was the Craw-Daddy Club, held on Sunday evenings at the Station Hotel, Kew Road, Richmond. The club's latest attraction – resident attraction, in fact – was a rhythm & blues combo called the Rollin' Stones, who Giorgio had met the previous year and had featured once or twice at his Piccadilly Jazz Club off Great Windmill Street, now closed and about to reincarnate as the Scene club.

Giorgio believed in the Rollin' Stones with missionary fervour and was also acting as their unofficial manager although no written agreement was in place. Giorgio could also talk…and talk…and talk he did to Peter Jones in DeHems, till Peter finally succumbed and travelled from his home in Wanstead to Richmond in Surrey one Sunday evening to check out Giorgio's boys. Giorgio probably never knew what an achievement it was to get Peter to do this.

The problem was that Peter wouldn't write about rhythm & blues. He left writing about rhythm and blues to me, the self-appointed rhythm & blues advocate.

Peter stood there looking down on me as I tried to hide myself pretending to be completely involved in designing some exquisitely difficult layout. I knew what was coming. Giorgio pesters Peter, Peter pesters me.

First, there was the sigh, the sigh of one attempting to be reasonable in the face of someone else's pathetic failure to grasp the obvious.

"Giorgio was there again."

I decided to cut him off at the pass.

"Peter, believe me, all British rhythm & blues is crap."

"Well they sounded good to me, they really know their stuff…"

"How would you know? Peter, you don't really like rhythm & blues, so how d'you know?"

"Why don't you just go down there and see them?"

"I know what they'll be like. They'll be rubbish."

Peter thought for a moment. "I can't stand it anymore. Giorgio's on my back all the time. I s'pose I'll have to write about them then."

"Yes, that's good, you've seen them, you write about them."

68

The trouble was that Peter really didn't want to write about them. He just wanted Giorgio off his back. He wanted me to write about them.

He turned his biggest gun on me.

"You're supposed to be the rhythm & blues expert..."

There was something the "supposed to be" that got me. I finally capitulated.

"All right."

He visibly relaxed with relief.

"I can tell Giorgio...?"

"Next Sunday, I'll take Bill and get some pictures."

Even better. Peter Jones was happy.

Bill Williams, photographer, caterer to the 'boys in blue', insisted I meet him en route to the Station Hotel the following Sunday. Jill and I hung around at the appointed rendezvous, Bill appeared, we jumped in his car and tried to jump out again. It stank.

"Spilt some bloody milk, can't get rid of the smell."

Retching, we drove the rest of the way with heads thrust as far out of the open windows as possible.

When we arrived, late, there was a crowd of kids outside the Station Hotel who couldn't get in – the place was packed full. In time-honoured journalistic style we elbowed our way to the front, flashed various press cards, cameras, demanded to see Giorgio. The noise was already fantastic – Giorgio appeared and just pushed us into the room where the Rollin' Stones were already playing.

It was one of those Bo Diddley songs with a Bo Diddley beat. I'd never heard anything like it in a live act. I'd never felt anything like it. The place shook, everyone in the audience was wet with sweat, the sound was bouncing off the walls, throbbing, utterly irresistible. It lifted me up and swept me along, song after song.

The personnel in the group were not entirely unfamiliar. I recognised a couple of them from playing on and off with Korner, and the singer I'd seen several times in the Star Cafe in Great Chapel Street which did a decent five-bob lunch. He was known to everyone there simply as "the rhythm & blues singer". I thought it was a joke till I saw him perform. But the sound they made together was nothing like Korner's worthy troupe. This was alchemy. It was perfect – rhythm & blues in Chicago couldn't have been any more exciting than this. I was almost in a state of shock. After the initial rush, my brain switched back on and my first thought was like, we could do it. White people could do it.

Well, that's how it seemed at the time. Maybe white people never got to do it any better than the Stones did in those early days, which is why the music changed and became rock music, that mulatto child of rhythm & blues that white people actually could do. After the gig, as the crowd melted away, Jill and I just stood there, looking at each other, silent. We knew what we'd heard. Bill had taken some pictures and told us he was going, did we want a lift? We couldn't bear getting back in his stinky car and anyway Giorgio was glad-handing me, what did I think, what did I want to do, come along with me and the boys we're going to see so-and-so.

Bill split and Jill and I hung around chatting to Giorgio, being introduced to the Rollin' Stones one by one as they ambled off-stage. Brian, the most intense character, was the chattiest, doing a PR job on me. What can you do for us? he asked. What could I say? Anything they wanted, really.

Their pianist, Ian Stewart, offered to drive us, so together with a couple of cars made our way to the house of "a producer". I was still in a haze, a blur, the impressions had overwhelmed me, I was disoriented. There was no indication what kind of producer he was; middle-aged, American, had a big dark pad, there were musical instruments everywhere. I got the feeling he was a film producer. All the Stones started picking up instruments and playing around on them. Drinks were poured, everyone relaxed, unwound, I started chatting to the guys. I was surprised to see Mick, the singer, trying out several instruments. He had the hardest job in the band, fronting that incredible sound and holding his own. He was polite, distant, not just from me but from everyone that evening. I spoke mostly with Charlie and Keith, who, like me, was a big Mary Wells fan – we shared our disappointment with "Laughing Boy" but hoped that "Your Old Stand-By" would be return to form (it was). Those were the kinds of conversations everyone had in those days. I arranged to see Brian, who seemed to be the group's leader and spokesman, up at Record Mirror the following week. Eventually Jill and I left. Ian drove us all the way home to Winchmore Hill, a fair trek from the house of "the producer" which was near Richmond. But it was the small hours of the morning, traffic was light.

Next day, Monday, I went straight to work from staying with Jill. The paper was put to bed on Tuesday, and as I had to finish the last layouts – generally the news pages – I spent the morning writing headlines for David's news stories, shuffling stories around on the page to fit, putting a few finishing touches here and there and then grabbing a cab to Marylebone for the train to High Wycombe. I'd made a few notes about the Rollin' Stones but there was no urgency to write the article. There was no record to tie it on, and anyway, Bill's photos wouldn't be ready till Tuesday. So the article, not yet written, missed the next issue of New Record Mirror.

I told Peter how wild and great they were, told him I'd write a rave story on them, and how wrong I'd been. This pleased him.

When I got back to the office that Wednesday, I sat down to write the article having the distinct feeling that I should be very careful in what I said. This had nothing to do with any premonition about how big the Rollin' Stones would become – how could anyone know that? – but more to do with the fact that there were certain expectations attached to the article: Peter's, Giorgio's, the group's. Also, it was the first time I could remember a feature article written in New Record Mirror about an act that didn't yet have a record – after all, that's why we were called 'Record Mirror'. So I wrote the article – carefully – and chose one of Bill's photos and scheduled it for either the following week's issue, or the issue after that. I don't remember which. The chronology of what happened at that eventful time in the career of the Rollin' Stones still doesn't make sense to me, no matter how many times I read everyone's reminiscences, go over and over the dates, and who did what, or saw whom, or said what.

But the most important thing, as far as helping the group, had little to do with me or my article. Peter Jones, sitting on his favourite stool and holding court that week in DeHems, was now being harangued not by Giorgio Gomeslky, but by Andrew Oldham, whose clients included Brian Epstein's burgeoning NEMS stable. As usual Andrew was hustling for coverage, and Peter advised him to check out the

Rollin' Stones, mentioning that they were about to get a rave write-up in Record Mirror – the first group without a record to be featured in our columns.

At that time I assumed Peter simply thought the Stones would make another fine client for Andrew's publicity stable, but many years later he told me that management was in fact what he'd suggested to Andrew, based, I guess, on what he'd discussed with the group when he'd met them a few weeks previously. The rest, as they say, is history: Oldham also went to see the Stones, experienced the epiphany, and moved in on them to become their co-manager together with agent Eric Easton, record producer, and crucially, all-round Svengali, essentially creating their image. Andrew was arguably more responsible than anyone else, including the band themselves, for the huge success of the Rollin' Stones – or, as he would shortly rename them, The Rolling Stones. Funnily enough the headline on my article prophetically misspelled their name as The Rolling Stones

That same week, after I wrote the article but before it was published, Giorgio and some of the Rollin' Stones visited Record Mirror to take me and Peter to see a film Giorgio had shot of the group performing Bo Diddley's "Pretty Thing". Giorgio had hired one of those little preview theatres around Wardour Street. I was a bit surprised because Oldham was already with the group, whisperings were going on, and he seemed to be getting on famously with them.

Whether or not Giorgio was deliberately ousted by Andrew Oldham is a matter for conjecture. Somehow I doubt it. Back-stabbing didn't seem like Oldham's style – I think he would have considered it beneath him. April and May 1963 were seminal months in the group's career: local reporter Barry May from The Richmond And Twickenham Times was the first journalist ever to give the Stones a write-up, in the April 13th issue of his paper. The Beatles, Peter Jones, myself, Andrew Oldham, all saw the group during April at the Crawdaddy. Andrew then moved quickly. By the time my article – their first national write-up and the first by a music reporter – appeared early in May, Oldham and Eric Easton had already formulated their master-plan, signed the group to a management contract, and would shortly sign a lease-tape deal with an eager Decca Records, still smarting over rejecting the Beatles. New Record Mirror hit the streets on May 8th with the Rollin' Stones' article on Page 2, and that afternoon three of the four major record companies phoned me to find out where they could contact the group. I told them to talk to Andrew Oldham who I now knew was involved in their management, although I was still under the impression that Giorgio was involved. The rise of the Rolling Stones was destiny, and destiny won't be denied: I don't think Oldham had any choice in the matter.

Incredibly, Giorgio had also managed to disappear for several days at this particularly eventful time without telling anyone where he was or for how long he'd be gone. In fact he was abroad attending his father's funeral. Andrew Oldham subsequently stated that during the management negotiations at this time, the group never even mentioned Giorgio.

A strange post-script to this episode occurred thirty-two years later in 1995 when Andrew co-wrote a book with Tony Calder and Colin Irwin titled *Abba – The Name Of The Game*. They launched the book at the big HMV store in Oxford Street and hired Abba tribute band Bjorn Again to perform there for the book signing. I was invited to the press reception by Calder, Oldham's one-time partner in Immediate Records, with whom I'd recently been in contact – but I hadn't seen or heard from Andrew since 1972 in New York, twenty three years earlier.

HMV was packed. I shoved my way in, took a book from the stack and waited in the queue with all the punters to get it signed by the authors before going out back to the press reception. As I approached the table where the three authors wearily sat signing, Tony Calder saw me and grinned and said to Oldham, "It's Norman Jopling!" Andrew glanced up, clocked me, and without a word scribbled in my book with big black marker pen. He wrote: "Norman, where was Giorgio?"

NRM w/e 11th May 1963
THE ROLLING STONES – GENUINE R&B!

AS the trad scene gradually subsides, promoters of all kinds of teen-beat entertainment heave a long sigh of relief that they have found something to take its place. It's Rhythm and Blues, of course – the number of R&B clubs that have sprung up is nothing short of fantastic.

One of the best-known – and one of the most successful to date – is at the Station Hotel, Kew Road, in Richmond, just on the outskirts of London. There, on Sunday evenings, the hip kids throw themselves about to the new "jungle music" like they never did in the more stinted days of trad.

And the combo they writhe and twist to is called the Rollin' Stones. Maybe you've never heard of them – if you live far away from London the odds are you haven't.

But by gad you will! The Rollin' Stones are probably destined to be the biggest group in the R&B scene if it continues to flourish. And by the looks of the Station Hotel, Richmond, flourish is merely an understatement considering that three months ago only fifty people turned up to see the group. Now club promoter, bearded Giorgio Gomelsky, has to close the doors at an early hour – over four hundred R&B fans crowd the hall.

GENUINE

And the fans who do come quickly lose all their inhibitions and proceed to contort themselves to the truly exciting music of the boys – who put heart and soul into their performances.

The fact is that, unlike all the other R&B groups worthy of the name, the Rollin' Stones have a definite visual appeal. They aren't the Jazzmen who were doing Trad eighteen months back and who have converted their act to keep up with the times. They are genuine R&B fanatics themselves, and they sing and play in a way that one would expect more from a coloured U.S. R&B team than a bunch of wild, exciting white boys who have the fans screaming – and listening – to them.

Line-up of the group is Mick Jagger, lead vocal and harmonica and student at the London School of Economics. The fierce backing is supplied by Brian Jones, guitar and harmonica, and also spokesman and leader of the group. He's an architect, while Keith Richards, guitar, is an art student. The other three members of the group are Bill Wyman, bass guitar, Ian Stuart, piano and maracas, and drummer Charles Watts.

Record-wise, everything is in the air, but a disc will be forthcoming. It will probably be the group's own adaptation of the Chuck Berry number "Come On" (featured on Chuck's new Pye LP). The number goes down extremely well in the club session on Sundays – other Chuck Berry numbers that are in the group's repertoire are "Down The Road Apiece" and "Bye Bye Johnny" – which is one of the highlights of the act.

DISC/FILM

Even though the boys haven't dead-certain plans for a disc, they do have dead-certain plans for a film. For club promoter Giorgio is best known as a film producer and has made several imaginative films dealing with the music scene. But for the Rollin' Stones film, there are some truly great shots of the team in action, singing and performing "Pretty Thing", the Bo Diddley number. The film itself lasts for twenty minutes and will be distributed with a main feature film.

The group are actually mad about Bo Diddley, although pianist Ian Stuart is the odd man out. Diddley numbers they perform are "Crawdad", "Nursery Rhyme", "Road Runner", "Mona" and, of course, "Bo Diddley".

They can get the sound that Bo gets too – no mean achievement. The group themselves are all red-hot when it comes to U.S. beat discs. They know their R&B numbers inside out and have a repertoire of about eighty songs, most of them are the numbers which every R&B fan in the country knows and loves.

The boys are confident that, if they make a disc, it should do well. They are also confident about their own playing, although on Sundays at the end of the session they are dead-beat. That's because on Sunday afternoons they also play the R&B session at the Ken Colyer club.

SUPERFICIAL

But despite fact that their R&B has a superficial resemblance to rock'n'roll, fans of the hit parade music would not find any familiar material performed by the Rollin' Stones. And the boys do not use original material. "After all," they say, "can you imagine a British-composed R&B number – it just wouldn't make it."

One group that thinks a lot of the Rollin' Stones are The Beatles. When they came down to London the other week, they were knocked out by the group's singing. They stayed all the evening at the Station Hotel listening to the group pound away. And now they spread the word around so much in Liverpool that bookings for the group have been flooding in –including several the famed Cavern.

All this can't be bad for the R&B group who have achieved the American sound better than any other group over here. And the group that in all likelihood will soon be the leading R&B performers in the country...

Everyone gets it right sometimes…

Like most teenagers I raced around hither and thither at an enormous speed. Staying in was not an option: television was for old or sick people. From the age of fifteen when my friends and I relentlessly trudged or biked through the streets, mooched around various youth clubs and played poker at each other's houses, the attractions of the outside world broadened to include coffee bars, the dance palaces, ever-more-frequent cinema, pubs, concerts, parties, rock hops; with Jill I also attended the theatre, jazz concerts, the ballet, and an assortment of 'soirees'. But, thus far, clubbing was not my game. Jill liked to go to London's French clubs like La Poubelle and Le Discotheque, but not moi. So she went to those places with her girl friends. And although the Flamingo was an exciting club, I was never fully at ease there. But I was shortly to discover a club I would love.

One morning that May an ebulliently bright-faced Guy Stevens arrived breathlessly at Record Mirror and announced proudly that he was now a dee-jay with a residency at the Scene Club, a month-old and according to Guy exciting-sounding basement dive in cobbled little Ham Yard, off Great Windmill Street, itself off Shaftesbury Avenue, conveniently not five minutes from Record Mirror. The premise had incarnated through countless transformations and was now run by Irish entrepreneur and idealist Ronan O'Rahilly and his business partner, genial South African Lionel Blake. It was unlicensed, featured live attractions, with the music policy more-or-less based around rhythm & blues. It opened from 7.30 or 8.00pm to 2.00am, or 3.00am at weekends – Friday and Saturday. Guy had been given the "dead spot" – Monday evening – in the hope of attracting a crowd that would flock to hear and/or dance to great rhythm & blues records, popular and obscure.

Guy's rhythm & blues (not to mention R&R, blues, jazz) record collection was already one of the best in the UK. This gig was his big break, his entrée into the music business. The following Monday I found the dingy entrance to the Scene and announced myself to the two guys on the door. True to his word Guy had left my name, my hand was stamped to glow in the ultra-violet light, and thus it was forevermore: I never paid to get into the Scene.

The Scene wasn't big, it was seedy, dark, and full of darker corners: Guy operated from an enclosed booth to the left of the entrance, and the stage was on the right. There was a bar which didn't serve alcohol, a dance floor, and not much else. The atmosphere was almost always good, easy-going. It was low-key, relaxed, modest and unpretentious, the focus was on the music so there was no brazen hip, no blatant cool, everyone was digging the same thing and that was all that mattered. You didn't have to dress up or dress down but could if you felt like it. It was an ideal place to meet like-minded friends and acquaintances. It wasn't a pulling club: there were generally far more boys than girls. For the next year, maybe eighteen months, the Scene club was the hottest little club in London: and in 1963 London was the centre of the world – even if the rest of the world didn't know it quite yet.

Monday nights at the Scene were fun. I'd spend most of the evening in the booth with Guy, who kept his precious records in a big wooden box which he'd sit on. The booth had twin turntables but no dee-jay address system, so punters were always knocking on the booth door to enquire about the record he was playing: "Who's 'Money Honey' is this?" "It's the Hollywood Flames!" "Great version!" Although Guy was another certified rhythm & blues apostle fanatically intent on spreading the word about this hitherto neglected music, he remained loyal to his rock'n'roll roots: if he felt like playing Jerry Lee – his first hero – he would. And Little Richard and Carl Perkins. Fringe jazz – Jimmy Smith, Jimmy McGriff, vocalists like Carmen McRae, Mose Allison – Guy would throw them all in. In a matter of weeks he became 'the man', London's top rhythm & blues dee-jay: actually he was the only London rhythm & blues dee-jay.

The Scene had good acoustics, probably by accident, and rhythm & blues records sounded big and brilliant pumped out loud on their sound system. Sometimes Mondays were moderately full, other times not. A bit of dancing, mostly young guys jigging around, drinking coke, slipping a drop of scotch in, mod pill-heads, suburban record fans, ordinary kids, young musicians, young music business people. But you didn't show up on Monday just for the social scene – it was for love of the music.

I never quite found out what Ronan O'Rahilly's agenda was, though Guy seemed to think it was something to do with the Kennedys and the IRA – a united Ireland seemed to be the city in the sky, with the Scene helping fund the wherewithal. Later, in '65 when purportedly the management unwisely stopped paying West End Central, there was a big police raid. The noise of the deafening clatter of pills hitting the Scene floor has passed into legend. It was serious: Lionel took the fall for Ronan and was banged up for a year. That was the end of the Scene. There was a "New Scene" but it wasn't the same. Yet I never saw Guy popping pills, and I certainly didn't; it was still just booze. But I was naturally twitchy and highly-strung and always getting hit on by some frazzled mod desperate for speed – blues, hearts, black bombers and other exciting-sounding stimulants, unknown to me but most familiar to another Scene regular, future legend Peter Meaden, fast becoming one of my bosom buddies.

The live nights at the Scene could be equally brilliant. Chris Farlowe – arguably Britain's best-ever blues voice – with the Thunderbirds;

78

Georgie Fame & the Blue Flames, also resident at the Flamingo, always a hot live attraction who managed to ensnare both jazz and rhythm & blues fans. Georgie was a unique performer who'd managed to slip away from Larry Parnes' pop-idol stable but kept the name Larry dreamed up for him. He wasn't the only one: despite the show-biz sniggers, most Parnes' protégés remained wedded to their monikers long after Larry's reign as Britain's top pop manager was over.

In June the Rolling Stones played a four-week Scene residency on Thursdays; the Roosters, featuring Eric Clapton and Tom McGuinness, also performed, albeit somewhat irregularly. Eric also played there during his brief stint with Casey Jones & the Engineers. That autumn when Bo Diddley toured – a God come down to earth – he too appeared at the Scene. I loved Bo Diddley more than any artist since Buddy Holly, so it was very clever of Guy to suggest that he should write a piece for New Record Mirror on the great man, accompanied by a discography, esoteric information only available to someone like Guy who, somehow, had this enviable data at his fingertips. Anyway, I was happy to raise Guy's profile by letting him freelance in Record Mirror and I made sure he got big by-lines like 'By Guy Stevens, R&B DJ'. It was all for 'The Cause'.

I used to come into the office most Saturday mornings and one Saturday Guy brought up Eric Clapton who just sat around saying not very much at all and looking extremely flash. Guy took me aside and whispered that this guy – I'm not even sure he knew Eric's name then – was a brilliant blues guitarist. I took an immediate dislike to Eric for looking so great and being so insouciant in my territory. A day or so later I felt very ashamed of myself for having such feelings with absolutely no proper cause. So when Eric got stranded a couple of times after gigs at the Scene, I'd give him a lift to wherever it was he lived in South London on the back of my scooter which I kept parked in Ham Yard. I felt this would neutralise my negativity, and so it did. Eric was always perfectly polite and amiable.

Guy was the best record-finder I ever knew. Lady Luck often holds hands with the fanatical (for a while), and so it was with Guy and his records. One day he phoned me in a state of feverish excitement saying I had to go to so-and-so record shop in Scala Street off Tottenham Court Road. Somehow he had discovered that in the shop's basement were thousand of pristine 45s, promotional copies sent out by all of the record companies since the advent of the 45rpm single in the mid-50s. This was a treasure trove. Guy had already been there, creamed the collection as far as rhythm & blues and rock'n'roll was concerned, but told me there were still plenty of goodies left. He had managed to buy these discs for a shilling each (5p) – the cost of a new 45 was then nearly seven shillings– and he had spent all the money he had and all he had been able to lay his hands on.

I raced along and the proprietor was happy to let me take the pick of Guy's leavings, which were considerable. Every one was a promotional disc: regular 45s with 'Demonstration' stickers, early A-labels, yellow Londons, orange Londons, some double-sided, the earlier ones single-sided. White EMIs, big and little A's, everything ever issued in the UK – and plenty that never even got played on the radio. It was an unbelievable stash – like a dream where you find desirable things. Who had they originally been sent to? How had the shop obtained them? No-one there seemed to know. I spent all my money too, laden-down I had to get a cab back to RM, and run inside for the fare.

Those demo 45s became an integral part of Guy's great collection. The following year, inspired by the success of a little basement business called Transat Imports in Lisle Street where he'd bought lots of rare US singles and albums, Guy would start his own record import business called Atlantic Imports, buying his stock from quirky American one-stop record shops with names like Stans and Ernies, whose catalogues were so thorough that they were virtual discographies of many obscure artists about whom no other reliable information was available.

Guy then decided to bring himself to the attention of the major record companies and was soon advising several of them on rhythm & blues releases. His first job was compiling EMI's Stateside label LP "Authentic R&B" from the Excello catalogue (Slim Harpo, Lazy Lester, Lightnin' Slim), but he really hit his stride a few months later with Pye's R&B series. Pye had managed an excellent initial batch of the R&B Series early in '63, but got little chart action: Guy's involvement then brought them mainstream success. The R&B series wasn't a separate label: it was simply the red-and-yellow Pye International label with regular numbering, but overprinted with 'R&B Series' – and the jewel in their crown was Chicago's Chess label group. Guy's advice concentrated on reissues: Chuck Berry, still in jail, was getting a second wind chartwise and would shortly cut some scintillating new sides, but it was Guy who brought Chuck back into the UK Top Ten that autumn with the reissue pairing "Let It Rock" / "Memphis Tennessee". It established Guy as an expert who could create big-selling releases from back catalogue.

On the charts that spring, the word was 'Merseybeat' and it was dominating UK pop. The Beatles' second single "Please Please Me" reached No. 2, and "How Do You Do It", debut single by NEMS stable-mates Gerry & The Pacemakers, had beaten the Beatles to No.1 but would itself be displaced when the Fab Four's "From Me To You" rocketed to the top early in May. The Big Three were in the lower end of the charts with a revival of the Cavern staple "Some Other Guy", a Richie Barrett original, while the first release from Billy J. Kramer with The Dakotas – the Beatles' song "Do You Want To Know A Secret" – was poised to chart, with John Lennon's comment "These boys can take over from Elvis!" bringing a predictably irate response from our readers. The first major Manchester hit was also in the Top Ten: well-established rock-comedy team Freddie and the Dreamers' chirpy revival of James Ray's recent R&B classic "If You Gotta Make A Fool Of Somebody".

That April, Dezo Hoffmann and our circulation manager Roy Burden finally managed to persuade Jimmy Watson that a trip to Liverpool would indeed be a worthwhile endeavour. Our editor had now glimpsed the Light From The North and realised (a) that the Beatles were special and (b) that "something was happening" up in Scouseland. The Beatles had scored a chart-topping LP, a No.2 single, and, from being the supporting act on the Tommy Roe/Chris Montez tour, they'd been promoted to bill-toppers. Their girl fans were already screaming wall-to-wall. They were now unstoppable.

Dezo's early passion for them had endeared him to the Beatles and caught the attention of Brian Epstein, who granted Dezo unlimited access on the condition that NEMS saw the photographic contacts first, granted approval or not, and had first pick for their own use for promotional purposes or as record sleeves. Dezo could then sell the approved pictures to anyone he liked. And as he was still the official Record Mirror photographer, we had the first pick of those pix. You'd have thought it would be a license to print money, but it didn't work out that way, thanks to John Lennon. But that was later.

Once the penny dropped with Jimmy, he exercised his editorial 'droit de seigneur' and decided that the editor himself would henceforth chronicle the rise of the Fabs. This was happening all over the place – jazz-era journalists, who previously hated and despised all Top Ten music, jumped on the Beatles' bandwagon grabbing as much reflected glory as possible.

The NRM team caught the train to Liverpool, and thus New Record Mirror became the first pop paper to venture up and report the Merseybeat phenomenon on location. Dezo took reels of iconic shots which even today resonate with the down-to-earth charm, humour, and sheer vivacity of the early Beatles: at Paul's home; Paul ironing; John making tea; in Allerton Golf Course jumping in the air; down in the Cavern; having their hair cut…these, and hundreds more wonderful photographs. Plus dozens of pictures of fans, and many other Liverpool bands, the known and the unknown.

The next issue of New Record Mirror featured the Beatles and Gerry & The Pacemakers on the front cover, and even EMI took out an unprecedented advertisement, congratulating Gerry on his No.1 hit, and announcing the release of the new Beatles single "From Me To You". That Liverpool trip merited the entire centre-spread, featuring Jimmy's report, a long article on The Cavern, plenty of little news items, and loads of great photographs.

Unfortunately Jim's cosy new relationship with the Beatles proved to be short-lived: on the way back from the Liverpool trip he arranged to meet the Beatles and drive them to a gig at Stowe School, the famous all-boys public school. Jim, as ever, was late and kept the Beatles waiting, then got lost, taking the long route to Stowe where they arrived very late. They were not best pleased. Fortunately Dezo was also there to chronicle the event, and captured plenty of on-stage and back-stage candids, as well as the Beatles mingling with the pupils, posing with classical instruments, and having tea with the headmaster and his family. The Englishness of the whole thing was marvellous.

One of those American rhythm & blues greats who'd inspired both rock'n'roll and the Merseybeat-led UK beat boom was Ray Charles – "The Genius", as he was constantly referred to. Unique and prodigiously talented, Ray was everyone's favourite, John Lennon famously saying that he really liked Ray Charles, but stopped when everyone else started liking him. Predictably, this brought a withering response from Cliff Richard, another Charles devotee. Although several other rhythm & blues acts had become huge international stars – Fats Domino, Chuck Berry, Little Richard – they'd done it via rock'n'roll. Charles became huge and never really went near rock'n'roll. Instead, he did it by adding ballads to his rhythm & blues repertoire, recording several decent specimens for the jazz/R&B Atlantic label. But it was his controversial move to ABC-Paramount that brought major pop chart action. Ray's early ABC single releases were eclectic, from his soulful string-filled interpretation of the ballad standard "Georgia On My Mind", to the hard call-and-response R&B of "Hit The Road Jack" or the jazz instrumental "One Mint Julep". All were hits. Then in 1962 Ray rocketed to even bigger global superstardom with his "Modern Sounds In Country And Western" LP, a concept combining full orchestral arrangements of country standards overlaid with his soulful vocals, but with full white choral backing instead of the funky Raelets. The LP hit No. 1 in the USA and was his first UK hit LP. Its debut single, the hitherto neglected Don Gibson B-side "I Can't Stop Loving You" became a chart topper on both sides of the Atlantic.

In fact Ray was only continuing the trend instigated by the Platters' manager and producer Buck Ram in '58, who'd realised that with ballads, a great black R&B voice (the sublime Tony Williams) set against classy orchestral arrangements showcased that voice to greater effect than a slow honkin' rhythm & blues arrangement. The concept was picked up by writer-producers Jerry Leiber and Mike Stoller with the Drifters on Atlantic and Sammy Turner on Big Top with equal success. Like the Platters, The Drifters' records crossed over from the black market to the far more lucrative white market. This classy black pop style then caught on big, with everyone from Dinah Washington to the Shirelles following the format and selling vast amounts of records to whites. Ray just took it all a bit further, his backings a bit whiter, his vocals, if anything a bit blacker.

And now, in May 1963, he arrived in the UK with his Revue for the first time and Jimmy decided I should review the show as I was "the rhythm & blues expert". Hmmm. I admit I was a trifle sniffy: my self-appointed role as the World's Number One Ace Teenage Rhythm & Blues Reporter had made me somewhat of a R&B purist and, pedant that I was, Ray Charles now seemed a bit too show-biz establishment. I guess I was like Lennon – now that the whole wide world loved him, I didn't anymore. I was still thrilled by his Atlantic work and listened to it avidly at home – but his recent ABC records would never get played at the Scene.

The Astoria, Finsbury Park, is now a Christian revivalist temple but for decades was both a cinema and a theatre, able to mount some of the best music events in London. Its interior was and still is an Art Deco Spanish-Moorish masterpiece with exotic motifs reminiscent of The Thousand And One Nights. Ray was dynamic and my trepidation rapidly overcome. Jimmy wanted my review on page three, the lead feature spot. And Ray hadn't sold out on his R&B roots – it was nice to be wrong.

NRM w/e 18th May 1963
GENIUS HITS THE STAGE...
After Ray Charles Fantastic Build-up Norman Jopling Finds Out Whether Or Not It Is Deserved

ALTHOUGH the audience at the Astoria, Finsbury Park, was told that the Ray Charles programme was to be split into two parts, it wasn't quite like that. We were told that before the intermission Ray's orchestra would play, and after, they would be joined by the Raelets and "the genius" himself, as some tend to call him.

Including the announcer, who modestly hailed him as "the greatest musical giant of the generation – the genius."

Ray was escorted on by a number of his very considerable troupe – in fact he is supposed to have more hangers-on than Elvis Presley. He was handed an alto sax and he played a somewhat interesting if rather mediocre number.

Then he was led back to the piano.

Ray looked, while he was standing up, a rather bewildered kind of "genius". He constantly had to push his sunglasses back as they gradually tilted off. When he was left alone he either stood dead still or groped his way around.

A smallish figure with exceptionally broad shoulders and an even broader grin, he was well settled as he started to play an instrumental, "One Mint Julep". Maybe his orchestra tended to drown him a little on that number, but Ray Charles began to come through...

When he started on the next number, everyone knew that Ray Charles had not been over-rated. "Sometimes I get a little lonesome..." and then he rocked away with his great classic.

SACRIFICE

After that, everything was jam for the man who has been offered an eye from a 22-year old girl, Grete Wiltscha, from Vienna. "Her sacrifice would be too much for any one man to ask," said Ray, who has been blind since he was a child in Albany, Georgia.

In extremely fine form vocally, and instrumentally in brilliant form, Ray romped through a selection of his hits and misses in a style that sounded better than on his discs.

The pseudo country stuff that he has recorded of late sounded better than it has ever done before as Ray gave it his unique treatment. "Born To Lose", "I Can't Stop Loving You" and "Careless Love" all sounded like classics. But in the latter song, you couldn't help feeling a pang as Ray deliberately repeated and emphasised the line, "Once I was blind, but now I can see..."

His rock numbers swung like anything. "Hallelujah I Love Her So", "Hide Nor Hair", "Don't Set Me Free", and his beat version of "You Are My Sunshine" – in which he was assisted more than ably by the Raelets, four girls who at times sounded like tom cats and at others like angels.

85

ON FIRE

But best of all were his blues treatments. "Without A Song" is an oldie that sounded so deep and sincere you just couldn't believe it. "My Baby" – again with some great backing from the Raelets – came through a jerky piece of passion-cum-spiritual fire.

Last and probably least was "What'd I Say" – his own personal favourite and a million-seller in the States. It didn't create the impression the others made, but it still managed to set the place on fire with the shrieking Raelets and the hoarse tones of Ray.

The crowds walked out of the place without even bothering to think that Ray didn't sing some of his best-known numbers. What he did sing was good enough.

Ray Charles himself was born in Albany 31 years back. His real name was Ray Charles Robinson. The latter name was dropped to avoid confusion with boxing champ Sugar Ray Robinson.

ATTENTION

The story of Ray Charles is rather tragic. He contracted glaucoma when he was six and within two years he was completely blind. He could have been cured – but because he was a Negro and he lived in Georgia he was unable to get the correct medical attention. That was in 1938 – and a year before another great blues singer, Bessie Smith, had bled to death after a car accident because allegedly no "white" hospital would admit her.

Now there are reports that Ray is not allowed to play in Georgia by the authorities – some say that Ray is not even allowed to go back there, to the place where he once had vision.

When Ray sings "Georgia On My Mind" you wonder whether he singing about the state or the girl. He has every reason to sing that about the place...

FRESHNESS

His parents died when was 15, but not before they had sent him to a blind school, where he entered the music class. At seventeen he left school and was going round the night clubs with his trio – sounding suspiciously like Nat "King" Cole. In 1954 Ray formed his own band – after making many recordings in the "Nat Cole style".

His contract with Atlantic Records enabled him to hit the big time he is still hitting. His attitude to the blues, to rock and country and western, is one of freshness and an out-of-the-rut approach.

GENIUS?

Whether or not he is a genius is not for me to say. A genius in the world of pop music is something of an impossibility. But then Ray Charles appeals to jazz fans, blues fans and rock fans. Pete Murray once introduced "What'd I Say" when it was first played on the radio as "... and here's a guy who makes Little Richard sound tame..."

From rock singer to genius in four years?

Could be. I went along to see Ray, expecting a let-down. Instead I came out feeling he could be what they all say about him. With his great wide grin and his attitude that he's thoroughly enjoying himself, Ray Charles gives the blues new meaning.

Unknown to me, my regular *Fallen Idols* column was about to meet a premature demise, the last two recipients of this dubious distinction being Tommy Edwards and Carl Perkins. Ironic that Carl was about to get rich beyond his wildest dreams, making more money than he'd ever dreamed of – including his mid-'50s royalties from his chart-topping rock'n'roll standard "Blue Suede Shoes" with cover version by the then-red-hot Elvis Presley: the Beatles, with their unprecedented global chart domination merely months away, would record an astonishing four of his compositions.

My other regular column *The Great Unknowns* continued apace, spotlighting Mary Wells, Jimmy Clanton, and the Marvelettes. Unfortunately I'd picked up (or made up) a piece of information about Mary Wells which had unforeseen consequences.

> *...but there's something a little tragic about the story of Mary. When she was very young she was a victim of the crippling ailment muscular dystrophy.*
>
> *She was cured later but she never forgot her ailment, and those who did not recover as well as she did. So she asked her manager, Berry Gordy, if she could contribute money from her first big professional engagement to the National Muscular Dystrophy Fund. Berry granted the request and since then Mary has been donating many sums of money to the organisation.*

The trouble with this heart-warming piece of 'information' was that there was and is no cure for muscular dystrophy. A reader suffering from the "crippling ailment" (which indeed it is) wrote in pleading for more information on Mary's miraculous cure. Was this some new American medical discovery which hadn't yet reached our shores? No. It was a piece of hack journalism which went wrong. Ashamed of ourselves, we (that is, editor Jimmy on my behalf), entered into a private and apologetic correspondence with our sadly misled reader.

I got to interview Del Shannon at the Mayfair Hotel for *"The Idol Who Can't Sleep"*. Teeth-grindingly intense, yet amiable and down-to-earth, Shannon was one of the few Americans who would be relatively unaffected by the UK beat boom and subsequent British Invasion of America. I profiled Dee Dee Sharp in *The Mashed Potato Girl* (should have saved her for *The Great Unknowns*), got Wesley Laine to profile Frankie Valli & Co in *Four Seasons Here*, and began a discography series kicking off with Cliff Richard, Elvis Presley, and Chuck Berry (the latter written by Chuck's ever-active Fan Club president Mike Bocock). The "new" Buddy Holly single "Bo Diddley" was announced in *Rockin' Buddy!*, although our freelancer Graeme Andrews had done a far more distinguished and informative job than me writing about Holly in recent months. There was certainly something serendipitous about the timing of Holly's latest two posthumous hits, "Brown Eyed Handsome Man" and "Bo Diddley", both big-selling top five singles. "Brown Eyed Handsome Man" was a Chuck Berry song, while "Bo Diddley", well, self-explanatory. Holly had been dead for over four years yet these singles were smack dab in the hot rhythm & blues genre. The prosaic explanation was simply that they were recordings from 1956 cut in producer Norman Petty's studio in Clovis, New Mexico, when Chuck Berry and Bo Diddley were scoring their rhythm & blues hits first time around. In 1962-3, three years after Holly's death, Petty overdubbed extra backing tracks by his studio band the Fireballs, to the eternal chagrin of the original Crickets. My final article in May was another piece of flannel by Wesley Laine – *Why A Vocal On The Flipside?*, a complete waste of space about the Shadows – known primarily as an instrumental group...thus the article.

Two offers tempted New Record Mirror readers, issue week ending June 1st 1963. On page 3, beneath Peter Jones' lead feature *Can This Disc Harm The Beatles?* ("My Bonnie" with Tony Sheridan) and next to *The Great Unknowns No. 7 – The Marvelettes*, a cut-out coupon advertised Guy Stevens' Rhythm & Blues Record Session at the Scene, enabling two readers to get in at half-a-crown each instead of the usual three-and-sixpence. On the coupon Guy listed some of his featured artists: "Listen or dance to records by – Bo Diddley, Chuck Berry, Jimmy Reed, John Lee Hooker, Howlin' Wolf, Muddy Waters, Fats Domino, Jerry Lee Lewis, Carl Perkins, Larry Williams, The Coasters and a host of other great R&B artists including many specially imported American discs". It certainly sounded exciting, but the inclusion of Jerry Lee and Carl Perkins gave the game away: Guy was not above chucking in some white rock'n'roll – and who could blame him? The "What Exactly Is Rhythm & Blues?" controversy had been running for weeks, if not months, in our correspondence columns; everyone seemed to have their own opinion, and fuel – high-octane fuel – had recently been added to this conflagration by the (wearisome) insistence of several of the Mersey groups that they played their "own version" of rhythm & blues, a boast which had brought out the best in our readers from other parts of the British Isles:

NRM w/e April 20th 1963
(Readers Letters)
R&B = HA-HA!

CAN any fan of the many Merseyside groups (Beatles, Pacemakers etc) tell me where their music differs from other British groups.

When it was first announced that Merseyside had its own brand of R&B I looked forward to hearing it.

Maybe it will be a mixture of Chuck Berry, the Coasters and the Bill Doggett Group, I thought. But no – after listening to all their records so far, it seems more like a mixture of Adam Faith, the Dallas Boys and The John Barry Seven.

Let's face it, the Merseyside sound is no nearer R&B than any of the other rubbish in the hit parade. – MR E. McDANIEL, 25 Warrington Road, Hanley, Stoke-on-Trent, Staffs.

The other cut-out coupon also mentioned Jerry Lee Lewis, and offered a huge 10/- (ten shillings!) off the 57/6d needed to board MV Royal Daffodil the following Saturday – Whit Saturday – for the "Rock-Twist-Jive Across The Channel" event starring The Killer himself. The impressive Royal Daffodil (she'd rescued nearly ten thousand troops from Dunkirk over seven trips) would leave Southend at 9.00am and sail to Boulogne ("Fabulous Day Out In France"). During the voyage, lesser acts on the bill who'd managed to drag themselves to Southend that early would entertain the revellers. The Royal Daffodil would then dock for several hours while Jerry Lee and co. played to fans, English and French, at the local Casino. Embarkation would follow, and Jerry would perform once again, on deck, for the multitude. I decided that this would be an event worth reporting.

The "biggest" supporting artists on the bill, according to the type size on the coupon, were Johnny Angel, Ricky Valence, and The

Outlaws. But who was Johnny Angel? I had thought it was a soppy record by Shelley Fabares. Actually, he turned out to be rather good. Ricky Valence had topped the charts three years previously with a cover version of the kitsch American death ballad "Tell Laura I Love Her", then nothing. Could anyone possibly be interested anymore? Much more exciting were the Outlaws, one of North London's best and busiest instrumental groups who not only backed Mike Berry but also worked as Joe Meek's house band – and included Ritchie Blackmore, later founder-member of Deep Purple, and Chas Hodges, later of cockney rocksters Chas & Dave. The Outlaws would also back Jerry Lee on this trip – a most satisfactory combination.

The other, lesser, attractions were Dane Roberts, Jimmy Marsh, Ted King, The De-Lormes, The Flee-Rekkers, Vicki Rowe, Nero & The Gladiators, Jeff Curtis & The Flames, Joe Bronkhurst and Colin Chapman. Most of these were as unknown then as they are now. They probably had to buy their own tickets.

The Rock Across The Channel coupon nestled in the corner of page 9 with the reviews of the week's new singles that included, for those interested in contemporary minutiae, Buddy Holly's "Bo Diddley", the Crystals' "Da Doo Ron Ron", Lance Percival's "Riviera Cayf"/"You're Joking Of Course" and Kyu Sakamoto's "Sukiyaki (Ueo Muite Arukou)".

That Saturday Jill and I fell out of bed at some unearthly hour, made it to Southend just in time and hooked up with Guy Stevens on the quay. Passports were not needed for these day trips. The Royal Daffodil sailed half-an-hour late, which was lucky for many, including our photographer David Magnus, one of Dezo's apprentices. Guy had seen Jerry Lee during his notorious tour in '58 at the Gaumont State, Kilburn, just before the tour was cancelled due to revelations Jerry had bigamously married his 13-year old cousin, accompanying him on the tour. Even 21st century eyebrows would be raised at that.

Built in 1939 by the General Steam Navigation Company, the Royal Daffodil was a fine-looking craft, twin-funnelled, twin screws, two thousand tons – the size of a small naval frigate – and could carry up to two thousand passengers. Plenty of space above and below decks. On her last trip to Dunkirk, a bomb had gone right through her hull and exploded outside – the crew had patched the gap with a mattress.

Weather at the Whitsun weekend can be dodgy, but this day of days was clear and sunny. The sea was calm. The excitement in the air was palpable. It could safely be said that in 1963 Jerry Lee Lewis was one of the last of the great rock'n'rollers. Many considered him the greatest of them all. His uncompromising music and lifestyle seemed to attract the most fanatical, eccentric and devoted of followers. And among the 800-or-so rockin' revellers aboard the Royal Daffodil were several Teddy Boys in full regalia. These magnificent creatures, preserved from a bygone age, commanded respect from all and sundry. At this point in time the enmity between "mod" and "rocker" had not yet been blown up by the press to Cavalier and Roundhead proportions. The tribes were not yet at war. The Teddy Boys, though rockers, were frequently expert music enthusiasts whose tastes were more or less coincidental with the new wave of rhythm & blues devotees. And today, all were united in their general hero-worship of Jerry Lee – all were brothers-(and the occasional sister)-in-rock'n'roll.

After exploring the ship, as you do, we stood and watched the couples dancing, mainly Teds and their girls, jiving on deck to records played on the tannoy system – so far, none of the advertised artists had performed. Later we learned that lots of them, including Ricky Valence, never made the trip.

"There's 'Breathless' Dan," whispered Guy.

"Which one, which one?" we asked quickly and eagerly. "Breathless" Dan Coffey was Jerry Lee's legendary Number One devotee and one of the notorious Newport Teddy Boys.

"Dancing with Frantic Fay!" said Guy admiringly, indicating a gyrating couple, he dark and handsome in immaculate Ted apparel, she blonde, pony-tailed, pretty but unsmiling, wearing a tight sweater embroidered with Jerry Lee song titles including "Whole Lotta Shakin' Goin' On", "Great Balls Of Fire", and the song which hubbie Dan had affixed to his monicker, "Breathless".

They were so perfect that I was slightly intimidated. They'd even named their first-born son Jerry Lee Lewis Coffey. But in fact I already knew of Dan from New Record Mirror; he was a regular and interesting correspondent on matters rock'n'roll, and had contributed a fine featurette to our long-running "When I Met..." series for our Readers Letters page. His subject, of course, was when he met Jerry Lee.

About half-way through the outward-bound trip we sat down on deck at a table with a friend of Dan's, Dick Brittan from Bristol, who Dan later described as one of his "street fighting friends". Dick was less in a "street-fighting" mood today and more in a "rapping about the blues" mood, and he and Guy began discussing the likes of Excello stars Slim Harpo and Lazy Lester.

I was listening to this discussion with considerable interest, as both Guy and Dick knew a whole lot more than I did about the subject, when I became aware that someone was standing next to me quite aggressively, leaning over and spouting some kind of diatribe in my ear. The fact that I had failed to notice this person and not immediately paid attention to his outburst had further increased his aggression, causing him to become scarlet-faced and even angrier. His name was Henry Henroid and he was explaining that he had sought me out deliberately with the intention of doing me harm.

"I don't know who you fucking-well think you are, putting Gene in your fucking *Fallen Idols*, Gene's not a fucking Fallen Idol, but you're gonna be a fucking fallen prick 'cos I'm gonna fucking throw you overboard..."

For reasons unknown, hearing this threat made me not at all fearful and I even felt strangely detached, thinking how odd it was I'd used my pen-name Wesley Laine for that particular article – no idea why – and yet Henry Henroid had known it was me nevertheless. He must be a regular reader, I surmised. The feeling that I was a character in a play being acted out in real-life had not yet completely worn off, and incidents such as this only reinforced that feeling.

Henroid was a known henchman of the promoter Don Arden, a fearsome man with a reputation for intimidation and violence. Arden specialised in rock'n'roll acts and had been very successful in bringing many fine artists to the UK – including Gene Vincent. Whether Henroid had been put up to this stunt by Arden I never discovered, but he seemed to have learned his lessons well at the feet of his master, coming across as a proverbial nasty piece of work.

Unfortunately for Henroid's plan of chucking me overboard, as soon as the others at the table – Jill, Guy, and Dick – picked up on what was going on, the two blokes, especially Dick, did that thing guys do when menace is in the air. They looked straight at Henroid, stiffened and moved slightly forward in their chairs as if about to jump up and seize him by the throat. Jill made the same move but fixed him with a hateful stare. Henroid could almost certainly have taken me, Guy and Jill with one hand, but not Dick. You don't mess with a Ted, especially one with half a dozen mates nearby.

Henroid backed off. The conversation resumed.

To paraphrase one of Lazy Lester's greatest recordings – "I'm A Lover Not A Fighter", and consequently I immediately resolved to knock *Fallen Idols* on the head. It wasn't merely that I didn't want to get bashed up by some ape. I just wasn't keen on saying anything hurtful in print or upsetting anyone with my articles, even though Breathless Dan later assured me that Henroid's gripe was more concerned with Gene Vincent's commerciality than with any hurt feelings.

When we reached Boulogne it was hot and sunny, and fascinating because I had never before been abroad. Jill, I knew, had been to Switzerland, Austria, maybe elsewhere, and certainly Guy was wider travelled than me. I decided to forsake my journalistic duty and skip the concert at the Casino in favour of wandering around Boulogne – I could always get a second-hand report of what went on from David Magnus, who was obliged to attend the concert and take the snaps. Despite his fanaticism for Jerry, Guy decided to join us: after all, Jerry would be performing on the way back.

We had a fun few hours drinking and sightseeing and when we got hungry we found a nice clean-looking restaurant.

"Look," I said, "at those lovely prints of horses in the window!"

"Do you know why they have those there?" asked Guy, rhetorically.

"Because they eat horses here," answered Jill.

I was amazed and horrified. Horses weren't for eating. That was like cannibalism. Nevertheless, as none of us had ever eaten horsemeat before, we duly ordered our pony steaks or whatever they were, and ate them all up. Never again though, we agreed.

Back at the ship, there was a minor fracas on the quayside between half a dozen UK fans and some French teenagers, which was reported the following day in the more lurid Sunday press as "teenagers crazed with drink fighting the French police on the streets". On board,

David Magnus told me all about the concert and it later turned out he'd snapped some fantastic shots of Jerry on stage, as well as Jerry walking through the streets of Boulogne escorted by a phalanx of Teds – and Henry Henroid. It seemed that H.H.'s master Don Arden was promoting Jerry's current tour, a short seven day stretch that took in Bath, Wallington, East Grinstead, Birmingham, Coventry, Stoke, The Royal Daffodil, and Liverpool. No London gig though.

The Royal Daffodil set sail back to Southend and anticipation mounted at the prospect of Jerry's homeward-bound performance. Unfortunately the weather turned increasingly inclement and the size of the waves also mounted. The sea got so choppy that it was difficult for the road crew to stabilise the piano, drums and amplifiers on the raised stage area. People were starting to be seasick, but Guy and I managed a few quick words below with Jerry before his performance. Eventually, after half an hour or so, Jerry and the Outlaws appeared on deck and started to play, but were obviously uncomfortable with the considerable swell. Jill was also feeling bad, but I ungallantly left her huddled in a corner to her own devices as there was no way I was going to miss Jerry Lee's battle with the English Channel. Fortunately, she was looked after by a very kind Johnny Duncan, he of the hauntingly high-and-lonesome skiffle hit "Last Train To San Fernando".

Jerry Lee's major fans, all blokes, like to crowd in close to him when he performs and at this point I lost Guy, who'd edged up to the front. But I was close enough. Jerry, as always, gave a terrific performance, but the rising swell affected him badly. He turned green. Trooper that he was, he would play and sing as long as possible, then break off to make his way in a dignified manner to the side of the ship, heave up, and return as formidable as ever, sometimes in mid-song. This was awesome. He performed for over an hour in these conditions, and the music and the excitement were exemplary. He was truly the King Of Rock'n'Roll.

When I wrote up the article for the following week's edition, I included a full discography contributed by "Breathless" Dan. But my article was shamed by David's photographs, many of which captured the true essence of a "Killer" performance.

NRM w/e 8th June 1963
JERRY LEE LEWIS ACROSS THE SEA...
The 'Rock Across The Channel' Story

PROBABLY the greatest white rockster still performing thrilled teenage fans on the "Rock Across The Channel" trip this year. The trip, which was much heralded by adverse publicity in the Sunday papers the next day provided many of Jerry's fans opportunity to see him at his best. Artists appearing on the star-studded bill included the Flee-Rekkers, Nero & The Gladiators, Johnny Angel, and many others.

But it was Jerry Lee Lewis who stole the thunder for one of the most memorable trips on record. Although many of the artists missed the early-departure boat, Jerry Lee was not one of them. During the journey to Boulogne, from Southend, Jerry rested as he had been travelling all night. But he didn't mind fans breaking his sleep and quizzing him on a thousand-and-one subjects.

When the 'Royal Daffodil' docked, the triumph was reached for Jerry and promoter Jimmy Moran, who laid the trip on. Jerry appeared at the Casino in Boulogne and gave what was considered by fans to be one of his best performances.

Singing all the numbers that have ever been associated with him, Jerry Lee sent British and French teeners twisting and bopping like mad to the strains of his great frantic piano playing and powerful singing – in fact on most of the songs Jerry sounded even better than the discs which had made him so famous. The fact is that every fan was pleased by Jerry's performance – but more was to follow.

When the boat embarked the weather was certainly a lot rougher. Before his performance on the way back we asked Jerry about his contract with Sun Records, which was due to expire in a few months time. "Well," he drawled, "I think I'm gonna sign a contract with RCA for a maximum of six months. They'll issue about two or three singles and one LP. If they plug them hard enough and manage to bring my name back into the charts I'll stick with them. Personally I think they'll be able to do that; but if not I'll change once again."

Coming back to Southend a rumour was spread about the 'Royal Daffodil' that Jerry Lee had been seasick and would not appear. It wasn't so. Despite the fact that many others on board were seasick, Jerry Lee soon took to his piano and amidst hoards of hand-clapping, cheering and yelling fans he proceeded to give everyone a really lively performance. "Down The Line", "You Win Again", "In The Mood", "Little Queenie", "Sweet Little Sixteen" were but a few of the numbers to which fans twisted and jived.

It was probably one of the best sessions Jerry has had here, so atmospheric and tremendous was it.

It was later reported that "the gentleman promoting the event went off with the money", but whether this referred to Don Arden or Jimmy Moran I have no idea. The Royal Daffodil had been making "no passport" trips to France since 1955, carrying skifflers, Trad fans, rock'n'rollers, and beat group devotees, but at the end of the 1966 season all efforts to sustain commerciality failed in the face of competition from the new cross-channel ferries, and she was sold for scrap. In 1967 she sailed to Holland under her own steam to be broken up.

Back on terra firma I was delighted to see Billy J. Kramer had stoked the fires of indignation with his comments on the kind of R&B he played. Once again, our gallant readers rose to the bait:

NRM w/e 8th June 1963
(Readers Letters)
BILLY J'S DIFFERENT KIND OF R&B

WE are just sick and tired of the records that are being issued at the moment with the tag "Rhythm and Blues".

Billy J. Kramer states that he and the Dakotas "play a different kind of R&B to that of Bo Diddley and Chuck Berry". How very odd! We, along with hundreds of other R&B addicts, thought that there was only ONE form of R&B but now it seems that we were misled. Rhythm and Blues of the 1963 calibre has such phrases as "I like the way you tickle my chin" and "The secret is I'm in love with you". Oh! How very, very authentic. We could well imagine artists like Muddy Waters, Howlin' Wolf, Jimmy Reed etc chanting out the above lines, we don't think!

So Mr Kramer, if you want to be a pop idol, then the best of luck, but please leave our Rhythm and Blues untouched, unspoiled, and most of all unmentioned! – 25 Hillside Gardens, Betchworth, Surrey

However, New Record Mirror's doyen of fair play, Peter Jones, gave Billy the right to reply (though not without reprinting the above letter in its entirety at the beginning of the article). According to Peter, "Billy's voice came through on the blower, loud, clear and deep":

"...It's difficult pointing out exactly where the differences lie...you could say it's a LIVERPOOL blues. Yes, that's it. It has a different sound and a different approach to it all. But, as far as I'm concerned, that doesn't make it any less authentic.

"Why shouldn't there be different styles INSIDE the R&B field? Why has it got to be that everybody has to work exactly like the Americans in order to be accepted? Liverpool R&B IS different. You've only got to listen to the records, or sessions, that come from there. But it's still R&B.

"And if you want a further difference it is that right now our R&B is obviously commercial. We're the ones who are in the charts, not Muddy Waters or Howlin' Wolf. But we all go for R&B. It's our kind of music.

"As far as I'm concerned we're all in the same field. And to say that this particular number is R&B and that one is not is only creating difficulties."

My own UK R&B faves the Rolling Stones now had their first record out, the predicted "Come On" and to my ears most disappointing. Brian Jones had taken to visiting the Record Mirror offices regularly and in addition to picking his brains on all matters R&B (on which he was truly expert – even more so than Guy Stevens, which is saying something), I got some up-to-date Stones info from him for a feature titled *Back To Britain's Big Beat Boys* which, in contrast to my first article on the Stones, was an unconvincingly stilted piece of PR. "Come On" simply didn't capture their magic and it was impossible to pretend it did. I couldn't slag it off in print, but couldn't enthuse either. "But the disc doesn't sound like the Stones", I wrote, "it's good, catchy, punchy and commercial but it's not the fanatical R&B sound that the audiences wait hours to hear. It's a bluesy very commercial group that should make the charts in a small way." Much later I was gratified that Bill Wyman in his definitive *Stone Alone* autobiography agreed with those comments: record-wise it would be months before the Stones really got into gear.

Brian was not only extremely knowledgeable, but erudite and charming, and the Rolling Stones were still – just – his group. Mick also took to popping into Record Mirror until Roy Burden took against him and threw him and some Stones' equipment out and down the stairs – so we never saw Mick again up at the RM. The June 8th issue also carried one of my worst articles, titled *Sad Sad Bobby – Has Bobby Darin's Latest Song Been Influenced By His Marriage Break-up?*, where I completely miss the point of Darin's current hit "Eighteen Yellow Roses". So bad was this piece of tripe that I invented a new pen-name for it: Perkin Giles. He was indeed a pretender.

My other nom-de-plume, Wesley Laine, penned an interesting piece *How To Get The Liverpool Sound In London…and the latest A&R idea* about music publisher Baton Music making its own records and leasing them to Oriole. Baton were hopeful for "There's A Place", the Beatles' song, cut with Brighton group Bobby Sanson & The Giants. It flopped, but nevertheless they were pioneers in UK independent recording. Yet what did that headline really mean? All the Liverpool hits were recorded in London. There was only one centre of the UK music business. If you wanted to make it, you came to London. But now that London had discovered Liverpool, London also discovered that there were lots of other great British cities that not only boasted great football teams, but also boasted great beat groups. By now most of the myriad Liverpool groups were signed up, with even little Oriole grabbing an unlucky handful (they never got a hit with any of them) by taking a mobile recording unit up to Liverpool.

The next city to invade the charts was Manchester: Freddie and the Dreamers were Top 3, and the Hollies were scoring with their debut single "(Ain't That) Just Like Me", a revival of a so-so Coasters oldie. Their manager, Tommy Sanderson, had been impressed by New Record Mirror's visit to Liverpool earlier in the year, and offered to show us around his own city. Manchester had the hit records, so we said Yes.

Jimmy and Dezo and Roy decided that one Northern city was enough for them, so me and lensman David Magnus were co-opted for this latest trip. We took the train up to Manchester the following weekend and straightaway met the Hollies, who proved excellent guides and hosts. I got on particularly well with Eric Haydock and Graham Nash, and there was something about their quality of enthusiasm I liked. They were proud of their city and proud of the whole Manchester pop scene, taking us to a club called the Twisted Wheel (where we saw the Hellions perform), and to a clothes shop called the Toggery in Stockport where the local groups bought their clothes. They took us to a nearby Lido for a swim, and they showed us around the city centre. It rained. Manchester with its solid civic buildings was impressive, and having met and interviewed several Northern beat groups, I now realised all this provincial beat music owed much of its freshness and appeal to the very fact that it had evolved far away from the London show-business-oriented music scene.

We ran the report in the next issue's centre spread, getting a nice batch of advertising in the bargain. It was a long puff piece, but I had no intention of coming on as a cynical Southerner:

NRM w/e 15th June 1963
THE MANCHESTER BEAT SCENE
An NRM Roving Report
A Conducted Tour By The Hollies

HALF an hour's fast drive from Liverpool lies a bigger and smokier city. Home of a ship canal, a test cricket ground, and the F.A. Cup winners – but a forgotten city when it comes to beat music. A city submerged by the publicity that comes from Liverpool just half an hour away.

And now, only now, is Manchester beginning to shine through the Liverpool-dominated charts, to bring some its own groups to national prominence. Names like Freddie And The Dreamers, The Hollies etc, are currently sharing the charts with The Beatles and The Pacemakers.

It was the Hollies, though, who took the NRM Roving Report Team on a conducted tour of the big one-million plus city - the city of smoke and grime - and hidden away in corners some fabulous music. Music like "Just Like Me" - the great R&B-styled number that the Hollies are pushing up the charts, and "If You Gotta Make A Fool Of Somebody" by Freddie And The Dreamers"...

On and on it went, redeemed mainly by David's photographs. Any ideas that I initially had – inspired by the Beatles – that the Northern groups might be hip clothes-wise, or indeed any-other-wise, had been sadly dashed over the past few months after realising that plenty of the Northern beat groups were just as naff as the London groups. The Hollies, though, were trendy dressers in the Beatles' style: Chelsea boots, tab-collar shirts, dark suits, leather & suede gear – but many of the others were still stuck in smart rocker mode.

I got on well with the beat groups, whether from London, Liverpool, Manchester or anywhere else, but they were usually boring to interview because at that time they were all the same. The line-up was generally identical (it was an event if they had a sax player or even a keyboard player), and they were mostly from the same sort of background and they all liked the same sort of music – rhythm & blues. I knew all about them because I was like that myself, except I was a journalist. But now, six months after the Beatles started it all, merely being from Liverpool was no guarantee of success. Pye Records had recently signed two big Liverpool bands, I featured them both, one made it huge, the other didn't. *Cheerful Undertakers – Norman Jopling Views The Latest Merseyside Beat Group On Disc* clumsily headlined my interview with Chris Huston whose group The Undertakers included Jackie Lomax, later taken up by the Beatles' Apple Records where he had no more chart success than the Undertakers did – one week at No.49 with their spirited revival of Roscoe Gordon's "Just A Little Bit". The other group was the Searchers: *The Liverpool Group With A U.S. Sound* They'd taken one of the Drifters' most unconvincing records, a pop confection called "Sweets For My Sweet", made it brighter and sharper and were currently on their way to the top of the charts with it. Their A&R man was the talented Tony Hatch, but the choice of song and arrangement was the group's, pinned down well before Pye signed them. Of the two groups, the Undertakers got buried; the Searchers went on to become one of the top five beat groups of the mid-'60s.

Many of the biggest Liverpool groups were never able to deliver chart hits. Rory Storm & The Hurricanes, the Undertakers, Kingsize Taylor, Faron's Flamingoes, the Big Three (after their small initial success)... all flopped. The A&R men had a lot to answer for – but it was new territory for them too. In the event, the major Liverpool record acts turned out to be the Beatles, Gerry & The Pacemakers, Billy J. Kramer with The Dakotas, Cilla Black (all NEMS acts) and the Searchers, with the Fourmost, the Merseybeats, and the Swinging Blue Jeans coming up at the rear. But the revolution had begun. As Peter Jones later wrote:

> *(History Of Rock Issue 27)*
> At the time when 'Love Me Do' was being released, the Beatles were playing as a support band, with the Big Three and eight other local groups, at a Little Richard concert at Liverpool's Tower Ballroom. That's the kind of all-action scene which had been going on for years – a scene of which the music moguls, lounging in their plush London offices, were completely unaware. But after the Beatles exploded on the scene nothing could be the same again.

How right he was. The first six months of 1963 had already transformed the UK record business and moved the talent focus from solo stars to groups, expanded the horizon from London into the provinces, the music itself from pop to white "rhythm & blues". That same explosion would, during the following year, reverberate around the world with huge and thrilling international success, moving to even greater creative heights as, inspired by the Beatles and soon Bob Dylan, the British groups began writing their own songs and thus sounding the death knell for the old Tin Pan Alley establishment.

I liked the music of the beat groups plenty more than I liked the music of the pretty boys, but I still liked rhythm & blues even better. My next *The Great Unknowns* featured the Majors ("She's A Troublemaker", "Wonderful Dream", "A Little Bit Now"), Guy got to run his *Bo Diddley Discography*, I profiled Sam Cooke's disc career in *Mr Cooke's Ups And Downs*, did *The Buddy Holly Discography*, and spoke to Cyril Davies again for the article *I'm Still Striving For My Sound*. The Cyril Davies All-Stars had a residency at the Marquee Club in Oxford Street and were pulling big crowds, not surprising considering the quality of his band which included Nicky Hopkins on piano and Long John Baldry on vocals. Cyril was an interesting guy, a singer and multi-instrumentalist, an old-school dyed-in-the-wool blues purist – in fact he was a purist among purists. He was perched at the opposite end of the R&B spectrum to the Rolling Stones – they loved stuff like Jimmy Reed, Bo Diddley and Chuck Berry; Cyril told me didn't like any of them. He didn't like any of the beat groups either – "pseudo R&B". He wouldn't sing any Ray Charles himself, but he did let Long John and his girl group the Velvets – like the Raelets – have a go. Long John did an excellent Ray Charles. Cyril, who was 32, was a dumpy bloke who looked middle-aged and sported a comb-over. Luckily the All-Stars looked good, especially Long John.

Cyril, whose background was trad and skiffle, couldn't stand rock'n'roll, and he was constantly admonishing his group to "get bluesier, stay steeped in the blues traditions", which wasn't always easy considering they were brought up with rock'n'roll. Muddy Waters was Cyril's god, and his ambition was to record an album of material at the Chess studios in Chicago. He knew there was a good chance of pulling it off because his label, Pye, were starting to sell Chess records in quantity in the UK. Cyril hoped that an LP would enable him to re-cut "Country Line Special" and run it for its full ten minutes. That would have been really something. Of course none of it ever happened because Cyril would be dead in six months from leukaemia.

On occasion, the best things about New Record Mirror were the readers' letters. The '63 summer silly season began with the July 6th issue and some corkers. Our readers would really get into the spirit of the thing and we loved them for it:

R&B PART ONE
I AM fed up with reading nothing but R&B in your paper. R&B can't be that special because nobody seems to know what it is. I refer to your letters each week where some claim Billy J. Kramer sings R&B and the next week somebody says he doesn't. You answered why "Bo Diddley" by Holly is in the charts calling it "blatantly commercial", while when released it was "great lyric", "top vocal form", "superb backing". Now Diddley's version is "more earthy", "way above other beat discs" and has "more beat", it is "better than any other version". So that lot on top of Holly's would make it the best disc ever, but I have heard it. I thought it was awful and the Holly version five times as good. I think your jury must be more than biased. Why all the space for R&B anyway. Chuck Berry hasn't been in the charts for five years, Bo Diddley never (according to your discography). I propose R&B fans shut their mouths and let us common types get a look-in. – RICHARD TAPP, 5 Colebrook Close, Worthing, Sussex.

R&B PART TWO
CONGRATULATIONS NRM on daring to print page after page of R&B. Don't stop! Please don't stop!! You are the only paper R&B fans can read that supports R&B in a big way. Please thank Norman Jopling especially for his articles on Mary Wells, etc etc. Tell him to keep writing. It's our only source of information on these unknown stars. Let's have more Fallen Idols too. More discographies, too.

How about an R&B poll? The other main weeklies both have pop or jazz polls. Do I have support for a poll – who seconds it?

How about a campaign to fight for air time on the BBC of our kind of music? - CLIVE DUNN, 72 Pwllygath Street, Kenfig Hill, Glam.

NAUGHTY NRM!

SHAME on the NRM. Having bought your paper for many months I was disgusted when I read the article on Ritchie Valens. I for one had never heard of Ritchie Valens and most definitely was not yearning for another disc from him.

Just because writer Jim Gains and a minority of others are gasping for more Valens material, it doesn't mean that NRM should fill its pages with subjects of such little importance.

Buddy Holly, as far as I'm concerned, is the only "late" singer worth listening to. No, Decca please stay asleep. - TERRY, 15 North Parade, Southall, Mddx.

GOOD OLD NRM!

HURRAH for Jim Gains and the NRM for giving Ritchie Valens some well-deserved publicity.

I am a fan of Buddy Holly but agree Ritchie and his fans have been given a raw deal.

The article was most interesting and factual and should be rewarding as far as future Valens' recordings go.

Now maybe more publicity concerning Ritchie will be put before us. Once again a pat on the back to all concerned. Keep it up, NRM. - PETER SLOCOMBE, 6 Franconia Rd, Clapham, London SW4

I saved the lead letter spot in that issue for a particular piece of mischief-making titled *HOLLY? IS IT A HOAX – TWO READERS ASK*. In light of Buddy Holly's recent extraordinary posthumous success, two readers – one from Norway – wrote in on a similar theme, with what must be one of pop's first conspiracy theories:

WITH the reappearance of another "Buddy Holly" disc in the charts isn't it about time someone found out if it really is Buddy singing, or just another copyist. If Tommy Roe, Mike Berry, Earl Sinks and many more can sound just like Buddy, surely it is possible for these "Buddy Holly" recordings of late to be by an impostor.

The last two releases "Bo Diddley" and "Brown Eyed Handsome Man" do not sound to me as if they were made pre-1959. We are told that the backings has been added, but the actual voice is so clear that it seems impossible to get this sound on an ordinary tape recorder, and after the tape has lain around for over four years!

Now comes the news that another Holly tape has been found and, of course, these will be released and sell like hot cakes, but would someone please explain how a tape that has been lying around for four years has only just been found?

Don't get me wrong. I'm a Holly fan and saw him when he came over, but are today's record buying fans sure it is their idol, or are we being taken for one of the biggest rides in modern record history? – JIM COSTELLO, 40 Stainton Road, Enfield, Mddx.

IT was very interesting to read your discography on Buddy Holly some weeks ago. But it's also interesting to find that except for "Baby I Don't Care", a hit in July '61, all Buddy's singles from "Peggy Sue Got Married" in September '59 to "Reminiscing" in October '62 have been flops.

In the last few months there has been much written about Holly and it has been written that Norman Petty back in the U.S. has plenty of recording material left of Buddy's – enough to have records released for many years to come.

But isn't it strange that these tapes haven't been issued as records many years ago when Buddy's releases all flopped in a row?

Is the reason that U.S. Brunswick needed a guy who sang so like Buddy that with some technical arrangements it was impossible to hear the difference? I find it very strange that Mr Petty has such a great number of unreleased tapes. In the discography Mr Norman Jopling said "A perfect tape had just been found by some U.S. dee-jays of Buddy singing 20 R&B standards."

Seems like Buddy has gone around and recorded whenever he had a spare minute. Tapes are found by his mother, by Petty, or just by some dee-jays!

Although I'm a keen Holly fan, I for one find this very strange. – PETTER KNUTZEN, Terrasseveien-14, Stabekk, Oslo, Norway

Everyone who knows Holly's records knows what a brilliant producer Petty was. But at the time of Holly's death, unknown to the press and public, Holly was escaping from Petty's control: tracks like "Rave On", "Early In The Morning", It Doesn't Matter Anymore" and "True Love Ways" had already proved Holly could make great records without Petty. Nevertheless, four years after Buddy's death, Petty was now working with the Holley family and in charge of sprucing up Buddy's unissued tapes…and making a fine job of it too. The recent hits "Reminiscing", "Brown-Eyed Handsome Man", "Bo Diddley" and the forthcoming "Wishing" were testament to that. It was understandable the Holley family would want to work with Petty – he was local, they knew him well, they trusted him. And when, in mid-'59, Decca themselves had attempted to spruce up Holly's demos for his final songs ("Peggy Sue Got Married", "Learning The Game", "That Makes It Tough" etc) they'd botched the job.

Predictably Petty rose magnificently to the dangled bait of our two lead letters. His reply was in the following week's issue: he'd telegrammed it. Air Mail wouldn't have been quick enough.

NRM w/e 13th July 1963
(Readers Letters)
BUDDY – NORMAN PETTY WRITES
And A New Disc Is On The Way

YOUR July 6th paper…page two…articles from two readers. It is most surprising to think how difficult it is for some people to accept the truth of any situation. Make something complicated...tell small stories...then it is easy to sell...but it is very difficult indeed to think that some of your readers still doubt the authentic voice of BUDDY HOLLY, True...there have been many who have tried to sound like BUDDY...but sound alone is not enough... regardless of what your readers might think.

The term "feel" must be brought forward...that is exactly what could not be copied...since BUDDY HOLLY did have his own feel and true record friends can spot the copies and the "real thing". Your readers have not been fully informed concerning the background of "all those tapes" you are now hearing about. The tapes have not just been found as some trade papers would have you believe...they have been around all the time...we knew about them...so did the record companies. Legal difficulties...not necessarily the problems of yours truly...but of all concerned, prevent the public from knowing the full story behind the tapes. You can rest assured that a record company with reputation of Decca would not be part of "a hoax"...at any cost. They could not care less for the money involved at this point. As stated before...Decca has known of these tapes for some time. The press has known of them. Now it seems a good time to sell more papers...thus all of a sudden more tapes are found. It makes this reader very angry to be blamed for vague stories about the tapes. It is my obligation and trust to dress up to the best of my ability ...all tapes concerning BUDDY HOLLY and this trust will not be "sold" to perpetration. In fact...we do not hold but a very few useable tapes and these will not be released until they are up to the standards we know were possible with the ability of Buddy Holly.

We did not arrange any of the release dates of "the flops"...or any other releases there. The very early tapes did not go through us but were sent directly from Decca here to your country. You and your readers should rest assured that much has been written among all parties concerned with these tapes and all can be authenticated. However, this seems pointless at this stage. The simple truth...all tapes that have been released are BUDDY HOLLY. Few remain...to be released only when completed.

As a matter of fact...Decca Records here and in England have had the recording of "WISHING" by BUDDY HOLLY, since the first of the year. It is a great record in my opinion and you will be able to hear it when the GREATER POWERS THAT BE decide to release it.

It was my rare pleasure to be the recording engineer... the musician...a co-writer of many songs...the manager...a friend associated with BUDDY HOLLY
Best, NORMAN PETTY

A week later a letter arrived from Buddy's parents. Petty had chided us for printing the two letters, but Mr and Mrs Holley were more realistic: "...naturally we do not consider you or your staff of reporters responsible for the opinions expressed by your readers..." The Holleys went on to write a long, gentle letter about their son and his music and the tapes. They concluded by stating "Please tell them (NRM readers) that when they are listening to Buddy's songs they may rest assured that they really are hearing Buddy and not another. We could not and would not betray the trust and love they have shown to his memory and to us also."

1963 was the year that UK pop really took off, and the second half of the year did not disappoint. In July I compiled a half-yearly survey: Cliff was top, up from No. 3, but the Beatles were in at No. 2 – and Elvis down to No. 17. My next two *The Great Unknowns* were Jimmy Reed and John Lee Hooker; Guy Stevens then profiled Howlin' Wolf for the column, and I returned to my beat with Arthur Alexander; my next scouser interview *This Group Gets U.S. Sound* featured Johnny Sandon & The Remo Four; *Top London Beatsters Inspire Liverpudlians* was a profile-interview with Cliff Bennett, a seriously good rock'n'roller and red-hot live act that seldom translated into hits; Wesley Laine castigated Dion DiMucci for the death disc "Be Careful Of Stones That You Throw" in

No More Like This, Please Dion!; The Searchers told me *We're Still Searching* (for a follow-up); and in July two articles on two enormously popular London bands, one of which achieved virtually no chart success – the Outlaws in *Rumour About The Outlaws Made Their Disc Company Panic* (vicious slanders that the group were splitting up) – and another that did: *Brian Leads The Big Breakthrough – and gives hope to all London groups*. That was Brian Poole & The Tremeloes, who'd cut some fine Holly-esque flops with sides like "Twist Little Sister", "Blue", "That's Alright" and "Keep On Dancing" over the past couple of years. But they were now established in the Top Ten with "Twist And Shout", the Isley Brothers original currently being immortalised by the Beatles. Said Brian: "In answer to the people who say we cashed in on 'Twist And Shout', all we can say is that we, and many other groups, were playing this number long before the Beatles popularised it again. Naturally if it hadn't been for the re-awakened interest in the song due to the Beatles version of it, ours probably would not have been released." Brian and the Tremeloes would shortly follow up "Twist And Shout" with a revival of the Contours' Motown classic "Do You Love Me". They'd top the UK charts with it, and no Beatles version in sight to dog them. On the distaff side (as we used to say) I had the pleasure of interviewing Little Peggy March – a real sweetheart – in *I Didn't Think I Was Good Enough To Make Discs*. And I did a track-by-track feature-review on A Brenda Bargain, Brenda Lee's Ace Of Hearts collection "Love You" containing (mostly UK unissued) rock'n'roll tracks.

High summer '63 was when surf music broke into the charts: Jan & Dean hit the top 30 with their US chart-topper "Surf City", future surf kings the Beach Boys crept into the top 40 with "Surfin' USA" (a timely rewrite of Chuck Berry's "Sweet Little Sixteen"), but the biggest UK surf smash was the Surfaris' frantically exciting Top 5 instrumental "Wipe Out", closely followed by Dot labelmates the Chantays' moodily throbbing "Pipeline", which reached a respectable No. 16. I squeezed out yet another Jan & Dean feature – *Five Years Of Hits In America: Now A British Success For Jan & Dean*, and profiled the two Dot groups in Let's Surf Again! – the same week that Presley hit the top with "Devil In Disguise", redeeming the forgettable "One Broken Heart For Sale" – but it would be a bumpy downhill ride for Elvis over the next few years. The King was dead…long live the Kings.

As far as the Kings were concerned, they were still No. 1 in the LP and EP charts with "Please Please Me" and "Twist And Shout" respectively, but "From Me To You" was falling rapidly – after a full five months in the singles chart. But if anyone had any doubts remaining about the power of the Fab Four, their new just-released single was about to blow away all opposition, top the charts globally, place the Beatles on a pinnacle where they'd remain for the rest of their career and beyond. Here's the review of the awesome "She Loves You" from the New Record Mirror disc jury:

> *THE BEATLES*
> *She Loves You; I'll Get You*
> *(Parlophone R 5055)*
> *THAT noise you hear is the Beatles' newie rushing straight into the charts – an advance order of a quarter of a million, for a start. Two Lennon-McCartney numbers. Top side is strictly fab, pushed along at precisely the right pace, with stack of vocal attack. Solid instrumental fair pounding along behind the vocal work. We just can't think of anything to have a go about. Flip is slightly slower and features another swingingly commercial slice of Merseybeat. A value-for-money coupling but top side will attract most of the attention. Just clear that Number One spot, that's all.*
> *FOUR BELLS*
> *TOP TWENTY TIP*

Much as I'd love to take credit – or even co-credit – for that spot-on review, it's a Peter Jones piece all the way. Peter was now officially New Record Mirror Features Editor, according to the little masthead on page 2, which gave our phone number and address, also stating (according to Jimmy Watson) who did what on the paper. Editor: Jimmy Watson / Assistant To The Editor: Norman Jopling / Features: Peter Jones / Advertising & Circulation: Roy Burden.

I hated that "Assistant To The Editor" with a vengeance. When he decided on those credits Jimmy was at pains to point out to me: "You're not the Assistant *Editor*...you're Assistant *to* the Editor." This I resented deeply. After all, in practise I was the chief sub-editor, did all the layouts, put the paper to bed, wrote half of the singles reviews, compiled *A Look At The US Charts*, had several regular columns including *The Great Unknowns* (our most popular column), was a feature writer, reporter, rhythm & blues activist and considered myself, rightly or wrongly, the hippest member of the staff. I worked hard. Jimmy, as far as I was concerned, did very little. He'd go over the final proofs at the printers checking for errors, libels, he'd answer letters from readers with a grievance, reviewed the LPs (badly) and didn't overmuch share them out. Fond of Jimmy though I was I had more than a smidgen of teenage gripe over that title. I would sooner have had no title – I didn't ask for one. I was happy to be a reporter.

But Jimmy did make some real changes that summer. Our circulation was going up, we were pulling in more advertising, Roy needed an assistant. My pal Bob Bedford, droll and dapper, still working as office-boy was the obvious candidate and happy to move up in that direction rather than towards the editorial desk. That left the office boy position free: the obvious candidate was my other best mate, Terry Chappell, a witty dandy who'd left school at 15 to work in the legal profession, dropped out, and was currently Ronan O'Rahilly's gopher at the Scene. Jimmy liked Terry, who was always hanging out at Record Mirror anyway, and offered him the job. He took it. Who wouldn't.

Dezo Hoffmann was busy photographing the Beatles. After the Liverpool trip he captured some nice candids in Soho near his studio. He also made some posed studio shots, where Jane Asher accompanied "the boys", as Dezo (and Brian Epstein) would always refer to them. The Liverpool Echo commissioned him to supply them with a photo-feature presciently titled "A Day In The Life". Dezo snapped them in Berwick Market, in their hotel, at his shirtmaker, and with the tailor Dougie Millings. This would be the last period in their lives when the Beatles could wander through London virtually unaccosted. Fans would recognise them, autographs would be given, but – just about – they were not being mobbed. Not yet settled in London, they were still a bit provincial. Dezo's first Beatles' picture book would be published in August, simply titled "The Beatles", containing 77 photographs and would, inevitably, immediately sell out.

From May 18th to June 9th the Beatles embarked on a major UK tour for the first time as headliners on a sensational triple-whammy bill also featuring Gerry & The Pacemakers and Roy Orbison. "From Me To You" was No.1 at the beginning of the tour, displaced late in May by Gerry's "I Like It". And Orbison was America's hottest act in the UK, probably the only performer in the world who could hold his own against the unstoppable Liverpudlians. But the tour couldn't have been comfortable. There were twenty-one venues spread over twenty-four days – three days off – and the itinery was crazy: Slough-Hanley-Southampton-Ipswich-Nottingham-Walthamstow-Sheffield-Liverpool-Cardiff-Worcester-Manchester-Southend-Tooting-Brighton-Woolwich-Birmingham-Leeds-Glagow-Manchester-Blackburn. The M1 was Britain's only motorway – and only 60 miles of it. The travelling was gruelling: Nottingham-Walthamstow-Sheffield indeed! Their next tour – The Beatles Autumn Tour – would be even worse. But by then "She Loves You" would have catapulted the Beatles into the pop stratosphere and other heavyweight attractions could be dispensed with. The Beatles would 'share the stage' this forthcoming November with instrumental combo Peter Jay & The Jaywalkers, the Kestrels, and the anachronistic pre-Beatles era duo the Brook Brothers.

The Brook boys got lucky with that tour, but the group they'd modelled themselves on, and who doubtless had been an inspiration to the Beatles and every other beat group who attempted harmonies, were themselves touring the UK that autumn. But with chart placings barely better than the Brook Brothers, the once-mighty Everly Brothers undoubtedly did need other heavyweight attractions to bolster the bill. And Don Arden – the man who wanted to kill me – was the promoter and did indeed make sure that the Everlys were well supported.

He brought over rhythm & blues god Bo Diddley, hired the Rolling Stones for their first major tour, and filled the cracks with Mickey Most (then a performer, ex-Most Brothers), Julie Grant, and The Flintstones. It still wasn't enough. When ticket sales for the first few dates looked disappointing he brought over Little Richard to share top billing. That did the trick.

Just before the tour started, Pye Records, who handled Diddley's US label Chess, threw a press reception for him. Eager to meet the legend among legends, Peter Meaden and I trooped along to a pokey little basement club hired by Pye. Like other press receptions of that era it was comparatively easy to get to talk to the artist as most of the journalists, especially from the nationals, were there only for the free booze and as many canapés as they could shove down their throats, and would studiously avoid talking to the artist at all costs. Guy Stevens was already at the reception, now an intimé of Bo's, having lured Diddley and his cohorts Jerome Green and the Duchess straight to the Scene club a few days previously, played loads of his records and watched the threesome dance with the fans. Frustratingly I'd missed all this, having had to stay overnight at High Wycombe that Monday putting to bed a troublesome issue of NRM.

For Bo, whose American career was on the slide despite scoring a useful US hit in '62 with the exhilarating "You Can't Judge A Book By The Cover", all his Sundays came at once when he suddenly discovered he now had a large and devoted UK and European fan following and was back in demand both as a live performer and recording artist. Meaden and I sidled up to where the great man was holding several of the Rolling Stones hypnotically captive with a mesmerising description of the broken carburettor in his car and the precise way the petrol drip-drip-dripped out of it. Awestruck I may have been in the physical presence of this R&B divinity, but I managed to get a few quotes from him, sussed out his opinions on this and that, and soon realised that Bo was a prickly character with grievances. And there was no doubt that some of these grievances were justified. Although Chess had released a series of wonderful Diddley albums in the States, they'd also released enough scrappy cash-ins to cast doubt on Diddley's own artistry and integrity, culminating in his latest US album "Surfin' With Bo Diddley", which was later discovered to contain only three or four Diddley tracks, the rest being performed incognito by equally-displeased rockabilly legend Billy Lee Riley who'd fondly imagined a batch of recordings he'd sold to Chess would at least be issued under his own name.

Bo was also irate about Buddy Holly's recent UK hit version of "Bo Diddley", complaining that his own record should have been reissued (it was), and also complaining that he should have been credited as a co-writer by Holly for the 'Bo Diddley'-style rhythm on "Not Fade Away". The Rolling Stones were taking particular interest in this. Then, just to rub it in, a young female cub reporter from the Daily Mirror elbowed her way through the worshipful throng of male rhythm & blues addicts, took out her notebook, and asked Bo what was obviously her prepared 'scoop' question:

"Bo, why did you name yourself after a hit record by Buddy Holly?"

The great man was for once rendered speechless – and his male admirers equally drop-jawed.

Bo was one of those artists simply unable to play the self-publicity game. It this respect he wasn't dissimilar to Chuck Berry, his equally-prickly fellow Chess artist and rock'n'roll pioneer. Chuck and Bo didn't get along, despite the public image perpetrated by Guy Stevens' successful pairing of them on a series of "Chuck & Bo" EPs for Pye International's R&B series. According to Bo, they'd also nearly come to blows recently after a stage contest which was judged on applause, and which Bo hinted he'd won. Chuck was more successful and financially shrewd than Diddley, but artistically they were more-or-less equals, though stylistically miles apart. Bo was more of an experimenter: Cyril Davies' opinion that Bo hadn't moved on just proved that Cyril hadn't been listening to him. Bo may have pioneered the famous 'Bo Diddley' beat but there was so much more to his music than that "shave-and-a-haircut, two-bits" rhythm. Aficionados still agree with Phil Everly's judgement on Diddley: "...the most under-rated rock'n'roller of the century".

But Bo was ornery. Whereas Chuck, soon to tour the UK, would come onstage and change the lyric in "School Day" from "Hail hail rock'n'roll" to what he considered to be the UK crowd-pleasing "Hail hail rhythm and blues" (it didn't please the rockers), Bo just couldn't help biting the trend that was feeding him.

NRM w/e 28th September 1963
'MY MUSIC'S NOT R&B' – BO
The Most Controversial And Colourful Figure On The R&B Scene Gives His Frankest Interview

"NO man, I don't sing Rhythm And Blues" said Bo Diddley, one of the greatest Rhythm And Blues singers alive today. That was typical of the man. For with Bo Diddley, everything has to be different. From his clothes, down to his cars, and up to his music.

And it's his music that's most different of all. There's no tag attached to Bo's music, as far as he's concerned at least. He admits he's a blues singer – and proud of it. But he doesn't like being tagged with anyone else.

"I've got my own sound. And my own type of music, and my own style. If I hadn't developed my style I wouldn't have lasted eight years. I know lots of singers who've had lots of hits and fallen down crash. Me, I'm different. I've worked on my sound and yet I try to be different all the time – even on my own performances."

Bo was a solid, dynamic presence onstage. The Flintstones augmented the missing members of his band, for this was the era when the Musicians Union ruled that if American musicians wanted to play for money in the UK, an equal number of British musicians must go play for money in the USA. Unfortunately we wanted theirs a lot more than they wanted ours – for the time being, anyway. Those rules didn't apply to a headline act like Bo, who did manage to bring in his maracas player and long-term buddy Jerome Green, and rhythm guitarist 'The Duchess', alias Norma-Jean Wofford, who Bo said was his sister but wasn't. Bo later confessed that the white lie helped protect the Duchess from unwelcome advances because she certainly was one glamorous and sexy guitarist, clad in her skin-tight gold lame cat-suit. When one journalist asked how she managed to get into it, the Duchess responded by producing an over-sized shoe-horn. Better still, she was an excellent musician, a worthy successor to Bo's previous lady guitarist Peggy 'Lady Bo' Jones, whose mastery of the Diddley beat had been indistinguishable from Bo's and who was a prime contributor to some of his finest work. Inexplicably, Arden only allowed Diddley to perform three songs per performance, which was infuriating for the fans, i.e. me. Maybe Arden thought they'd buy more tickets for another venue.

Every week of the tour, each of the Rolling Stones wrote a column for NRM, and interesting they all were too. Brian called Bo "the exciting, off-beat, zany but very hip king of R&B...much more 'primitive' (I'm sure he won't mind me saying this) than I expected... Don & Phil the epitome of polished white performers...this is really the tour to be on." Mick reported the following week when Little Richard joined the tour: "...he played to two packed houses and drove the whole audience into a frenzy...his hypnotic hold on the audience was reminiscent of an evangelist meeting...we get on like a house on fire with the Diddley threesome and travelling on the coach with Bo and Jerome makes the otherwise tedious journey great fun as they are the life and soul of the party." Next came Bill: "We took a day off to record our new single which the Beatles offered us some weeks ago, Brian plays steel guitar on 'I Wanna Be Your Man' and it is an entirely new sound for a British disc...our new van arrived last week and already it has been attacked by eager fans and bits and pieces disappear every night. Last night we lost three letters from the front and now it just displays OMM." Reported Keith: "We should like to thank the girls who sent us the cigarettes. Brian announced he has given up smoking – in fact he has only given up buying them...we met a party from the Bradford Food Fair and now Jerome sports a big badge on the lapel of his very English sports jacket announcing he is a representative of a well-known butter firm...we listened to playbacks this week of our new record and are all knocked out at the sound Eric Easton has got for us." On the fifth and final week Charlie summed things up: "Mickie Most always gives a tremendous opening; Little Richard is a consistently great performer and, as an avid R&B fan, it is great to see the fabulous Bo Diddley going down so well...finalising the report made two weeks ago, the number plate has now entirely disappeared and we are a complete mystery to the AA and RAC".

Charlie was right, Mickey Most was a tremendous opener, a good all-rounder and a convincing rock'n'roller. I was so impressed I spoke to him during the tour, for *Do-It-Yourself Mick!* He'd just had a minor hit with "Mr Porter" and had cut a follow-up, "The Feminine Look", which was even better. Mickey was a shrewd likeable guy – he'd been around since the late '50s, cut singles for Decca as the Most Brothers (with Alex Murray) with a band that featured future UK instrumental

luminaries Hank Marvin, Bruce Welch, Jet Harris and Pete Chester –
three-quarters of the Shadows. But no chart action. Then he married a
South African girl and decided to try his luck there. The SA pop scene
was nowhere: Mickey managed to notch up 11 straight Number Ones in
a row and became rich reviving oldies like "Johnny B. Goode". But not
without effort: "The studios there were just about as out-of-date as you
can get. The studio men want to make all your songs sound like waltzes
– that's how with it they are! It was grim trying to get everyone to get
a good sound, but eventually we succeeded and made some passable
discs." Mickey was now doing something similar to what Andrew
Oldham had pioneered – producing his own records and selling them
to the major companies. He added that he wanted to be a producer of
good records. His wish would shortly come true, in spades.

The autumn tours were a regular fixture and '63 was a vintage
year. Not only was the Everlys/Little Richard/Bo Diddley/Rolling
Stones package wending hither and thither, not only were the Beatles
experiencing full-on frenzied Beatlemania, but an in-demand Roy
Orbison was back after his summer success with the Beatles and Gerry,
heading a package that included three hot beat groups: Mancunians
Freddie & the Dreamers, Liverpudlians the Searchers, and Londoners
Brian Poole & the Tremeloes. That autumn I profiled Roy in *An
Unexpected US Hit For Roy ("Mean Woman Blues": he dares to follow Presley
and Jerry Lee!)*, and a week or so later caught up with the man himself:

NRM w/e 28th September 1963
WHY I LIKE BALLADS
*Roy Orbison tells Norman Jopling About His Song Tastes
In A Frank Interview*

*AN enchanted audience watch Roy Orbison sing a
succession of big-ballads – an audience who normally go
for the big-beat numbers and usually don't want to know
about anything you can't twist to.*
*But with Roy Orbison it's different. Very different. For
on a bill that includes such giant names as Brian Poole*

and the Tremeloes, Freddie and the Dreamers, and the Searchers, it is Roy Orbison who is THE star, the one who gets the most applause and screams.

Why?

Why can this man sell his records and himself at a time when the popularity of American artists has never been at a lower ebb? Why does he succeed with a type of song that is notoriously out-of-the-rut?

To find the answers to these questions I talked with Roy backstage at Tooting Granada last Wednesday.

"I'm singing the type of song I've always wanted to sing," Roy told me. "The big-ballad is MY type of song – and I don't think I'll do another one of those exotic things like 'Only The Lonely' again. I like that sort of song but I'm on my own ground now.

"When I started out singing, my manager and my A&R man all wanted me to do the big beat type of number – rock'n'roll all the way. So I made some rock discs – they were moderately successful – but it wasn't anything like the stuff I liked.

"About that time I had plenty of free time to compose songs for other people as well as myself. Nowadays, well, I may have a spare hour or two – then I had a spare week or two or even more.

"I wrote 'Claudette' – one of my biggest songs, that's my wife's name – for the Everly Brothers. But now I just about get time to write my own songs.

"There's no plan for my songs. I just pick up my guitar and strum away and maybe get a few ideas. They don't always work out – a melody may sound great for the first few bars but after a minute or two it doesn't sound so good. Some of my songs I don't write myself. One side of my latest is of course "Mean Woman Blues". We took a chance on that one – giving it a bit of a push – but it paid off. I think it's good to have changes in style every now and then. But I won't make a regular thing of recording numbers like that.

"I still prefer the slow big-ballad – I prefer performing that kind of number as well on stage.

"My favourite song of any artist is 'Limelight' by Charlie Chaplin from the film. And my favourite song of my own things is 'Running Scared'."

It doesn't only seem to be Roy's favourite song either. At many of the places where he has performed it has been called for three times.

Another change in Roy since his last visit here some months ago is the change of glasses. Instead of the normal thick horn-rimmers, there's a pair of tinted lenses. The reason for the change – which is somewhat of a surprise after years of wearing the same specs, is a pretty simple one. Roy accidentally broke the glasses he usually wears and the other tinted pair were made in a great hurry – and it just so happened that Roy liked them. They also tended to protect him from the savage flare of the stage lights – not a pleasing experience for any performer.

This interview didn't exactly reveal the answers to the questions posed so provocatively at the beginning of the piece. Blame can fall on that professional maniac Freddie Garrity, acting up all over the place backstage, annoying everybody with his tediously "zany" antics and putting me off my interview. Orbison also told me – and I have no idea why I didn't include it in the feature – that he'd work on a song in the evening (he was talking about "In Dreams") then go to bed, and if he remembered it the next morning he knew it was a hit. If he'd forgotten it – well, he'd forgotten it.

Other big tours that autumn included Cameo-Parkway dance queen Dee Dee Sharp, supported by Heinz, just off a Joe Meek-produced Top Ten smash with "Just Like Eddie", and Johnny Kidd & The Pirates, arguably the UK's finest rock'n'roll group who were hitting big with Liverpool pastiches like "I'll Never Get Over You" and "Hungry For Love". Stars dropped in and out of this tour, including the Caravelles, Joe Brown, Vince Eager, the Big Three, and even the mighty Gerry & The Pacemakers if they happened to be in town that night, I guess, and weren't doing anything else. Little Richard hung around after the

Evs/Diddley tour wound up, and joined the Duane Eddy-Shirelles package, dropping out after four dates to be replaced by either Gene Vincent, Jimmy Justice, or the Evs' popular bassist Joey Page, then later by Gary U.S.Bonds. Yes, it was a Don Arden package. Helen Shapiro, still a bill-topper, toured with Bobby Rydell, the Spotniks, the Chants, the Trebletones, and a guest star at every gig, among who were Brian Poole & The Tremeloes, Heinz, the Searchers, the Hollies, and the Fourmost.

I was blasé about gigs. When you can see them for nothing, as many as you like, you get that way – at least, I did. But I did make an effort to catch "The Greatest Record Show Of 1963" – after all, it boasted five big US hitmakers – Timi Yuro, Dion DiMucci, Lesley Gore, Brook Benton and Trini Lopez. Didn't enjoy it though:

NRM w/e 26th October 1963

ALTHOUGH it's billed as "The Greatest Record Show Of 1963" the first performance at Finsbury Park Astoria last Sunday didn't exactly bear witness to that. Nothing was wrong with the line-up which included some of the biggest U.S. stars on the scene at the moment.

The thing that was missing was atmosphere. The reasons were pretty obvious. For a start there was so much talent the whole show was rather rushed. Therefore some of the big chart names didn't get the build-up they deserved.

Secondly and most important, it was the backing. Timi Yuro, Dion and Lesley Gore were backed completely by the Ken Thorne Orchestra. The effect was the same as if Victor Silvester had been backing Little Richard. There was no beat, the orchestra just couldn't 'feel' the music, and result was a host of wishy-washy backing that, for me at least, spoiled the show.

This was strong stuff for me, normally Mr Anodyne. I did commend Ken and his Ork for their solo spot, and further commiserated with the big names whose acts were frustrated by "inappropriate accompaniment". Predictably, the most enjoyable act was Trini Lopez:

Next was Trini Lopez, who definitely was the biggest success in the show. His polished original versions of old numbers triumphed mainly because of the fact that his recordings are made 'live' anyway, so on stage he was the same, probably better than on record. He also brought his own drummer who laid down the first solid beat on the programme, and his own bass player. First was "La Bamba" which he does so well it wouldn't surprise me if he brought it out as a single. He then went through numbers like "Unchain My Heart", "America", "That'll Be The Day", "What'd I Say", and finally "If I Had A Hammer". Trini also managed to get the audience participating not only with handclapping, but also singing, quite a feat.

Other autumn scribblings included *Are We Clairvoyant?* (self-congratulatory piece on the Rolling Stones with comments from Mick and Brian); *A Hit Despite JBJ* (that's "Juke Box Jury" – the hit was "Searchin'" by the Hollies, who I was still championing); *The Tired Tremeloes – Brian & the Boys Begin To Feel The Price Of Being London's Hottest Group* (not sure about that phrase "feel the price" – but do make the most of being London's hottest group, Brian & the Trems, because the Dave Clark Five and the Rolling Stones are looming); *Why Dig Up The Old Songs?* inquired Wesley Laine (revivals in the current chart: "It's All In The Game" – Cliff, "Sweets For My Sweet" – Searchers, "Dance On" – Kathy Kirby, "Come On" – Stones, "Twist & Shout" – Beatles, Brian & Trems, "Searchin'" – Hollies, "Still" – Karl Denver, vintage oldies "Confessin'" – Frank Ifield, "Whispering" – Bachelors, "Frankie & Johnny" – Sam Cooke.) Then there were further instalments of *The Great Unknowns* (Solomon Burke and the Contours written by me, Muddy Waters written by Guy Stevens, and James Brown by Jes Pender); *The Bachelors' View* (likeable Irish trio consolidate their success and comment on the beat group scene); *Malayan Popster* (profile of Dave Ventura).

Our latest Readers Letters controversy concerned the noticeable and much-commented-upon absence of Elvis from our shores. This was a topic which had usefully filled many column inches, in features and letters pages, since Elvis completed his tour of duty for Uncle

Sam. A reader, Alfred Riley from Accrington, suggested a boycott of Elvis' records might get him over sharpish: "…only when he is on his way out will he come". In point of fact Elvis was well on his way out and still never came – now, of course, we know why. Riley's letter enraged other Elvis fans: "Just how childish can some people get? Grow up, Alfred, your nappies are showing" (Winn Hall, from Whitley Bay). Others suggested that the then-enormous sum of three million quid put in a pot from all the countries in Europe might be enough to tempt the King. But the most controversial reply to Riley's letter sparked off a nice mod-rocker spat which ran for several weeks:

> *…if he ever did come he would not be such a success as people think because he is a 'rocker' and we don't wear drainpipes, black shirts and Brylcreemed hair any more, and I for one would rather pay to see a modern group like the Hollies or the Rolling Stones.*
>
> *No, I'm afraid Elvis would get rather a big shock. – A MOD (M.O.M.F. Member of MOD'S Federation, Walthamstow, Essex.*

Cat was set among pigeons.

> *THE MOD who wrote a letter in NRM 19th September doesn't know what he is talking about. He says "we" don't wear drain pipe trousers, black shirts and Brylcreemed hair but "we" Rockers do. Anyway, Elvis doesn't wear those kinds of clothes much. He says he doesn't like dressing up like that. But all the same I'm sure there are many "Rockers", "Mods" and "Mids" that would welcome Elvis if he came to England. – A ROCKER, 23 The Ridges, Orpington, Kent.*

> *THE un-named goon of a mod who thought that Elvis would flop because Elvis dressed like a rocker must be off his (rocker).*
>
> *If he judges singers by the clothes they wear he should have his head examined.*

I hope when he says "we" he isn't referring to the public in general, because not only mods (or slobs) buy records.

Personally I prefer Buddy Holly to Elvis but when some twisted goon starts saying this it makes my rocker blood boil. – GRAHAME MORRISON (A ROCKER), 104 Maybank Road, South Woodford, London E.18

REGARDING "A Mod's letter", while I am indifferent to Elvis, I must point out that "modern" groups like the Hollies and the Rolling Stones are issuing very inferior imitations of original songs by Rock'n'Roll groups and singers (Chuck Berry, the Coasters etc) lately called Rhythm & Blues singers.

The so-called Rhythm & Blues revival is merely Rock'n'Roll coming to the forefront again. How many true Rhythm & Blues singers (Muddy Waters, John Lee Hooker, etc) have made the charts of late?

More power to Rock'n'Roll and its High Priests, Jerry Lee Lewis, Chuck Berry and Gene Vincent. – E.J. TOWNSEND, Crewe, Cheshire

Winter approached and I sold my scooter. I couldn't face the cold, I was drinking more, I'd stopped going to Tottenham Royal and the Lyceum. The mods, as opposed to modernists, had taken up scootering in a big way and suddenly it seemed like such a juvenile thing to be riding around on a scooter. The bike had been expedient in the summer, but even then I'd stripped off the chrome, chucked away the dead fox I'd had on my saddle, tail waving in the wind, got it down to basics. I was slowing up a bit.

There was something in the air that autumn: big things were about to happen and there was a new kind of confidence, an exuberance. British pop music was moving on to new levels of artistry and was poised to conquer the world and sound the next note of the Sixties, this thrilling decade that would mark everyone who lived through it. But in the USA, Kennedy's Camelot was about to come crashing down, taking America's hopes with it.

All this didn't stop me churning out the usual column-fillers. As Wesley Laine I profiled the four contestants in *The "I Who*

Have Nothing" Battle, a lot of fuss about a big-voiced Italian ballad anglicised by those versatile rock'n'roll moguls Leiber & Stoller for Ben E. King, covered here by Shirley Bassey (who had the UK hit), Dick Emery (yes, he had a "voice of operatic proportions" which was being heard nightly on ITV on the Esso commercial), and Ken Kirkham, another "big-voiced gent". It was all a mite kitsch. Not so *Rock'n'Respectability: After 8 Years Beat Music Is No Longer Considered Rebellious*, a piece about the music establishment's now-fervent embrace of the once-despised beat music. That October, Brian Epstein's new press officer Tony Barrow called me about NEMS latest hitmaker Cilla Black and asked if I'd like to interview her. I was curious, I had no real opinion about her record "Love Of The Loved", a minor Lennon-McCartney number – but there was something about Cilla that seemed interesting. So I wandered up Shaftesbury Avenue and met her in a little café close to Monmouth Street. She was there with boyfriend Bobby and we sat at one of those little chipped formica-topped tables with cramped bench seats facing each other over a cappuccino and bun. Cilla was very much all right, bright, down-to-earth, instantly likeable.

NRM w/e 2nd November 1963

THERE'S much more individuality to Cilla Black than just being the only girl in the NEMS stable – a fact which hasn't exactly been over-exposed.

For example her hit "Love Of The Loved".

"As everybody knows it's a John Lennon-Paul McCartney composition", she told me, "but that didn't exactly commend it to me when I first heard it. John and Paul wrote it with me in mind but when I heard their demo I nearly died. I mean, demos are bad at the best of times, but this one!"

I reminded her she was talking about the most commercial sound in the land.

"It just wasn't my sort of song. But after I'd listened to it a few times I decided to make my own interpretation of the number. I realised that if the Beatles HAD made a great

demo job I could only have copied it – making a second-rate version. As it was I was more or less forced to be original.

"Mind you I didn't have any idea it would be a hit. Even with NEMS handling me.

"As it is I'm so pleased my disc has made it, even if it doesn't go any higher I'll be pleased." The fact that Cilla's disc has made it has personally chuffed her so much because she's a bit of a pessimist. For example she's currently embarking on her very first tour – of course she worries herself silly every night that the fans won't like her.

But every night they do.

"I even get fan letters," she confessed, "not many, mind you, and even then they're mainly from girls. My first was from a lady of 81 who was also named Cilla. She told me she hadn't heard of anyone who had our name! I've got some more girls who start off with 'It may seem funny me writing to you, being a girl.' But I like to reply to all the ones I've received. Quite a lot are very crafty and ask me if I can get them Gerry's autograph or something.

"Someone even asked me to get them into the Beatles hotel..."

It surprised me that Cilla hadn't had more fan letters from blokes – although I must admit she's only been on release for three weeks. In fact she's an extremely attractive girl – but like all girls she has a complex about not being photogenic.

"It worried me a lot about my photos. Please use a nice one," she asked me. Currently, Cilla is touring with Gerry and Co. and Del Shannon – "a wonderful bloke", she says. And she's also booked for several TV spots and, of course, the Beatles' Xmas Show, together with Billy J., The Fourmost and Tommy Quickly. After that she's STILL reasonably well booked up.

Twenty-one year old Cilla first started singing some three years back when a singer in the 'Pool thrust a mike in her hand during the middle of "Fever". Ever since she's been singing for her bread but the style is slightly changing.

"I want to go on more to the jazzier, bluesier sort of stuff. If possible I would like to break into the cabaret field – but that would be in about ten years time of course! You have to be prepared, you know..."
Cilla hasn't looked back since the day that mike was thrust in her hand. I don't think she'll need to because Cilla Black probably has more chance of breaking into the adult entertainment audience than any others in the NEMS stable.

Was I right or was I right? Cilla went into cabaret a mere five years later. I saw her at the Savoy in '68 and she was fantastic. A bunch of hoorays in the audience started barracking her and after five minutes of banter they were eating out of her hand.

But if there were big global changes taking place there were changes closer to home too. The Cilla Black interview was the last I'd do for New Record Mirror.

The paper's name was about to change and so was much else about it. And it was all because one of the most powerful newspapermen in the land had taken an interest in us.

The Labour MP Woodrow Wyatt, as far to the right as anyone in the Labour Party could ever be without falling off, was also a capitalist, a minor press baron who had recently built a printing plant in Banbury, Oxfordshire. The factory was called Papers and Publications and was located on some rough waste ground half a mile from famous Banbury Cross. Access to this sparse field was across a large humpbacked bridge which spanned the Oxford Canal and which had caused much intake of breath in 1962 when Wyatt brought in a state-of-the-art Goss web offset printing machine which had to be driven over the bridge extremely slowly and extremely carefully. A lot of digging and levelling had also taken place, but the result was a printing plant with a theoretical capacity to print large runs of newspapers – with full colour.

Among his other publications, Wyatt owned the local Banbury Guardian and the Birmingham Post, but their circulations hardly exceeded 15,000 copies apiece weekly. Wyatt needed several outside clients to turn a profit at the plant, and his socialist contacts handily provided him with his first client, the propaganda weekly Soviet News, whose small yet dedicated readership would doubtless be even happier to see the happy citizens and scientific triumphs of the USSR in full colour instead of mere monochrome.

Wyatt was a man with powerful contacts on all sides of the political spectrum, and two of his Tory friends were Decca boss Sir Edward Lewis, and the editor of the Sunday Express, John Junor. We shall never know the genesis of the arrangement, but it was probably over one of the many lunches such men enjoyed in each other's company: Wyatt, extolling the virtues of his high-capacity, large print-runs-in-colour, state-of-the-art web offset printers; John Junor, intrigued, dreaming a vision of the Sunday Express boasting glorious colour, the first major paper in Fleet Street to take such a technological leap; Sir Edward Lewis, scion of the mighty Decca empire, remembering his farthest-flung outpost, a little pop paper printed in black-and-white but whose circulation had mysteriously risen from less than twenty thousand in 1961 to almost sixty-three thousand in late 1963.

Could this web-offset process be used to print the Sunday Express? Junor knew he would need to experiment on a guinea pig to find out. That pig was to be us. So he bought a percentage of Cardfont Publications, New Record Mirror's holding company, from Sir Edward Lewis with the intention of discovering the practicalities of printing the Sunday Express in colour. Much has been written about John Junor, editor of the mighty Sunday Express. But "John Junor – The Rock'n'Roll Years" is a neglected chapter I shall forthwith explore.

Reactions at New Record Mirror to the news of our takeover were mixed. Peter Jones, the only "proper" journalist among us, was excited at the prospect of hob-knobbing with other "real" newspapermen. But Roy Burden and Jimmy Watson, both of whom were on a cushy number, were not happy at what would undoubtedly be a major disruption to their groovy lifestyles. Roy viewed the whole thing with trepidation. As circulation and advertising manager, he could take some credit for the rise in circulation, but our advertising revenue was still pathetic. Editor Jimmy, who presumably knew of Junor's scheme before anyone else, was decidedly dour about it. His lack of enthusiasm was to manifest itself in phoney bonhomie towards the new regime – and it showed. The one member of our staff who was absolutely delighted was Dezo Hoffmann. He'd been shooting in black-and-white and colour for years. Here was a potential showcase for his talents.

I was suspicious. John Junor, Woodrow Wyatt, The Sunday Express, Fleet Street, all meant nothing to me. Fleet Street was not hip to pop. It would rub off on us, I knew. Everyone was concerned about the practicalities of changing printers, and Jimmy told us he'd suggested to Junor that our regular men Dan and George from Merritt & Hatcher be given jobs at Papers and Publications. But that didn't happen. Jimmy had no power in this situation. And Junor wasn't merely changing printers. He sent in a team of his top Sunday Express lay-out men to redesign New Record Mirror and, for the first colour issue, put it to bed at Papers & Publications. We just provided copy and pictures and they did the rest. But it couldn't have been easy for them: they knew as much about web offset as we did, which was nothing.

The plan was that they'd set the new house style, teach it to us, and then we'd carry on ourselves under their supervision, which would decrease as we became more expert. This was more or less what happened. Their chief lay-out man was Jack Andrews, a genial middle-aged chap (they all seemed middle-aged), highly regarded in Fleet Street, who, like the rest of his team, soon decided that they rather liked working on location – in Soho. They'd all troop up to our offices to get on with the lay-outs and teach us amateurs – well, me – how to do it 'properly'. The real reason they wanted to work on location was that it got them out of the Express Building in Fleet Street for half a day and, with the exception of leader Jack, they'd perfunctorily inspect what we'd done, then wander round Soho for a few hours, visit strip clubs, soft-porn cinemas, exotic coffee bars and everything else Soho had to offer the middle-aged man freed from his nine-to-five. Who could blame them?

The newspaper and print business was then heavily unionised, and the Sunday Express production team soon decided that it didn't look good for Record Mirror, as they re-re-re-christened us, to have merely one layout man who also doubled as a journalist, i.e. me, while the Sunday Express seemed to have legions of them. Terry Chappell was swiftly promoted to layout and design duties, while a new office boy, Marvin Brown, was conjured up.

Junor and his team were boasting that they'd double the circulation of Record Mirror with the first colour issue. I wasn't so sure. The final black-and-white issue of New Record Mirror was the November 9th edition and I put it to bed at High Wycombe alone because Jimmy was at Banbury, preparing the first colour issue together with the Express team, all of them learning about web offset. I was sad. I knew I'd never again have the kind of influence over the paper that I'd been allowed over the previous two years. I knew we'd still never be able to compete with NME in terms of breadth of features and news coverage. They had lots more writers and there was a settled confidence about them. They had big circulation, lots of advertising and made money. But New Record Mirror had been more cutting-edge: we were on to rhythm & blues in a big way long before anyone else; none of the other papers dared to take the chances we did; no-one had the chart coverage we did. Peter Jones, David Griffiths, Alan Stinton, were all good journalists. Our regional coverage was superb. Our readers loved us and knew we loved the music. I was unsure whether a pop weekly with colour pictures as the selling-point would prove as commercial as the Fleet Street experts predicted.

Nevertheless the first issue under the new regime certainly looked good. It was beautifully laid out, clean and crisp, very professional, colour front and back. But my worst fears were confirmed. Because of the new style of visual presentation, especially the size and scale of the headlines, there was less space for actual articles. Our features, reviews, regular columns, got shorter. The Fleet Street team ruthlessly chopped our articles to fit the space available. I wondered if a new readership, enticed by the colour pictures, would compensate for the eventual loss of the dedicated readership we'd built up over the past few years – readers who were interested in the music and the artists, in our discographies, in reading about great unknowns and fallen idols. Or could there be room for both?

The problem was soon solved. The first colour issue, minus any mention of rhythm & blues in it, sold 120,000. The second colour issue didn't. The circulation fell back to 65,000, just above what it had been for New Record Mirror. Readers who saw the writing on the wall wrote in begging us not to drop the rhythm & blues coverage just because we'd gone colour. So we put back the rhythm and blues and everyone was happy. I wondered what John Junor thought about those circulation figures. Did he still think that colour was the way to go for the Sunday Express?

But now, in for a penny in for a pound, whatever he thought about RM's roller-coaster circulation, it didn't stop him and his team from enjoying their Soho sojourns. For the next few years we'd see a fair bit of JJ and a lot of Jack Andrews. JJ was also fond of Soho, but his destination was the famous restaurant L'Escargot in nearby Greek Street. He would regularly visit us on Thursdays, and then be escorted by our editor to the doors of L'Escargot. Our editor would then trudge back to RM while JJ would enter alone, to meet and dine with the rich, the interesting, and the powerful.

John Junor was tall, slightly stooped, often ruddy-faced, wore suits – tonic in summer like Peter Jones – and charismatic. What JJ made of me I never really knew, but he was always perfectly pleasant. He liked Peter Jones, didn't much like fellow-Scot Jimmy Watson. Jimmy's attempts at ingratiation with JJ tended to hit all the wrong notes, like Jim's jokes about 'poofters', a subject which Junor, far from finding funny, viewed just this side of frothing at the mouth with righteous disapproval.

It wasn't long before I discovered the advantages of association with power and success. Unlike the High Wycombe letterpress stint, Record Mirror at Banbury was a two-day job and Junor was quite happy for whoever put the paper to bed to stay overnight in the four-star Whately Hall Hotel near Banbury Cross, a congenial and historic establishment with a memorable restaurant and menu. The second time I went to Papers and Publications, Junor arrived mid-morning with his son Roderick, then studying at nearby Oxford. JJ was driving a beautiful Aston Martin DB4 and I was so impressed I blurted out my admiration to him at his fantastic car.

"I'll drive you to lunch," said Junor, "we'll go at quarter to one, with Roderick".

At quarter to one I stopped work and walked over to Jimmy.

"Junor's taking me to the Whately in his Aston!" I declared.

Jimmy's hackles rose. "No he's not, there's too much to do here. Go and finish those pages off!"

I couldn't believe it. Jimmy was jealous of me getting a lift with JJ.

I ran round to where JJ was waiting and told him I couldn't come, that Jimmy had said he needed me here. JJ hesitated for a moment then, being an editor himself, decided not to undermine Jimmy's authority. He gave me a look that said it all, muttered something like "some other time", and drove off with Roderick. I thought Jimmy was making a mistake by being so petty – I knew very little about Junor but he seemed like an expansive kind of bloke who wouldn't much like what Jimmy just pulled. And I never again got the chance to ride in that Aston and have lunch with JJ and Roderick.

The comp (composing) room at Papers and Publications was the nerve centre of our new printers and the place where I would work for almost two days a week for the next several years. A huge bright shed, rows of light tables back-to-back running along the middle of the room with pages from Record Mirror, Soviet News, Banbury Guardian, all in various stages of completion attended by hovering journalists, editors, ad-men and compositors. The pages were made up as positives, with copy, headlines, typography, screened (pixillated) photographs, captions, advertisements – all of which were generated elsewhere in the building – pasted on meticulously by the white-coated operatives following the layout design previously submitted by the sub editors. By the time we arrived late on Monday morning, most of the pages – with the exception of the news and chart pages – were already provisionally made up and ready for us to finish off. Features which were too long would need to be cut, or the last paragraphs re-set in smaller type, or when too short insert extra crossheads and little house ads or extra illustrations; trim here, fill in there, and everything so much easier than working with hot metal. When we were satisfied the page looked right, we'd do a final proof-read, make any necessary corrections, then sign it off – one editorial signature, one advertising signature – and it would be carefully taken to be photographed ready for block making. There was no ink in the room. "This place should be as clean as a surgery", Jack Andrews would say – glumly, as it usually wasn't.

The process, with its attendant scalpels, cow gum, Letraset and other accoutrements of the post-hot metal/pre-computer era, was the print syndication technology of my generation, of our magazines, newspapers, graphic designers. The hot metal process inspired by Gutenberg lasted maybe five hundred years and evolved to a state of awesome technical sophistication. It was replaced virtually overnight by a cleaner, quicker, and cheaper process that would barely last thirty.

There was a rivalry between the compositors. Some were local lads, others had been lured from London by Wyatt. Naturally the Londoners considered themselves superior to the yokels, who in turn were determined to show us clients they were every bit as efficient as the boys from "The Smoke" (and they were). Union regulations forbade us from even touching the page, let alone chivvying out bits and pieces here and there and doing the work ourselves, of which anyone with a decent eye and steady hand was capable. However, this rigorous closed-shop regime was soon to crumble as entropy, laziness and familiarity, not to mention the unspoken connivance of the union shop-stewards, began to kick in after a few months.

Junor may have been in for the long(-ish) haul, but his trips to Banbury ended after a mere month. Then, for the next half-a-dozen issues, it was Jack Andrews and me from Monday through Tuesday, with Bob Bedford coming up just for the day on Tuesday to check the adverts. Jack, like Junor, soon got bored with the Banbury trip and decided that Soho was as far as he would venture from Fleet Street on behalf of Record Mirror.

Freed from the constricting eyes of the oldies, the junket expanded rapidly. For the next two years, me, Terry and Bob became "the regulars", travelling up by train on Monday mornings from Paddington, and returning late on Tuesday. That gave us two meals at the Whately Hall. We courageously worked our way through the sumptuous menu, the impressive wine list, collapsing in a stupor in the warm historic rooms. We learned about decent food and drink quicker than we'd ever learned about anything at school. On Monday evening we'd sometimes hang out at the local disco, helpfully located within staggering distance of the hotel, and chatted up the local birds. Or we went horse riding, to clear our heads.

The bills for our indulgences were paid in full for the first six months at Banbury until a terse memo arrived from Decca's accountants: "We have noticed that the bills for alcohol at the Whately Hall exceeded the total amount for food and accommodation". The bills for food and accommodation would continue to be paid, but no bills for alcohol. Fortunately we'd already worked our way – several times – through the wine list.

The novelty of Record Mirror's invasion by Fleet Street professionals notwithstanding, the show nevertheless had to go on: the Express team had taken over our layouts, but we pop pundits still had to pen the prose. Articles had to be written, pop stars interviewed, reviews dashed off, news gathered, lead letters chosen: we now gave an LP to our lead letter writer, an impulsive act of generosity by Jim which didn't noticeably improve either the quality or quantity of our correspondents – it was still essentially the same old love-hate fan mail.

My first piece in the new-look Record Mirror was the *Duane Eddy Show Review*. I was lucky enough to catch the second house at that late-lamented deco palace, the Regal Edmonton. Lucky, because Duane and the Rebels hadn't played the first house due to "faulty amplification" (actually their equipment arrived late, so it wasn't exactly a lie). There were only three acts on the show, but mighty acts indeed. My girlie favourites the Shirelles kicked things off and fantastic they were too, in "transparent black chiffon dresses", singing loads of their hits perfectly and sending everybody mad with delight with a barnstorming "Saints" closer. Then Duane and the Rebels socked it out as only American rock'n'roll musicians could, laying on tons of moody twang, punchy sax, rebel yells, the lot – exactly what the instrumental R&R fans craved. And just when you thought things couldn't possibly get better, on came Little Richard, superbly backed by the UK's Flintstones, strips to the waist, jumps on his piano, sings hit after hit giving a performance better than anything he did on the previous Everlys/Diddley/Stones package. What a show!

I caught up with Duane and his then-wife Jesse Colter who was wearing a rather fetching hat, a few days later in the Mayfair Hotel. With him were two other ace guitarists, Al Casey and Britain's Bert "Play In A Day" Weedon. It was a 'guitar talk' interview *titled The 'Twangy Guitar' Man Hits Town*. Bert and Duane both used Guild guitars, and Guild had just made a special "Bert Weedon" model. Al and Duane tried it out: "I think I'll stick to my guitar", said Duane, "Mine's easier to play – and Bert's a better player than I am. If anyone wants to learn to play the guitar they'd do better to try mine, not Bert's!"

When Duane and Richard returned to America after the tour, it was no longer the same. JFK had been assassinated.

My reputation as a young meteor in the pop journalism field must have spread, because that was the week I first got head-hunted, at the tender age of 19. Approached by the editor of a forthcoming pop music monthly titled Rave, I was told how great I was, and offered £16.00 a week – £6.00 more than I was earning with Record Mirror. But I didn't want to leave RM, thinking that Rave would be too pop-oriented for my tastes, yet the money was too good to refuse. I told Jimmy and he said if RM could match the offer, would I stay? Yes, I said. He went to Junor, the raise was agreed, and I stayed.

Beat group-wise, Bern Elliot popped in the office for *Sure We Like 'Money'*; Bern and his Fenmen had the UK hit single of Barrett Strong's R&B staple "Money", a song which appeared to be obligatory for all groups to include in their repertoire. Bern beat off a fair amount of competition on the song, and it didn't hurt that the Beatles had included their own dynamic version of "Money" on their second LP which, that very week, had toppled the first Beatles LP from the top of the LP charts, while three Beatles EPs headed the EP chart, and "She Loves You" topped Britain's Top 50 – for a second time – after 4 months on the chart. Phew! I profiled Phil Spector in *The 'Ronettes' hits and Phil's Flips* which was a kind of hors-d'oeuvre to Phil's long-anticipated arrival in the UK, scheduled for early in '64. Unfortunately, the headline demonstrated the utter squaredom (cubedom, even) of the Express production team – their insistence on putting certain group names in single quotation marks. Similar crimes they committed included: *The 'Shadow' Who Quit* (Rostill replaces Locking) and *Going Commercial? Rubbish say the 'Stones'*, which was particularly galling for me. I interviewed Brian Jones for the article, who revealed that Gene Pitney was planning a Jagger-Richard song as his next A-side, and "a U.S. artist" was planning to use a composition by Brian for his next A-side – no name given. Maybe Brian was just making that bit up, starting to display the insecurity that would eventually destroy him.

I adopted the currently-popular house monicker Ken Graham for *Big Dee Irwin's Hit Swings Up The Charts* (Dee's duet with an anonymous

Little Eva on an extremely groovy pop-R&B version of a Disney classic). We tended to give these imaginary scribes like Ken their moment in the sun, and for a few weeks Record Mirror would be full of articles by James Craig, or Perkin Giles, or some such make-believe scribe, then they would fall out of favour and their efforts appear only spasmodically.

We scored a sort of victory over the Sunday Express gang that same week by persuading them to print our singles and LP reviews in a smaller typeface: we crammed in a lot more reviews that way. The main text body size in the redesigned Record Mirror was 8pt, so the reviews went down to the next available size which was 6pt. The 'old' New Record Mirror was all in 7pt, a size that Woodrow Wyatt's organisation seemed not to possess. Really, though, the 6pt size was too small. We also printed the charts in 6pt for the next six months, then managed to hike the size in summer '64 using the same amount of space – and the chart looked really good from there on in. But my next *The Great Unknowns* – Hank Ballard – looked dreadful, set in 8pt, tiny picture, no by-line, the copy cut by a third. I was cross about that, but they probably left off my by-line because I had the lead article on the same page, *It's The Song, Not My Name Which Sells*, a long-ish interview with Johnny Kidd that was more-or-less completely summed up by the headline.

What a year 1963 had been. The Profumo Scandal, the Great Train Robbery, Martin Luther King's inspirational 'I Have A Dream…' speech and the Civil Rights rallies, the terrible death of John Kennedy. In entertainment, the Beatles had seized complete domination of the UK pop scene, with Merseybeat marking the moment that British popular music began to stop sounding like a slavish and usually inferior imitation of the American original. Of course, the beat groups were still trying to capture the energy and authenticity of American music, but it was their gallant failure that created something of our own. The UK beat boom was undeniably fuelled by a love of American Rhythm & Blues, an unsophisticated black music style already superseded in America by the sound of Soul. Yet the potent combination of callow yet inventive British white boys and hard Black urban rhythms and hip attitude had given birth to what would become Rock music in all its wonderful (and not-so-wonderful) varieties.

The top ten record artists for '63 – according to the charts point system – were:

UK	USA
The Beatles	The Four Seasons
Cliff Richard	The Beach Boys
Frank Ifield	Bobby Vinton
The Shadows	Elvis Presley
Gerry & The Pacemakers	Lesley Gore
Roy Orbison	Dion
Billy Fury	Ray Charles
Jet Harris & Tony Meehan	Chubby Checker
The Springfields	The Crystals
Brenda Lee	Skeeter Davis.

Not one crossover. Predictably, I penned a two-part end-of-year R&B survey with *Rhythm & Blues Made The News* and *A Year Of Rhythm& Blues*, while the fictitious RM Disc Jury chose their personal faves of the year. Mine were Rufus Thomas' "Walkin' The Dog", Bo Diddley's "Pretty Thing" (actually seven years old) and Dionne Warwick's "Don't Make Me Over", with honourable mentions for Jimmy Reed, the Jaynetts, the Impressions, Mary Wells, and the Kingsmen. Nom-de-plume Wesley Laine chose "Blowin' In The Wind" from Peter, Paul & Mary, "Easier Said Than Done" by the Essex, and the Crystals' "Then He Kissed Me", with honourable mentions for Dion, Darlene Love, Buddy Holly, Chiffons, Ronettes and UK beat groups the Marauders, Mojos, and Triffids. Also mentioned was the comic "Little Eeefin Annie" from Joe Perkins. "Eeefing" was a (very) short-lived American record craze, a crazy craze indeed – a vocal sound made by panting violently, noisily and extremely quickly, which felt dangerously self-harming when you attempted it yourself, which you invariably did after listening to one of the eeefing records. But it was

137

such a puny craze that it couldn't really stand on its own feeble legs, and relied on being associated with something else, a sort of parasitic craze: "Little Eeefin Annie" was a parody of the comic strip Little Orphan Annie, while another eeefing hit "Eeefenanny" parodied the current US folk "Hootenanny" movement. Later I discovered that Joe Perkins, who was black, had used a white "eeef-master" called Jimmie Riddle (sic) to do the actual eeefing. And apparently the technique had originally developed in the Appalachians where musicians tried to imitate the grunts of their hogs.

More 'humour' in the pages of Record Mirror that Christmas came via John Junor. He persuaded one of his posh mates, a toff called Lord Massereene and Ferrard (Maserati and Ferrari?) to scrawl a few lines on House Of Lords notepaper, which we were commanded to use as our lead letter. Our headline was *Elvis, his Lordship and the Beatles* and the note read: "I cannot understand this Beatle mania. I appreciate they have attractive personalities but when it comes to a question of rhythm, Elvis Presley has it all the way. Yours faithfully, Massereene and Ferrard". It was accompanied by a photo of his Lordship looking a little like a raffish version of the Duke Of Windsor. I don't know if Junor thought this would garner us some welcome publicity, but hardly anyone commented on it except for a few puzzled remarks from music-biz insiders mildly wondering what nonsense we were up to.

I got to see the Beatles perform in the final month of their first big year – saw them but hardly heard them. "The Southern Area Fan Club Get Together" was held on a cold Saturday at Wimbledon, and for three shillings and sixpence the fan club members, 90% female, could queue up and shuffle past the Fab Four, shake their hands, get their autographs, exchange a few words. I wrote it up in *Oh! What A Day It Was For The Beatle Fan*, but the accompanying pictures told the story better than any words. There were faintings galore, and even the burly attendants couldn't stop a few determined fans, momentarily unhinged in the presence of their objects of worship, from leaping over the tables and caressing their particular fab fave. It was a hypnotic spectacle.

You had to hand it to the Beatles who were the souls of good humour and patience throughout what must have been – for them – an ordeal that went on for hours and hours. They smoked a lot of cigarettes. And when every fan was satisfied, they got up and played for nearly three-quarters of an hour, longer than for any gig, serenaded by continuous cacophonous screaming rising and falling, orchestrated perfectly, as if controlled by some sort of telepathy. "Phenomenal" was the only word. And, troopers that they were, they played the Wimbledon Palais that same evening. This was also the first year the Beatles sent out a specially-recorded Christmas record to their fans, a thoughtful tradition that would be kept up to the end of their career. Epstein certainly knew about building fan loyalty – I guess because, really, he was the biggest fan of all.

My final scribblings that year included *The Southern Sound – Presented By The Paramounts* (who included future Procol Harum stalwarts Gary Brooker and Robin Trower), *Pop Stars On The Big Screen* ("Summer Holiday" had been No. 2 at the box office, next to James Bond, and there were plenty of future contenders in the can), and finally an interview with Cliff Bennett, whose flop-filled record deal with Joe Meek had expired. EMI were delighted they could now A&R one of Britain's top in-person rock'n'rollers, but Bennett's eventual record success would never reflect the sheer power of his stage act.

Another fine performer, albeit one who was more famous as a songwriter, was Mort Shuman, briefly in town and flying back to New York for the New Year. Luckily, he left the song "Little Children" with his publishers, which would prove useful to Billy J. Kramer and the Dakotas. If you bought pop records between '59 and '65, and – like me – you studied the names in brackets under the song title, you couldn't help but notice that the name 'Shuman', almost always linked with the name 'Pomus', appeared with enviable regularity beneath some very fine pop songs including "Save The Last Dance For Me", "A Teenager In Love", "Sweets For My Sweet", and, strictly for Elvis, "His Latest Flame", "A Mess Of Blues" and "Surrender", though neither Shuman nor Pomus ever met Elvis. Mort was an interesting interview, an imposing presence. I'd seen him perform years before on UK rock'n'roll TV shows like "Boy Meets Girls" and "Drumbeat" when he pounded out his own versions of a couple of songs he'd written with Doc Pomus for Fabian, "Turn Me Loose" and "I'm A Man", singing different, more adult, words than the recorded Fabian version. Being a fine musician, primarily a keyboardist, he would also frame their song demos with his own highly-distinctive arrangements. He told me that the memorable arrangement on Andy Williams' million-selling Pomus-Shuman classic "Can't Get Used To Losing You" was taken in its entirety from his demo.

We got to talking about other New York songwriting teams, and naturally enough, he was full of praise for Jerry Leiber and Mike Stoller, who'd been mentors to Doc and Morty, recognising a pair of kindred spirits and encouraging them accordingly. But when I asked him what he thought about the current red-hot team of Goffin and King, Mort didn't seem to understand my accent, didn't know who I was talking about. No matter how many times I said "Goffin and King! – Gerry Goffin, Carole King", and throwing in the titles a few of their hits, things that Mort Shuman couldn't possibly not have heard – "Take Good Care Of My Baby", "The Locomotion", "Will You Love Me Tomorrow", he professed bafflement at my English accent and declared he couldn't make out who I was talking about. *The Man Who Writes Hits For The U.S. Stars* appeared in the first issue of the new year, 1964, but, true to the fan-based journalistic ethics of the era, I didn't mention the most interesting part of the interview – Mort's refusal to admit he'd heard of Goffin and King – or was it simply my unfamiliar limey accent? I think not. My intuition at the time was that Mort felt that if he didn't feel like saying anything nice, then he wasn't going to say anything at all. So the easiest way out was to pretend he didn't understand me.

1964

Fearsome promoter Don Arden seemed to have forgiven my *Fallen Idols* on Gene Vincent, possibly because of the enthusiastic ravings I'd printed for several of his recent package tours. He told me for a January 11th news story that after considerable effort he'd booked Chuck Berry to tour the UK in May (Chuck being incarcerated during negotiations), supported by new and highly-touted beat group the Nashville Teens and rockabilly hero Carl Perkins.

The Great Unknowns continued into 1964 featuring Marvin Gaye and Martha & The Vandellas, both from Berry Gordy's Motown stable. Despite Oriole's commendable release schedule, Motown was still hitless in the UK and would stay that way till May when the breakthrough would come with Mary Wells' "My Guy" – marketed by Motown's new outlet, the EMI group, first on Stateside, then on the new Tamla-Motown label.

Times were tough for American pop in the UK since the advent of the beat boom – there were only so many chart places and there were lots of good local beat groups who could be seen regularly live, on TV, and heard on the radio. Yet at this moment when the British beat boom was poised to invade America, one established American artist, with only two minor hits here, was enjoying a breakthrough in the UK which would consolidate a hit career that would last throughout the '60s and give him a fan base for the rest of his life. Gene Pitney was a songwriter-turned-singer; his writing credits included "He's A Rebel" for the Crystals and "Hello Mary Lou" for Ricky Nelson, both global million-sellers. Pitney had decided he preferred performing to songwriting, possessed a uniquely singular voice, a likeably boyish demeanour, had a distinctly "post-Elvis" image, and was favoured by such luminaries as Phil Spector and Burt Bacharach. It was Bacharach's "Twenty Four Hours From Tulsa" that gave Gene his UK breakthrough. I spoke briefly to Gene for *Why 'Tulsa' Made The Charts*, and slightly less briefly to Mick Jagger who told me he was hoping that the "Tulsa" follow-up would be "That Girl Belongs To Yesterday", which he'd written with Keith in twenty-five minutes, information I'd somehow also gleaned from Brian Jones some weeks previously.

Cyril Davies died suddenly that January. We were fortunate enough to get Alexis Korner to write a tribute, and I also wrote an obituary, titled *Cyril's Death Leaves A Big Gap In R&B*.

RM w/e 18th January 1964

THE sudden death of R&B star Cyril Davies from leukaemia last week came as a terrible shock to all his friends and fans. In the short space of a year Cyril had established himself and his band the All Stars as Britain's top rhythm and blues team. Together with Alexis Korner they had engineered the great rhythm and blues boom that now dominates the music scene so fully.

The obituary continued with a resume of Cyril's career, but his real contribution, together with Alexis and the Stones, had been to finish off trad jazz as a major live attraction and usher in the rock era. The Cyril Davies Memorial Concert held at the Flamingo that February boasted the all-star line-up of Georgie Fame & the Blue Flames, the Yardbirds, the Animals and Manfred Mann. In the audience were some of the Rolling Stones. Cyril's own brand of purist British R&B was torrid and excitingly overpowering in the clubs, but the future of R&B lay not with his brand of 'authenticity' but with the innovation and personal statements of the Rolling Stones. Rhythm & Blues would be the main club attraction for the next few years, with the coming year heralding the dramatic evolution of these R&B-inspired beat groups towards the great artistic accomplishments of the mid-late '60s.

None of it could have happened without the Beatles, and the Beatles were everywhere. Our man David Griffiths even filled up an entire page with *It Seems Impossible In Pop Journalism But BEATLES? I've Never Met Them, Confesses Pop Writer.* Peter Jones's DeHems buddy Fraser White, who had a sideline as a handwriting expert, managed four articles in a row using the alias Bill Hogarth, analysing the mop-tops' scribblings. The headlines to these fan articles were: *John – The Live Wire, Paul – The Courteous, George – The Businessman and, most interesting, Ringo – I'm Not Conceited. Ringo denies an interesting aspect of his handwriting.*

An interesting interview that month was Georgie Fame, whose debut LP "Rhythm and Blues At The Flamingo" was just released, with edited versions of two of the tracks – "Do The Dog" and "Shop Around" – on a single. It wouldn't be a hit; in fact, Georgie wouldn't chart for almost a year but when he did, he would hit No. 1 with "Yeh Yeh", first of his three chart-toppers. Georgie was a dynamic live performer, very groovy, jazzier than the R&B-inspired beat groups, and more authentic-sounding too. Articulate and intelligent, he said some interesting things about rhythm and blues in the article.

RM w/e 18th January 1964

…*"Don't let anyone tell you there isn't a difference between rock'n'roll and rhythm and blues," he told me. "Although the beat's still there, there's a world of difference. And it's the BLUES that makes the difference. Makes the difference between a twangy, echo-y sound, and a sound that means something. That has 'soul', if you like. Many of these young groups nowadays say they play R&B – they don't. If they play rock they should say so – not cash in. After all, there's good rock'n'roll too. I began several years ago playing Jerry Lee stuff – I was mad about Jerry Lee. There were various group changes, but the big change came when I decided to include an organ in the band instead of piano – and to dispense with guitar.*

"That was the big step. The difficult bit came when I had to play the guitar bits on organ! However, we managed it, and our sound evolved to what it is now. And it's still progressing.

"People ask me to describe the type of music we play. Well, it's difficult to explain. But take the early rock. They were trying to put soul and excitement over. They did it by using loud noise and brashness. Then came groups like the Beatles who were slightly subtler but still striving for the same result. The Beatles were one step ahead. And we are one step ahead of the Beatles – we put the same thing over with a lot more subtlety and less noise and twang – no twang at all, in fact!

"Although my tastes veer towards jazz, there isn't much likelihood I'll stray off playing rhythm and blues – but again, I feel my sound could become more uncommercial for today's R&B fans."

Georgie's residency at the Flamingo in Wardour Street attracted a big following, especially West Indians, black US servicemen, and plenty of mods. The London clubs were now buzzing with R&B. Cyril Davies's group became Long John Baldry and the Hoochie Coochie Men and continued their residency at the Marquee, together with future hitmakers the Yardbirds, who, under Giorgio Gomelsky's guidance, had taken over the Stones' residency at Richmond and now boasted Eric Clapton in their ranks. The Animals, as yet without a record deal, were down from Newcastle and playing at Jazzshows in Oxford Street together with Jimmy Powell and the Five Dimensions, while the Flamingo not only featured Georgie Fame, but also John Mayall & His Blues Breakers, and Zoot Money's Big Roll Band, neither of whom yet had a record deal.

On page one of the 25th January issue I reported the biggest news story of the month, in fact the biggest pop music story of the '60s:

RM w/e 25th January 1964

BEATLES TOP IN THE U.S.

THE impossible happened. The Beatles crashed the U.S. charts right up to number one – with a jump of 42 places. And it was of course "I Want To Hold Your Hand" that did it.

But it looks as though there could be a Beatle battle at the top. For "She Loves You" has leapt in, first week at number 51, just missing this week's charts. "Hand" is issued on Capitol, while "She Loves You" is on Swan. Also "Please Please Me" and "From Me To You" have been re-released by Vee-Jay, who had the original rights to them.

The Beatles are all set for TV dates in the States after their trip to the continent, in fact it was their appearance on "The Jack Paar Show" singing "She Loves You" that started it all off. "I Want To Hold Your Hand" is Capitol's hottest single ever. In New York everyone is raving over the British foursome, and the disc was selling at ten thousand per day.

Only once before has a Beatles disc made the charts. That was several months ago when "From Me To You" made the top 150, but Del Shannon's cover version moved a lot higher.

Over the next few months the Beatles would set awesome chart records in America still unbroken, and the legendary 'British Invasion' would turn American pop music on its head, completely revitalising it. But on the UK singles chart "Glad All Over" by the Dave Clark Five had displaced "I Want To Hold Your Hand". And a new EP titled "The Rolling Stones" was released in late January and in two weeks would end the Beatles' domination of the UK's EP chart. It would also be the first number one record for the Rolling Stones.

Predictably, John Junor soon replaced Roy Burden of his role as Advertising Manager but retained him as Circulation Manager, and in stepped Brian Harvey, large, genial, round-faced, dynamic. Almost immediately Record Mirror started boasting at least 400% more advertising per issue. Predictably, Brian immediately became Junor's golden boy and was allowed to hire himself an assistant, Barry Hatcher. In addition to Hatcher, Brian Harvey also had Bob Bedford under his command, and reported not to Jimmy Watson but directly to Junor.

One Saturday morning late January Andrew Oldham brought record producer Phil Spector to DeHems for me to interview. I was a big fan of Phil's work, but nothing like as big a fan as Andrew, who was uncharacteristically subservient and generally hero-worshipping towards the diminutive maverick of the US music business. Over the past two years Spector's productions had enjoyed massive global success, but his independent record label Philles, released here through Decca's London-American label, was not merely a hit factory. His productions were of a very high quality and they were unique. No-one else could – quite – get his sound. "Teen symphonies", Phil called them, and he had created his distinctive "wall of sound" using the best LA session musicians, the eccentric arranger Jack Nitzsche, and some marvellous vocalists who he treated like puppets. Phil had followed in the footsteps of his mentors Leiber and Stoller by framing black voices against a modern orchestral backdrop – but raised the game by making the contrast even more extreme, casting younger teen vocalists on a series of pounding densely-layered "Wagnerian" productions. People were already calling Phil a genius, although Phil's musical mentor jazz guitarist Barney Kessel, who often played on Spector's sessions, famously remarked "If you're going to call Phil a 'genius', then what word do you use for Tchaikovsky?"

Phil was in London "looking after the interests of his artists", which meant checking up that his girlfriend Ronnie Bennett of the Ronettes, Phil's latest hot girl group on tour in the UK behind their "Be My Baby" hit, didn't get too friendly with the long-haired UK beat groups. Plus he was checking out the scene – hip Americans knew something important was happening here and Phil had managed to be in London just as the Beatles were poised to lead the British Invasion across the Atlantic.

Spector wasn't keen on hanging out at DeHems and being ogled and wanted to go somewhere quieter, so we sloped off round the corner to the Record Mirror offices, which were deserted. Phil was happy to sit down at an old desk and rap with me about music, his records and the way he produced them, his history, and just about anything else. We were on the same wavelength – at least when it came to music. It was like discussing music with one of your pals. However, I'd already noticed that American artists – and Phil really was the artist on his productions – were far more wised-up to the business end of music than British artists, and a lot more educated about the money, Phil even more so. His other noticeable character traits included a glint of paranoia, although, as with all paranoia, there's usually a sliver of truth somewhere: a gleefulness at what he'd got over on this one or that one, the conspiracy of the American record business against him, the times he'd been shafted, the secret way he did things so no-one could copy him, and all the rest of it. He was an intriguing study; sophisticated, brilliant, a bit mad, yet still youthfully enthusiastic with real charm – and a dedicated pop music fanatic. He was also quite a dandy.

What particularly amused me was his rationale for putting instrumental flips on some of his biggest hits *(The Man Behind America's Big Hits Comes To Britain)*.

RM w/e 8th February 1964

"Why do I put instrumentals on the flip? Several reasons. The main one is that I like to give value-for-money singles. I think that if the flip is inferior to the top side it's bad. Rather than have an inferior flip side I'd sooner have my studio musicians do an instrumental. And do you know what? When I first started doing this, some promoters thought the girls must be superb musicians. When they wanted to book them they said '...and tell them to bring their instruments'."

So now you know, buyers of London American 45s by the Crystals, Bob B. Soxx, the Ronettes. Straight from the horse's mouth, the logic behind those tracks like "Brother Julius", "Dr. Kaplan's Office", and "Tedesco And Pitman", which were seldom off our turntables.

I thought that was the last I'd see of Phil, but no. The following week Decca threw a press reception at their offices in Great Marlborough Street for Ben. E. King, also on their London American label. Being a big fan of Benny, I went along and immediately observed it was one of those receptions where everyone was standing around drinking and talking to each other and stuffing their faces with canapés, while the artist – the guest of honour, in fact the raison d'etre of the entire proceedings – was sitting ignored, alone and lonely in a corner. Seizing this opportunity, I spoke for a good ten minutes with Ben including getting his opinion on his successor in the Drifters, Rudy Lewis. Then suddenly, in the middle of the interview, up rushed Andrew Oldham, a look of intense seriousness on his usually groovy visage, and barked an order at me: "Phil's in the boardroom! He needs to talk to us – now!" Andrew dragged me to into an adjoining room with a big table and lots of polished wood, where the only other occupant was Spector, sitting at the table, face like thunder.

As Phil explained his predicament, I confess I was both baffled and flattered that he considered me, a mere pop reporter, to be an ally and potential advisor in this the latest of what must have been a lifelong series of contretemps with the record business establishment. Andrew and I sat glued to Phil's every word, both slightly fearful at the evident extent of his passion. The problem, it seemed, was his group the Crystals. For the past two years the Crystals had been one of the hottest of the new wave of American girl groups, scoring half a dozen big US hits including the No.1 "He's A Rebel", and three big hits in the UK including the classics "Da Doo Ron Ron" and "Then He Kissed Me", both in the past six months. This was a lot of revenue.

Phil's story was that Decca supremo Sir Edward Lewis, the current subject of his vituperation, had visited the Philles office in Los Angeles in Phil's absence and, impatient at Phil's failure to supply Decca with a follow-up to "Then He Kissed Me", snuck off with a master tape of a Crystals track called "Little Boy". This was entirely understandable because "Little Boy" was the Crystals' new American single on the Philles label. Regrettably for all concerned, "Little Boy" was a mediocre record that barely scraped into the US chart and virtually finished off the Crystals there. Phil, realising his error, was dead set against it being issued in the UK – but Decca had already scheduled it and sent out review copies. Phil explained that he could persuade Sir Edward Lewis to pull "Little Boy" if there was an alternative single. But he had no new Crystals' tracks in the can. What advice could we offer?

Anxious to please Phil, Andrew and I spoke in conspiratorial whispers for a few minutes, then suggested he replace "Little Boy" with the unreleased Crystals US hit "Uptown" from 1962 and a very good record indeed – though the arrangement was far more redolent of Leiber-Stoller-Drifters than Phil's more recent wall-of-sound innovations. Phil thought about it, agreed, relaxed, and set the wheels in motion. A week or so later demo pressings of "Uptown" with "Little Boy" on the B-side were sent out to reviewers. Meanwhile, Phil returned to the States on the same flight that took the Beatles to New York, where the hot teen songwriting team Ellie Greenwich and Jeff Barry, writers of "Da Doo Ron Ron" and "Then He Kissed Me", presented him with their new song, "I Wonder". Phil immediately cut it with the Crystals, withdrew the "Uptown"/"Little Boy" coupling in the UK, substituting the "I Wonder"/"Little Boy" coupling. In the event, although "I Wonder" was a better record than "Little Boy", it was no "Da Doo Ron Ron" and only managed to creep up to No. 36 in the UK charts. He should have stuck to "Uptown". That was the end of the Crystals in the UK too, a shame because they were shortly due to tour. The truth of the matter was that Phil's creative energies seemed best focussed on one act at a time, and by 1964 that act was the Ronettes. "Be My Baby", "Baby I Love You" and the following three Ronettes' singles showed Phil Spector's pop genius at its most creative, and he even went on to wed lead singer Ronnie Bennett. No happy endings there though.

As this Crystals debacle was an exclusive, I wrote it up as a news story, checked it with Phil, or Andrew, I can't remember which (they were beginning to merge a bit), who said it was fine – the story diplomatically let Sir Edward Lewis off the hook – and it was published in the February 8th edition of RM. And Oldham's fruitful association with Pitney and Spector paid off big time when, at the Stones' February '64 recording session, the American twosome sprinkled their magic on to the new Stones' single "Not Fade Away" which became their first

UK Top 3 single and, more importantly, the first single that captured their unique excitement.

While in Britain, Phil expressed an interest in meeting Joe Meek who could loosely be called his British equivalent. Meek refused to see Phil – typically, in case Phil stole some of his 'secrets'. Years later, shortly before blowing his own brains out with a shotgun in 1967 after killing his landlady, Meek expressed regret that he hadn't taken that opportunity to meet Phil. He'd since realised that they were birds of a feather.

There is a post-script to my brief association with Phil. When I interviewed him, one of his gripes was that he never received any royalties from his first hit record, the Teddy Bears' "To Know Him Is To Love Him", a US No. 1 smash hit on Doré Records in '58. Decades later I happened to be talking to Lew Bedell, owner of Doré Records, and I mentioned what Phil had told me.

"He's a lying so-and-so," Lew exploded, "I remember perfectly well paying him those royalties, because he'd send his sister up to get the cheques – and she was the foulest-mouthed broad I'd ever come across. When I met Phil he was still at school, and when I told him I'd record him it was all 'Yes sir, thank you sir'. Then when we were cutting the record it was 'Yes Mr Bedell, of course Mr Bedell'. When it started to climb the charts it was 'Yeah, Lew, great, Lew'. And when it got to No.1, it was: 'Hey, you!'"

But we must not leave my encounter with Phil Spector on a negative note. Before returning to the States, he took out a quarter-page advertisement in Record Mirror with a nice photograph of himself looking like a young Disraeli and with his grumpy "little old man with a top hat" logo perched on his shoulder. It read: "Thank you for making my visit to your country so enjoyable – Phil Spector".

Phil wasn't the only American enjoying success in the UK. Chuck Berry had been released from jail and rushed into the Chess studios by label scion Marshall Chess, who was understandably friendly with Guy Stevens who'd done so much for Chuck in the UK. Marshall revealed to Guy that the first of Chuck's post-incarceration recordings to be released would be "Nadine" – and following Guy's enormous success in the UK with Chuck's back catalogue (four hits in a row), Marshall was issuing "Nadine" in the UK prior to US release. The

British music scene was indeed beginning to be taken seriously by the Americans.

This wasn't altogether surprising, especially considering America was going Beatle-crazy and their pundits predicting "...it won't be long before every group with long hair will be sought by American companies". How right they were. The Fab Four themselves were still in Paris, where Peter Jones reported they were unloved by the French establishment yet worshipped by the teenage French boys – in every other country it was mainly girls. In France the parents wouldn't let the girls even go to the concerts. "We do miss the screams," said George, "but the French audiences are still great. Now it's roll on America". Across the Atlantic, "She Loves You" was heading to topple "I Want To Hold Your Hand" from pole position.

Another massive group emerging from the London R&B club scene was Manfred Mann, about to become one of the most popular and influential groups of the decade. Drawn from various blues, jazz and R&B units throughout '62 and '63, the hit line-up had finally coalesced in January when Tom McGuinness joined on bass. I'd run into them individually at clubs such as the Marquee and Studio 51, and they were poised to become the formidable hit-making unit that would contribute much to the soundtrack of the '60s. They were bright, opinionated, and fine musicians, and Manfred himself gave me a great headline for my first interview with them – well, with him and charismatic lead singer Paul Jones.

RM w/e 1st February 1964

WHY R&B CAN NEVER BE AS BIG AS TRAD

"5-4-3-2-1" YELLS Paul Jones and, in a few seconds, the rest of Manfred Mann, one of Britain's best and most popular R&B groups join in on the throbbing, exciting number that's shooting up the charts.

Just who are Manfred Mann and why the choice of name?

151

Well, they're a competent bunch of musicians who have been playing R&B more or less in the same way for nine months. Before that, their music verged more on the jazz and blues side of things – but a gradual change of style and the R&B boom thrust upon them the responsibilities of a top group in this country.

CONFUSING

The name, well, that derives from the group's organist and pianist Manfred Mann. "I just happened to have a fair old name," he says modestly. I'm definitely not the leader of the group – but things do tend to get a bit confusing sometimes."

Despite the fact that Manfred Mann are now recognised as one of the country's top R&B teams, their views on the scene tend to be a lot more off-beat – and franker – than most.

For example: –

"When I get into the studio , I'm just not the same. My voice dries up and goes completely different. Our discs aren't any good – to my way of thinking anyway. And it's all my fault..."

That's Paul Jones, lead singer, harmonica player extraordinaire.

"They say there's a big rhythm and blues boom. They may be right, but it won't be, can't be, anything like the trad boom. Why? Because trad was a form of music that sounded completely different to any other. It was totally different to rock, modern jazz or blues. If you were a trad fan you were different, and so was your music.

"But R&B is very close indeed to rock'n'roll. The line that separates them is variable and who can tell what is rock'n'roll and what is R&B. Thus, rock groups can easily palm themselves off as R&B groups. Nowadays, anything with a beat is called R&B. This type of music – even though it's our type of music – isn't different enough to create the sensation that the trad boom did."

ORIGINALITY

That was Manfred No. 3, Manfred Mann himself.

But the rest of the group are equally outspoken. Take the example of the surprise vibes and flute on both sides of their hit.

"A lot of people have misinterpreted that. They say we shouldn't have done it. But our vibes player (Mike Hugg, also on drums) and our flautist (Mike Vickers, also guitar and alto) are excellent. So we added a touch of originality. The cool sounds of those two instruments against the earthy sound of the rest of the disc comes off well – at least we think so. But then others disagree."

EARTHY

Other member of the group is Tom McGuinness, ex-scriptwriter from Wimbledon. The group have had two previous discs, "Why Should We Not", an instrumental, and "Cock-A-Hoop", a Bo Diddley-type vocal beater.
"5-4-3-2-1" is the theme tune of "Ready Steady Go!", and already the team have made a couple of appearances on the programme. They're featured on the Joe Brown/ Crystals spring tour, and can be seen at a lot of London clubs including the Marquee, where they have been bringing the house down. And it's no wonder when you listen to some of the most exciting, earthy sounds in the land, performed by one of the most exciting groups – Manfred Mann.

It was a privilege being able to interview most of the big beat groups of this period, but I rarely got to talk to the Shadows, our greatest instrumental group. But that February I did get to speak to their ex-drummer Tony Meehan – who wouldn't talk about the Shadows, and indicated that his recent highly-successful chart partnership with the group's ex-bassist Jet Harris was permanently finished, thanks to Jet's instability. In *The Unusual Perfectionist*, Tony indicated that if his latest disc "Song Of Mexico" wasn't a hit (it reached No. 39), he'd probably pack it in and concentrate on producing. Which he did.

The next beat group interview was a four-parter: *The Searchers One By One*. They were No. 1 again, this time with "Needles And Pins", a more-than-decent version of the sublime 1963 US hit by Jackie DeShannon, and far better than their previous record "Sugar And Spice", a follow-up cash-in confection penned by their producer Tony Hatch following their debut chart-topper "Sweets For My Sweet". I got on well with the Searchers, they were very Liverpool, very funny, but Tony Jackson was the funniest, and the frankest:

RM w/e 15th February 1964

"I was glad when we turned pro. Mike and John weren't keen at all, in fact we almost had to force them at gunpoint to leave their jobs. But I was glad. I hurt my arm and hand in an accident at work and I can't play guitar with it. I can use it normally but I have to play left-hand bass. I never want to go back to manual work. I'd sooner have no money and be a tramp or something. When I get older I'd like to stay in show business in London. Or even write features for magazines.

"I don't want to go back to Liverpool. I can't stand it, it's much better down here."

I churned out yet another Holly piece, *Buddy & The Faithful Fans* – "...a man who rose above any petty fad or craze to produce some of the greatest pop records in the world, and a host of faithful fans who will be his fans until the day they die." Can't argue with that, even now.

A big new UK record craze at the beginning of '64, riding on the back of the R&B boom, was "blue beat", a misnomer for Jamaican ska music (the word "ska" was seldom mentioned then), misnamed after the Blue Beat label, owned by Emil Shallit's indie Melodisc Records and A&R'd by Blue Beat founder Siggy Jackson. Jackson had recognised the power of Jamaican music in the late '50s, and after signing a deal with producer Duke Reid had the prescience to release titles like "Madness" by Prince Buster and – as credited on the Blue

Beat label – "Carolina" by the Folks Brothers ("Oh Carolina" by the
Folkes Brothers). Not unimportantly, Blue Beat also had a desirably
well-designed deep-blue-and-silver 45 label. This new fad, the mods'
darling for some months, was not without controversy, and long after
the Blue Beat label was forgotten by all but hard-core aficianados, a
new record company, a tiny operation which also shot to prominence
on the crest of the blue beat wave, would become an international
music force: Island Records.

RM w/e 15th February 1964

*A Look At The Latest Craze To Take The Record Industry
By Storm*
IT'S THE BLUE BEAT CRAZE

*THE record industry thrives on new crazes and sounds.
And at the moment three record companies are thriving on
the Blue Beat craze which is being taken up by the industry
in general as a potential money-spinner for all concerned.*

*Just for the record, and for those who probably haven't
heard it yet, just what is blue beat? Well, it's a strictly
Jamaican sound with a pulsating on-beat played with
stop chords throbbing mercilessly through the disc. Most
of the discs are down-to-earth items that don't usually
deal with love, and the songs are strictly secondary to
the beat. The craze has been 'in' with the mods since
last summer because of the marvellous dance beat and of
course has been bought by the West Indians in Britain for
many years now. But it was only when the larger record
companies heard of fantastic sales for such blue beat discs
as "Madness", "Carolina", and "Blazing Fire" that they
realised it could mean something.*

ORIGINS

*Anyway, let's take a look at the small blue beat companies
– after all, one of the attractions the music had for the*

mods was that it was exclusive to the smaller and virtually unknown labels.

First there's the Blue Beat label itself. Owned by Melodisc Records run by Siggy Jackson, this label was formed two years back. It boasts many of the biggest blue beat artists including Prince Buster, Derrick Morgan, and the Folks Brothers.

"The blue beat rhythm itself was started by Prince Buster", says Siggy. "He had been singing it in Kingston for a while then invented this new rhythm. His success since then has been phenomenal. He has packed halls in Brixton and his 'Madness' has sold over 120,000 copies. That's our best seller that's top of our own little chart. Other good discs for us are 'Carolina' by the Folks Brothers and our new one 'Tom Hark Goes Blue Beat'. Although Buster invented the blue beat rhythm, I invented the name for our label."

The other two blue beat labels don't agree about the origin of blue beat. Both Island and R & B say that the rhythm has always been predominate in Jamaican Music.

Island is run by Chris Blackwell, an enterprising young white Jamaican who was fascinated by blue beat and started his own company here well over a year ago. His best seller is "Blazing Fire", while another good one is "Housewives Choice". Most of his numbers are recorded in Jamaica, unlike Melodisc who record here. But recently Island have been recording some of their best artists here including one Millie, who had a disc issued recently by Fontana.

"So far all of our discs have done well and we haven't had a flop", Chris told me. "My aim is to see a blue beat disc in the charts – even if it was only at No. 50."

Chris also owns two more labels. One is Sue, the great US R&B label which Chris bought when he was last in the States. The other is Black Swan, more of a Calypso type label.

The other record company is R & B, the smallest of the three. Like Island, they are selling very well to the Jamaicans, while Melodisc are selling more to the Mods. Run by Ben

Isen, who also runs the R & B Record Shop in Stamford Hill, sales have been picking up considerably. One of their top discs is "Orange Street" by Georgie Fame & The Blue Flames.

They are the smaller companies, the ones who pioneered blue beat. How about the larger ones? First of all, Decca has put out a disc called "The Blue Beat" by the Beazers. All of the small companies unanimously say "This isn't blue beat. And if people think it is it will do us harm". The record itself is sung by Chris Farlowe and backed by Cyril Stapleton. And no-one anywhere seems to think it is blue beat. Decca are also reported to be leasing some tracks from Melodisc and next week will be recording some genuine blue beat groups to be put out on Decca.

PRIORITY

EMI are issuing two discs in February by Ezz Reco and the Launchers with Boysie Grant and Beverly as vocalists. This is a genuine blue beat group and if the discs are fairly successful, EMI will be issuing more. But it is certainly an unprecedented step for a big record company to issue two discs by the same artist within two weeks!

And so far no word from any other companies. So it looks as if the Blue Beat craze is destined to catch on in a big way with the two biggest record companies giving it top priority. But once it starts breaking big nationally, it looks as if the mods are going to have to find something more exclusive. Keep your eyes open, record companies...

Back on the world stage, the Beatles landed in New York at the newly-renamed JFK, famously conquered the hard-bitten America media at the airport press conference with their wit and vivacity, and began, in person as well as on record, to take America by storm. The love affair between planet Earth and the Beatles began to bloom in earnest. Record Mirror featured several correspondents reporting the phenomenon from the States, including impresario Larry Parnes, whose praise for the Fabs, who he'd once turned down, managed to be as grudging as possible, while still predicting US success for a host of other UK acts including his own Billy Fury. Unfortunately for Larry – and Billy – America already had Elvis Presley.

A couple of weeks after I'd helped Andrew Oldham placate Phil Spector at the Ben E. King press reception, the interview with Ben E. King appeared under the imaginative heading *Ben – The Drifters And I*. Ben was a distinctive and enormously successful singer, forever associated with such classics as "Spanish Harlem", written by Jerry Leiber and Phil Spector, "Save The Last Dance For Me" and "Stand By Me". A great R&B vocalist, he was a beneficiary of producers Leiber and Stoller's unique talents, but despite his innate soulfulness would not achieve the same degree of success with the emerging phenomenon of soul music. Neither, for that matter, would Leiber and Stoller.

RM w/e 15th February 1964

"...my favourite type of music? Well, as you could guess from my discs, I love the Latin sound. My favourite of my own discs is 'Spanish Harlem'. I'll tell you a story about that one. When I cut the first session without the Drifters, it was because New York was hit by one of the worst snowstorms for years. I was the only one of the Drifters who turned up, so the engineers and I thought we wouldn't waste the recording time, and that we'd cut a disc. The result was 'First Taste Of Love' which we were pretty pleased with. But they wanted a Phil Spector composition 'Spanish Harlem' on the flip. We recorded it but I wasn't happy. 'You're mad' I said, 'You can't release that thing.' I just didn't think it would sell. Instead it was the side that did the best business anywhere!

"Well, that's my favourite form of music. You could tell that by my LP 'Spanish Harlem'. A lot of people, myself included, find it surprising that a Negro artist like myself goes for this sort of music. But I do. I dig R&B too, of course

– Chuck Berry is a gas. My kids rush out and buy it, R&B, all the time, and I can't stop them. The flip of my disc here is from a live LP "At The Apollo". I did it with other Atco artists. That's more R&B than most of mine.

FAVOURITES

"My favourite artists come from the Berry Gordy labels. I love Martha & The Vandellas, and Smokey & The Miracles. Record-wise I haven't any further plans except to record some standards later on here in Britain. I try to vary the styles as much as I can. I know that I can sit and listen to an artist for a day if his songs are varied and his styles are different.

"I try to be like myself. There have been a lot of remarks about me and the Drifters. Well, the fact is that we are all still personal friends. And although a lot of people say that the present lead singer sounds like me, I can assure them it's not deliberate. For when I heard their first disc without me I thought he was trying to sound a bit like me. So I went along to the studio to find out. And he sang as naturally as can be! Their style hasn't varied because they have a successful formula.

"I started with the Drifters in 1958. It was a completely new group then because the old group had broken up when Clyde McPhatter went solo. We were previously the Five Crowns but when we signed to Atlantic Records they changed our name to the Drifters. Our first disc was of course 'There Goes My Baby' which I wrote. I do a bit of writing sometimes – well, not exactly writing. I sit down with this old guitar which I have that's missing all but three strings – no-one else could possibly play it but I pick out tunes and when I have something I'll play it for someone who can write it..."

Ben was being modest about his writing. He not only wrote "There Goes My Baby", but also penned, together with Drifters' road manager

Lover Patterson, three other songs cut at the same '58 session: "Oh My Love" – the B-side of the million-selling "There Goes My Baby" and a substantial copyright in its own right, and two lesser songs, "Baltimore" and "Hey Senorita". After the session, Ben, who was experiencing some financial difficulties, sold his part of the songs to manager George Treadwell and accountant Louis Lebish of Drifters Inc., who tightly controlled the group's finances.

Later, Ben confessed "I know now how naive I was, but I needed the money then, I was still only twenty, and a hundred bucks was a lot of money to me at that time. No one knew how big those songs would be – except perhaps Lover," (who sensibly held on to his interest in all four songs). Ben also wrote the follow-up, "Dance With Me" – but the writing credits on that song, a Top 20 smash in the USA and the UK, are now registered with MCPS as: *L. Lebish, G. Treadwell, I. Nahan.*

Ben fared better in 1961 when his biggest solo smash "Stand By Me" was first released. He wrote that too, but the writing credit (and royalties) would be shared with one Elmo Glick, an alias for producers Jerry Leiber and Mike Stoller. Now – at the time of writing – the credit reads: *King, Leiber, Stoller,* so perhaps Ben's share has shrunk even further – from half to a third. However, "Stand By Me" was not a completely original creation. Ben admitted he was "inspired" by a gospel standard when he wrote it: de-sanctifying gospel music was by 1961 a tried-and-tested tradition, inspired by the success of Ray Charles.

"Little Boy" or no "Little Boy", the Crystals were still hot, and they also were here. I caught up with them backstage at Finsbury Park Astoria, and interviewed them in their dressing room. They were all wrapped in white towels, and wigless with close-cropped hair, really cute. They told me how much they'd hated their third US single, the lame Goffin-King song "He Hit Me (And It Felt Like A Kiss)", but Phil kept insisting on its potential. The girls were proved right when the Parent-Teachers Association cried "masochism!" and got it banned from radio play, so Phil was forced to pull it. He then cut Gene Pitney's "He's A Rebel" with Darlene Love and issued it as a Crystals single, but the girls didn't tell me that, a fact unknown at the time. In fact, they told me it was the favourite of all their singles. La La Brooks had gone on to sing lead on "Da Doo Ron Ron" and

"Then He Kissed Me", immortalising her voice. The girls had made half a dozen truly great pop records, but could have been even bigger. They'd cut the original versions of "It's My Party" and "Chapel Of Love", but Phil didn't release them. But then without Phil, how big would the Crystals have been?

John Junor sacked Jimmy Watson early in 1964. Jimmy never came back to the office. Wherever the axe fell, it fell on him somewhere else. Junor had one further meeting with the Record Mirror staff about the editorship decision the following week. Brian Harvey wanted the editor's chair, but that didn't happen. He was too valuable to Junor as advertising manager, so Junor made Peter Jones editor. Peter was also allowed to maintain his free-lance connections and activities. When he next spoke to me, Junor said "I can't make you editor Norman, because you're too young." That was it.

I was too young, but that didn't stop me being disappointed about something I never expected anyway and had never thought about. The fact that Junor had even considered it was interesting. I knew, and Junor knew, and everyone there knew, that I could have edited the paper as well as anybody, maybe better. But he was right – I hadn't the maturity or expertise for the non-journalistic facets of the job. But from that day onward I knew I would never be editor of Record Mirror, and my attitude inevitably changed.

For the past three years, '61 to '64, I felt I was on a mission. Suddenly, for various reasons, I stopped feeling that way. Those reasons included the realisation that my career could now go no further at Record Mirror. Just to rub it in, Rave magazine, which had offered me a job as star reporter, was now publishing its second very successful issue – and advertising it heavily in RM; also, the emergence of rhythm & blues into the musical mainstream and its role as the engine behind the global success of the British beat boom was the fulfilment and culmination of my crusade using the columns of New Record Mirror. The musical Jerusalem had been won – end of that story. Also, I wasn't the only journalist of my generation now working on the pop press. For a couple of years I'd been the only kid in the sweetshop, but lately the job of being a pop hack had got groovy. NME and Disc now both boasted staffers of my age – I was no longer unique. And I wasn't even the only young writer on Record Mirror anymore. Peter Jones recruited Barry May, he of the Richmond & Twickenham Times, as news editor and feature writer, freeing David Griffiths to concentrate on high-profile articles. I had no idea Peter was pally with Barry. I missed Jimmy, I felt I wanted to go somewhere else, do something different...but my present routine was so attractive: all those new records to review, pages to lay out, headlines to think up, articles to write, pop stars to interview, trains to Banbury and free gourmet meals in four star hotels, hand-made suits and shirts, and best of all, being in the middle of Swinging London where, without exaggeration, it really was all happening.

Resignedly, predictably, I sank back into the routine, swept away by the fascinating demands of producing a pop paper week after week after week. Who could give that lifestyle up? Not me. Not at 20 I couldn't. There were new compensations, too. The small raise that came with Jimmy's exit was followed by considerably more precious cash-in-hand. Peter Jones, with characteristic generosity, decided he and I would now review the LPs, so we kept the ones we personally wanted, gave away what anyone else in the office had the gumption to ask for, and sold the rest.

Our main man for offloading LPs was the guv'nor at Lee's Record Stall in Earlham Street, just off nearby Cambridge Circus. Not only was "Lee", alias Bob Daniels, later – in the '70s – rock'n'roll revival singer 'Rocky Rhodes', a straight-up payer and all-round good guy, but he also regularly and mysteriously acquired from sources obscure plenty of unissued LPs imported from the USA, including highly desirable rhythm & blues LPs, the kind with the thick board sleeves, oh bliss. And he was quite happy to do a two-for-one swap – that's two of our UK LPs for one US import.

So I partied more, clubbed more, bought more clothes, drank more, spent more. I also managed to write a lot of uninspired articles as the year progressed: *Invasion By The Unexpected Army* (minor hit from Salvation Army's own beat group the Joystrings revives the Regal Zonophone label – "I can't stand the slow, slushy religious songs" said Captain Joy Webb), *The Label-Change Gamble* (what happens when big-name hitmakers change record labels. Answer: usually more money,

less hits), *How Big Dee Likes Touring Britain* (the "Swinging On A Star"
man, loquacious, ambitious, and, as seen at Tottenham's Noreik Club,
an entertaining live act), *It's The Animals* (short profile on soon-to-be-
major group), *Should A Pop Star Marry?* (NJ and PJ co-write a piece
of fluff more suited to Boyfriend magazine), *Will 'HITSVILLE
U.S.A.' Hit Britain Now?* (history of Berry Gordy's Tamla Motown,
following UK chart debut with Mary Wells' "My Guy"), and *Meet The
Mojos*, (half-ways decent interview spread over two issues with one of
the last big Liverpool groups, currently charting with their rave-up
single "Everything's Alright"). Meanwhile, everyone else on Record
Mirror was writing great stuff, and Guy Stevens even got himself a
four-page special following a recent trip to the USA. He'd been to
the Chess HQ in Chicago as a guest of the Chess family, and at their
recording studio took a photo of Chuck Berry recording "Promised
Land", which we printed. What a scoop! Guy was big friends with
Chuck, not surprising after his sterling efforts on Chuck's behalf.
Chuck, shortly to visit the UK, gave Guy a smashing interview, and
if Guy were here today he'd be delighted for me to quote from it. So
here's an excerpt:

RM w/e 4th April 1964

Chuck Berry Tells Guy Stevens About
'HOW I WRITE MY SONGS'

*...I questioned Chuck about his songwriting methods.
"I concentrate on the lyrics usually," he replied after
considerable thought, "and then I work out the song on
my guitar when I have the lyrics on paper. Then I tape it
to get an idea of the overall sound, after which I record it.
Most of my songs come from either personal experience or
other peoples' experience or from ideas I get from watching
people. I would say that I aim specifically to entertain and
make people happy with my music, which is why I try to
put as much humour into my lyrics as possible."
I asked Chuck if he would describe himself as a rhythm
and blues artiste, telling him of the major controversy*

over here at the moment about what is authentic rhythm and blues. "No," he said firmly, "I would like to think of myself as an artiste who can sell to any type of market. In America I am considered a rock'n'roll artiste, as are most of the artistes that you would call rhythm and blues. Our idea of R and B over here is groups like the Moonglows, the Flamingos, the Dells etc., whilst singers such as Muddy Waters or Howlin' Wolf are considered to be folk blues artistes."

We were still plugging rhythm & blues like crazy. Peter and I reviewed the first Stones' LP which quickly displaced "With The Beatles" at the top of the LP charts, at the same time their EP "The Rolling Stones" pushed the Fabs' "All My Loving" from pole position in the EP chart. I kicked off my new series of *The Great Unknowns* with Dionne Warwick, as yet hitless in the UK (though "Walk On By" would chart that same week), following through with dynamic duo Ike & Tina Turner, and then the fabulous Impressions. On April 25th 1964 we ran our R&B Poll Results. Here's the top three in each category: Best Female Singer – Mary Wells, Etta James, LaVerne Baker. Best Male Singer – Chuck Berry, Marvin Gaye, Jimmy Reed. Best Male Group – Miracles, Coasters, Rolling Stones. Best Female Group – Shirelles, Marvelettes, Martha & Vandellas. Best all-time disc: "Smokestack Lightnin'" – Howlin Wolf, "Green Onions" – Booker T & The MGs, "What'd I Say" – Ray Charles. Best British Artist – Georgie Fame, Long John Baldry, Cyril Davies. Best Instrumental Group Or Artist – Booker T. & MGs, Chuck Berry, Bo Diddley. Pye Records immediately released "Smokestack Lightnin'" on a single and it hit the charts.

As Chuck Berry was coming to the UK, we ran a 4-page special, including a full-page ad for his tour, scheduled to open on May 9th at Finsbury Park Astoria. The bill was interesting. The two main support acts were The Swinging Blue Jeans, just off a huge hit with their unstoppable version of "Hippy Hippy Shake" which made the Chan Romero original sound like a demo, but presently doing so-so chart business with their rather less successful revival of Little Richard's "Good Golly Miss Molly" which, needless to say, couldn't hold the proverbial candle to Mr Penniman's original. They shared second billing with the Animals, recent arrivals in the Top 40 with their first single "Baby Let Me Follow You Down", and who'd come down from Newcastle a couple of months back with a hot reputation, blown away the crowd at the Scene club, and were about to cut one of the finest and most influential singles of the Sixties – "House Of The Rising Sun". Further down the bill were Kingsize Taylor & The Dominoes, a highly-regarded Liverpool rock'n'roll act, the Other Two, whoever they were, and – Carl Perkins. This was astonishing. Perkins may have been vaguely remembered by pop fans as the originator of "Blue Suede Shoes" (the Presley cover was – marginally – bigger here), but the spectrum of rock'n'roll, blues, R&B and rockabilly devotees knew that Carl was someone very special indeed. He was the all-time King Of Rockabilly, a title held since Elvis long ago abdicated the crown. Carl could boast a series of awesomely perfect sides cut for the legendary Sun label including "Matchbox", "Boppin' The Blues", "Honey Don't", "Dixie Fried" and many more. The Beatles would go on to cover four of his compositions, making him far wealthier than "Blue Suede Shoes" ever did. Carl may have been at the bottom of the bill, but Chuck would feel the heat from the competition.

The Beatles themselves had now finished filming "A Hard Day's Night", and under the guise of Perkin Giles I cobbled together a Page 3 article with quotes from Dick Lester and Alun Owen. Everyone seemed very happy indeed with the film, but it wasn't fun for everyone. What I didn't know at the time – and didn't find out till over twenty years later – was that our chief photographer and Beatles confidante Dezo Hoffmann had fallen out with John Lennon. Here's how Dezo tells the story.

From JOHN LENNON
by Dezo Hoffmann and Norman Jopling (Columbus Books 1985)

"I stopped photographing the Beatles so frequently during 1964, and the reason was silly, really silly. I could kick myself because it sounds so childish. One morning

I went to Twickenham film studios where the boys were already shooting for the third or fourth week on 'A Hard Day's Night'. I'd been quite busy on a tour with Cliff Richard and was looking forward to seeing the Beatles again. When I got to the studio I saw John and he was talking to a pretty girl. He was always talking to pretty girls! He saw me and, and suddenly became very angry and began ranting at me like I was his running boy. He completely lost control of himself in front of all those extras, electricians and cameramen: at that time I was the official of ACTT, the cinematographic union. He was angry because a picture of him had been published where his hair, blown by the wind, revealed his forehead. I had taken it in Miami while he was water ski-ing. Now, the background story to this picture is that every time I went somewhere, I always got assignments from papers which paid me in advance, and in this case I was paid by Tit-Bits. The Beatles, or NEMS, never paid me for pictures, even though they used them all over the world. As soon as I got back from America I sent Tit-Bits the pictures immediately I printed them, everything from everywhere, so they had about twelve pages of pictures of the Beatles in America – a lovely feature – and John picked on that one picture. I still think it's a lovely picture, full of life, as if he's saying 'Look, I can ski already!' The instructor was not even holding him. John couldn't understand why I released this picture because before then I never released anything I believed was not really their image. That was the point and he was hurt. Yet that picture was one of the best from the whole clip.

"I felt so humiliated in front of all those people that I couldn't even answer him. I just turned my back on him and walked out. And I obviously finished with the Beatles also. In my imagination I had thought of myself as a father figure to them, I couldn't believe that John could talk to me as though I were a 6-year old kid."

166

Poor Dezo. But business was business and their master's misfortune didn't stop his apprentices henceforth snapping the Beatles at every available opportunity.

Guy Stevens was always coy about how much he was paid by Pye Records to mastermind their R&B Series, probably because it was a pittance. It certainly wasn't enough to live on. He wasn't paid a lot for his articles for Record Mirror, if anything, and Ronan and Lionel at the Scene were still only using Guy's DJ skills on Mondays. The change in his fortunes came when Island Records' supremo Chris Blackwell obtained the UK rights to the hot US R&B label Sue by offering its volatile owner Juggy Murray its own UK imprint: Sue was formerly one of the many labels handled by Decca via their London-American umbrella. Chris's operation was still tiny – together with partner David Betteridge they were selling their records to specialist shops out the back of their cars – but Chris knew all about Guy and respected his drive, his knowledge, his enthusiasm and his ability to make things happen. So Guy became label manager for Sue Records. He was now in the music business, full-time. It was a dream job for him.

Sue's roster included two dynamic male/female duos – Ike & Tina Turner, and current hitmaking brother-and-sister act Inez & Charlie Foxx, Foxx being an appropriate name for the gorgeous Inez. Their US Top Ten smash "Mockingbird" launched the new UK Sue label... but despite good sales didn't chart here, and it wasn't till "Hurt By Love" later in the year – and with Inez and Charlie touring the UK – that they'd get that UK hit. Other Sue notables included jazz-funk organist Jimmy McGriff who'd scored in the US with a spectacular instrumental version of Ray Charles's "I Got A Woman", and yet another duo, The Soul Sisters, who'd recently charted in the US with "I Can't Stand It", a frenzied soulful shout-up not a cigarette paper away from pure gospel. Sue was on a roll.

Guy got to work, but soon got bored just releasing titles from the Sue catalogue and began to license unissued and now-deleted (in the UK) R&B classics, old and new, and releasing them under the Sue imprint. In the process, he created one of Britain's most legendary record labels catering for rock'n'roll, rhythm & blues, and blues fans.

When Juggy Murray found out what Stevens was up to, he took his label back to London-American, but by then it didn't matter. Juggy's roll was over, the US Sue label cut no more hits, and UK Sue, under Guy's guidance, thrived.

Island Records, Sue's parent label, still specialised in Jamaican music, and another label getting action in this area was R&B Records, whose proprietor, Benny Isen, got cross with me for not saying enough about his label in my original Blue Beat article. Benny ran a famous local record shop in Stamford Hill together with his wife Rita (Rita and Benny – R&B!), and a few months back they'd branched out with the R&B Records label, not only releasing Blue Beat (Ska), but also everything from rhythm & blues to country. Their customers were mainly black, but the hip white kids had also latched on to Benny's cottage operation. Later in the year Benny's King label would score a hit by Irish country star Larry Cunningham – "Tribute To Jim Reeves" – a lachrymose Irish-C&W homage to "Gentleman Jim", the country superstar destined to die in a plane crash in July. Reeves, strangely (well, it seemed strange at the time), was always a big favourite with black audiences. I made good my previous omission by profiling Benny's R&B label in more detail on the same page as my *Meet The Manfreds (Part One – Mike Hugg and Tom McGuiness)*. I'd intended to profile all five Manfreds, but for reasons long forgotten, David Griffiths stepped in to do Mike Vickers and Manfred Mann, then I returned to do Paul Jones. That same week I got a call from the States from the Crystals, who'd been summoned back by Phil Spector for a new session – but, to my knowledge, nothing from it was ever released. La La and Dee Dee had flown back first, followed by Fran, Barbara, and their road manager Arthur. They said they loved England and wished Phil hadn't hurried them back. 'Perkin Giles' reported the conversation, pondered on *Mystery Of The Crystals' Flop*, but it was no mystery at all really. Phil was giving his best material to the Ronettes, and that was it for the Crystals.

Phil Spector wasn't the only American checking out Swinging London. In April, TV rock'n'roll guru Jack Good, now working in the USA, brought over Texan-born California-domiciled P.J. Proby and entourage including the eccentric Kim Fowley to guest in his Rediffusion TV production *Around The Beatles* spectacular. Pony-tailed Proby, alias James Marcus Smith, looked great, sounded great,

caused a sensation. In *Is This Man The New Elvis?* I interviewed him –
he was informative, enthusiastic, interesting. In America, Proby had
been cutting demos for Elvis and had written some good songs: the
Searchers made an EP hit headlined with his "Ain't Gonna Kiss Ya",
while Johnny Burnette had charted here and in the USA with Jim's
surreal "Clown Shoes".

That same week, Chuck Berry arrived in the UK and on Saturday
morning was hauled up to the RM office by Peter Meaden, his official
UK publicist, a gig doubtless due to Meaden's friendship with Guy
Stevens. The Chuckster, as Meaden called him, was with his lawyer, and
seemed most un-R&R-like, wearing a black shortie mac and a bemused
disposition. I didn't interview him (that was Guy's prerogative),
just exchanged a few words of polite, respectful, greetings. In fact,
Meaden, as usual firing on all cylinders, had only brought Chuck up
the office to escape from the hoards of fans, all blokes, mainly Teds,
whose rock'n'roll radar had located him publicising the Sound City
instrument shop a few doors down the street and were pestering him
with bothersome questions of an arcane R&R nature.

Chuck's concert that evening was a classic. The Teds were in force,
team-handed. The Swinging Blue Jeans were booed offstage. But
the Animals, despite having only one single release, met a different
reception. Their power was undeniable. It was the first time I'd heard
"House Of The Rising Sun", as yet unrecorded, an obvious, instant,
masterpiece. When Dylan heard it a few months later it would inspire
him to change the course of rock music. Carl Perkins wisely stuck to
his rockabilly repertoire: "King o' Rock" yelled the Teds; "Wheel 'im
on" yelled some wag, but he sounded somewhat more country-tinged
than on the records. That was unsurprising considering that since
rockabilly died in the USA he'd had to revert to his country roots to
make a living. But it would take him no time at all to rediscover his
rockabilly genius, helped, no doubt, by meditations on his forthcoming
bank balance following the Beatles' enthusiastic covers of his songs.
Kingsize Taylor & The Dominoes, an unknown quantity in London,
were professional and impressive, covering songs by everyone from
the Four Seasons to Little Richard.

When Chuck walked on he had plenty to live up to and live up to
it he did. Chuck was currently red-hot in the UK and the USA, he

169

was a born-again star and knew it. The Dominoes backed him, Chuck played plenty of his hits, offended the Teds terribly by changing the line "Hail hail rock and roll" in "School Day" to "Hail hail rhythm and blues", and demonstrated a mastery of rock'n'roll guitar that left everyone yelling for more.

Behind the scenes occurred a great rock'n'roll moment, never forgotten by those who witnessed it. Guy Stevens, Peter Meaden, me and Jill, ran backstage directly the last applause began. It was packed back there. Chuck, sweating, triumphant, came off after the ovations. Opening his dressing room door he saw Carl Perkins in there getting changed.

In a quiet but firm voice he said, for all to hear: "Carl, you're in my dressing room, Carl." Poor Carl slunk out in front of everyone. The bill-topping Berry walked in, closing the door behind him.

Another fine guitarist re-emerged that same month. Eric Clapton, formerly of the Roosters, then Casey Jones – and already a guitar hero – had now joined the Yardbirds, whose debut single "I Wish You Would", a decent enough version of a Billy Boy Arnold original, demonstrated the edgy garage-blues sound that the Yardbirds would never entirely lose. They'd taken over the Craw-Daddy residency when the Stones outgrew it, were managed by Giorgio Gomelsky (who made sure he had papers on them), and I profiled them in *The Blueswailers With The Mod Appeal*, mocking the Daily Telegraph who'd called them the Yardsticks. Actually I'd made – and was to make – far bigger blunders with group names but I wasn't owning up.

A blunder I did make that month, and a big one, was the worst thing I ever wrote in my life, not for Record Mirror, but a little magazine called Jazzbeat, which in May 1964 featured an R&B Supplement. My brief was to write a staunch defence of "British R&B", and the subsequent article included the following:

Jazzbeat May 1964

BRITISH R&B? OF COURSE IT EXISTS
says top R&B man Norman Jopling

"...And as for those fanatics who say that R&B can only be played by long-suffering over-worked under-fed negro musicians, what do they think the more authentic British R&B groups were doing for the years before they became famous?

They played ridiculously long hours in sweaty clubs for fees that school kids would sneer at as pocket money. They travelled themselves sick in decrepit vans not having enough time to eat properly, and altogether had more cause to wail the blues than many of the spoon-fed negro R&B musicians in the States today."

No-one at the time commented on it. But decades later an American academic chastised me in a scholarly book about the British blues boom, saying *"...that it seems utterly ludicrous that anyone would suggest that riding in a van and missing an occasional meal was comparable to a lifetime of institutionalized discrimination or that African American musicians had become a pampered elite".* No arguing with that, although her earlier assertion that I was questioning whether African Americans even retained the right to sing the blues was (I think) inaccurate: what I was positing was that white British musicians had as much artistic right to sing the blues as black Americans. But any defence I moot pales against the naivety, ignorance, and incipient racism of the piece. What made it even worse (though my critic didn't know it) was that I didn't even believe myself what I'd written – which makes it worse. I'd played devil's advocate; much as I supported and wrote about British R&B, and much as I liked and admired its participants, there was never any contest as far as the music was concerned. The criticism served me doubly right for not even being true to my own love of American R&B.

Whoever was promoting nearby instrument shop Sound City was doing a good job, because the week after Chuck's visit, along came Little Richard. Dezo's apprentice Vincent Hayhurst took a great picture of Richard playing the drums, and I re-aquainted myself with the first star I'd ever interviewed, for our current *Off The Cuff* series which was little more than an excuse for not bothering to write a decent article. But sometimes you could read between the lines:

RM w/e 30th May 1964

LITTLE RICHARD – OFF THE CUFF

CURRENTLY enjoying a renewed spell of popularity in this country, the fabulous Little Richard is back with his new disc. Little Richard was one of the first real rock'n'rollers, and has inspired many British artists including the Beatles who are good friends of his. At one time in 1957 Richard, real name Richard Penniman, had no less than five sides in the British Top 20.

He writes his own material and is now 32. He records for Specialty Records – and is still contracted to them. He recorded many gospel numbers in the six years he was in retirement, but he has finally decided to make an out and out attempt at the beat field again with his disc "Bamalama Bamaloo". Here, he answers questions on a variety of subjects put to him by Norman Jopling.

BRITISH TELEVISION – Like it, it's the greatest. And I dig the novel techniques.

PROFESSIONAL BOXING – I don't know much about it. But Cassius Clay is a good friend of mine. But I don't know whether he is a better boxer or a talker.

SOUNDS INCORPORATED – They're the best backing group in England – I'd go as far to say they're the best backing group in the world. But I don't think they'll ever be REALLY big as a hit solo group though.

POETRY – I don't know nothin' about it – but I sure like it.

COLOUR PREJUDICE – I hate it. Birmingham, Alabama is my most un-favourite town. Everybody's bad to me there.

ELVIS PRESLEY – He's a good friend of mine. He's also the greatest solo entertainer in the whole wide world.

ICE CREAM – I like it when it's called "Tutti Frutti"

BRITISH AUDIENCES – Man, they're the greatest. They're so full of life that they make an artiste get carried away, and go really wild.

AUSTRALIA – It's very much like Britain – the people, I mean. I hope to go back in a few months time.

THE BEATLES – The greatest in the whole world. You can't say anything against the Beatles because their success speaks for itself. They love me and I love them. And they're the greatest things ever for the record business – they've done more for the business than anybody else including myself! They've brought back the old wild rock, and they've made it possible for ugly people to be appreciated and screamed at instead of just the pretty ones.

GOSSIPS – They need to hush themselves and tend to their own business. They need six months to get the facts straight and the other six months to rest.

CHINESE FOOD – Man, I love Chinese food. But I don't always know what I'm eating!

STRIP TEASE – Well, if it's female it's all right I suppose. But when I strip on stage it's because I get carried away. I see a pretty girl or a nice feller in the audience, and they're lovin' me, so I want to throw my clothes to them.

BRITISH TEA – Man, it's great. All the American teabags should be thrown in with the trash and they should drink English tea. But American coffee is best. British tea and American coffee!

DON ARDEN – He's the greatest agent there is for bringing over American stars.

MARRIED LIFE – Just wonderful. I only wish my wife was with me on this tour.

GOSPEL SINGING – I love it. Mahalia Jackson is the greatest, and I've done a lot of it myself. There's so much soul and feeling put into it you know.

That spring I got a call out of the blue from John Allison of "Are You Sure" fame. We'd kept loosely in touch since my The Sad Scene article nearly three years earlier had upset the Allisons by suggesting there was a possibility they might turn out to be one-hit wonders. John was calling on behalf of a friend who managed a London-based

R&B group called Blues By Five. I met up with the manager, Geoffrey, who asked me if I'd write a piece on his group. I said we didn't write pieces on groups without a record deal, to which Geoffrey replied, "You did it with the Rolling Stones and they got a record deal out of the article, so if you write about Blues By Five, then maybe they'll get a deal too". Geoffrey invited me to see the group perform at the Purley Orchid ballroom. This was way off my beaten track but I went anyway, as I had the feeling this would repay my non-existent debt to the Allisons for jinxing their career. And who knows, maybe Blues By Five might be the next Rolling Stones. Besides, Geoffrey didn't seem like the usual pop group manager. I liked his style – he was an extreme dandy. As far as I could ascertain he was "something in the city", and was the most fastidiously and beautifully-dressed City gent you could imagine, absolutely immaculate, over-immaculate even, verging on the style of Hardy Amies' legendary director Bunny Roger.

The Orchid was enormous, and Blues By Five were dwarfed in it. It was no venue for an R&B group – but they weren't bad at all. They had a sax player, and a charismatic Anglo-Indian singer. I figured they were sufficiently different to write about, so I compromised and told Geoffrey I'd write the article for Peter Jones' New Faces page, and it would be the lead profile. Geoffrey seemed happy with this, then revealed that the lead singer, who he explained he managed under a separate agreement, was shortly leaving the group and that Geoffrey was transferring his management interest in this handsome lad to Robert Stigwood, who intended to do great things with him. How interesting, I thought...but then, what business was it of mine, the passing around of pretty boys?

The article appeared and a week or so later so did Geoffrey at the Record Mirror office. It was lunchtime, I was alone in the editorial office, and he said how grateful he was for the article and that Decca were now interested in signing them. It was rare to get thanks for an article, other than from the readers, so in all sincerity I said that's great, good for you all. Geoffrey then handed me an envelope, wished me all the best, and left. I opened the envelope and inside was a cheque for forty pounds. I was astonished. I had no inkling this would happen. I felt compromised. Confused, I wondered what should I do? I considered calling John Allison, finding out Geoffrey's address and returning the cheque. Then I thought, fuck it, I wrote the article in all innocence. Besides, forty pounds was good money then. So I kept the cheque and never heard from Geoffrey, John Allison, or Blues By Five again. It was the only time I ever got money for writing an article other than from the paper I was writing it for. No-one else ever offered!

Blues By Five went on to support Big Dee Irwin on his UK tour, then cut a version of John Lee Hooker's "Boom Boom" for Decca which was released later that year but didn't trouble the charts. Their former lead singer became Simon Scott, and Robert Stigwood spent an awful lot of money on him, including sending round Beethoven-style busts of his protégé to the music press as publicity items, presumably to be used as paperweights, but which visiting NME wild child Richard Green, a.k.a. "The Beast", jammed down the RM loo in the hope that it would get regularly shat upon, but it blocked the drainage and had to be removed. 1964 was the year of gay managers lavishing disproportionate attention on pretty boys who didn't really make it – Larry Parnes with Daryl Quist, Stigwood with Simon Scott, and Brian Epstein with Tommy Quickly. They came as quickly as they went.

Blues By Five may not have been the next Rolling Stones, but then a group appeared that actually were. It came about through Peter Meaden and his complex relationship with Andrew Oldham. Back in '61 Meaden and Oldham had teamed up to form a PR outfit called Image. When Image sank, Meaden went back to advertising, Oldham on to pop PR – then the Rolling Stones. They were both stylish hustlers: Andrew was cool, sharp, very bright, very aware; Meaden, two years older, was more artistic, a bit mad, a bit brilliant, always flailing around. But when Meaden was "on", no-one could touch him. He generated excitement. Fuelled by pills and whiskey, on a roll about his latest scheme, his latest discovery, his latest project, and you'd stand there listening to him with your jaw dropping at the awesome, crazy connections he'd be making. And believe him, too.

When Oldham made it with the Stones, he attempted to bring Meaden back into the fold but it didn't work: Meaden, who craved his own success, found it hard to be around the now-successful Andrew and they fell out. Because Oldham was so successful, everyone assumed Meaden had once been his protégé. It wasn't till Oldham's memoirs in 2000 that I – and several others who'd known Meaden intimately – realised that in the early years it had been the other way around, as Andrew made clear with his generous and detailed reminiscences. Meaden, strangely, never disabused anyone of this misconception.

Meaden then figured that if Oldham could make it big with a group, why not he? Early in '64 he found that group. The Who, formerly the Detours (three-quarters of the Who) were being managed by Helmut Gorden, and Peter became their publicist, then co-manager. Musically, they were perfect, a spiky R&B-covers band, but without a distinctive look. Peter's brainwave was to reposition them as THE mod group. He gave them a mod name – the High Numbers – then worked on their image. One warm day in early summer he brought the High Numbers, now including Keith Moon, up to Record Mirror en route to Austin's hip men's wear emporium along the road in Shaftesbury Avenue to buy them imported American gear. I tagged along with them. I was wearing a three piece blue chalkstripe wool suit, a beige herringbone shirt with a high starched collar. Meaden and the boys looked so casual, so cool, so comfortably stylish that I felt heavy and outdated. It was the first time I'd felt that way since my style epiphany at Art College in 1960 and I didn't like the feeling at all.

Stylistically, Meaden was fixated on casual, classy American gear. His model was Steve McQueen. For Meaden, mod for the High Numbers was the means to an end and he pursued it with his usual all-consuming enthusiasm. He got them a residency at the Scene, got them talked about everywhere, and after a couple of months got them a one-off record deal with Philips, one of the big four record majors, on their Fontana imprint.

I caught the High Numbers at the Scene whenever I could. The Stones, the best live group I'd ever seen, generated real wildness, but it was controlled wildness. The High Numbers seemed to lose control frequently, yet demonstrated dynamics that already marked them as major performers. The Miracles' recent single "I Gotta Dance To Keep From Crying" was a forgettable slice of Motown, a minor US hit follow-up to the smash "Mickey's Monkey". But in the hands of the High Numbers it was a rave-up and then some.

Meaden's first mistake, other than changing their name from the Who, was not to have cut the High Numbers on an R&B cover which had been audience tried-and-tested. Even better would have been an LP on the lines of the currently successful "Georgie Fame Live At The Flamingo", but maybe Fontana just weren't that hip. Their first session was booked for June, no material had been rehearsed specifically for the record, so on the day before the session Peter, together with his pal Mickey "The Face" Tenner, borrowed a dozen or so of Guy Stevens' 45s, took them round to Mickey's, and they re-wrote in mod-speak cliché the lyrics of a couple of R&B classics. Slim Harpo's "Got Love Is You Want It" became "I'm The Face"; the flip was "Zoot Suit", modelled on the Dynamics' recent "Misery". Next day the High Numbers performed at the session as well as could be expected on the lame material newly presented to them, but the result was a so-so record that no more represented the High Numbers than "Come On" had the Stones. Nevertheless I penned a rave review:

RM w/e 18th July 1964

THE HIGH NUMBERS I'm The Face; Zoot Suit (Fontana TF 480)
THE sensational new mod group and an atmospheric wailing item with a jerky danceable beat and an ultra-commercial blues-flavoured tune that grows and grows on you. Interesting lyric about mod fashion and good vocal all leads up to a first class disc from this new team, who are kicking up a storm in London clubs. With enough exposure it could click in a big way. Flip is a smoother also-beaty item with another good lyric.

TOP FIFTY TIP

I think Meaden knew it wasn't a good record, but he had to go along with it and brave it out. He dashed off a piece for Record Mirror which I minimally subbed, then plonked into Peter Jones' New Faces page – at the top. It was the first article on the group. Dezo did a location photographic session that included the famous shot of the High Numbers posing by a whelk stall. Meaden fixed the press launch for the Scene club, and with his genius for hustling got everyone there, Fleet Street, the lot.

RM w/e 11th July 1964

HOW HIGH WILL THESE NUMBERS GO?

HAILED as "the first authentic mod record", four hip young men called The High Numbers are out right now with "I'm The Face" backed with "Zoot Suit" – a Fontana disc. Two numbers penned by co-manager Peter Meaden.

How mod are this mod-mad mob? VERY mod. Their clothes are the hallmark of the much-criticised typical mod. Cycling jackets, tee-shirts, turned-up Levi jeans, long white jackets, boxing boots, black and white brogues and so on to the mod-est limits.

Says Peter Meaden: "After all, the Mod scene is a way of life. An exciting quick-changing way of life. The boys are totally immersed in this atmosphere. So they have this direct contact with thousands of potential disc buyers.

SWITCHED

"And the reaction is already very strong indeed. Take places like the Scene club in London. The fans are mad about the disc – both sides of it!" In fact, "Zoot Suit" was originally planned as the "A" side, being switched only at the last moment.

In a way the High Numbers sound swivels directly round the vocals and harmonica-wailing of Roger Daltry. His blond hair is styled in a longish French crew cut and he buys clothes in the very latest styles. Currently he's modelling Zoot Suit jackets. He digs the blues and Buddy Guy...and is glad he no longer has to work as a sheet-metal worker.

Lead guitarist Peter Townshend originally wanted to be a graphic designer having been to Ealing art-school.

A near six-footer, he has cropped dark hair, piercing blue eyes – and says: "I used to spend a fortune on bright and in-vogue clothes. I go for the 'West Side Story' look and the Ivy League gear." Musically he's for Bob Dylan and the Tamla-Motown-Gordy label.

AMBITION

On bass is John Allison. He went to School with Roger at Acton County Grammar School. "I used to be in an income tax office. This gave me an ambition: to get OUT of the tax office." John is certainly the most conservative of the group, really preferring classical music to most other kinds. He is an accomplished musician.

Come in now, drummer Keith Moon. He's the youngest of the group – only seventeen. A Wembley resident, he went to Wembley technical college and was a trainee representative before turning professional musician. Is the smallest of the group too, has black hair and brown eyes – and says: "I spend all my spare time listening to music in various West End of London clubs."

Record Mirror colleagues are convinced the boys stand a good chance of getting away with "I'm The Face". And one thing is for sure: the phraseology is good and authentic. Mod, in fact.

Interesting to see how the disc sells.

We all wanted it to work for Meaden. The High Numbers performed sensationally, the Press, unable to get a drink at the "dry" Scene, later congregated upstairs where Meaden sat strangely morose, nursing a bottle of Scotch. It was all very puzzling. Kit Lambert and Chris Stamp were there. The rumour, a few weeks later, was that Lambert and Stamp wanted to promote a High Numbers tour, and when Meaden signed their tour papers that evening at the Scene over his bottle of Scotch, he failed to notice it was also a management contract: he'd signed away the High Numbers. This was a false rumour. Later we heard that Peter had been paid £500 (or £200 or £250 depending on who tells the story) by Lambert and Stamp for the High Numbers. It was all a mystery and I never asked him subsequently for details, as he was ashamed of having lost them. Whatever did happen, in hindsight it's obvious that Lambert and Stamp were destiny's choice to manage the Who. And the sheer calibre, not to mention aggression, of the four individuals in the group would soon have caused friction with Meaden with his overwhelming Svengali tendencies. As it was, Meaden and the Who (as Lambert and Stamp re-re-re-named them) remained friends for the remainder of Meaden's life. They were always supportive of Peter and his future enterprises, always praising his early efforts on their behalf, his successful repositioning of them in the mod arena.

Midway through '64 came Record Mirror's 10th birthday Pop Poll, as voted by our readers. Here's the top three in each category: Male Vocalist – Elvis Presley, Cliff Richard, Roy Orbison. Female Vocalist – Brenda Lee, Mary Wells, Cilla Black. Male Vocal Group – Beatles, Rolling Stones, Searchers. Female Vocal Group – Crystals, Ronettes, Shirelles. Instrumental Group – Shadows, Sounds Incorporated, Booker T. & The MGs. Solo Instrumentalist – Duane Eddy, Jet Harris, Chuck Berry. Best Disc Of '63 or '64 – "She Loves You" – Beatles, "Not Fade Away" – Rolling Stones, "Anyone Who Had A Heart" – Cilla Black. British-only section – Male Vocalist – Cliff Richard, Billy Fury, Mick Jagger. Female Vocalist – Cilla Black, Dusty Springfield, Kathy Kirby. Vocal Group – Rolling Stones, Beatles, Searchers. Best Dressed Artist – Cliff Richard, Billy J.Kramer, Adam Faith. Disc Jockey – Jimmy Savile, David Jacobs, Alan Freeman. Individual Group Member – Mick Jagger, Hank B. Marvin, George Harrison. Large Band or Orchestra – Joe Loss, Ted Heath, Andrew Oldham. Radio Or TV Show – Ready Steady Go!, Top Of The Tops, Thank Your Lucky Stars. Most Promising New Singer – Lulu, Millie, Cilla Black.

Before returning home, Carl Perkins made himself available for interviews. He was staying at a plush London hotel and when I arrived, the concierge, a fan, told me in an awed voice "He's in the restaurant". Carl was indeed in the restaurant, sitting alone in a huge empty rococo room waiting for me. He was bigger than he'd seemed backstage at Finsbury Park (probably because he'd been diminished

180

by the Chuckster's humiliation) and my first impression was of an air of Southern menace, but in fact he was most likeable. The tour had gone well for him, he'd been lauded everywhere as he deserved to be. Carl was also still grateful to be alive and working: in '56 his career had stalled after a bad car accident just as "Blue Suede Shoes" was racing up the US charts in tandem with Presley's "Heartbreak Hotel". Elvis got the TV spots; Carl got the hospital bills. Here are Carl's quotes from the article:

RM w/e 20th June 1964

I NEVER HAD THOSE SHOES! CONFESSES CARL PERKINS

"...I was playing with the boys at a High School dance. I was looking at the audience and right at the front there was a slick boy dancing with his partner, a good looking girl. But he didn't care about her – all he was worrying about was that she didn't step on his new pair of blue suede shoes.

"I started thinking about this, and I couldn't get it out of my mind. When I went to bed that night I couldn't sleep for thinking about this boy. So I got up in the middle of the night and I wrote 'Blue Suede Shoes'

"It was my biggest hit. In 1957 you could buy 16 versions of that song. Altogether it sold over four million copies including Elvis's version, so they tell me.

"After a while I left Sun Records. There was something wrong with that company. After all a record label that's OK doesn't go around losing artists like Presley, Roy Orbison, Jerry Lee Lewis and Johnny Cash. They've got nobody now. And they had the biggest names in the country at one time.

"When I moved to Columbia they tried to make a ballad singer of me. But it didn't work and I drifted back to country music for a while. Then came this tour news of Britain. I didn't think I'd enjoy it. I'd heard of British people being very snooty and upper-crust. I didn't think

anyone in Britain would want to talk to someone like me. But I was wrong. I've never had a better time. The people in Britain are great. In fact this tour has been the best of my life – even better than when 'Blue Suede Shoes' was at the top of the charts.

"The other night I had a great thrill. Don Arden told me that there were four friends who wanted to see me. They put me in a car and we drove round to a flat. When we arrived I went upstairs and there were the Beatles!

"I've never been so thrilled. We all went down to the recording studio, and there they recorded my song 'Matchbox' for their new EP. It was Ringo who sang on it – he's a real clown.

"Although I've had misfortune, I've been very lucky. And I'd like to say that I'm a firm believer in God and I thank Him for all my good fortune."

That recording of "Matchbox" would feature on the Beatles EP "Long Tall Sally" which remained in the UK EP charts for a record 63 weeks. It would also be issued as a stop-gap single in the USA, make the US Top 20, and be released on no less than four Beatles' American LPs. Nice one, Carl. And indeed what a time this was for Beatles' LPs: their latest, "A Hard Day's Night", eventually proved to be the Fabs' second-biggest US LP hit, topping the charts for over three months. Unsurprising though, especially as the US film critics couldn't resist the Beatles' debut movie: we reported the raves as a top-of-the-page news story:

RM w/e 22 August 1964
U.S. RAVES FOR BEATLES PIC

AMERICAN film critics have gone overboard for the Beatles' first movie, "A Hard Day's Night"
Everywhere, columnists have been giving it "rave" notices.
The New York press gave the Beatles a unanimous "Yeah, Yeah, Yeah".

182

The New York Times said "This is going to surprise you – it may knock you right out of your chair – but the film with those incredible chaps the Beatles, is a whale of a comedy."

The New York World-Telegram and Sun – " 'A Hard Day's Night' turns out to be funnier than you would expect and every bit as loud as the wildest Beatle optimist could hope."

New York Herald Tribune – "It really is an eggheaded picture, lightly scrambled, a triumph of the Beatles and the bald".

New York Daily News – "The picture adds up to a lot of fun, not only for the teenagers but for grown-ups as well. It's clean wholesome entertainment."

New York Journal American – "The picture turned out to be a completely wacky off-beat entertainment that's frequently remindful of the Marx Brothers comedies of the "30s."

New York Daily Post – " 'A Hard Day's Night' suggests a Beatle career in the movies as big as they've already been in stage and dancehall. They have the songs, the patter, and the histrionic flair. No more is needed."

Washington reviewers found it difficult to assess the merits of the film because of the teenage audiences.

The Washington Post said "The main thing about it is that you can't hear it, because the audience sort of over-participates."

And the Washington Evening Star reported "The film appears to be a genuinely funny British comedy though nobody may ever really know. Its stars appear to be agreeable personalities with a zest for spoofing themselves and their idolators and it looks as if it might be fun if you could hear it as well as see it."

Down below in the same news spread was buried a story which was to change the balance of the British music industry: "...from usually reliable sources in New York", we learned that the American giant

Columbia Records, itself a division of the major CBS-TV network, had acquired the UK independent Oriole group, together with its pressing-plant, warehouse, distribution, and West End offices. Under the banner CBS Records, a new major record company was now set to join the four existing majors the following February. It was a blow for former CBS distributors Philips who were not even to be allowed a selling-off period.

My next *The Great Unknowns* featured Inez and Charlie Foxx, finally here, and booked as support on the new Stones' tour, plus a week of club dates including Liverpool's Cavern, Manchester's Oasis, and London's Flamingo. Backing them were the Spencer Davis Group, already under the wing of Island's Chris Blackwell. Chris had produced Millie's current Top Ten ska smash "My Boy Lollipop" which he'd leased to Philips, the manufacturer and distributor of Island/Sue Records, for their Fontana label. Chris would go the same label route with Spencer Davis, but despite some small hits it was to be nearly eighteen months before Spencer's group, featuring the voice and keyboards of the prodigious Stevie Winwood, would score their first major hit.

Meanwhile, Inez and Charlie finally charted Guy's Sue label with their new single "Hurt By Love", which could have been a lot bigger if a TV technicians' strike hadn't prevented them plugging the disc on Ready Steady Go!. Shame about that, but they did go down a storm on the Stones' tour:

> *"Stones apart, the biggest surprise of the evening was the sensational reception accorded the American rhythm & blues artists Inez and Charlie Foxx. Despite going on in the most difficult part of the show (just before the Stones), their wild singing and dancing brought a fantastic response from the audience. They opened with 'Mockingbird', which must be a hit for them during this tour, then ran through an exciting version of 'Hi-Heel Sneakers', and 'He's The One You Love'. The duo finished with a pounding version of 'Hurt By Love', after which the audience brought them back for three encores."*

That summer controversy dogged the Searchers, the most popular Liverpool group after the Beatles. Despite fervent denials from management and record company, there was a rift in the group, serious nastiness between Chris Curtis and Tony Jackson: it was the first of the "musical differences" splits, soon to become a cliché. Tony had sung lead on their first two hits, but not on the massive "Needles And Pins", as he had laryngitis at the session. Tony's version of events – at the time – was that Chris then told Tony he didn't want him singing lead anymore as Chris was planning on moving the group in a softer direction away from R&B. Musically, Chris was right, and the Searchers would go on to become the first beat group to pioneer folk-rock. But Tony, a staunch R&B devotee, considered himself firstly a singer, then a bass player, and felt hurt and rejected. Threats were made, Tony was forced to quit. His popularity was such that Pye Records, the Searchers' label, offered him a solo deal immediately. Tony and his new group The Vibrations covered Mary Wells' US debut single "Bye Bye Baby", but it became only a minor hit. Covering, or more usually reviving, American R&B hits, even in late 1964, was already becoming passé. Only dead-cert hitmakers like the Rolling Stones (currently topping the charts with their superior cover of the minor US R&B hit "It's All Over Now") and Manfred Mann (ditto with "Do Wah Diddy Diddy") were getting away with it.

The Searchers weren't the only Liverpool group to change their line-up. Some of the biggest live groups on Merseyside were floundering after failing to find chart success now that the A&R stampede to Liverpool had abated. The Big Three split up and re-formed with ex-Faron's Flamingo Bill Faron in the line-up, and he had his own sad tale to tell me: "We didn't have a bad group. But it wasn't as good as the Big Three are now. I was choked that Oriole didn't issue our version of 'Do You Love Me' as a top side though. Mind you, it wasn't their fault – they asked twelve teenagers walking down the street to come into their studio and they played them 'See If She Cares' and 'Do You Love Me'. They all voted for 'See If She Cares'. But it didn't do anything. Later Brian Poole reached number one with 'Do You Love Me'..."

The Beatles apart, the writing was on the wall for the major Liverpool groups. Gerry & The Pacemakers and Billy J. Kramer would enjoy a further year of diminishing hits, the Searchers another two years. The rest of Britain had caught up and overtaken: the UK beat boom was now a global phenomenon, and a glance at the quality of the hits that autumn showed why. Here's a sample: "It's All Over Now", "Do Wah Diddy Diddy", "House Of The Rising Sun", "The Crying Game", "You Really Got Me", "Have I The Right", "She's Not There", "Downtown", "Tobacco Road". The UK charts hadn't been this vibrant since the hey-day of rock'n'roll six or seven years previously...but then the hits were American.

The four Kings themselves, topping every chart worldwide with "A Hard Day's Night", were in the US and Canada for their first "proper" tour, as opposed to the two-gig publicity visit earlier in the year. Here's a sample of how RM reported their amazing reception:

RM w/e 29th August 1964

> *...the latest incredible riot was at Vancouver, British Columbia, Canada on Sunday when the Beatles' concert at the Empire Stadium almost turned to tragedy.*
>
> *Thousands of teenagers rushed from their seats onto the playing field towards the group, crushing hundreds of young girls against a restraining fence in front of the stage.*
>
> *Police handed dozens of girls suffering from broken ribs over the heads of the others to first-aid men, while others milled around the first-aid station, "apparently lost, hysterical and emotionally over-wrought".*
>
> *In the vicinity of the Hollywood Bowl where the Beatles played after the Vancouver concert, residents were issued with passes to get to their homes. Police and firemen set up roadblocks.*
>
> *At Seattle, Washington, the car that was to have taken the Beatles from the Coliseum was damaged so badly by fans that it could not be used. After playing to an audience of 14,000, they left by ambulance.*
>
> *When the Beatles opened their tour at San Francisco's Cow Palace last Thursday, fifty were hurt, two arrested, and fifty others forcibly prevented from climbing on to the stage. At the end of their 30-minute concert, after being*

hit by jelly beans and stuffed animals, the Beatles dropped their instruments, left the stage and ran straight into a car, to be whisked away from the Cow Palace before the fans had hardly realised that the show was over.

At their San Francisco hotel girls dressed as maids tried to bluff their way past detectives and guards and thirty-five girls were rounded up on the 15th floor – assigned solely to the Beatles.

At the gaming centre of Las Vegas, gaming by the Beatles had been limited to playing two slot machines carried to their rooms. During the group's concert before 7,000 at the Convention Centre, some youngsters tossed peanut shells onto the stage to be ground up by the stamping Beatles and collected in pieces as souvenirs. At one stage during the concert the group could only be "heard" by people who could lip-read.

Today (Thursday) the Beatles will be protected by five policemen standing by their side on stage at the Cincinnati Arena with more than a hundred others nearby. At press-time, RM was told that the Beatles will break their journey from Dallas, Texas to New York on September 20th to play a single performance at Kansas City, Missouri, for a fee of $150,000 (£53,600).

The deal was arranged after the owner of the baseball park at Kansas City had travelled to California to personally plead with the group to appear in the park.

According to the American show-biz paper "Variety", the Beatles might make as much as a million dollars (£357,000) on their current tour of USA and Canada. "A Hard Day's Night" in America has grossed more than a million and a half dollars (£571,000).

In less than two years, the Beatles had become the biggest attraction in the history of world entertainment, and British music become a creative dynamo, a global phenomenon that had eclipsed America's long-held supremacy in popular music.

America, however, was fighting back. Although it would be a further year until Beatles-inspired US groups such as the Byrds and the Lovin' Spoonful would demonstrate their unique magic, two established American groups were holding their own domestically and internationally against the UK onslaught. The Beach Boys, moving away from surf and drag-racing themes, topped the US charts and scored their first UK Top Ten hit with the sophisticated "I Get Around". Similarly, and equally clever, were radical doo-woppers the Four Seasons whose "Rag Doll" – arguably their best record to date – had also topped the US chart and given them their fifth UK hit.

But the real challenge to UK hegemony was not from white groups but from 'The Sound Of Young America' – Motown. Berry Gordy's R&B hit factory in Detroit was about to shift gear and move up into the international pop market – the white market – thanks to the combination of the writing-production team of Holland-Dozier-Holland plus the "no-hit Supremes", as they were known in Detroit.

Motown's creativity had never been in doubt. Since 1960, Smokey Robinson and the Miracles, Martha & The Vandellas, the Marvelettes, Marvin Gaye, the Temptations, girl-goddess of R&B Mary Wells, and many others had together cut a breathtaking body of work that was already the envy of every other independent label, black or white. Their hits had inspired the Beatles, the Rolling Stones and every other British beat group. Gordy's company was already worth millions, but still perceived as an R&B label, a black label, despite substantial forays into the pop charts. Gordy knew how good his product was, knew how clever and creative his artists, musicians, songwriters and producers were. The boost and the plaudits from the British beat boom had reinforced his long-held instinct that the white market was ripe for his music – all he needed was an unstoppable artist.

It was almost Mary Wells. But at the very moment Wells topped the US charts with "My Guy" and propelled Tamla-Motown into the UK charts, the story goes that her new husband, Herman Griffin, talked her to into making one of the worst business decisions in the history of pop music. As she became 21, Griffin's lawyers declared her Motown contract was null and void because Wells had signed it as a teenager, and – for a substantial advance and a vague promise of movie stardom – Griffin persuaded her to quit Motown for the new 20th Century Fox label. Gordy fought the ruling but lost. Mary Wells never scored another big hit, never made a movie. Even at the time it seemed a grotesquely foolish move. Apart from her self-penned debut "Bye Bye Baby", all of Wells's hits had been written and produced by Smokey Robinson. She became, in effect, his female alter ego, able to tame her natural raucous delivery in order to more subtly and sexily vocalise Smokey's clever songs. All her biggest hits – "The One Who Really Loves You", "Two Lovers", "You Beat Me To The Punch", "Your Old Stand-By", "What Two Can Easily Do", "My Guy" were virtually Smokey Robinson in drag. He produced, he wrote, he told Mary exactly how to sing them. Griffin's greed had sunk the girl-goddess of R&B.

Fortunately for Gordy, his hit factory contained plenty more talent. The previous October as a last resort he'd paired the so-called "no-hit Supremes" (they were a joke at Motown) with up-and-coming producers Brian and Eddie Holland and Lamont Dozier. Late in 1963 they scored a modest hit together with "When The Lovelight Starts Shining In His Eyes"…then nothing. But at the next recording session, despite the group's reservations at the "simplicity" of the material, HD&H cut them on a selection of songs including "Baby Love" and "Where Did Our Love Go", a song rejected by the Marvelettes. Gordy released the latter title first, propelling the "no-hit Supremes" to immediate global chart success, a US No.1, the first of a dozen, Diana Ross to eventual superstardom and, best of all, taking Gordy's group of record labels and all its artists – marketed with that superb slogan 'The Sound Of Young America' – into the worldwide white record market.

Gordy's music had long been championed in the UK by Dave Godin, a veteran writer of readers' letters to Record Mirror, a male nurse, and a key figure on the UK R&B scene. Dave, who looked a bit like the Bloomsbury Set writer Lytton Strachey (and seemed to share some of Strachey's witty waspishness and other idiosyncrasies), was the kind of fan to whom R&B was more than a music – it was a cause. The cause was Civil Rights in the USA, and Dave was one of an increasing number of hard-core white R&B fans for whom the plight of blacks, both here and in the USA, was a matter of personal conscience. R&B, which was evolving into soul music, was their banner, and he had no truck for white R&B. Dave despised the Rolling Stones, even though he claimed he'd introduced the younger Mick Jagger to black music at Dartford Grammar School.

I didn't share Dave's involvement with the politics of the music, and neither did most other R&B fans I knew. Nevertheless we got on famously – we both loved the same sort of music, and when I interviewed a black artist he sometimes accompanied me. He was probably about seven years older than me and his views and his knowledge were always interesting and informative. He dressed well, was a skinny six-foot dandy, and had his own coterie of admirers. One day he came racing up to the office and told me that in his capacity as founder-member of the Tamla Motown Appreciation Society And Mary Wells Fan Club he'd received a personal invitation from Berry Gordy to visit Detroit – and Motown's HQ "Hitsville USA". He wanted to know if we would publicise his visit on his return, so I said, yes, of course. It would be a scoop.

When Dave returned, we gave over the entire centre spread to his visit, with photographs picturing him with various Motown artists including Mary Wells, Martha Reeves, Kim Weston, Stevie Wonder, Marvin Gaye, Motown's live review backing band Choker Campbell's Band, and Gordy himself.

RM w/e 4th September 1964

A GREAT VISIT TO HITSVILLE USA
By DAVE GODIN as told to Norman Jopling

IT was probably the biggest surprise in the life of Dave Godin, founder-member of The Tamla-Motown Appreciation Society and Mary Wells Fan Club when he received a telegram from the States. The telegram asked Dave to visit the Tamla-Motown set-up in Detroit, all expenses paid, and see the Motortown review.

Needless to say Dave accepted – and when he returned he told Record Mirror the full story of his exciting and revealing trip to the home of the greatest modern blues label in the States.

This comes at a time when EMI are expecting to launch Tamla Motown as a separate label in the near future.

"When I arrived in the States I was met at the airport by a bevy of photographers. In fact I had more pictures taken during that trip than in the rest of my lifetime.

"They whisked me off to Hitsville USA. It was there that I met Berry Gordy Jr. who told me that all the stars at Tamla had chipped in towards my visit , which had been engineered by Miss Margaret Phelps of Hitsville USA Artists' Fan Club.

"The Tamla set-up is magnificent. They have two recording studios – one is their 'soul' studio, personally supervised by Berry Gordy. "...this studio is the one where they produce the music that you like," Berry told me. In the other studio most of the string-filled and ballad numbers are cut. Although it sounds corny, Berry Gordy always refers to the sound he is striving for as 'soul – there's no other word for it...'

"But the most fantastic thing about the Tamla-Motown labels, and organisation, is the close-knit atmosphere. It all started with Berry Gordy and his sisters. Berry had been writing songs, managing artists, and producing discs for various companies and artists for several years and was well acquainted with artists such as Jackie Wilson and Marv Johnson (Marv will probably be returning to Motown as soon as his contract with United Artists expires).

"Berry produced some discs, including Barrett Strong's 'Money', for his sister Anna's label, named after her. Anna, incidentally, is now married to Marvin Gaye. Berry's other sister Gwen is married to Harvey Fuqua. Harvey was not too long ago a very big name in his own right, when he sang with the Moonglows – and of course with Etta James as Etta and Harvey. But Harvey was probably one of the most interesting people I met there.

"Berry Gordy Jr. is married of course – and he has four children. I also met Claudette Robinson, one of the Miracles and married to Smokey Robinson, leader of the

Miracles and Vice-President of Tamla Motown. Berry met the Miracles when he produced two singles for them at Chess Records. When he started his own label he signed them up. Berry signed Marvin Gaye after Harvey Fuqua discovered him at a talent contest – it was shortly after that Anna and Marvin fell in love and married.

AMAZED

"Incidentally Marvin has a new female backing group – the Andantes. They were on Marv's 'You're A Wonderful One', but there was one of the Supremes on that session. When 'You're A Wonderful One' was issued I wrote to Tamla saying that I thought I heard a Supreme on the disc. They were amazed at that, but it seems I was right...

"That brings me on to the Motown Sound. Every master tape must be finally signed for by Berry before it's passed, and pressed. One of the hits Berry didn't produce was 'Every Little Bit Hurts' by Brenda Holloway which was recorded in California where Tamla have a new studio.

FALLACY

"Smokey Robinson was once quoted as saying that Tamla didn't know how they got their sound. Well, that's wrong. They DO know how to get it. And another fallacy is that they consider cover versions to be tributes. They get every cover version of every Tamla disc, and the Tamla artists greatly resent them.

"When a vocalist or group are going into the studio to record their next disc and they haven't a song already written, it's often written as they go along and the finished disc lasts about twenty five minutes. Then they cut it until they're finally left with the best bits and that's the record. The main songwriters at Tamla are Berry, Smokey, and Eddie Holland, who had a big hit with 'Jamie'. The sessions there are edited and as Berry says, "...it's usually

192

at the end of the session where the actual disc is cut from that everyone is getting a groove on."

"When I was in Hitsville USA, Berry took me to where there were four new sides cut by Martha and The Vandellas. He asked me to pick their next single. I said I thought that two were about as good, but he made me actually pick out one track ('Dancing In The Street') and he said it would be Martha's next single!

"While I was in the States we visited a Playboy Club, a fairground, and, of course, the fabulous Motortown Review, which is now split into two shows as there are so many stars going around now.

DECISION

"I met Mary Wells finally backstage after the review. She was very nice, and she was with her secretary Maye Hamilton. I didn't ask her about the rumours that she's leaving Tamla Motown, but there should be a decision and a statement soon one way or the other. I must say how nice Marvin and Martha were – the latter being one of the most soulful people I've ever met.

"Berry is very concerned with the British market. He thinks that British fans are the most faithful and the best in the world."

Of course Dave knew full well the situation with Mary Wells. He knew another secret, too, one which we couldn't publish. Following on from the success of their double-sided duet smash "Once Upon A Time"/"What's The Matter With You Baby", Mary Wells and Marvin Gaye recorded the album "Together", a collection of duets. The album was in the US charts for four months. But Mary hadn't sung all her parts when she stopped recording for Motown. So on some of the tracks, "Mary Wells" is in fact – Smokey Robinson!

In the same issue I profiled the Supremes, who had hit the UK charts that week with "Where Did Our Love Go", using information cribbed from a Tamla-Motown press hand-out, a not uncommon occurrence among journalists. The article finished with the following paragraph: "…and apart from singing, the three girls have interests outside music. Diana still makes her own clothes, and those for the group's appearances. Florence still likes to go down to the ten-pin bowling alley for a quick game. And Mary still likes to sit around reading quietly and quoting Latin!"

Two days after that issue hit the streets, the Beatles played Detroit's Olympic Stadium. At the press conference reporters asked them what they liked about Detroit. "Tamla Motown records and their artists" was the reply. Hours later Berry Gordy announced he would be bringing the Supremes to the UK for a seven-day promotional visit and recording them on a new album to be titled "A Bit Of Liverpool". They arrived the following month and at the party EMI threw for the members of the Tamla Motown Appreciation Society (the 'Mary Wells' bit had now got dropped) Dave Godin introduced me to Berry Gordy. The photo of me with Berry Gordy Jr and Dave Godin taken on that occasion is still one of my treasured favourites. I also met the three Supremes, who were terrific girls and seemed very down-to-earth. I didn't formally interview them, but spent ten minutes or so chatting, a bit of flirting. My instant impression was that Mary was the pretty one, Florence the sexy one, and Diana was like a cheeky sparrow, a bit gawky and highly-strung, but the most vivacious.

Lots of readers had written complaining about some recently well-publicised gaffs by prominent DJs, so with the strangely mis-titled feature *Dee-Jay Sensation!* Peter Jones and I deliberately took opposing positions in this controversy: I frothed at the mouth at their ignorance, while Peter praised their professionalism. This particular kind of discussion was, anyway, the sort of banter that went on in the Record Mirror office on an almost daily basis: me, the fan, Peter, the pro. In retrospect those DJs may just have been having a joke – or were they? On a recent Juke Box Jury, Pete Murray had heard a Shirelles record, then said their previous record was "Sherry". David Jacobs then said "No, 'Sherry' was by the Purcells." That was what started it.

That autumn Peter and I also co-wrote, under the by-line 'RM Disc Jury', *'Our EP, The Inside Story'* (Stones' tracks cut in Chicago's Chess studios for the "Five By Five" EP, which immediately displaced the Beatles' "Long Tally" EP at pole position); I profiled Major Lance and Bobby 'Blue' Bland for *The Great Unknowns*; met Dave Berry ("taller and bigger than anyone would have imagined via his TV appearances") for *How Dave Got That Gimmick!* (hiding behind his coat and moving his hands in a weird way); finally met local lads the Kinks for the Page One feature *'You Really Got Me' Was A Jazz Song! Say The Kinks;* interviewed Georgie Fame yet again for *A Theory Disproved* (the 'theory' being that in order to have a big reputation you needed a big hit record – though for him this was indeed about to happen); and met the already-legendary Burt Bacharach. Burt was in London ensconced at the office of music publisher Franklyn Boyd when we got the call he was available for interviews – right now. Unfortunately I was not wearing my usual dandy-ish gear, but instead old jeans and casual shirt. So was Barry May, who also wanted to meet Burt, but nevertheless we both trotted along to see the great man who at first seemed a bit huffy at these two young scruffs pretending to be journalists. This was long before the era of casual in this kind of situation. But, pro that he was, Burt forced himself to give a good interview – *Time Is My Enemy* – and spoke movingly of his admiration for the recently-deceased Rudy Lewis, lead singer of the Drifters and one-time heir to Ben E. King.

Not at all huffy was the genial Mickey Most, who I'd interviewed a year previously when he impressed everyone as one of the supporting acts on the Little Richard / Bo Diddley / Everly Brothers / Rolling Stones tour. Mickey had happened to mention his ambition to be a producer of good records. Maybe he found a magic lamp, or sold his soul, or was just staggeringly lucky, but in the space of a year he'd become the hottest independent record producer in the world. He was currently topping the US chart with the Animals' "House Of The Rising Sun", and in the UK his top 50 hits were "I'm Into Something Good" by Herman's Hermits (3, and it would be No.1 next week), "Is It True" by Brenda Lee (23, going up), "Tobacco Road" by the Nashville Teens (27, going down), "Seven Golden Daffodils" by the Cherokees (38, going up), "I'm Crying" by the Animals (40, first week in with a bullet). Mickey was becoming seriously rich – an independent producer earns percentage points from each record sold, as did Andrew Oldham and Eric Easton on the Rolling Stones, whereas George Martin, who produced all of EMI's NEMS acts (including the Beatles, Gerry, Billy J., Cilla) and other Parlophone hitmakers such as Matt Monro, were salaried employees. Here's part of the interview with Mickey talking about the major groups he'd recorded:

RM w/e 18th September 1964
HE'S THE MOST SUCCESSFUL

"...I'd made all our own records in South Africa and recorded a few other people there, so I knew the mechanics of A&R work.

"I heard the Animals at the Scene club in Soho and was knocked out. They are my favourite group, still. Anyway, everybody wanted to record them but I got the job. Immediately I started work on an album – funny way to start, I know. 'Baby Let Me Take You Home' was put out as a single and was fairly successful – got to about 12 or 13. Then 'House Of The Rising Sun' was released and went to the top. I wasn't a bit worried about it being four minutes long – the controversy got the disc talked about. The album is already out in America. A British version (with substitutes for 'House' and 'Baby') will be released here in November to catch the Christmas trade."

Next, Mickey went to the Cellar Club in Kingston to hear the Nashville Teens. He thought they were a good group and set about the task of recording them. "You know, some groups are good on stage and not so good in the recording studio. Others are fine at records, poor on stage. In the studio we had a lot of problems with 'Tobacco Road'. We recorded for nine hours and changed studios because I couldn't get the right sound. We did countless takes – unlike 'House' which the Animals did in one take.

"Eventually we got 'Tobacco Road' sounding right and we were all satisfied. Then I tried Herman's Hermits, another fine group, but frankly, I wasn't sure that 'I'm Into Something Good' was as good as they were capable

of. I was a bit reluctant at releasing it but it seems to have turned out all right."

In the middle of September I took a break, went on holiday to Egypt with Jill. As soon as I got back to the office I reviewed the Kinks' debut LP in depth. The four Kinks were interesting and quirky people so it was an apt name they'd given themselves, even if Ray didn't much like it. The article began thus: "Kurrently the Kinks look like krashing the LP chart with their kommercial new album kalled simply "Kinks". The kover of the album is kovered with krazy kampaign notes on the restoration to its rightful place of the letter 'K'". That same week in October my frank-and-fearless *Searchers And DeShannon* probe commented on Kinks' Pye label-mates the Searchers, who were the subject of great vituperation from Record Mirror girl-group addicts because they'd predictably revived yet another Jackie DeShannon record, this time "When You Walk In The Room". Jackie D, like Peggy March, Little Eva, Leslie Gore and Darlene Love was a sort of "honorary" girl-group by virtue of her sound, which was – on these early hits at least – in the same bag as the US girl-group sound which, for the moment, was surviving the British Invasion. In fairness to the Searchers, "When You Walk In The Room" had only been a minor US hit for Jackie months before the Searchers revived it – the Liverpudlians certainly hadn't stomped on Jackie's UK or US chart chances. And as she'd written "When You Walk In The Room" – and it became a major global hit for the Searchers – if she did have any complaints, at least she would have been grouching all the way to the bank. The article was a cut-and-paste job, with quotes from Jackie taken from a letter she'd sent Peter Jones, a big fan and personal friend. On the Searchers' side I quoted what they'd said about "Needles And Pins" from the recent Radio Luxembourg Book Of The Stars, an major annual pop publication.

"A time comes when you decide that you can do different things with tunes, so you DO them. Normally with an orchestra there's an arranger, but a group has to work out its own arrangements. You know your own limitations. Ideas simply come like with 'Needles And Pins"

"Turning 'pins' into pinsa' just came. The original version was an American record. It had a musical phrase in the background which we went for in a big way, and took as our start. The phrase was, originally, so far in the background that it was virtually indistinguishable. We always try to pick something in a song or record we hear and develop it to suit our style.

"So that's what we did with the original Jackie DeShannon record of 'Needles And Pins' – we took out the piano phrase on the record and changed it to a guitar phrase. We felt the tune get stronger as we went on, so we began with a single voice, then at that particular point where it begins to build emotionally, we added vocally to give it still more emotional wallop."

Well, not quite, guys. The Searchers made a good beat group version of "Needles And Pins" but Jackie's version was better. And that "musical phrase" was far from indistinguishable on the original version – in fact it's first played on guitar, then gets taken over by the piano, by which time Jack Nitzsche's inspired arrangement – as good as anything he did for Spector – provides the bedrock for Jackie's exceptional vocal performance, which packs a lot more emotional wallop than the Searchers' version and which the guys didn't even – couldn't even – try to emulate.

Co-incidentally Jack Nitzsche was in London that week plugging a film process called "Electronovision", a cheap way of making movies using TV cameras, and hoping to sign up the Stones, Gerry, and Billy J. for the next Electronovision project. And, as he told David Griffiths, "I'm also supposed to find a British girl group. They want me to bring back a female version of the Rolling Stones but I haven't heard anything remotely suitable."

The late Jim Reeves currently had seven LPs in the LP Top 20, an astonishing feat, and in *Mary Was Jim's Inspiration* I spoke to RCA's Pat Campbell, who'd chosen Reeves' UK singles with far more success than RCA-Victor in the USA had with their choices. Pat also cleared up the rumour that he had withdrawn the proposed single "This World Is Not My Home" following Jim's untimely demise: "It was for Ireland only," he told me. That was a pity, because it would have fitted in nicely with the "spooky singles" phenomenon, whereby a late great's waxing at the time of death eerily echoes their doom, e.g. "Three Steps To Heaven" by Eddie Cochran, "It Doesn't Matter Anymore" by Buddy Holly, and, spookiest all, Chuck Willis's double-deathly "What Am I Living For"/ "Hang Up My Rock And Roll Shoes".

Holly himself was back in the charts with his rather good original version of "Love's Made A Fool Of You", a studio demo he'd cut for – but never recorded by – the Everly Brothers back in 1958. His former manager and record producer Norman Petty was in town, so I took the opportunity of meeting him. Petty, a smooth round-faced man looking more like a bank manager than a rock'n'roll record producer, told me he was working on the forthcoming "Holly In The Hills" album but that very little else of any quality was left in the vaults. At that time nobody in the UK knew about Holly's falling-out with Petty. "...as well as being his manager, I was also a friend of Buddy's, a close friend," he told me. Petty seemed decent enough, but despite his wonderful work with Holly, their less than harmonious parting and its subsequent tragic ramifications must have given him plenty pause for thought over the years.

The Great Unknowns continued that autumn with Chuck Jackson (penned by reader Andrew C. Dyke), followed by Doris Troy and Betty Everett. A new regular column also started: RM Readers Club. This was an idea of Dezo's which was to prove highly popular for the next several years. We printed a coupon with the following categories to be filled out: Name, Address, Age, Stars, Hobby, Anything Else Of Interest. It was a little coupon, so brevity was essential. The reader would fill in the coupon and, together with a photograph (booth pics were now common), send it to RM. We devoted two columns every week featuring ten readers, and we got thousands of coupons. It was really a pen-pal idea, but over the years several readers wrote and told us they'd married after meeting up through the Readers Club.

One of my favourite places to interview artists was in the Italian House restaurant next to the Columbia Cinema, opposite Record Mirror in Shaftesbury Avenue. You could sit there with a coffee for hours and they didn't mind. Heinz, still scoring small hits, was back from an Australian tour and I bought him a coffee or two over the interview. After we finished he had the cheek to cadge the money from me to get his car out the car park. I guess he was used to getting his own way with blokes but I wasn't one of those blokes and resented his wheedling…but coughed up just the same as he was "the star". The car park was on the corner of Shaftesbury Avenue and Gerrard Place, a razed bombsite that remained undeveloped for about thirty years after the war. How much must that slice of land be worth now! The article came out as *Heinz's Hat, Some Surfing & The Sharks!*, a reference to Heinz's rather fetching white straw hat which he'd worn throughout the interview. A month or so later Heinz changed labels, from Decca to EMI's Columbia imprint, and EMI threw a big bash at Manchester Square to launch his new 45, a rocked-up version of the country-blues standard "Diggin' My Potatoes", where EMI supremo Joseph Lockwood, delighted (and florid) to be in the presence of Heinz, personally did the honours introducing his new artist. The gimmick, as these press receptions often had a gimmick, was some unfortunate dressed up as a giant potato standing at the door, greeting the visitors. The giant potato greeted me by name and newspaper… but I never found out who he was.

The following week I profiled Tommy Tucker in *The Man Who Made An R&B Standard*, scheduled to tour the UK on the strength of his global smash earlier in '64, "Hi-Heel Sneakers", one of the last great authentic blues hits. Years later I came across an unauthorised version of the record, the hit take, but with an extra verse and instrumental break. Couldn't make out the lyric though – maybe that was why it got cut out. Talkin' 'bout the blues, we ran a news story announcing the new Stones' single would be the Willie Dixon song "Little Red Rooster", popularised by Howlin' Wolf and Sam Cooke. Prominently featuring Brian's bottle-neck guitar, it was the Stones' finest blues performance to date with everyone on top form, and would deservedly top the UK chart. In fact we'd announced "Little Red Rooster" would be the Stones' new single some weeks earlier after a premature announcement from Decca, but had to withdraw it the following week after Andrew Oldham complained, in a fit of Spector-ish pique, that Decca had no right to make the announcement.

Manfred Mann were always good for a controversial opinion – some might even say "opinionated" – so I went to the ABC-TV Studios in

Teddington to talk to them while they were recording the Eamonn Andrews Show. *"Follow-Ups Are Finished"* they told me, which was a bit rich considering their current hit "Sha La La" was the follow-up to the equally meaningless but catchy "Do Wah Diddy Diddy", but their diatribe was in fact a paean to the first pirate radio station Radio Caroline and its current power in breaking singles by new groups. They were also moving away from R&B:

RM w/e 14th November 1964

"...but we're really fed up with the R&B scene at the moment," said organist Manfred: "Just about every group in the business is playing the same old Chuck Berry, Bo Diddley and Muddy Waters numbers. We just cringe when we hear 'Got My Mojo Working' now. We can't play it any more.

"And another thing that gets on our nerves are the bigots of the R&B scene...they're so narrow-minded about everything. Long John Baldry goes around telling everyone what is and what isn't R&B." It was then that Paul Jones interrupted: "After all, who DOES know who plays R&B. Is it Berry or Diddley, is it the Miracles or Supremes, is it James Brown or Bobby Bland.

"Then the artists come over and tell us they're not R&B," exclaimed bass guitarist Tom McGuinness: "Diddley says he doesn't play R&B, Howlin' Wolf says he's a folk singer..."

Meanwhile the tastes of the whole group are widening all the time. Paul is going for numbers like "I Wish You Love" and "These Foolish Things", while Manfred himself is thinking of instrumentals in terms of Cannonball Adderley and Mongo Santamaria.

"But we'll keep on playing R&B", said Paul: "Although the R&B we'll play and record will be wider, musically, than what is accepted now."

If the Manfreds were moving away from R&B, the Animals certainly weren't. That same week I did a track-by-track review of their new album – *Bluesy New Animals LP* – and in addition to a couple of interesting originals, particularly Eric's "Story Of Bo Diddley", there were versions of songs by John Lee Hooker, Fats Domino, Larry Williams, Little Richard, Ray Charles and Chuck Berry. They'd honed these numbers in clubs for months and the result, produced by Mickie Most, was a sensational debut album. R&B was still on the menu with *Martha's Mad On Fashion* (Martha & The Vandellas here on a nine-day promo trip following a modest UK hit with "Dancing In The Street"). And, still on the R&B kick, in *Stones – "Our Obsession"*, I reviewed a new book on the Rolling Stones: "Our Own Story – By The Rolling Stones", as told to Pete Goodman, and published by Corgi Books at a mere 5/- a copy. "Pete Goodman" was an alias for our editor Peter Jones.

I churned out another "list" feature in *Odds Are Good For The Yanks* (proving American chart-toppers by American artists were still statistically likely to make the UK Top 50, despite the UK beat boom). And the Honeycombs told me *Our Image Needs To Change* (singer Dennis D'Ell confessed he didn't like the flop follow-up to their "Have I The Right" smash – their latest "Eyes" wasn't going to make it either). Alter-ego Wesley Laine profiled Zoot Money's Big Roll Band in *What's A Big Roll Band?* (revealing their name should actually be 'Paul Williams with Zoot Money's Big Roll Band'. What a mouthful).

Beginning his descent into infamy was P.J.Proby, whose earlier triumph on Jack Good's "Around The Beatles" TV show was already becoming slightly tarnished. Following the inconvenient revelation that his new UK Decca record deal where he'd scored two major hits with rocked-up oldies "Hold Me" and "Together" was invalid because he was still contracted to the US Liberty label, P.J. – or "Jim", as he was known to his familiars – was currently shooting up the charts with a third oldie, a quiveringly mannered version of the "West Side Story" ballad standard "Somewhere", which vocally owed not a little to Billy Eckstine. The side had been cut for Decca, but handed over to Liberty in lieu of damages. Now, at the end of '64, Jim had also acquired a reputation for unreliability: purportedly, he hadn't shown up for several gigs (the onstage trouser-splitting was yet to come), and so he decided to defend himself in our columns.

RM w/e 12th December 1964

'I'M BROKE AND DISGUSTED'
Says P.J. Proby to Norman Jopling

P.J. Proby was down in the dumps to say the very least. "I'm broke and I'm disgusted..." he said glumly. I asked him why.

"Simply because of the raw deal I've been getting from the British promoters, agents, managers and press," he explained. "Everybody calls me a bad boy. And the press only want to know about the dates that I've supposed to have broken. Nobody wants to know about my side of the story.

"In fact all these stories about me are a pack of lies. I didn't turn up at certain dates because the promoters threatened me NOT to turn up. They knew I wanted cash for these performances, and they weren't prepared to pay me. They thought I was easy.

"My managers – and they were against me – linked me with the promoters and tried to get as much work as possible out of me, with no money. When I said that I wanted paying in advance they told me not to bother to turn up and they posted bouncers on the doors to keep me out. I even tried to get in but I couldn't. I didn't even want the money for myself, it was the group then. Now I DO need money.

"My agents booked me dates, and signed my name for me, without my knowledge. When I refused to play those dates they gave the stories to the national press who lapped it all up."

OPINIONS

Then, Jim talked about another subject. Opinions of him, by the fans, by the press, and by the rest of show business.

"People say I'm big-headed. But in fact I'm not – I'm a believer in the star seniority system. I believe that a star of my status should be treated with the respect that status deserves. I've been misquoted on that.

"My ambition, professionally, is to be on the same par as Elvis Presley or the Beatles. I'm not interested in a career on the scale of Gerry, or Billy J. Kramer. That's all very nice, but if my career can't be as big as the Beatles, then I'm not interested in a career.

"With me it's all or nothing. Unless I can have twenty suits in my wardrobe, then I'll just knock around in blue jeans. I came to this country with one pair of pants, one pair of shoes and one shirt. I'll leave that way if necessary, but I don't want anybody else pushing me around and treating me like dirt.

"I'm just about getting bookings now, after all that bad publicity. And I'll keep them. I would have kept that entire tour with Robert Stigwood which he had planned with me on the top – even if I had been cheated I would have gone on to the last show, and then left this country.

"As it was, Stigwood was scared of me not turning up so he hired Chuck Berry, who didn't turn up, and a lot of money was lost. I would have turned up for every date.

"I like touring though, especially with artists from whom I can learn. I learn from all the stars that I work with. A little bit of everything rubs off on me. But I don't think I've ever been genuinely influenced by anybody.

"That is, except when I was a lot younger. Then I was all for James Dean. One day, when I had my black leather jacket, washed out jeans, motor-bike, and bleached hair, I rode into a Hollywood bar. I walked in, and seated there were half a dozen exact replicas of myself. I rode out, back home, and washed my hair. I kept original from then on!

204

MIX UP

"I'm broke, because I've had no work recently. And as for my records, well, there's such a mix up that nobody knows what's happening about royalties yet. After my money for 'Hold Me', I don't know what's happening.

"The biggest mistake I made in my career was to refuse a tour with Arthur Howes. He's a great promoter, and I refused it because I didn't understand British money then. I regret that.

"And the biggest break was meeting Jack Good in the States, where he signed me up for the 'Around The Beatles' show.

But what Jim said next could well strike deep into the hearts of his fans. "I've even drawn up plans for leaving the country – and a list of the reasons why." Jim then produced a sheaf of documents, all signed, sealed and not yet delivered.

"But if I DO leave it, it won't be the fault of the teenagers and the people who buy my discs. They're great."

Jim was on his way to becoming a rock'n'roll tragedy. Blessed with a distinctively impressive voice, considerable charisma, good looks, and a fine songwriting talent, his "personal demons" would ensure, over the next few years – then decades – a succession of broken tours, many managers (no-one doubted his talent or potential for superstardom), and a handful of very good records. The biggest blow would fall this following February when the pants-splitting incident at the ABC Luton would lead to a ban on performances in all major theatre chains and both ITV and BBC TV channels.

I interviewed two more Californians that week, but this pair was more grounded than Proby. Dick St. John and Deedee Sperling, alias Dick & Deedee, who'd greatly impressed me and about two million others with "The Mountain's High" three years back and who were still scoring modest US hits, were currently in Billboard's Top 20 with "Thou Shalt Not Steal". They were an attractive ex-couple, and Dick explained that their unique vocal sound was a "sandwich" concocted in the studio – Dick sang high falsetto and low register, Deedee sang in the middle. I got on so well with them that we hung out during their UK trip. One memorable occasion was at the Royal Garden Hotel in Kensington where Burt Bacharach was throwing a big party. It was a splendid event: Dusty Springfield was there, plenty more British and American stars, Brian Jones getting tired and emotional. Halfway through the party the news broke that Sam Cooke had been shot dead, putting a major damper on Burt's celebrations.

Dick St. John had an interesting take on the British Invasion earlier that year:

> *"...so many American groups and artistes suffered when the British boom hit. In fact almost every white act suffered both in popularity and record sales. If they say they didn't, well, they're covering up. Every radio station was playing British tunes and groups all the time. We didn't release a disc then. It wouldn't have sold. We just kept touring.*
>
> *"The only artists it helped were the coloured American groups and stars because the stations that played Rhythm & Blues didn't play white American music, nor would they play British music. The Tamla label especially did very well out if it. Now, things have calmed down a bit more..."*

It was now the end of 1964, possibly the most important year ever for British pop music. We published our usual end-of-the-year surveys, and the event-by-event diary of the year was written by a familiar name now freelancing for us: Richard Green, aka "The Beast (666)", now no longer working for NME, and currently cosying up to Peter Jones at DeHems. Beastliness was to follow…

The top ten record artists for singles in the UK for 1964 were:

UK
Jim Reeves
The Beatles
The Bachelors
Roy Orbison
The Searchers

Cliff Richard
The Rolling Stones
Manfred Mann
The Hollies
The Dave Clark Five.

So why was Jim Reeves at the top? I had to explain in an editorial:

BEFORE any comment on these chart results, a word of explanation on how they were compiled. The chart used was of course the "Record Retailer" top 50, published every week in the RM. Each chart entry was then given a certain number of points, depending on which positions it reached during its spell in the top 50. The points system, of course, is based on fifty points for a week on top, and down to one point for a week at number fifty. Thus, with all the positions reached by each chart entry added together, the final total is reached.

Although this is OBVIOUSLY not a guide to best-selling discs, we at the Record Mirror think that these charts are of considerable interest to you, the reader, as you will see just which discs were the most successful chart-wise.

Thus, although a certain disc, e.g. 'A Hard Day's Night' may be well below 'The Wedding' in the single discs category, this means that the Beatles shot up very quickly to the top spot, accumulating a very small number of points on the way up. When they reached the top the disc sold in such vast quantities, that the disc dropped from the top spot relatively quickly. Whereas 'The Wedding' gradually climbed up, remained there for a long time, and took its time going down.

And so it was with the late Jim Reeves' singles "I Love You Because" and the posthumous hit "I Won't Forget You" – they lingered and they won, like the tortoise and the hare. In America the top ten artists for 1964 were:

<u>USA</u>
The Beatles
The Four Seasons,
The Dave Clark Five,
The Beach Boys
Bobby Vinton
Jan & Dean
Elvis Presley
The Impressions
Marvin Gaye
The Supremes.

I couldn't help commenting on those results either:

THERE can't be enough adjectives in the dictionary to describe the overwhelming success of the Beatles in this poll. Although they had over twice as many top fifty entries as their nearest rivals, the Four Seasons, the Beatles have won by a margin that may never again be repeated.

As a comparison, the top artists last year were the Four Seasons with a total of one thousand four hundred and odd points. This means that not only the Beatles, but the Seasons themselves, and the third contender, Britain's Dave Clark Five beat the last year's top total.

The points totals referred to were a staggering 5324 for the Beatles, with the Seasons at 1907, and the DC5 scoring 1856. In the UK (using the same points system), Jim Reeves had scored 2391, the Beatles 2098, and the Bachelors 1727. What a year! And the music was getting better and better.

Isadore Green, *Record Mirror* founder and editor from 1954-1961 (left) with actor and comedian Ben Lyon in 1958. *Rex Features*

Jimmy Watson, *New Record Mirror* editor from 1961-1964 (above) on a *Thank Your Lucky Stars!* judging panel, together with guitarist/ 'one man orchestra' Wout Steenhius, and Starlite Artists' supremo Peter Walsh. *NJ personal collection*

Record Mirror's Peter Jones (left) in 1958 interviewing Johnnie Ray. Jones was later editor of Record Mirror from 1964-1977. *Rex Features*

Apollo Music's office boy-turned- pop star Bobby Shafto (above) happily enlists in *New Record Mirror's* dynamic publicity machine. *Rex Features*

Joe Brown with help from Pamela Blee (left) manages to flog a few copies of *New Record Mirror* outside 116 Shaftesbury Avenue in 1962. *Rex Features*

Left to right: Guy Stevens, Norman Jopling and Dick Brittan aboard *SMS Royal Daffodil* on Whit Saturday, 1st June 1963 for the Jerry Lee Lewis-starring *Rock Across The Channel* event. *Rex Features*

The Beatles in January 1964 at the George V Hotel in Paris, with *Melody Maker's* Mike Hennessey (seated) and legendary lensman Dezo Hoffmann. *NJ personal collection*

Record Mirror inaugurated a (short-lived) award imaginatively titled "The Topper", for records which reached No. 1 in the UK chart. Below, NJ and top EMI executive Arthur Muxlowe bathe in the radiance of "The Topper" presented for the Supremes' "Baby Love" late in 1964. *Rex Features*

Left to right: soul music pioneer Dave Godin, Norman Jopling, and Motown supremo Berry Gordy Jr. at the first Tamla-Motown press reception at EMI House in September 1964. *NJ personal collection*

Record Mirror / NEMS / Radio Luxembourg co-promotion in February 1965. With Elkie Brooks (celebrating NJ's 21st birthday en route to Luxembourg); with Billy J. Kramer; with Gerry Marsden; with Dodie West and Radio Luxembourg DJs Barry Alldis and Chris Denning; (opposite) with the NEMS team being entertained in-flight by their press officer Tony Barrow. *All photographs Dezo Hoffmann, Rex Features*

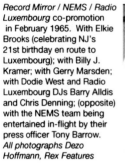

Below: with Johnny Terry of the Drifters at a Decca Records press reception in April 1965. *Rex Features*

With Paul McCartney on the set of Help! at Twickenham in May 1965. *NJ personal collection*

With Paul McCartney and Gail Forsythe on the set of Help! at Twickenham in May 1965. *NJ personal collection*

With Scott Walker at a Philips Records press reception for the Walker Brothers in April 1966. *Rex Features*

Interviewing the Four Tops at the NEMS office in Argyll Street, London, November 1966. *NJ personal collection*

(Left) Trevor Churchill, Dave Godin, and Terry Chappell outside the original *Soul City* record shop in Deptford, South London in January 1967. *Rex Features*

NJ in New York, September 1972. *Norman Jopling personal collection*

RECORD MIRROR CHARTS PAGE

CASHBOX TOP 50

AIR MAILED FROM NEW YORK

1 HOUSE OF THE RISING SUN*
 (1) Animals (MGM)
2 WHERE DID OUR LOVE GO*
 (3) Supremes (Motown)
3 EVERYBODY LOVES SOMEBODY*
 (4) Dean Martin (Reprise)
4 BREAD AND BUTTER*
 (5) Newbeats (Hickory)
5 A HARD DAYS NIGHT
 (6) The Beatles (Capitol)
6 UNDER THE BOARDWALK*
 (7) Drifters (Atlantic)
7 G.T.O.*
 (8) Ronnie & Daytonas (Mala)
8 OH, PRETTY WOMAN*
 (2) Roy Orbison (Monument)
9 BECAUSE*
 (7) Dave Clark Five (Epic)
10 MAYBE I KNOW*
 (14) Lesley Gore (Mercury)
11 SELFISH ONE*
 (18) Jackie Ross (Chess)
12 MAYBELLENE*
 (12) Johnny Rivers (Imperial)
13 REMEMBER (WALKIN' IN THE SAND)*
 (23) Shangri-las (Red Bird)
14 CLINGING VINE*
 (9) Bobby Vinton (Epic)
15 C'MON AND SWIM*
 (10) Bobby Freeman (Autumn)
16 HOW DO YOU DO IT*
 (26) Gerry & The Pacemakers (Laurie)
17 HAUNTED HOUSE*
 (16) Gene Simmons (Hi)
18 WALK DON'T RUN 64*
 (15) Ventures (Dolton)
19 SAVE IT FOR ME
 (21) Four Seasons (Philips)
20 IT HURTS TO BE IN LOVE*
 (29) Gene Pitney (Musicor)
21 YOU NEVER CAN TELL*
 (15) Chuck Berry (Chess)
22 DANCING IN THE STREET
 (28) Martha & Vandellas (Gordy)
23 IN THE MISTY MOONLIGHT*
 (19) Jerry Wallace (Challenge)
24 FUNNY
 (27) Joe Hinton (Back Beat)

25 IT'S ALL OVER NOW*
 (10) Rolling Stones (London)
26 DO WAH DIDDY DIDDY*
 (1) Manfred Mann (Ascot)
27 AND I LOVE HER*
 (14) Beatles (Capitol)
28 BABY I NEED YOUR LOVIN'*
 (28) Four Tops (Motown)
29 WE'LL SING IN THE SUNSHINE
 (42) Gale Garnett (RCA)
30 OUT OF SIGHT
 (2) James Brown (Smash)
31 WISHIN' AND HOPIN'*
 (12) Dusty Springfield (Philips)
32 I'M ON THE OUTSIDE (LOOKING IN)*
 (38) Little Anthony & Imperials (DCP)
33 SUCH A NIGHT*
 (17) Elvis Presley (RCA Victor)
34 RAG DOLL*
 (26) Four Seasons (Philips)
35 JUST BE TRUE*
 (37) Gene Chandler (Constellation)
36 SAY YOU
 (38) Ronnie Dove (Diamond)
37 SOMEDAY WE'RE GONNA LOVE AGAIN*
 (47) Searchers (Kapp)
38 MATCHBOX*
 (3) Beatles (Capitol)
39 YOU'LL NEVER GET TO HEAVEN*
 (43) Dionne Warwick (Scepter)
40 RHYTHM
 (4) Major Lance (Okeh)
41 PEOPLE SAY*
 (22) Dixie Cups (Red Bird)
42 (YOU DON'T KNOW) HOW GLAD I AM*
 (24) Nancy Wilson (Capitol)
43 AIN'T SHE SWEET*
 (25) Beatles (Atco)
44 ALWAYS TOGETHER
 (31) Al Martino (Capitol)
45 THE LITTLE OLD LADY (FROM PASADENA)*
 (33) Jan & Dean (Liberty)
46 STEAL AWAY*
 (44) Jimmy Hughes (Fame)
47 I'LL CRY INSTEAD*
 (33) Beatles (Capitol)
48 WHEN YOU LOVED ME
 (5) Brenda Lee (Decca)
49 WORRY
 (43) Johnny Tillotson (MGM)
50 HE'S IN TOWN
 (1) Tokens (Philips)

* An asterisk denotes record released in Britain.

A blue dot denotes new entry.

TOP TWENTY 5 YEARS AGO

1 ONLY SIXTEEN
 (1) Craig Douglas
2 LIVIN' DOLL
 (2) Cliff Richard
3 LONELY BOY
 (3) Paul Anka
4 CHINA TEA
 (5) Russ Conway
5 HERE COMES SUMMER
 (7) Jerry Keller
6 BATTLE OF NEW ORLEANS
 (5) Lonnie Donegan
7 HEART OF A MAN
 (8) Frankie Vaughan
8 FORTY MILES OF BAD ROAD
 (12) Duane Eddy
9 LIPSTICK ON YOUR COLLAR
 (4) Connie Francis
10 MONA LISA
 (11) Conway Twitty

11 SOMEONE
 (6) Johnny Mathis
12 JUST A LITTLE TOO MUCH/SWEETER THAN YOU
 (9) Ricky Nelson
13 DREAM LOVER
 (10) Bobby Darin
14 PLENTY GOOD LOVIN'
 (19) Connie Francis
15 TILL I KISSED YOU
 (—) Everly Bros.
16 ROULETTE
 (13) Russ Conway
17 THREE BELLS
 (16) The Browns
18 PEGGY SUE GOT MARRIED
 (—) Buddy Holly
19 JUST KEEP IT UP
 (—) Dee Clark
20 BIG HUNK O' LOVE
 (17) Elvis Presley

BRITAIN'S TOP LPs

1 A HARD DAY'S NIGHT
 (2) Beatles (Parlophone)
2 THE ROLLING STONES
 (1) The Rolling Stones (Decca)
3 GENTLEMAN JIM
 (3) Jim Reeves (RCA Victor)
4 WONDERFUL LIFE
 (5) Cliff Richard (Columbia)
5 THE BACHELORS & 16 GREAT SONGS
 (4) Bachelors (Decca)
6 WEST SIDE STORY
 (6) Sound Track (CBS)
7 MOONLIGHT AND ROSES
 (8) Jim Reeves (RCA Victor)
8 KISSIN' COUSINS
 (7) Elvis Presley (RCA Victor)
9 WITH THE BEATLES
 (9) The Beatles (Parlophone)
10 A TOUCH OF VELVET
 (9) Jim Reeves (RCA Victor)
11 GOOD 'N' COUNTRY
 (12) Jim Reeves (RCA Victor)
12 BUDDY HOLLY SHOWCASE
 (10) Buddy Holly (Coral)
13 A GIRL CALLED DUSTY
 (15) Dusty Springfield (Philips)
14 GOD BE WITH YOU
 (12) Jim Reeves (RCA Victor)
15 IT'S THE SEARCHERS
 (11) The Searchers (Pye)
16 IN DREAMS
 (18) Roy Orbison (London)
17 JAZZ SEBASTIAN BACH
 (14) Swingle Singers (Philips)
18 DANCE WITH THE SHADOWS
 (17) The Shadows (Columbia)
19 PRESENTING DIONNE WARWICK
 (20) Dionne Warwick (Pye Int)
20 HE'LL HAVE TO GO
 (16) Jim Reeves (RCA Victor)

BRITAIN'S TOP EPs

1 FIVE BY FIVE
 (1) The Rolling Stones (Decca)
2 LONG, TALL SALLY
 (2) The Beatles (Parlophone)
3 WONDERFUL LIFE
 (3) Cliff Richard (Columbia)
4 FROM THE HEART
 (6) Jim Reeves (RCA Victor)
5 THE ROLLING STONES
 (4) The Rolling Stones (Decca)
6 PETER, PAUL & MARY
 (8) Peter, Paul & Mary (Warner Bros.)
7 IT'S OVER
 (12) Roy Orbison (London)
8 ALL MY LOVING
 (7) The Beatles (Parlophone)
9 LOVE IN LAS VEGAS
 (15) Elvis Presley (RCA)
10 WELCOME TO MY WORLD
 (10) Jim Reeves (RCA)
11 THE BACHELORS VOL. 2
 (10) The Bachelors (Decca)
12 SPIN WITH THE PENNIES
 (—) Four Pennies (Philips)
13 THE BEST OF CHUCK BERRY
 (20) Chuck Berry (Pye)
14 ON STAGE
 (9) The Merseybeats (Fontana)
15 C'EST FAB
 (7) Françoise Hardy (Pye)
16 LAWRENCE OF ARABIA
 (16) Sound Track (Colpix)
17 THOSE BRILLIANT SHADOWS
 (13) The Shadows (Columbia)
18 WALKIN' ALONE
 (14) Richard Anthony (Columbia)
19 SONGS TO WARM THE HEART Vol 2
 (—) Jim Reeves (RCA)
20 IN DREAMS
 (—) Roy Orbison (London)

BRITAIN'S TOP 50

NATIONAL CHART COMPILED BY THE RECORD RETAILER

1 YOU REALLY GOT ME
 (2) The Kinks (Pye)
2 HAVE I THE RIGHT
 (1) Honeycombs (Pye)
3 I WON'T FORGET YOU
 (2) Jim Reeves (RCA Victor)
4 I WOULDN'T TRADE YOU FOR THE WORLD
 (5) The Bachelors (Decca)
5 THE CRYING GAME
 (4) Dave Berry (Decca)
6 DO WAH DIDDY DIDDY
 (3) Manfred Mann (HMV)
7 I'M INTO SOMETHING GOOD
 (8) Herman's Hermits (Columbia)
8 RAG DOLL
 (7) Four Seasons (Philips)
9 AS TEARS GO BY
 (7) Marianne Faithfull (Decca)
10 A HARD DAY'S NIGHT
 (6) Beatles (Parlophone)
11 IT'S FOR YOU
 (10) Cilla Black (Parlophone)
12 SHE'S NOT THERE
 (—) The Zombies (Decca)
13 SUCH A NIGHT
 (14) Elvis Presley (RCA)
14 I LOVE YOU BECAUSE
 (9) Jim Reeves (RCA-Victor)
15 I GET AROUND
 (10) Beach Boys (Capitol)
16 THE WEDDING
 (19) Julie Rogers (Mercury)
17 IT'S ALL OVER NOW
 (11) Rolling Stones (Decca)
18 WHERE DID OUR LOVE GO
 (21) Supremes (Stateside)
19 CALL UP THE GROUPS
 (16) Barron Knights (Columbia)
20 TOBACCO ROAD
 (18) Nashville Teens (Decca)
21 EVERYBODY LOVES SOMEBODY
 (22) Dean Martin (Reprise)
22 RHYTHM 'N' GREENS
 (13) Shadows (Columbia)
23 YOU NEVER CAN TELL
 (17) Chuck Berry (Pye)
24 I SHOULD HAVE KNOWN BETTER
 (15) The Naturals (Parlophone)
25 TOGETHER
 (20) P. J. Proby (Decca)
26 I JUST DON'T KNOW WHAT TO DO WITH MYSELF
 (26) Dusty Springfield (Philips)

27 ON THE BEACH
 (21) Cliff Richard (Columbia)
28 IT'S GONNA BE ALRIGHT
 (25) Gerry & The Pacemakers (Columbia)
29 IT'S ONLY MAKE BELIEVE
 (24) Billy Fury (Decca)
30 IS IT TRUE
 (41) Brenda Lee (Brunswick)
31 I FOUND OUT THE HARD WAY
 (24) Four Pennies (Philips)
32 YOU'LL NEVER GET TO HEAVEN
 (39) Dionne Warwick (Pye Int)
33 HAPPINESS
 (43) Ken Dodd (Columbia)
34 TWELVE STEPS TO LOVE
 (34) Brian Poole & The Tremeloes (Decca)
35 FROM A WINDOW
 (36) Billy J. Kramer & the Dakotas (Parlophone)
36 OH PRETTY WOMAN
 (—) Roy Orbison (London)
37 MOVE IT BABY
 (47) Simon Scott (Parlophone)
38 HOUSE OF THE RISING SUN
 (12) Animals (Columbia)
39 BREAD AND BUTTER
 (—) The Newbeats (Hickory)
40 THE LETTER
 (33) The Long, and the Short (Decca)
41 WISHIN AND HOPIN
 (31) The Merseybeats (Fontana)
42 THE GIRL FROM IPANEMA
 (—) Stan Getz & Joao Gilberto (Verve)
43 THE FERRIS WHEEL
 (38) Everly Bros. (Warner Bros.)
44 SEVEN DAFFODILS
 (35) The Mojos (Decca)
45 (THE BEST PART OF) BREAKING UP
 (47) Ronettes (London)
46 WHAT AM I TO YOU
 (27) Kenny Lynch (HMV)
47 SHAME, SHAME, SHAME
 (3) Jimmy Reed (Stateside)
48 SEVEN GOLDEN DAFFODILS
 (42) The Cherokees (Columbia)
49 KELLY
 (45) Wayne Gibson (Pye)
50 LOVE'S MADE A FOOL OF YOU
 (—) Buddy Holly (Coral)

1965

The beginning of 1965 saw some major personnel changes at Record Mirror. News editor and feature writer Barry May, after less than a year on the job, was booted out, and Richard Green ("The Beast") installed as a full-time RM journalist. This was the result of Richard's scheming and schmoozing of Peter Jones at DeHems, Barry not being such a heavy-duty DeHems habitué. Despite his beastly reputation, Richard was a talented and enterprising journalist and would heroically drink himself and everyone else under the table for a good story. Another point in his favour was that he socialised with the artists much more than me or Peter.

Our other editorial addition was Tony Hall, who would write us a terrific regular column over the next few years. Tony was the same age as Peter Jones, and was also tall, dark and handsome and looked great in a tonic suit. He was a label manager and DJ, mainly for Decca, was an expert on a wide spectrum of music from jazz through R&B, blues and pop and he picked up on new trends quicker than anyone, and he had more contacts than the rest of us put together. He was also a fine enthusiastic writer and was respected throughout the music business. We were lucky in having him. Also like Peter Jones, it was rumoured he'd had affairs with various starlets, which didn't hurt his reputation.

Our other major change involved gung-ho advertising manager and sometime journalist Brian Harvey. One day he was there, next day he was gone. "Why?" I asked Bob Bedford, who worked in Brian's

217

department. Bob explained that although Record Mirror had been filled with advertising since Brian's tenure, he'd given everyone so many discounts and freebies that the game wasn't worth the candle: we'd added extra pages, which cost money, because of the extra advertising, but we didn't get the money that we expected from it. The decision to get rid of Brian had been Junor's, made after consulting with Decca's Mr Frankham, who still visited us regularly every Thursday to go over "the books" with Pat Farnham.

Brian was replaced by Barry Hatcher, with Bob as his deputy. Barry was a bright chirpy guy but didn't stay long either. Thirty-five years later when Barry was a top executive at Sony Records he told me with some residual bitterness that he had been elbowed out by Roy Burden who had taken against him and worked continuously towards his downfall. Barry added that he had been very unhappy at Record Mirror. I was amazed, not just because I liked Roy enormously, but because, as far as I knew, no-one at RM ever had an inkling of these Machiavellian tendencies.

Another personnel change occurred with my old mentor Ian Dove, who left his job as Features Editor at NME to join the music trade weekly Record Retailer as joint editor in tandem with the soon to be legendary-in-his-own-lunchtime Frank Smythe, all of which sounded like a peculiar arrangement. This arrangement had taken place following the death of Roy Parker, director, editor and founder of Record Retailer, which would later change its name to Music Week.

Early that year I did a track-by-track review of the new Stones album "Rolling Stones Vol. 2", had a quick word with the group and a long rave in print. I profiled Jimmy Radcliffe, a Gene Pitney protégé currently scoring a minor hit with Bacharach-David's "Long After Tonight Is All Over". And I also did a couple of interviews with Del Shannon – *My Success Changed My Friends* and *The Unseen Side Of Del Shannon* – over to promote his new UK and US Top Ten smash hit "Keep Searchin'", a terrific record and his best since "Runaway", which was saying something, especially considering his high-quality singles output since '61. Del had also penned a catchy song called "I Go To Pieces", shooting up the charts in the USA for the hot UK duo Peter and Gordon but which, mysteriously, wouldn't click here for them. Peter and Gordon had previously been the lucky

218

recipients of some Lennon-McCartney originals, including a song called "Nobody I Know", the first line of which had been dashed off somewhat thoughtlessly, by Paul or John: "Nobody I know could love you more than me…" But the real Del Shannon story wasn't in either of my interviews, and wouldn't be known for many years; the story of one of the most spectacularly inept and crooked management deals ever to handicap a major star, and its effect on an intense yet vulnerable performer whose mood swings would eventually lead to gunshot suicide.

Currently also in London were the Righteous Brothers, latest recipients of the Phil Spector magic following on from the Crystals, the Ronettes and sundry smaller acts. "You've Lost That Lovin' Feeling" was heading for No. 1 in the USA and the UK, but Bill and Bobby weren't at all happy with Cilla Black's cover version. I interviewed them at their hotel and they were both stern-faced and adamant: *Sorry Cilla, said the Righteous Brothers to RM's Norman Jopling, but WE DON'T LIKE YOUR RECORD!* Worth quoting a couple of paragraphs from the article:

> *"What do we think of Cilla's version of 'You've Lost That Lovin' Feeling' said America's Righteous Brothers when I posed them the question. "Well, we don't like it… for a start we don't think she sings the song in the way that it's meant to be sung. When we first heard that Cilla Black had recorded it we were pleased and complimented – especially as Cilla was one of Britain's top singers. Also, we went mad over her recording of 'You're My World'.*
>
> *"But it was quite a while after we arrived here before we heard Cilla's version – and we just don't think that there's enough, well, soul there. Can't say any more about it, really…"*
>
> *Then Bill told me how the pair met and how they got their unusual and distinctive name.*
>
> *"We both had separate groups to start with, and as we both worked around the same area, we would go and see each other on our nights off. We liked the way the other one worked, so eventually we joined forces. But we*

didn't have a steady name. Anyway, the audiences we'd play to would be largely coloured. At that time everyone, everything who was hip, with it, switched on, call it what you like, was tagged 'righteous' by the coloured set. And when they started to really dig our sound they'd shout out 'You're really righteous, brothers.' It sounds corny, but that's how we got our name."

The story goes that when Spector first presented the song to Bill Medley (deep-voice) and Bobby Hatfield (high-voice), Bobby realised there was very little for him to sing. "What do I do then?" he demanded. "You go to the bank," Phil replied.

At the end of January I churned out a piece of rubbish titled *Death Of A Dynasty – NJ takes a hard cynical look at the declining beat boom and makes some frank comments.* Every now and then I felt I had to prove myself by writing a 'hard-hitting' piece. As I was no hard-hitter, the result was usually squirmingly bad. The only good thing about it was an accompanying colour picture of Manfred Mann playing a grand piano with the rest of the group standing round it and singing. I was back on more solid ground with *Not So Much A Label*, profiling Guy Stevens's Sue label. It was a straightforward plug piece – Island Records were a regular advertiser, thanks to Guy's insistence – but anyway Sue was hot, so why not?

Latest "bad boys" on the scene were the Pretty Things, a decent enough R&B group following in the footsteps of the Stones and even featuring ex-Rollin' Stone Dick Taylor, but who never quite managed to get the commercial songs. *The Things Hit Back* was the first of several articles I'd pen in defence of the group's mildly boorish behaviour. The Things had read my *Death Of A Dynasty* piece from the previous week, and rightly scoffed at my predictions – which I didn't even believe myself – of a beat boom crash.

My big treat in February was getting to meet and interview Goldie & The Gingerbreads, who'd recently been discovered by the Animals in a New York club, whisked back to the UK, signed by their manager Mike Jeffery and put in a studio with Mickie Most to cut a single called "Can't You Hear My Heartbeat", currently a modest hit. It was a girl-group record but Goldie & Co. weren't a girl group, per se. They were a beat group who happened to be all-female. They played their own instruments on stage. At the beginning of a damp February I dragged the girls to Trafalgar Square for a photo session and interview where we did a lot of running around and yelling and pushing and pulling each other. The girls all wore different varieties of Chelsea boots, black slacks, roll-neck jumpers and suede or leather coats. They also wore wigs, like the black girl groups did. They were sparky chicks and I fell for them all, particularly Goldie. Here's an extract from the article:

RM w/e 13th February 1965

FOUR TOUGH BIRDS

THERE isn't much that scares Goldie And The Gingerbreads. Being an all-girl group in a male-dominated scene helps to toughen up the so-called weaker sex.

However, there was one thing – or things – which frightened the girls considerably. Namely, pigeons. I took the girls along to Trafalgar Square for a photo session, when swarms of the feathery beasts descended upon the girls and almost buried them.

Screams of horror and confusion resulted and eventually both the group and the pigeons were pacified. Still, one couldn't blame the feathered birds for fancying four birds of the less feathery variety. For Goldie & the Gingerbreads are four very attractive young Brooklyn girls, brought from the States by the Animals during their recent U.S. tour.

"The reason we don't like pigeons", explained Goldie, "is that in New York they found that pigeons were disease carriers. So the authorities poisoned them all. Now every New Yorker is frightened of pigeons..." Goldie went on to explain how they had been discovered in New York by the Animals.

COLOURED

"Well, we were playing in a little club and the Animals were passing by. They heard us playing and thought it must be a coloured group. When they told us this afterwards, we were very complimented.

"Anyway, they came in, and pounced on us, saying 'Have you a manager? Have you a recording contract? Are you signed up? When did you last see your father?' and all that.

"We hadn't anything really. We did make a record once but then the Beatles crashed the scene and it got lost. So they took pity on us and brought us over.

"We didn't really like the Beatles until we learned they wrote all their own material, but when we met them they weren't at all conceited. In fact it was Ringo that got us on 'Not Only...But Also' on BBC-2. Other groups that we like are the Stones, Them, and of course the Animals.

"We try to get a belting soulful sound – our record 'Can't You Hear My Heartbeat' isn't really us, but we're really pleased with it."

Goldie and the group have been together now for almost two years – all of them except Goldie were trained musicians playing in male groups before. Goldie was a secretary.

"But I was a clown. Everyone would say to me, 'Goldie, you should be in show business.' I never guessed I would be. But I met up with the other girls, one by one, and we decided to form an all-girl group.

The piece continued with the obligatory 'no-time-for-boyfriends' declaration, and described their various ambitions...which included the equally obligatory 'getting married'. But despite touring for the next three years in the UK and Europe supporting the biggest British groups, the Gingerbreads never made it again on to the UK charts. Nor on to the US charts – Mickey Most, weighing the odds, re-cut "Can't You Hear My Heartbeat" with Herman's Hermits, just off their initial No. 13 US hit with "I'm Into Something Good". In America "...Heartbeat" rocketed the Hermits to No. 2 and launched them on a superstar run of eleven Top Ten hits, sinking the Gingerbreads' version in their home territory. To be fair, Most only released the Hermits' version in the UK as the B-side to "Silhouettes". Nevertheless, for the next three years Goldie & the Gingerbreads became a permanent fixture on the UK scene, stars without a big hit. Someone should have bothered: they were the first all-female group to perform on Ready, Steady, Go! playing their own instruments, they were talented and attractive and sounded great. Goldie & the Gingerbreads – Carol, Margo, Ginger – would return to the States in '68 but thereafter soon split up. Goldie would become Genya Ravan and keep singing and producing, Carol and Ginger would form all-girl Isis.

EMI announced that Berry Gordy's roster, previously on their generic Stateside imprint, would now be released on the new Tamla-Motown label, and at the same time Pye Record launched the new Chess label following their spectacular successes over the previous eighteen months. But the Chess heyday was over. They would struggle to get hits in the new, slicker, era of Soul music, competing hopelessly against Gordy's hit factory which was now churning out dozens of million-sellers one after the other. But the party Pye threw for the launch was fun. I spoke to the always-interesting Marshall Chess, son of Chess founder Leonard Chess, to singer Jackie Ross, just off a big US hit with "Selfish One", and most interestedly to Billy Davis, Chess A&R supremo who'd worked with Berry Gordy in Chicago during the Jackie Wilson period in the late '50s, and who now re-iterated a familiar current theme:

> *"I think the chief difference between making pop and R&B records, is what's called 'soul'. I can make pop records but it's a good deal harder making R&B. Of course we have to aim for the commercial market, and I'm afraid I might lose the blues touch if I lean over too far. I have done sometimes. There's not much trouble in finding material for established Chess stars such as Chuck or Bo. But we also keep a look out for songs for the others.*

> *"There is a Chess sound, of course. But basically, R&B is very different from pop. The markets for the two types of discs are really different in the States. That's why the British invasion only harmed American pop artists"*

Billy said more or less exactly what Dick St. John told me two months earlier. Except that Dick, who was white, evidently felt able to say the words "coloured" which was not at that time politically incorrect, and "white", whereas Billy, who was black, omitted those words, referring only to "R&B" and "pop". But they were both talking about the same thing.

In the Sixties one "came of age" at 21, and my coming-of-age, whatever that meant, took place en route to the Grand Duchy of Luxembourg, a tiny and much-overrun (mainly by the German Army) piece of Western Europe squeezed into the corner where Belgium, France and Germany collide, and whose main claim to international fame was its powerful and influential radio station. But Radio Luxembourg had just started to feel the breeze from the offshore UK pirate station Radio Caroline and, anxious to hit back, was wide open to various novel promotional and marketing initiatives. Our circulation manager Roy Burden had handily taken advantage of this and hooked up a deal with Radio Luxembourg and Brian Epstein's NEMS empire, whereby we took several NEMS artists to Luxembourg and devoted a four-page supplement to the event.

Three RM staffers went on the trip – me to write it up, Dezo to take the snaps, and Roy – for the ride. The NEMS artists were Gerry Marsden, Billy J. Kramer, Elkie Brooks, Dodie West and Dutch star Connie Van Bos. Dezo, Roy and I met up with Elkie at London Airport, as it was then, while the others flew out later. I liked Elkie – she was a lot of fun – and when Roy discovered it was my 21st birthday we ordered and sunk several bottles of champagne on the outgoing flight. We were all squiffy when we arrived and stayed that way for just about the entire trip. Luxembourg Airport, which is situated outside the city, is built on a hill and taking off and landing was like using an aircraft carrier – but safer. Amazingly, our visit was headline news in the pop-starved Duchy and we were greeted by a handful of teenage autograph seekers who insisted on my signature despite my feeble bilingual protestations that I was merely a journalist, much to Elkie's amusement.

The impressive city of Luxembourg, built on cliffs, spanning ravines, boasting ancient fortifications, breathtaking bridges – and expensive shops – was freezing. Luckily we were booked into a huge warm, plush five star hotel and spent the next few days in a hazy blur of sightseeing, taxi visits galore to the radio station located just outside the city at all hours day and night, having hundreds of photographs taken by Dezo, enjoying car trips hither and thither courtesy of DJ Chris Denning, eating and drinking in plentiful luxury, running in and out of each other's rooms, and generally having a fine old time. One evening we all wrapped up and trooped to the town's big cinema which was still showing "A Hard Day's Night" – the first time I'd seen it – and which was partly obliterated by the two sets of sub-titles that came half-way up the screen, one in French, the other in German. The men then all went to a strip club, also the first time for me, which was erotically a big let-down but rescued fun-wise when Roy got so sozzled he attempted to pull the star stripper and had to be forcibly restrained.

The NEMS artists were an interesting bunch. I'd never met Gerry, who proved to be a very bright and amiable guy. But with Merseybeat on its way out, he would score only one more UK top 20 hit – "I'll Be There" – although his US chart success would continue for another year. Billy Kramer also had only one hit left in the bag –Bacharach's "Trains And Boats And Planes". Dodie West was just off a small hit with a cover of Little Anthony and the Imperials' Bacharach-inspired "Goin' Out Of My Head", but despite her flourishing future European career would score no more hits despite cutting some fine records. Elkie – even then rated as one of our best female vocalists – would probably have been more than slightly disheartened to know she'd have to wait another twelve years before Leiber and Stoller would launch her decade-long solo chart success in the late '70s and '80s.

RM w/e 6th March 1965
STATION OF THE STARS
SECRETS BEHIND THAT LATE-NIGHT POP
Record Mirror special investigation – Norman Jopling reports

THE way of life of the British contingent of dee-jays at Radio Luxembourg could be compared in a way with Robinson Crusoe. Certainly, the Record Mirror party were welcomed more than any Man Friday would have been.

"After all, we don't see many British people here," said Chris Denning, "And unless you're married, life can be pretty dull..."

The four British dee-jays are a very small percentage of the hundreds of disc jockeys and announcers who work for the five different language broadcasts at Radio Luxembourg. And Luxembourg, as one of the smallest countries in Europe, doesn't offer much in the way of entertainment...

There isn't much in the way of local news either, so when our party arrived, there were big newspaper splashes, the lot. All the works in fact. And there to meet us at the airport were two of the British lads, Barry Alldis and Chris Denning.

Barry Alldis has been with Radio Luxembourg British section for eight years now, and he's the leader of the pack. Barry's a good-looking intense sort of guy who married a Luxembourg girl and settled down in the city of Luxembourg. Chris has been with the station slightly less than a year, and he's only 23, unmarried, and leads a wild sort of life around the Grand Duchy, driving around in a red Mini (they have great prestige on the Continent). I turned an envious shade of green when I saw his Institute of Advanced Motorists badge...

Back in our hotel, Barry and Chris told us about the general set-up at the station, or to more precise, the English language broadcasts.

General Manager – working in London – is Geoffrey Everitt, who was sent to Luxembourg after the war to train a Luxembourg army. He became a part-time dee-jay on a small mid-day programme for British servicemen, built the service up to an enormous peak of efficiency and ended up as General Manager in 1959.

SPONSORED

Most of the programmes are sponsored, some, like the record company programmes, are virtually an entire ad. Money-wise, 1964 was the best year to date with a record return of £640,000. Seven million people listen to Luxembourg in Britain, and the same number listen on the Continent to the English broadcasts, making a total of fourteen million listeners. Radio Luxembourg is also the second biggest industry in Luxembourg, next to steel.

Nearly all the big dee-jays started off in Luxembourg. Pete Murray, David Jacobs, Alan Freeman, Jack Jackson et al. And Jimmy Savile made his name with Luxembourg broadcasts.

Some of the programmes are recorded in London and sent over to Luxembourg, while others – especially request programmes – are performed live. The building which houses the station is a large affair.

"I thought it was a little shack," said Gerry. "But now I've seen it, well, it's huge."

One interesting thing is that the Radio Luxembourg transmitter is situated outside the city, and because of some mountains in the way, reception in Luxembourg is about the same as reception in London!

The other two British dee-jays are Johnny Moran and Bill Hearne. Johnny is 21, quiet, and like the others, completely dedicated to his job. Bill is a Canadian, a big friendly man, imported especially from Canada to be an announcer on the programme. All four dee-jays are great blokes – and just to reassure everyone, their voices really ARE like they sound on Lux...

Perhaps one of the most popular Luxembourg programmes is 'Music In The Night'. This two-hourly show is announced in rotation by the four guys, who sit alone in the studio. In front of them is a table equipped with levers, buttons (including the one that makes the famous Luxembourg gong. That one fascinated Billy...) and a powerful microphone. There are also two clocks – one showing London time, and one showing Luxembourg time.

REQUESTS

The discs and running order are prepared in London, but none of the dee-jays use written scripts. Just ad lib... in the studio next door is a technician whose job it is to put on the records and tapes. And of course all the ads.

Another aspect of Luxembourg is the mountain of requests and letters that the dee-jays receive. Some letters are really very funny. One girl, asking for a Beatles disc, wrote "...and I didn't like cheese until I found out Paul loved it. Now I quite like it."

Ace advertiser Horace Batchelor is often the butt of letters. "We know how to spell Keynsham," wrote one listener, but how do we spell Bristol?" Many listeners wrote to Horace saying he was an excellent mimic, after hearing his pools successes on the radio. Nevertheless I can assure any sceptics they were genuine, although Horace has taken them off the air now.

All in all, the English language section of Radio Luxembourg is efficient, entertaining, and far less complicated than you might think – at least at the actual Luxembourg end. The London studios at Mayfair seem to be in a constant turmoil day and night, with such personages as Jimmy Savile rushing to and fro.

But next time you return, weary from a night out, and with your last remaining ounces of strength switch on the *radio to 208, spare a thought for the dee-jay, propping up his eyelids with matchsticks, earphones around his head, and ad-libbing like mad for you...*

Chris Denning was particularly amiable, once even driving me across the border to Germany so I could get a German stamp in my passport, as that kind of thing mattered to me then. On one bitterly cold evening I went bar-hopping with Dodie West and, both of us tipsy, decided to visit Chris who was presenting 'Music In The Night'. It was around two in the morning and snowing and we staggered from the taxi and into the radio station, made our way to the broadcast studio and began waving to Chris through the glass panel in the door. He was on air but straightaway beckoned us in and immediately announced to the listening millions that some visitors had dropped by: "...and here's Norman Jopling from Record Mirror to introduce the next record", thrusting a 45 single – "Eddie My Love" by The Teen Queens – into my hand and pointing to the microphone. Luckily I was so inebriated that my natural inhibitions vanished and I made a reasonable job of announcing the record, even cracking a feeble joke about it being on the R&B label "...but which doesn't stand for rhythm & blues, but Rita and Benny... from Stamford Hill". When I got back to London, half a dozen people including some old school chums called to say they'd heard me on air, which surprised me somewhat to think that so many people must be frittering the night away glued to groovy Radio Luxembourg.

The reason I was so impressed with Chris Denning's Advanced Motorists' badge was that I'd passed my un-advanced driving test the previous month and bought myself a nippy Mini-Cooper with sunroof. So now I had wheels again, which was all very well, but I was also going out every night and drinking every night. Drinking and driving in the mid-'60s, though not acceptable, did not quite carry the stigma (and penalties) it does now. There were no breathalysers, neither had the seat belt laws been passed, so the death-and-serious-injury toll was horrific. But as far as I was concerned I could now visit even more pubs, clubs, parties, go further afield and generally speed the whole lifestyle up several notches, which I straightaway proceeded to do.

1965 was the year that folk music, which had been enjoying an international revival for over ten years, would enter the UK pop mainstream and add its considerable – mainly lyrical – influence to the spectacular artistic flowering of British and American pop. Unlike rhythm & blues which was essentially populist, folk had become elitist and intellectual. Its British practitioners were no longer posing as horny-handed sons of the soil singing traditional songs, or in America railroad-riding bums protesting against depression iniquities. The UK folk establishment were mainly well-educated socialists for whom "authenticity" was the byword. They considered themselves keepers of a sacred flame. But there was also a new UK folk movement, followers of the guitar genius Davy Graham, with a more modern agenda – and many of them wrote their own, often more personal, folk songs. And this new folk scene, thriving in the coffee bars, cellars and upstairs pub rooms in London, New York and every British and American city with a college campus, now had its genius. For the past three years Bob Dylan had gradually built up an international following and currently had three albums in the UK LP chart: "The Freewheelin' Bob Dylan", "The Times They Are A Changin'", and "Another Side Of Bob Dylan". In America his success was even more profound – he was considered the legitimate heir to Woody Guthrie and the musical spokesman for the black Civil Rights movement. No self-respecting pop star anywhere could now leave Dylan's name off his list of favourite artists.

Dylan's American record label Columbia had just done a very clever thing in the UK and bought up the small independent Oriole label, thus obtaining a West End office, a pressing-plant, a distribution set-up and some knowledgeable staff in one fell swoop. What Oriole didn't have was consistently commercial product or lots of money, and Columbia, itself owned by the giant US CBS-TV network, did. Because EMI Records in Britain already used and owned the 'Columbia' name, the new label in the UK was christened CBS, and overnight became a major player in the British recording industry. CBS decided to market Dylan not only as an esoteric folkie selling LPs to students and folk fans, but as a pop artist and singles chart-maker selling to the masses. The tiny UK specialist folk label Transatlantic was currently enjoying a minor hit with the Ian Campbell Folk Group's stately version of

230

Dylan's anthemic "The Times They Are A-Changin'", so CBS rush-released Dylan's own version of the song as his debut single.

But Dylan's real competition wasn't the traditional sound of the Ian Campbell Folk Group with or without a Dylan song, but an artist much closer to Dylan's own look and sound. Pye Records had just signed Donovan Leitch, superficially a Bob Dylan look-and-soundalike, and was rush-releasing his first single, a haunting ballad and original composition titled "Catch The Wind".

Pye threw a press reception in March for Donovan at a less than salubrious rendezvous, and a handful of less than enthusiastic journalists turned up, including myself and arch-cynic Richard Green. Donovan wandered in wearing his Guthrie-esque gear, strapped on an acoustic guitar and clambered up on to the small stage. The press were bored, but slightly curious.

Donovan was a Glaswegian. "What would y'like me to'sing – any subject y'like, topical, whatever…"

No-one said anything at first, then someone shouted out a headline from a current news story. With only a flicker of a pause, Donovan improvised and performed a more than passable folk song on the subject. Now he had everyone's attention. This game went on for about twenty minutes, after which Donovan clambered down to talk to the journalists.He still looked like a Dylan clone, or, to be fair, he may even have been inspired directly by Woody Guthrie, and although there was something slightly risible about Donovan's get-up and his earnestness, there was no denying his talent. He sang and wrote and played guitar beautifully. And he was only 18.

On March 27th 1965, Donovan's "Catch The Wind" hit the Top 50 at number 22 and would eventually reach No.4, Dylan's "The Times They Are A-Changin'" entered at No.36, eventually peaking at No.9, and the following week the Ian Campbell version, which had dropped out of the charts, got enough of a fillip to climb back into the charts for another few weeks. But what only insiders knew was that "The Times They Are A-Changin'" was merely a stop-gap, and that Dylan's first real commercial single had already been recorded and would be released in less than four weeks. It was titled "Subterranean Homesick Blues", it was loosely based on the Chuck Berry song "Too Much Monkey Business", and it was inspired by the artistic and commercial successes of the British R&B-fuelled beat groups, who had reciprocally impressed Bob Dylan. It was performed on electric instruments. It was rock'n'roll. The most important poet-lyricist of his generation had, in effect, already left folk music behind.

Folk-rock was looming, but rhythm & blues was still the staple attraction. My next four *The Great Unknowns* featured Huey 'Piano' Smith, Irma Thomas, Otis Redding, and Maxine Brown. In *America Hits Back With Tamla Motown Attack* I profiled – yet again – the Berry Gordy label stable in preparation for the all-star Tamla-Motown Revue, scheduled to tour the UK the following week. And I caught up with the legendary Larry Williams in a Soho drinking den: "No man, I'm not basically a rock'n'roller," he said straightaway. News to me, but as Larry was now on a soul kick with Johnny 'Guitar' Watson and recording and producing for Okeh in the USA and for Guy Stevens here, it was a forgivable rewrite of history. He was also purportedly one of the most dangerous men in rock'n'roll – or whatever he considered his scene was – so I wasn't about to argue the finer points of musicality with him. In person he was friendly and funny, not least because he'd already banked several hefty royalty cheques for the Beatles' version of his song "Slow Down". Plus, his song "Bad Boy" was due to be released in two months on the US-only "Beatles VI" LP: "Bless those Beatles!" he would say. Here's how Larry explained why he had been wrongly branded a rock'n'roller:

> *"It so happened that the feller who ran my record company (Art Rupe of Specialty Records) had a fixation about one kind of sound. That was the Little Richard sound and the sound on my early records like 'Bony Moronie' and 'Short Fat Fanny'. Everything else that I recorded he wouldn't release! Maybe he was right commercially speaking, but man, after three years of that I was glad to sign up for another record label"*

Even more legendary than Larry were the Drifters, touring here for the first time. I spoke with lead singer Johnny Moore for an article I mystifyingly titled *The Big Daddy Group* and a few days later caught their British debut at the Lyceum – and they were terrific. But, with mentors Leiber and Stoller now departed from Atlantic Records, the Drifters were at the tail end of their twelve-year hit streak and it would be another seven years before their UK chart comeback. Meanwhile, several ex-Drifters were about to form their own versions of the 'Drifters' and tour Britain and Europe: writs would fly and confusion reign.

When the Tamla-Motown Revue did arrive, everyone raved, especially our reviewer Alan Stinton. We also got a huge postbag from enthusiastic readers, and our columnist Tony Hall stated that he "had never enjoyed a show more in his life". There was a lot of argument whether Tamla Motown was R&B, or black pop, or soul…but it didn't much matter when records as great as the Temptations' "My Girl", Martha & The Vandellas' "Nowhere To Run", the Supremes' "Stop In The Name Of Love" and Marvin Gaye's "I'll Be Doggone" were currently flying the Detroit flag. Motown's slogan was "The Sound Of Young America" and there was a growing awareness that Berry Gordy and his artists had propelled black music into the global pop mainstream, leaving behind the blues, which, despite its artistic integrity, reflected an older and more oppressed black experience. But not everyone enjoyed the tour. I spoke to the Kinks in the new office of their publicist Brian Sommerville, who had recently formed his own PR outfit after working for Brian Epstein and handling the Beatles, most famously at their American press conferences.

RM w/e 17th April 1965

'THE TAMLA FANS THAT HATED US'
The Kinks talk to RM's Norman Jopling

GROUPS as a species have calmed down, both in mind, body and music. But there are exceptions. And one such exception is the Kinks, rated as Britain's third most popular outfit after the Beatles and the Stones. The Kinks are raw and uninhibited, straight-talking and pulling no customary punches. They talked to me in Brian Sommerville's office about themselves, and the pop scene in general.

233

"We were disappointed with the Tamla Motown show as a whole," said Dave, "although we weren't put off any of the artists. I think that after such a mammoth build-up, everyone expected something out of this world. We all liked Martha & The Vandellas best" (as did Tony Hall).

"But there was one thing which was pretty unpleasant," said Pete. "During the show we went backstage to have a quick chat with some of the Tamla-Motown stars. Anyway, I wandered into the dressing room and some of the Tamla fans recognised me. Well, they were really nasty. They started carrying on as though I wasn't good enough to be in the same room as the Tamla artists. That was the end in prejudice."

SCREAMERS

Then the Kinks started on about their own fans.

"Of course we take a lot of notice of our fans. The ones who scream, well, they tend to scream more to be noticed than anything else," remarked Pete.

"If we had an audience of one girl, all alone, she wouldn't scream. I personally like to think that the girls who just stand there and quietly listen are more interested in us."

"We also get a lot of satisfaction if there are a lot of blokes in the audience," said Dave, "nothing kinky about that though, most groups realise that blokes dig a group purely on the sound and not on visual effect."

"Then there are the fans who have to take things," said Ray. "The girls take personal possessions and the blokes, for a different reason, take our van and guitars. But some of the girls are really cheeky. We often let loads of them swarm into our backstage dressing room, and we have to keep our eyes open. I caught one girl with a bottle of brandy the other day.

RUDE

"And then there are the rude ones who come up to you and say, 'Sign your autograph here, three times, with love'. They also tell you they want a button from your jacket and proceed to twist it off. Their attitude is they're your bread and butter, therefore you should do what they want."

The Kinks are currently in Denmark for a three-day trip, but they've recently been to Australia where feelings were mixed about them.

"The blokes in Australia try to give out the rock-hard image," said Ray. "Much the same as in the North of England. Naturally the girls are all down-trodden and they look forward to a chance to let off steam at a beat show. Their blokes don't like this. They threw sand and stones at us on the big beaches, so when we tried surfing we had to use a little beach.

"It wasn't used much because the sewers opened out there. We didn't discover that until we were swimming about. Most unpleasant. We turned up for surfing in overcoats and the Australians went berserk, with anger that is. And some bloke spent half an hour explaining about surfing. We weren't really interested by then."

The Kinks will be appearing on 'Thank Your Lucky Stars' on Saturday. They talked about the new spate of 'live' shows.

CLIMAX

"Really, R.S.G. reached its climax some time ago," said Mick. "It's past its peak now. 'Lucky Stars' has got more atmosphere, in fact it's like R.S.G. used to be. The trouble is that R.S.G. has picked audiences. They don't want to hear the groups. They just want to be seen on television. There's no inspiration there to play well live. And anyway, the mikes are all in the wrong place at R.S.G. They're

*everywhere, so they pick up every little sound, whether
or not it's made by the group or the audience."*

*Just before I left the Kinks, Ray started telling the others
off. "Now listen," he said, "and remember that next time
play 'All Day' FASTER than 'You Really Got Me'. That's
how it should be..."*

What I didn't mention in the article were the Kinks' complaints
about the Who's first record "I Can't Explain", currently in the Top
Ten. "I Can't Explain" had been produced by Shel Talmy, who also
produced the Kinks. They were upset with Talmy because they
considered "I Can't Explain" a rip-off of the Kinks' style – and they
blamed Talmy, not the Who.

Also in the current Top Ten was Bob Dylan, who had been signed
to Columbia in '61 by John Hammond, the legendary producer who'd
joined the CBS organisation in '57 after championing and recording
Billie Holiday, Benny Goodman, Count Basie and countless other
jazz and blues acts. Hammond then signed many more major acts to
Columbia, but wouldn't sign his own son, John Hammond Jr. John
Jr. was a friend of Dylan's – they'd even been flatmates – but unlike
Dylan he didn't sing folk. He was a white blues purist, imitating at
first the black traditional country blues singers, and later the Chicago
electric blues. In 1963, after appearing at the Newport Blues Festival,
he got signed to the prestigious folk-blues Vanguard label, whose roster
included Buffy Sainte-Marie, Phil Ochs, the Weavers, the Rooftop
Singers, Buddy Guy, and their star turn Joan Baez. Vanguard was
released in the UK via the Philips group, and John Jr. had recently
turned up on their doorstep, at his own expense, to check out the
UK scene which he'd been told was "happening" by both the Stones
and Cliff Richard during their recent US tours.

Philips wasn't getting much media interest in John, so their press
office put the bite on Mr Easy-Touch, Peter Jones, who then ordered
me to go and do an interview. I wasn't sure that I was interested either,
but I figured the Dylan connection, which the Philips press office had
– naturally – stressed, would merit an article. I met John at a coffee bar
near the Philips building in Stanhope Place. He was very tall, gangling,
a bit awkward, and likeably sincere. The Hammonds were a wealthy

family and John had been educated at the finest schools, graduating in painting and sculpture, but this silver spoon had evidently not been entirely to his taste. After discovering his love of the blues – and the fact that he could play it convincingly (his singing was another thing, all a matter of opinion: he was no worse than the British blues imitators) – he hit the road, playing bars, clubs, passing round the hat. Hammond was a blues purist and that was it. His favourite British group was, unsurprisingly, John Mayall & The Bluesbreakers, now featuring ex-Yardbird Eric Clapton on lead guitar at the beginning of his "God" period. Hammond did say a few words about Dylan, though I suspected it was with some reluctance. "Let's say he gave me confidence when I needed it the most. And believe it or not Bob can sing and play blues well. His blues piano playing is nothing short of brilliant". That kicked off the article, *Folk And Blues Friends*. The real story, of course, must have been Hammond's relationship with his father, though he barely mentioned legendary dad. But that would have been too deep for Record Mirror, even assuming I knew what questions to ask, and assuming John felt like answering them.

Other articles I penned than month were more straightforward: yet another interview with Dennis d'Ell, lead singer of the Honeycombs, for *The Honeys Have Changed* (two flops after "Have I The Right" – but soon to hit the top 20 again with the d'Ell-Ann "Honey" Lantree duet "That's The Way"); *The Easter Tragedy* (5 years since the Eddie Cochran car-crash tragedy; retrospective on the late-great); *The Imitators* (knocking Hermans Hermits' "Wonderful World", the Animals' "Bring It On Home To Me", and various other such inferior revivals currently in the charts); *The Two Happiest People* (interview with Peter and Gordon, "two nice public school boys", a hot act globally, understandably baffled why their "I Go To Pieces" didn't chart in the UK); *The Return Of Rock* (recent in-concert successes of Chuck, Little Richard, Carl Perkins and Larry Williams); *What The Animals Found In America* (racial and musical discrimination, said Chas Chandler).

From 1963 onwards the Beatles were not only the undisputed world-wide kings of pop music, but the veritable Kings of the Sixties – the masters of the decade. By mid-'65 they were a well-oiled hit-making and performing machine that could annually churn out two LPs and three singles – more in America where their LPs had fewer tracks – with every one a global multi-million seller. It was impossible not to admire their accomplishments, their bright intelligence and their likeably natural personalities. Musically, many of their innovative melodies blasted right through the clichéd rock'n'roll-era chord progressions, making them sound tired and hackneyed. This was a step forward in the evolution of pop music, and it was loose and fun and exciting and well played. Together with the music of such other contemporary innovators as Burt Bacharach and Curtis Mayfield, the Beatles were a breath of musical fresh air.

But, try as I might, I still couldn't much dig what they were doing. It was so-superior pop, but it was still pop. I even preferred the latest discs by the Stones, the Kinks, the Zombies, the Beach Boys and a host of others, not to mention the wealth of black music pouring out of America. But all that was about to change.

The Beatles were currently topping the singles charts with "Ticket To Ride", the EP and LP charts with the respective "Beatles For Sale" albums, and finishing off their second movie "Help!" The powers-that-be at Radio Luxembourg were so pleased with their recent Record Mirror coverage that a new tie-up was arranged: a competition for RM readers and Radio Luxembourg listeners in which the prize was to 'Meet The Beatles'. Both lucky winners predictably proved to be girls, Wendy Stevens and Marian Armstrong, and I was given the task – reluctantly, I might add – of chaperoning them when they actually met the Beatles. Unfortunately, this was not set to take place at Brian Epstein's NEMS office or somewhere convenient, but, due to the Beatles' enormous work-load, somewhere on the set of "Help!" at the Twickenham film studios. My instructions regarding the actual meeting weren't very specific…in fact they were vague. Fortunately I was not alone in this mission, as I would be accompanied by Record Mirror's Girl Friday Gail Forsythe, a delightful young American presently proving very useful at Record Mirror, and photographer Feri Lukas – his compatriot, Dezo, now, alas, persona non grata with the Fabs.

On the allotted day, Gail rendezvoused with the winners and then with me, we joined up with Feri at Twickenham…and when we got there, nobody on the set of "Help!" knew anything about the competition. Until, that is, we were rescued by a charming Paul McCartney who, miraculously, recognised me, an unbelievable three years after our first and only meeting. Then, over the next hour or so, everything fell into place once Radio Luxembourg's Chris Denning finally arrived.

I'd only ever spoken to John on the phone, and on the set Paul introduced me to him in person. John was sitting with Cynthia looking moody, and was surly and uncommunicative. George, on the other hand, introduced himself, was very funny, and complimented me on my tie stick-pin, a gorgeous little cameo set in a gold surround. But I never met Ringo.

"Would you like an interview?" asked Paul, after leaving the winners with the other Beatles. What could I say? This was a scoop. And the two winners, with the other Beatles making a fuss of them, were still in heaven.

RM w/e 15th May 1965

HOW THE BEATLES SPEND AN EVENING
Norman Jopling talks to PAUL McCARTNEY

IT was a typical quiet evening at London's Savoy Hotel. Quiet that is until the Beatles turned up to see Bob Dylan. They all trooped down to the restaurant and ordered Porridge and Pea sandwiches.

They got them. Then one of the boys spotted Owls Legs on the menu. They ordered them as a joke. It didn't take too long before the Owls Legs were served, piping hot, to the group.,

"But we wouldn't have known if they hadn't been Owls Legs," said Paul.

An evening out for the Beatles is something of a rarity nowadays. The boys are leading almost entirely self-contained lives and the latest development of theirs to entertain themselves are film projectors.

"We've all bought 16mm film projectors with sound and everything," explained Paul. "And we hire loads of films. It's surprising but you can get some of the really

*latest top films. For example I've got 'Topkapi' and 'Tom
Jones'. And we hire some of Elvis' films too...I like them
in the same way I like 'Double Your Money'.*

JOHN'S HOUSE – LIKE A CINEMA

"*The projectors cost a lot of money, about two hundred
quid I think. But they're worthwhile to us at least, because
we don't get a chance to go out and see these films. John is
the really keen one. He has it all organised, showing two
films a night now. It's just like a cinema round his place.
We all sit there eyes glued to the screen. And he doesn't start
showing them till late, well, after television has finished
and none of us get to bed until fantastically late hours.*

"*We all sit bleary-eyed in front of the screen making
signs with our hands on the screen – little animals and
all that...*

"*So far we haven't got a copy of 'A Hard Day's Night'.
Not that it bothers me. I didn't like the film anyway.
Seriously, I mean that. The original novelty of seeing
yourself on screen wears off. You know, like home movies
of yourself at the seaside. The good thing is that at least
you can come out with anecdotes every ten seconds about
what happened behind the scenes.*"

Paul talked about the Beatles' next film "Help!"

"*I like this one better. It has been great filming it. But
all the residents of the Bahamas hated us. Really. They're
so rich there and they were so rude to us that we just didn't
care. We all rented Triumph Spitfires and drove them
around the island. They didn't like that either.*

"*But there are some good scenes from the film. There are
some shots of us in a disused quarry, using it as a race track.
We found it when we were waiting for the technicians. We
were screeching around it like mad. Well, they filmed it
slyly and put it in the film. Just like that.*

"*There are no speeded-up shots, like in 'A Hard Day's
Night', but there are some other visual gimmicks. Like*

standing on a rock in the middle of the ocean playing our instruments. And the next shot of us up to our necks in water, still playing. And one of Ringo, lying on his stomach on the beach swimming in the sand."

PAUL DIDN'T LIKE "TICKET"

Then Paul started to sing the Beatles next disc "Help!" to us, taking the part of all the voices, and even the backing. He maintains it's much better than "Ticket To Ride".

"Can't say I liked 'Ticket' much," he stated. "But this new one is – in my opinion – good. I hope I don't sound big-headed. But I like it. It's certainly the fastest record we've made and it's very different. It's a bit like the middle eight in 'It Won't Be Long'...

"I think that John and I are writing different sorts of songs to what we were a couple of years back. I can't say whether they're better or worse but they're certainly different. And that is OK by us because we wouldn't want to stand still, to stagnate musically."

Somehow I can't imagine the Beatles ever doing that.

What I didn't know was that the Beatles were now smoking pot and that together with the lyrical influence of Bob Dylan, their music was set to reach unimaginable levels of creativity. Their current LP "Beatles For Sale" was probably the worst 'proper' Beatles album. Their next would be the film soundtrack LP to "Help!", but before the year was out they'd release their first masterpiece, "Rubber Soul". Their singles would also become more interesting and meaningful: "Help!", which indeed was a new direction, would be followed by the magnificent double A-side "Day Tripper" / "We Can Work It Out". Suddenly I would begin to like the Beatles' music.

Dylan finally knocked "Beatles For Sale" from the top of the LP charts in May with "Freewheelin'", but unluckily for Bob, his soon-to-be-released "Bringing It All Back Home" would never reach pole position. The unbeatable newly-released "The Sound Of Music" soundtrack would keep Bob's electric/acoustic masterpiece stuck at number two for months. In America seven of the top ten singles were British, including four by Manchester groups: one each from Freddie & The Dreamers and Wayne Fontana & The Mindbenders, and two from Herman's Hermits (currently a sensation in the US) including their chart-topping "Mrs Brown You've Got A Lovely Daughter" – which producer Mickie Most didn't even bother to release as a single in the UK.

Transatlantic telephone calls were very expensive in the mid-'60s. But early that summer I managed to get in a couple of phone interviews with two established American hitmakers who were enjoying their debut UK hits. The first was Bronx-born Shirley Ellis, the perkily-voiced soulstress who'd been notching up big US hits for 18 months and was currently heading for the UK Top Ten with "The Clapping Song".

> *IT TOOK Shirley Ellis about seven minutes to realise that she actually had a hit in Britain. She was, literally, flabbergasted. "I didn't think people like me had hits in Britain," she stated. "You know, I always thought that me, and Maxine Brown and Esther Phillips, well, we weren't quite the thing over there."*
>
> *It took me a full two minutes to explain to Shirley that if Mary Wells, Dionne Warwick and Doris Troy could have hits here, she certainly could.*
>
> *Now let Shirley tell you, in her own words straight from the transatlantic telephone about herself.*
>
> *"I guess that any success I have is due to 'being prepared'. No, I wasn't a girl guide or anything. But for nearly six years now my manager has been Mr Lincoln Chase. And he managed me and tutored me pretty extensively until he wrote my first hit which was called 'The Nitty Gritty'.*
>
> *"They tell me the Beatles liked that one..."*

She went on to tell how she got started by winning the amateur night at Harlem's Apollo, and first sang with the Metronomes, where she met her husband, Alphonso Elliston, a group who covered all bases from rock'n'roll through calypso to jazz . "I'm certainly not a rhythm & blues singer", she said firmly.

Lincoln Chase, her manager, record producer and songwriting partner, was an interesting guy: he'd been around since the early '50s and written "Jim Dandy" for LaVerne Baker and, more importantly, "Such A Night" for Clyde McPhatter & The Drifters. "Such A Night" was now a standard which had also hit the Top Twenty in both the UK and USA for Johnnie Ray (a UK No.1) and, recently, for Elvis. Unfortunately, Chase was painting Ellis into a corner, stylistically speaking. My article was slightly unkindly headed *Shirley's The Nonsense Hit Miss*, referring to her nursery-rhyme styled hits "The Name Game" and "The Clapping Song". On the phone she seemed quite a serious person, but her next single "The Puzzle Song" would flop, and eventually she'd be reduced to recording stuff like "Ever See A Diver Kiss His Wife While The Bubbles Bounce Above The Water".

The other transatlantic call was to somebody equally serious, a truly great artist. Nine years after his first record release, Johnny Cash had finally been propelled into the UK charts – via Dylan-mania, with his jaunty version of Bob's "It Ain't Me Babe".

RM w/e 19th June 1965

FIRST HIT FOR A LEGEND

FOR ten years Johnny Cash was the legend without a hit. Now he makes a hit here with a Bob Dylan song. The picture above was taken nearly a decade ago. It shows Johnny with three artists who recorded for the same label. You may recognise them as Jerry Lee Lewis, Carl Perkins and Elvis A. Presley.

Now Johnny still mingles with the mighty. "I don't think anyone around has so much to offer as him," he says of Bob Dylan. "There's a chance he may come to Nashville and let me produce an album with him if the A&R men agree. I've got my own ideas about the Nashville sound and I'd like to try it with Bob.

Dylan thinks highly of Cash, but then so do El, Carl and Jerry. Johnny Cash has been mingling with the musical mighty for ten years now – mainly because he's one of the mightiest of them all.

Ten years ago he plucked up enough courage to see Sam Phillips of Sun Records. The results were hits like "I Walk The Line" and "Ballad Of A Teenage Queen". Then Johnny, like all the other Sun stars, moved to other labels. He continued the hit chain on CBS with "Don't Take Your Guns To Town" and "I Got Stripes". Recently his hits have been "Understand Your Man", "It Ain't Me Babe", and "Orange Blossom Special".

Johnny has a cause. Indians. He's part Cherokee himself and got interested in the Ira Hayes statue (part of the Iwo Jima statue) in Washington. He says...

"But I know how the people feel about Indians. It bugged me. So I told the story in 'The Ballad Of Ira Hayes'. I wrote it bitterly, and I did an album full of Indian protest songs called 'Bitter Tears'. No one has ever said anything about the Civil Rights Bill applying to Indian.

"I'm recording a Western album soon. I'm writing a lot of the stuff for it including a song called 'Mean As Hell'. When I saw the president of CBS Records he asked me what I was going to record next and I told him 'Mean As Hell' was the title of the album and he was a bit worried about that. Actually it'll probably be 'True West'.

"But some day," said Johnny, "I'm going to start writing a book, and disappear into a cabin in the west, which will be science fiction. I'm a bug on that anyway. The second, if ever I have time to finish the first, will be all about what I've seen and learned about people and that will be a lot!"

The "True West" – or "Mean As Hell" – LP never appeared, and Cash would go a full year without another hit in America and over four years in Britain. Not until his "Live At San Quentin" platinum-seller in '69 would Cash's record sales reflect his talent and authority. But 1965 was not his best year: apart from drug busts, his truck caught

244

fire and accidentally burned down a California forest: to this day, Cash is the only man ever prosecuted in California for starting a forest fire.

That same month I received a preview copy of the Stones' new live EP and duly reviewed it via a rave front page article *Stones EP – Exciting & Different*: unfortunately my review titled it "We Want The Stones", which got changed to "Got Live If You Want It" shortly before actual release. Another highly-rated UK R&B group were the Artwoods, named after the group's leader, brother of future Rolling Stone Ronnie, and with a line-up that included Jon Lord and Keef Hartley. *'We Aim To Excite!' say the ARTWOODS*, and excite they did, with a club residency and big following. They even became a bit legendary, but Art did say to me, "Of course we'd love a hit" – and that never happened.

The UK R&B boom was starting to put serious dollars into the pockets of those black American singers and musicians lucky enough to be lauded and have their songs recorded by their limey admirers. There was also a solid core live audience here for the real thing, and if a fading US R&B star did not have the good fortune to get one of his or her copyrights covered by a Beatles or Stones, there was always a stint in UK clubland, a new record contract with a hopeful but usually disappointed British label, and the chance to see Swinging London in all its early glory. With British groups in huge demand in the USA, the reciprocal Musicians Union agreement was now able to allow many more American performers into the UK. Many came, many saw, a few conquered. One such hopeful was the unique Screaming Jay Hawkins:

RM w/e 5th June 1965
KING OF ROCK AND HORROR
Norman Jopling talks to SCREAMING JAY HAWKINS

EVERY once in a while someone different comes along. In January, none other than the legendary Screaming Jay Hawkins entered Britain, and established himself as a performer with something new to offer.

That "something new" was a skull named Henry, wild jungle costumes, flames shooting from fingertips and the wildest and most macabre act in the land. Now, Jay has settled here more or less permanently. He talked to me about his career, his act, his views and himself.

COFFIN

"Well, it all started when I was in the army. That's when I started singing. A little while later I dreamed up all the macabre stuff. In the States I used to lose half the audience when I leapt out of my coffin in clouds of smoke and mist. They all rushed up the aisles screaming in terror. So in the end I would give boys money to sit upstairs in the balcony and drop elastic bands down on the ones who were running away, and whisper 'Worms, worms, worms...' They used to get even more frightened feeling these slimy elastic bands all over them!

"My aim has been to be recognised as a performer. When I go on stage the audience won't be disappointed. So many performers think to themselves, well, I'm so-and-so and that's good enough...I don't need to work hard because I'm well known.

"Well, even though I haven't had any hits lately, it doesn't worry me as long as I know that I'm a performer. And if I do get a hit I'll still go wild on stage. In the States I've had some 30 or more singles. Over here I've only had two – the first 'I Put A Spell On You' and the last 'The Whammy'. In between they've all been macabre with the exception of one or two. There was one called 'Feast Of The Mau Mau' for which I had a good stage act, with me pulling my wife out of a coffin by her hair. It's so long that it'd last all through the record before her head finally appeared on the end...but unfortunately the record wasn't released here."

CRITICAL

Jay is a very critical man. He criticises other stars and even more he criticises himself. Talking about Solomon Burke and Little Richard he says:

"They're both a pair of nuts. But then so am I. I guess we wild ones are all like that. Then there's your Screaming Lord Sutch. Now, I don't rate him. But then I think his Juke Box film of 'Jack The Ripper' is the greatest.

"When I first arrived here I had colds, flu and even pneumonia. But when the climate changed for the better I decided to stay. I can't say that I REALLY like it here though. Before, my wife and I were living on a Pacific island all by ourselves. Can you imagine it. No-one else around at all.

"When I first arrived here there was a good crowd at the Flamingo during my first three appearances. It was great there, and I think I gave my best-ever performances there."

SNAKE

At home, Jay is different. There are no wild clothes, but chambermaids don't like coming into his apartments. For one thing one of them was changing the bed once when she saw a pet snake curled up. She fled, screaming.

Another time Jay was practising his act, with ghastly blood-curdling screams, waving Henry around,, when a maid who was passing heard the din and nearly fainted.

Anyway, watch out for another disc from Jay soon, and even more appearances from the macabre king of rock and horror. And don't get too frightened...

But if, in my naivety, I thought Jay critical, he was mildness and reasonableness itself compared with the next legendary R&B star I interviewed. The mighty Solomon Burke, "The King Of Rock & Soul", arrived in the UK, the same Solomon Burke whose "Everybody Needs Somebody To Love" was featured on the new Rolling Stones EP, whose "Cry To Me" was being covered by Barry St. John, and whose latest single, astonishingly, was a cover version of Bob Dylan's "Maggie's Farm" from "Bringing It All Back Home". Burke was already a legend: he'd preached and broadcast as "The Wonder Boy Preacher" from his own church "Solomon's Temple", founded for him by his grandmother, in Philadelphia from '45-'55, he'd worked as a mortician and started his own chain of funeral parlours, and he'd been a major US R&B hitmaker since '61 – and many of his great records had crossed over to the US pop chart.

Hitless in the UK, his record company Atlantic evidently decided to jump on the Dylan bandwagon and flipped his latest US smash "Tonight's The Night" and made the B-side "Maggie's Farm" the plug side in the UK. Nastily, CBS in the UK then decided to release the original "Maggie's Farm" by Bob Dylan as the follow-up single to "Subterranean Homesick Blues" (it wasn't released as a single in the States), prompting my article *CAN DYLAN BE BEATEN? The answer is probably no – but all the stops are being pulled out for Solomon Burke's version of the Dylan number "Maggie's Farm"*. The article itself was of little interest, the headline really saying it all, and it ended up with the paragraph: "Although CBS may achieve their objective in respect of 'Maggie's Farm', it may make other artists steer clear of Dylan numbers. And that could mean a loss of royalties to Bob and a general decline in the standard of pop music…" which was possibly one of the most ludicrous paragraphs I ever penned. The one interesting thing in the article was my describing Solomon Burke as a "soul attraction", the word "soul" now being used as part of a descriptive noun ("soul singer") rather than an adjective ("his soulful vocals"). Over the next few years the term "R&B" would be used less and less in the UK to describe black American singers, although in America "R&B" would continue to be the descriptive generic term. Of course, as any dedicated UK soul fan will testify, rhythm & blues had started to metamorphose into soul music long before 1965, with such artists as Jackie Wilson, Sam Cooke, Ray Charles, Little Willie John, Clyde McPhatter and Curtis Mayfield with the Impressions all cited as standard-bearers in the oft-virulent arguments on the subject of soul music: i.e. "What is soul?", "What was the first soul record?" and other thorny questions with no definitive answer.

Part of "all the stops being pulled out" for Solomon included an eight-day visit to the UK covering radio and TV appearances galore. Our columnist Tony Hall, wearing his promo-chief-for-Decca hat (the Decca group handled Atlantic in the UK), personally supervised

Solomon's visit, accompanied him everywhere, and the following week devoted an entire column to the great man's exhausting schedule and universally rapturous reception. Tony arranged for me to have a few words with Solomon on the set of the hip TV pop show Ready Steady Go! where I immediately put my foot in it because someone had wickedly advised me to ask Solomon about James Brown, and unwisely I did:

RM w/e 3rd July 1965

THE BURKE v BROWN FEUD
Norman Jopling reports...

"Tell me," I said, "all about you and James Brown. There was a two-second hush, and then Solomon Burke, king of rock & soul, launched into a torrent of attack upon fellow-R&B singer James Brown.
Here's the printable, edited version.
"Man, you wanna know about James Brown? You must be crazy. Listen, this James Brown, he wouldn't come within 500 miles of me. On or off stage. I know all about him.
"He says he's sold over a million records in Britain on the Ember label. He says that he don't record for America anymore, only for Britain. Well I found out that James Brown doesn't sell any records over here on any label. And in the States no-one wants his records, that's why they don't release them.
"He was the only man in America to bet on Sonny Liston. And do you know why Liston lost? Because he trained to James Brown's 'Night Train'. I could have told Sonny that he'd lose, listening to James Brown.
"A few years ago James Brown used to be the sweetest, humblest and most dedicated of men. Now that's all changed. He don't even talk to his group the Famous Flames anymore. He just keeps them around as lucky mascots.

CUT OUT

"And once I was on his show. At that time I had a big record hit called 'Goodbye Baby (Baby Goodbye)'. I had six numbers to do. James Brown cut them out completely and left me with one shortened song.

"Ask any other American singer what they think of James Brown. They'll all say what I'm saying. And if you wanted to meet James Brown! You're the press but that wouldn't matter to Mr. James Brown. Oh yes it has to be MR. James Brown. Well, you'd have to make an appointment which he probably wouldn't keep, and if he did, he'd keep you waiting. But if you kept him waiting – even for a second...then he wouldn't see you."

I managed to get a word in edgeways. "Everyone over here talks about the three B's. Burke, Brown and Bland..."

Solomon nodded in disapproval. "Not Burke, Brown and Bland," he stated. Just Burke and Bland. Or Bland and Burke. And talking about James Brown, he said, "there's the question of his records. I don't think he's made one good record. Except that is "These Foolish Things'. But then he messed that up by screaming at the end."

And so Solomon Burke continued.

LEGEND

Now, there's a peculiar thing about this feud, which at the moment seems to be one-sided. That Solomon rates James Brown as a performer. Which shows he's not entirely bigoted.

And what is the truth about James Brown, the man who has become something of a legend with R&B fans?

Your guess is as good as mine. But one thing is sure. No-one will truly know until he visits these shores. Which could be in one year or ten years...

Soul was certainly becoming the catchword because I'd also spoken to the Soul Sisters: Anne Giffendanner and Theresa Cleveland, look-alike sisters from Harlem, whose exciting "I Can't Stand It" had been one of the major US hits released on Guy Stevens' Sue label. They were here on a flying visit playing the Flamingo and the US bases, and told me: *"We Couldn't Stand Our Biggest Hit".*

> *"...we started singing in church, like so many others. Then again like so many others we were told we could make a lot of money singing if we took it up professionally. So we did. But we didn't make a lot of money, at least not straightaway!*
>
> *"Although our biggest record was 'I Can't Stand It' we never really liked it. In fact we can't stand it. It was originally written as a hill-billy song and we sort of moulded it to our own style. Probably the only time we liked it was when we saw the royalties.*
>
> *"We have to be careful not to be ill. After all if a member of a group is ill they can carry on with a replacement. But then when there's only two of you, then you can't. Mind you we tried. Both of us have been ill at some time or another and we tried to carry on...sort of as 'The Soul Sister'. It just didn't work out."*

Among the pop papers we were still the bible for serious R&B fans: our newest initiative, thanks to reader Keith Yershon (later responsible for the innovative Old Gold re-issue label) was the instigation of an R&B Top Twenty. Keith did the compiling, later admitting to the same problems which beset all chart compilers. We got letters about the chart, plenty of them. So we printed an editorial response, penned by me and Keith, which seemed, amazingly, to satisfy everyone:

EDITORIAL

IT'S been a long time since we received so many letters on one subject. The subject in question is, of course, our new R&B Top Twenty. All the letters praise. But many of them have two intelligent well-founded queries about the chart which will now be answered.

Firstly, why aren't the top R&B discs in the same order in the R&B chart as in the top fifty?

Because the dealers' returns which make up the R&B chart are all from shops which sell mostly R&B records. The top fifty is made up of returns from dealers which sell mostly pop records. As these pop dealers are only selling one or two R&B titles it would be senseless to take returns from them. As it is, the R&B chart is, in fact, far more advanced than the top fifty. For instance "I Can't Help Myself" is rising in the top fifty but falling in the R&B chart because the R&B fans had put this disc on top of the R&B chart for several weeks previously. Most of them have now bought it, but in the meantime the song has caught on with the pop buyers.

The other question is who are we, at the Record Mirror, to say what is – and more importantly what isn't – R&B. The answer is that we leave it to the dealers concerned. They are primarily R&B dealers, therefore we leave it to their judgement. We don't censor. We hope the fact that this chart is as accurate as it could possibly be more than compensated for any dubious songs which may be included.

There you have it!

Mid-'65 brought the annual Pop Poll, as voted for by Record Mirror readers. Here's the top three in each category. World Section: Male Vocalist – Elvis Presley, Gene Pitney, Cliff Richard. Female Vocalist – Brenda Lee, Dusty Springfield, Sandie Shaw. Male Vocal Group – Beatles, the Rolling Stones, Everly Brothers. Female Vocal Group – Supremes, Martha & The Vandellas, Shangri-Las. Instrumental Group – Shadows, Sounds Incorporated, Ventures. Solo Instrumentalist – Duane Eddy, Hank Marvin, Bert Weedon. Best Disc – "Crying In The Chapel" – Elvis Presley, "The Last Time" – the Rolling Stones, "House Of The Rising Sun" – the Animals. British Section: Male Vocalist

– Cliff Richard, Billy Fury, Mick Jagger. Female Vocalist – Sandie Shaw, Dusty Springfield, Marianne Faithfull. New Singer – Donovan, Tom Jones, Vashti. TV Show – Top Of The Pops, Ready Steady Go!, Thank Your Lucky Stars. Large Band – Joe Loss, Sounds Orchestral, Sounds Incorporated. Radio Show – Pick Of The Pops, Saturday Club, Presenting Elvis Presley. Vocal Group – Beatles, Rolling Stones, Animals. DJ – Jimmy Savile, David Jacobs, Tony Hall. Best Dressed – Cliff Richard, Dusty Springfield, Mick Jagger.

That summer I was sent to report on the annual European Singing Cup Contest at Knokke-Le Zoute (Knokke-Heist), a harbour town on the Belgium coast up near Holland, a few miles north of Bruges. Since its inception in 1958 this was one of those favourite annual jaunts – or junkets – beloved by artists, journalists, and assorted music business people. The British team in 1965 was sponsored by Decca Records, and the team, the journalists and the assorted music business crew all stayed in the same hotel. At the head of the table in the grand dining room sat the contest organisation's PR executive David Wynne-Morgan, whose larger-than-life presence considerably livened up the conversation, though the same could not be said for his lovely then-wife, model Sandra Paul, who demurely smiled throughout but barely said a word.

Mostly I hung out with Dave Berry and his roadie Mick, and Adrienne Posta and her friend Gloria. Dave Berry was just off a top 5 hit with "Little Things" and had racked up his all-time classic "The Crying Game" the previous year. Dave Berry was an interesting performer who was originally influenced mainly by Chuck Berry, from whom he took his name, and Gene Vincent. Chuck, unfortunately for Dave, did not appreciate imitation being the sincerest form of flattery. When RM's David Griffiths brought together Dave Berry and Chuck Berry for a chat and photo-session in late '63, Chuck pointedly ignored Dave, which wasn't altogether surprising given the Chuckster's sometimes curmudgeonly attitude and the rather more compelling fact that Dave had spent three months on the charts with his version of Chuck's "Memphis Tennessee", which just happened to be Chuck's latest reissued – and comeback – single. Needless to say, Chuck won the chart battle hands-down.

Dave Berry was a subtle and distinctive singer, but not a particularly powerful one. His strength was in his personal charisma, and he was able to transmit that charisma through a genuinely weird and unique stage act. Black leather-clad (there's the Gene Vincent influence), Dave would prowl cat-like around the stage, hiding behind stage props or curtains, shielding his face with his hands, trailing the microphone cable behind his back and demonstrating other such moody gimmicks which remained remarkable effective for him for many years. His act was successfully copied ten years later by Alvin Stardust, and famously explained by Alan Price to a bemused Bob Dylan in the movie "Don't Look Back". Hanging out with Dave during the four days of the contest it was impossible not to notice his effect on women. His roadie told me it was always like that wherever Berry went.

The Singing Cup Contest would prove to be an important and influential moment in Dave Berry's career because his impact that year at Knokke-Le Zout launched him as a major star in Europe, creating for him a fan base which exists to this day. Unfortunately we provoked a minor international incident at Knokke. Following Dave's triumph, several of the the English contingent went to see Sacha Distel in a crowded cabaret room. Distel, all Gallic charm, did his usual sophisticated act, but Dave, Mick and me, finding this swinging ring-a-ding-ding stuff with a French accent excruciatingly irritating, got up and walked out. It was noticed, offense was taken, and Dave later forced to apologise. I left that bit out of the article:

RM w/e 24th July 1965

THEY CALLED DAVE 'IMMORAL'!
Norman Jopling reports on the Knokke-Le Zoute Contest...

"HE'S immoral!"
    That was the verdict of the German judges on Dave Berry last week at the European Singing Cup Contest held at Knokke-Le Zoute in Belgium. That wasn't all they said.
    "He's a bad influence on the German people. He can't sing. He's sick!" At this point tempers frayed to breaking point. British judge Alan Freeman stepped in.

"Listen. The greatest entertainer in the world is German. But she can't sing a note. Her name is Marlene Dietrich," he pointed out.

The Germans were crushed. But it didn't stop them from marking Dave down. They gave him two out of ten. The rest of the judges gave him nine.

Just one of the incidents at Knokke where everything opens peacefully and ends with a third world war in sight. We didn't win, although we had the best team. Really. Even the other teams and the foreign journalists thought so. Unfortunately the judges didn't. On our first heat we only clocked up 372 points losing to France. There was such a sensation that the judges had to re-think for our next heat with Holland. We won with 406 – the highest mark during the whole 7 years of the contest.

PRAISE

The continental press went wild, praising Dave's marvellous act, Adrienne Posta's charm and bounciness, Eleanor Toner's moving style, Clarke Robinson's swinging smoothness and everything about Joy Marshall, the coloured gal who had the best voice in the contest. But the next heat between Belgium and Italy gave Knokke's home country enough points to push us out of the finals; which took place between Belgium (who lost) and Holland (who rightly won), but who were nearly booed off stage by the disgraceful Belgian audience.

During the week of the contest some interesting things happened. Like when Dave was doing cabaret and singing "I Can Get It From You" making mock amorous advances to a pretty coloured lady in the audience. "I love you, baby", she yelled.

Dave was amazed when he found out it was Dionne Warwick. "She looks different," he complained.

New boy Clarke Robinson had only been singing in pubs before this. When the first heat came up, with a huge audience and TV live to five countries Clarke was more than nervous. After, he said "It was my fault we lost." It wasn't, but Clarke could do better. In the next heat when we won, Clarke wore his grandfather's cufflinks and found out the stars were OK for him. And Joy Marshall sat him down and told him, "Don't sing to the audience when you go out there. Sing for someone you know, who you like." Clarke did, and was great. Afterwards backstage Ade, her friend Gloria, and Dave's sister Julia all planted great kisses on Clarke who realised there were more than financial rewards to singing.

Adrienne appeared firstly in a white trouser suit which slayed the audience. But she was told to wear a dress for her next appearance. So she did. An ultra-short light blue one with frilly bloomers showing just below the knee. All the men young and old in the audience were straining their necks to look.

WILD

When Eleanor did "All Cried Out" and "Danny Boy" the audience went so wild it was obvious we'd won this heat. Joy clinched it.

The evenings at Knokke were spent in a mad flurry of dancing, watching the cabaret (such stars as Dionne Warwick, Sacha Distel and Pet Clark were there), drinking – although at a quid a drink our ration of two free drink tickets a night were more precious than gold, and signing autographs. Dave entered Belgium barely known and left amidst five-column newspaper headings such as "Dave Berry Worth A Thousand Beatles".

CHAMPAGNE

The days were spent Go-Karting, sleeping, and riding those four-man bicycles which are as big as a car.

We heard news that we had been pushed out of the finals while Dionne was singing "Who Can I Turn To", singing it fantastically and poignantly. Everyone nearly cried. Afterwards, Decca's Dick Rowe and Marcel Stellman bought everyone champagne to console them. They too needed consoling, as they had both nearly flogged themselves to death working for the team.

PRIZE

But it was a great contest. Dave won the Press Prize hands down and appeared on the last night with the winners. The Belgians wanted to nominate the whole British team for the Press Prize but unfortunately the rules stated that only one artiste was allowed.

The reason we lost was because of inconsistency in the judging – not because we were the inferior team. Even the other teams admitted that. But we went down in a blaze of glory anyway.

Just watch out for us next year, Knokke...

I'd always got on well with Dick Rowe, Decca's top A&R man, who'd sometimes invite me to the recording sessions he was supervising at Decca's West Hampstead studios. Dick was a nice guy as well as a fine producer who could consistently create hits across the pop spectrum: he'd been producing hits for over a decade, and over the past couple of years been responsible, among much else, for Billy Fury's string of major chart successes – mainly ballads – and for the Bachelors' string of huge international hits. He'd also recently produced a future rock classic: "Gloria" by Them, the B-side to their debut UK hit "Baby Please Don't Go", an A-side boasting US hitmaker Bert Berns on production credits. But "Gloria", Van Morrison's first classic song, would be the side which would go down in rock history.

Dave Berry consolidated his Knokke success with another even bigger continental triumph a few months later at Le Grand Gala Du Disque Populaire 1965 in Amsterdam. Dave was on a roll, and on superb form because his competition included the Supremes, the Everly Brothers, Wayne Fontana and the Mindbenders, Cilla Black,

Vera Lynn, Wanda Jackson and a host of Euro-talent. His moody act, we reported, "stole the show".

That summer I got to interview Hank Marvin in *Why The Shadows Quarrel* (Hank wasn't happy with the Shad's recording sessions, or their current records, but liked being back on the road touring); in *Now The Ivy League Hit Back*, the hot Carter-Lewis-Ford vocal and songwriting combo dug themselves out of the mire a recent Richard Green article had dumped them in (Ivy's disparaging backstage touring conditions, thus infuriating promoters); Ray Davies lamented the (as he saw it) lack of success for "See My Friends" in *"I'm So Worried" – Ray Davies talks to NJ* ("I'm not a great singer, nor a great writer, nor a great musician. But I do give everything I have…and I did for this disc") – Ray considered a No.10 hit a flop, so hot were the Kinks; Pretty Things drummer and wild thing Viv Prince rebutted NZ press libels about his bad behaviour down under in *Viv – It's All Lies!*; I profiled James Brown in *Mr Dynamite Explodes!*; in *The Star Who Keeps Out Of 'The In Crowd'* Billy Fury turned up early for his interview at the Record Mirror office to the amazement of all, as artists were usually late, and as usual was reclusive modesty personified. Of his ballad hits he stated: "I've never done a rock number as a top side. I wouldn't mind, but I've never found a song strong enough." And the Bachelors, who'd been globally huge in '64, now maybe grumpy from a poor chart year lashed out in *The Bachelors Slam Dylan!* Tottenham's finest the Dave Clark Five also came in for a piece of their mind, too.

I also managed to squeeze in a small piece on the latest club sensation Jimmy James & The Vagabonds, co-managed by Peter Meaden who'd bounced back after several months in the doldrums following the High Numbers debacle with this, on the face of it, unlikely and unwieldy prospect. Peter had "discovered" the Vagabonds when they performed at one of his many drinking haunts, the Overseas Visitors Club in Earls Court, and there experienced one of his many epiphanies. The Vagabonds were a nine-piece show band who'd formed in Kingston, Jamaica, in '61 and teamed up with lead singer Jimmy James in '63 following Jimmy's two solo Jamaican chart-toppers "Come To Me Softly" and "Bewildered And Blue". After getting as big as they could possibly get in Jamaica, they arrived in Britain in mid-'64 to concentrate on US-style R&B.

Peter flipped when he heard them, and shortly afterwards signed them up. Jimmy James & The Vagabonds were a large untidy unit of all shapes, sizes, colours, but became an integrated and fiercely exciting soul machine when they performed. It took the strange genius of Meaden to recognise their potential. Said Pete Townshend, who had remained friendly with Meaden: "I wouldn't have looked twice at the Vagabonds, had it not been for the way that Peter sold them. He used to say, 'The Count's elegant, he's sophisticated, he knows about style, and Jimmy's got this voice'." Ready Steady Go! co-producer Vicki Wickham was equally impressed, saying she'd never seen such an exciting version of the Contours' "Do You Love Me" as the Vagabonds' performance.

"Count" was Count Prince Miller, the band's cheerleader and support vocalist. And Jimmy James was "the voice"...in fact, one of the great yet under-rated soul vocalists of the '60s. With contacts like the Who, impresario Harold Pendleton, Andrew Oldham, and dozens more "movers and shakers", Meaden soon had the Vagabonds resident at the Marquee, and regularly gigging at the Whiskey A Go Go, the Rikky Tik, the Cromwellian, and nearly every other London venue of note. And in a matter of months they would be touring up and down the UK – the biggest live soul attraction in the country. But record-wise it wasn't happening. A deal with Decca, signed pre-Meaden, fell through after some unrepresentative releases, and a one-single EMI deal wasn't renewed. Luckily for Meaden and the Vagabonds, Pye Records' A&R supremo John Schroeder was about to get involved.

Situated as it was in the heart of the West End, the small-but-convivial Record Mirror office was still the obligatory pit-stop for a vast cast of publicists, promoters, producers, managers, musicians, photographers, agents, fans, friends, and other assorted riff-raff, high and low, of the thriving and quirky mid-'60s UK music scene – which had not (quite) yet been transfigured by the flood of dollars now being generated by the British beat groups. The democracy of poverty still reigned – just about – although by the end of the decade the lawyers and accountants brought in to control the inevitable squandering and profligacy would be busy taking over the operation, and henceforth it would indeed be "The Music Business", for better or worse. From my very first days at Record Mirror, the cast of eccentric characters popping in and out had been an education – from old Howard with his astonishing memories and anecdotes of such of his youthful contemporaries as Crippen's 'murdered' music-hall star wife Ethel Le Neve, to current regulars such as Jack Reilly whose sole claim to fame seemed to be the fact of his attendance, often at considerable distance and expense, to every show-business funeral.

A recent visitor on several occasions was an amiable young Cambridge student named Kenneth King, who'd bring us his demos and sit on the floor, student-like, while we listened to them. They were good. We predicted he would go far, and indeed he did, though not precisely in the direction we thought. Ken King shortly became Jonathan King and signed a contract with Decca – not only for performing, but for producing. The 'folk boom' was still booming but the writing was already on its wall, thanks to Dylan's new electric sound and fantastic lyrics. One legacy of the boom was its progeny the 'protest' craze, and this mini-movement, though spawned by the socially concerned lyrics of Dylan, Phil Ochs, Tom Paxton, Buffy Sainte-Marie et al, was not restricted to folk music. Big protest hits included Manfred Mann's version of Dylan's "With God On Our Side", and, currently, Barry McGuire's million-selling stomper "Eve Of Destruction". The prodigious Jonathan was soon up on the protest bandwagon, hitting the UK top 5 both with his own "Everyone's Gone To The Moon", a dreamy ballad with a quizzically interesting lyric, and a month or so later with his song "It's Good News Week", a sharp piece of contemporary satire performed by Hedgehoppers Anonymous. It was an auspicious start to King's career, and here's how that strange career got started:

RM w/e/ 7th August 1965

PEOPLE, PLACES & MR. KING

THOUGH he's not yet 21, Jonathan King has been to quite a few places and met quite a few people. Also, his new record "Everyone's Gone To The Moon" looks as though it's going places too.

Buddy Holly: While still at school (Charterhouse), Jonathan heard Buddy's record "It Doesn't Matter Anymore" and became a pop fan. Since then Jonathan has been told he looks a bit like the late Buddy.

Winston Churchill: This was the name of the camel that Jonathan rode for five hours in the Sahara. At the time, he (Jonathan, that is) was on a round-the-world trip shortly after leaving school. On the same trip he also met

Brian Epstein on the beach at Honolulu, and

Barry Goldwater at the San Francisco Republican Convention. After his return to England, Jonathan was so tired that he went away on a two week holiday in France. Staying in the next hotel room was

Victor Silvester! Then Jonathan went to Cambridge University to study English. He also produced a record on which the singer was

Terry Ward. It was called "Gotta Tell" and sold a respectable 3,000 copies on Fontana this spring. Jonathan also tried to make a record of his own voice and sent a demo disc to

Joe Meek. But nothing happened. Then Jonathan met Decca publicist (and RM columnist)

Tony Hall who introduced him to

Ken Jones, a skilled arranger who was interested in becoming Jonathan's recording manager, especially when Ken saw Jonathan's song "Everyone's Gone To The Moon". Ken's music publishing partner

Joe Roncoroni was also impressed and the resulting disc was sold to Decca. Asked what what his thinking behind this haunting, dreamy, somewhat poetic number, Jonathan said "It started off as a take-off of

Bob Dylan who seems to me to use a lot of adolescent truisms in his songs. But while I was writing it the number became more serious. I particularly like the vague, wishful airy-fairy recorded sound. I know my voice doesn't sound too clear but then I don't think I've got that much of a voice though it's as good as quite a lot of

Other people."

The following month Jonathan arrived again at Record Mirror armed with several more acetates. We'd printed a colour picture of him complaining in the caption that he hadn't been up to see us since he'd had a hit…though, in fairness, he did send us a special acetate explaining his absence. Here's some excerpts from the interview:

RM w/e 18th September 1965

X-CERTIFICATE JONATHAN KING

…Jonathan's next disc is "Green Is The Grass". Let him talk about it.

"We made it at the same time as 'Moon' he explained. "In fact, this was the demo which made several agents want to sign me up. But whereas 'Moon' had lyrics which meant something to some people – though not me – the words of 'Green Is The Grass' are completely banal. I hope it will appeal to a wider audience.

…(his) next production is a song called "It's Good News Week" by Hedgehoppers Anonymous.

When Jonathan wrote this he showed the lyrics to Decca chief Sir Edward Lewis.

"Change it!" thundered Sir Edward, eyebrows raised. So it was changed. Here's the original verse in the rock-protest song and the substitute:

"Lots of blood in Asia now
They've butchered off the sacred cow
They've got a lot to eat"
Was changed to:
"Famine's checked the need for coal
By stimulating birth control
We're wanting less to eat"
Jonathan is hoping the record will be a hit. It almost certainly will be. His own disc, after "Green Is The Grass", is very likely to be a song with lyrics more in the meaningful vein.

That follow-up was the tellingly-titled "Where The Sun Has Never Shone" and, like "Green Is The Grass", was a flop. Jonathan's cynicism wrecked any chance of him becoming a serious artist, if indeed that was ever really on the cards. Not until five years later would he return to the charts, straddling the '70s with a decade of bubble-gum and gimmick hits, as well as guiding the early careers of Genesis, the Bay City Rollers and 10cc, and becoming a rich, respected and influential though eccentric member of the music business community – for a while.

Not everyone approved of the protest boom as I discovered when I got to meet two of my early musical heroes that autumn – the Everly Brothers:

THE Everly Brothers gave each other peculiar looks when I asked them what they thought about protest records. For a moment I thought they'd start talking about something else.

But they didn't. They just told me precisely what they thought about protest records.

"They irritate me," said Don quietly. "This anti-war attitude is really usurping the authority of the U.S. government. Boys are dying out there – and someone's got to do the fighting. If they must sing anti-war songs they should go and sing them to the enemy.

"My idea of a protest song would be a song about muscular dystrophy, cancer, or any of those terrible things which should be brought on home to the public. But then this 'protest' craze won't last for ever..."

The Everly Brothers themselves aren't normally as fierce. In fact one's first impression of them is that they are startlingly pleasant and un-big time. It may be because they are SO big they can be themselves.

"When we started we were heavily influenced by Bo Diddley," they said. "Of course, our main source of inspiration came from our C&W roots. We had been singing since we were 6 (Phil) and 8 (Don). Eventually we were caught up in the rock boom, and started recording for Cadence. We always used to see the other Cadence stars

like Andy Williams and the Chordettes there. In fact we all came over to Britain together in 1958."

Did the boys regret leaving Cadence for Warner Brothers?

"There were some regrets. But career-wise it was the best thing for us. We're still very close to Archie Bleyer though, who owned Cadence. He's Phil's father-in-law!

"But sound-wise it makes no difference. What many people don't know is that Nashville, where we record, there's only one studio and about 15 studio musicians. We still record in the same studio with the same musicians for Warner, as for Cadence. Mind you, those musicians make a lot of money – many of them such as Chet Atkins and Floyd Cramer are big stars in their own right."

The boys spend about one-third of their time at home – that includes recording time – and the rest on tour. They don't know why they have lasted so long at the top – it could be because their sound has never sounded dated.

"But we've got to find a sound to make the U.S. singles chart," they said. "We haven't been doing much lately. Our albums are going great...of course we were very pleased when 'The Price Of Love' made it here. It's a different kind of song we think. The lyrics aren't teenage either, but then not many lyrics nowadays are. Our best song, copyright-wise, has been 'So Sad', believe it or not. We were forced to start writing our own songs out of necessity really, but we've been very lucky in that many of our songs still sound OK. We still think 'Bye Bye Love' is good."

Protest singer Barry McGuire elicited, to the best of my knowledge, the only flicker of interest in music ever shown by our Fleet Street supremo John Junor. During one of his weekly visits he drew me to one side and whispered conspiratorially, "Norman, can you get me the record of 'Three Wheels On My Wagon'." This was not a question but a command. "Three Wheels On My Wagon" was a popular western romp performed and recorded by the big commercial American folk group the New Christy Minstrels, featuring a rousing lead vocal from

Barry McGuire shortly before he quit the ensemble to go solo. I was on the phone to the CBS press office in a flash and the EP was duly delivered in time for the next visit by the mighty editor of the Sunday Express. The bizarreness of the request convinced me this song was a personal favourite of Junor's, rather than a favour for friend or family – it certainly suited his style. I hope he enjoyed it, and also hope he enjoyed one of the the perks of owning a pop paper.

The times were indeed a-changin' and I was no exception. My times were a-changin', too. Something was in the air but I didn't yet know what it was. Dylan seemed even more fascinating now he'd gone musically electric and lyrically surreal. From Lee's record stall I acquired all Dylan's earlier acoustic LPs, swapping them two-for-one for albums I'd reviewed for Record Mirror. I immersed myself in Dylan's music and especially those lyrics. He was taking pop music on to a higher level and everyone knew it and everyone was listening. This cross-fertilisation between British and American songwriters and musicians was beginning to bear tasty fruit and would progress exponentially over the next few years. If there was an anthem for the changing times it was the Byrds' awesomely groovy "Mr Tambourine Man", a global chart-topper, a new Dylan song. In one week that August three heavyweights lined up with major new single releases: "(I Can't Get No) Satisfaction" from the Rolling Stones, "Like A Rolling Stone" from Bob Dylan, and "California Girls" by the Beach Boys. The following month Dylan's all-electric "Highway 61 Revisited" LP consolidated the new vision. By the end of the year the Beatles would catch up and join the race with their first album masterpiece "Rubber Soul".

Black music was also changing but in a different way. The down-home sounds of rhythm & blues had metamorphosed into gospel-inflected soul music, which was proving more attractive to mass white audiences – as Berry Gordy could testify. Soul was about to hit the musical mainstream big time, in tandem with the black Civil Rights movement. But for me, the attraction of rhythm & blues had always been that it wasn't part of the pop mainstream. It had been created by blacks, for blacks. Much soul music would now be recorded with an eye fixed firmly on the white market. And why not?

However, much as I loved the new sounds of white and black music, I discovered I loved Nina Simone most of all. Her 1964 Philips' LP "Broadway, Blues And Ballads" had prompted me to go back and get all her earlier Colpix and Bethelehem LPs, and the release of her second Philips LP "I Put a Spell On You" in 1965 set the seal on a life-long affair. I couldn't help feeling that compared with Nina, nothing else in black music for me had quite that intensity, that musicianship, that voice, and that integrity. For weeks I played little else but Dylan and Nina Simone. Years later when Nina was recording for RCA, she visited the UK and there was a press bash. RCA's press officer led me to Nina, sitting aloof like a queen, and attempted an introduction, but Nina failed to acknowledge me: "because you're white", whispered the press officer. I thought it was a bit silly of Nina even to bother to show up, as almost everyone there was white, but I guess she had her reasons. I didn't take it personally – I still loved her.

Around this time there was a lyrical trend in a lot of American pop songs celebrating difficult romances between rich boy and poor girl, or vice versa. These "across the tracks" songs may have been metaphors for mixed-race relationships, but I suspect were more likely sentimental Tin Pan Alley corn masquerading as something more profound. But commercially the format worked. Culprits – and also hits – included "Looking Through The Eyes Of Love" and "Princess In Rags" by Gene Pitney, "My Block" by the Four Pennies, "Down In The Boondocks" by Billy Joe Royal, "Dawn (Go Away)" (rich girl, poor boy) and "Rag Doll" (rich boy, poor girl) from the Four Seasons, and many more. The trend infuriated one of our readers:

RM w/e 27th November 1965
AFTER PROTEST – THE POVERTY SONG?

WHY do many famous singers still make records which have completely ridiculous and far-fetched words? Gene Pitney's "Princess In Rags" is just a joke – is she one of the Beverley Hillbillies or something? And the Animals "It's My Life" is almost as bad, I mean does Eric Burdon REALLY sing about changing his rags to sables, as though he lives in Alaska, or the House Of Lords? And then

there's Billy Joe Royal with his ludicrous "Down In The Boondocks". With every other TV programme and article going on about the new working class elite I'm sure that Billy would be well away in real life with his girl from the proverbial 'other side of town'. Even protest songs have more relation to real life than these infantile squawkings, and that's saying something. Grow up fellas, you'll still make plenty of money without singing about your bird's worn-out Dad.
Anthony Hamilton, Chase Side, Southgate, London.

In November '65 we came across an unusual collection of photographs of Elvis: kiddie pix, teenage pix, family snaps and early career shots. These artefacts were then rarely seen, so we devoted three full pages including the centre spread to *Elvis Then* which featured the best photos together with informative captions. The spread looked great. Elvis still had a huge following, was still a massive album seller globally, and was still busy churning out those terrible films. But his career and his music lately seemed hopelessly square. It was nice to be able to print something about him which was reminiscent of the era when everything about Elvis mattered. Tom Jones first met Elvis late in '65, and told me all about it in DeHems Oyster Bar:

RM w/e 11th December 1965

ELVIS CAME DOWN FROM THE SKY TO MEET TOM!

ALTHOUGH Tom Jones isn't quite the all-American boy that his critics are currently painting him, he's certainly fascinated by the American scene in general. He walked into the Record Mirror offices wearing a buckskin Buffalo Bill-type jacket ("bought it at a Wild West sale"), and when we decided to have a quick drink he asked for a tomato juice with Worcester sauce ("Last night was TOO wild").
Then he started talking about America.

"Quite obviously I've been spending too much time there. I was there for three months solid at one time because I had a lot of things to do. I won't do that again. Any more trips I make to the States will be timed carefully.

"It was on a film set that I met Elvis. He was up in a studio helicopter, with all wires holding it up from the ceiling. I asked someone if I could see Elvis and they phoned up. Then Elvis came down from the helicopter and we shook hands and started chatting. He told me he had just bought 'With These Hands' and he started singing it. It's funny, but Elvis isn't a character, so to speak, like a lot of other stars. He's just a regular sort of feller, really pleasant, and completely different to what you'd expect.

OUT OF BED

"Now I didn't meet Jerry Lee Lewis there, I wanted to very much. I met him once when he came to Britain, but I was a fan then – I sort of shook his hand and told him how great he was and all that. I was determined to meet him in the States but I kept missing him. When he was up North I'd be in Memphis, and when he was in Nashville I was in New York. So I phoned him up – it was about four in the morning and his wife answered the phone. I asked if Jerry was there and she said he was in bed asleep but who was calling? I told her and about five minutes later Jerry came to the phone.

"He drawled Hello and how was everything. Well, we had a chat and I said I'd like to get together with him for a session. And guess what he said? Great, there'll be a whole lotta shakin' goin' on, he said! What a cat!"

In his spare time Tom visited various night clubs and stage shows. Including the Chuck Jackson show at Harlem's Apollo Theatre.

"I went in with Dionne Warwick to watch the show. You have to go in with someone coloured, because, well,

you'd never get in being white by yourself. I was the only white man in the theatre, and I went onstage to watch the show from the wings. It was great, and when Chuck Jackson had been on for a while he said to the audience that Tom Jones was here. He introduced me and the audience cheered, thank goodness! We all sang together then, Chuck, Dionne and me, and then Chuck asked me to do a number by myself. I was petrified. I sang 'Long Tall Sally' though, and to my amazement the audience loved it, I was really relieved.

"I used to spend a lot of of time in the discotheques. The Sybil Burton place, Arthur, is very show biz, and everyone just goes there to be in. But there's no décor – the walls are plain but there's a good atmosphere. And you get a kind of cabaret there, something which British clubs could do. There are far more things to do in American discotheques than in the British ones. It doesn't cost any money to get in – and anyone can go in. But the drinks are expensive. It cost us two dollars for two beers!"

Tom's own tastes in music are still very rock'n'roll. Of his own records he says he likes them, but they aren't strictly him. Of the Joe Meek singles, what he says is unprintable. But neither his manager nor his record company want Tom to jump on the rock or R&B bandwagon.

"They say there are enough R&B groups", said Tom. But despite his status as one of the world's top new adult singers, it's interesting to know that beneath it all Tom is a frustrated rock'n'roller...

And that was 1965 that was, and the top ten record artists – according to the charts point system – were:

UK	USA
The Seekers	The Beatles
Cliff Richard,	Herman's Hermits
Sandie Shaw	The Supremes
The Rolling Stones,	The Four Tops
The Beatles,	Elvis Presley
Peter and Gordon,	Gary Lewis & The Playboys
Bob Dylan,	The Rolling Stones
The Byrds,	Sonny & Cher
The Kinks	The Dave Clark Five
The Hollies.	Sam The Sham & The Pharaohs

Reader Miss Berry Wilson from 'M' Street, Belleville, Kansas, USA, conducted a "best hair" poll and the winners were:

Best hair Guys	Best hair Gals
Keith Moon	Twinkle ("she won hands down")
Stu James	Lulu
Billy J. Kramer	Marianne Faithfull
Brian Jones	Dusty Springfield / Patti Boyd (tie)
Graham Nash	Helen Shapiro
Zoot Money	Cilla Black
Paul McCartney	Sandie Shaw
Cliff Richard	Cathy McGowan
Keith Richard	Jane Asher
George Harrison	Cher

Several of those best-hair gals were regulars at the succession of pop-biz parties hosted around that time by the Moody Blues at their rented house in Roehampton. I usually went with Richard Green, who could generally be relied on to embarrass and insult the likes of Twinkle and Lulu. The parties were always fun, and the police waiting outside would wait until any Beatle had exited before making their presence known to the revellers. Not for long, though.

1966

Nineteen sixty-six would prove to be a high-water mark in pop music here and in America, crammed with masterpieces that still resonate. But for me, the year began badly. I'd recently broken up with Jill and one night in January I got a call saying she'd taken an overdose. I rushed to the hospital: Jill was unconscious, busy having her stomach pumped. She survived, but the event led to my falling out with Andrew Oldham and the Rolling Stones. The following day I got a call from Andrew asking if I'd like to come over for an advance listen to the Stones' new single, so I did. He didn't tell me what the title was. Andrew, standing, with Mick and Keith seated in the room smoking, treated me to a full-volume "19th Nervous Breakdown". They all loved it. Not me though. Still reeling from the night before, I told Andrew what had happened – he'd known Jill from way back – and said that under present circumstances I didn't think it was a particularly nice subject for a song.

That did it. The atmosphere froze, I was speedily ushered out. To them, I guess, I was first and foremost an appendage to their publicity machine, someone who'd always praised them, always championed them – extensively, in print – and had thus enjoyed a mildly special journalistic status, due also, maybe, to my early part in their rise to fame. But now I'd stepped outside my allotted role and, even worse, criticised them. The idea that my personal concerns would have any relevance to them was simply naïve. The lesson I sort of resolved to learn after that incident – as if I hadn't already known – was that it was not "me" that was of any interest to the people I wrote about – just those columns of praise-laden print I was able to deliver.

I'd been scheduled to do a big interview with the Stones later that month, but Andrew called Peter Jones and told him he didn't want me doing it. But I did manage a certain amount of schadenfreude when "19th Nervous Breakdown" failed to reach No. 1, a position enjoyed by its five predecessors. In RM's chart, supplied by Record Retailer, it hit No. 2, as it did in the USA, but was kept off the top by Nancy Sinatra's "These Boots Are Made For Walking". Interestingly, it performed worse in the New Musical Express listings, and according to the man who fixed the NME chart, someone coughed up several hundred quid in order to hike the record up a few places in the NME top five. I found "19th Nervous Breakdown" uncomfortable listening for a few years…then, after a while, it didn't matter anymore and I was able to hear just what a good record it really was.

But Mick must also have been having problems with women, for 1966 was not only the year of "19th Nervous Breakdown": the Stones' would go on to release a slew of "misogynistic" material that year, infuriating the burgeoning women's liberation movement with songs like "Under My Thumb", "Out Of Time", and "Stupid Girl".

There was plenty else happening that winter for me not to give too much thought to any unpleasantness, let alone to anguish, either about Jill, the Rolling Stones, or anyone or anything else. I was still buzzing around town in my now beat-up filthy Mini-Cooper, with parties and clubs galore, mini-skirted creamy-thighed dolly birds everywhere, great, great music, tons of booze, hand-made suits and shirts, the very model of a swinging Londoner; young, successful, great job, self-centred in the extreme, still only 21, confident yet insecure at the same time. I felt compelled almost as a duty to grasp this present slice of dolce vita for all it was worth, not only for its own sake but also symbolically because it was such a universe away from my Dad's factory job-for-life in dreary Edmonton, a fate I'd loathed and dreaded. And I also knew that compared to most 21-year olds I was privileged, and I appreciated it. But that February I took it all too far.

One Saturday night three of us went pub-crawling in Chelsea; me, my close buddy Chris Evans who ran his own insurance brokerage, and Miki Hayes, a model friend of Jill's. We were already heavily inebriated by the time we got a casual invite at one of the pubs to go to Lady So-and-So's coming-out 'do' that evening at an address just off the Kings Road. We zoomed round and immediately had to face off a bunch of hoorays who weren't keen on uppity working-class oiks crashing their party. There was nearly a fight, which would have been interesting because Chris, though he didn't look it, was rock-hard, having been a schoolboy boxing champion. But the hoorays were mostly students about our age and after the initial jostlings soon got fascinated by our expensive clothes and our trendy jobs (which never failed to impress), and of course our ability to trail gorgeous models like Miki in our wake.

The party was noisy, and after an hour or so Chris and I both noticed a curious thing. Someone outside was throwing stones which were rattling against the kitchen window. We decided to investigate, and there at the side of the house we discovered the old dowager duchess herself, mistress of the mansion, decked up in ancient furs and drunker than either of us, keyless and trying to get into her own house. As she could barely stand, Chris and I supported her limp old frame between us and took her up to her room and put her to bed. Before collapsing, she enthused gratefully as to what nice boys we were, and told us to take whatever we wanted from "behind the painting". "Behind the painting" referred to a concealed, but unlocked safe. Upon opening the safe we were slightly disappointed to find it empty of money, but nevertheless stashed full of alcohol stretching back into the distance. Making the best of it, we armed ourselves with a couple of bottles each and crept out the bedroom while the old duchess snored peacefully away.

My current tipple of choice was vodka and Dubonnet, a horrible and lethal combination, and I'd taken from the safe a bottle of each and proceeded to mix and drink for the next several hours until each bottle was empty. From this point onward things became strange. Chris vanished, I knew not where, and eventually I left the party with Miki and drove her home to her flat in Barons Court. I was feeling distinctly unwell. "You look green", she said, "You really should come in for a coffee". The prospect of heaving myself out of the Cooper's all-embracing black leather bucket seats, staggering into the flats, clambering up the stairs, reluctantly hanging out with a coffee when all I wanted to do was get to bed, was just too daunting. "No, I'm alright," said I, and shot off homeward.

Next thing I woke up in the dark. I thought I was in bed. I couldn't see anything and after a second or two knew something was wrong, that I wasn't in bed. Then I realised I was upside down and warm liquid was dripping on to my hands. I came to all of a sudden and knew the liquid was blood from my face and that I was in a car wreck. I started yelling, heard footsteps running towards me, passed out, then woke up again, on an operating table beneath brilliant lights with masked faces bent over me. I passed out again, then woke up, in bed, in hospital: the old Royal Northern in Holloway Road.

My legs were badly gouged and my wrist was broken but my face fared worst. Yet I'd been lucky, really, all things considered. I don't know how fast I'd been going: the last thing I remembered was dropping off Miki. I'd crashed miles away, on the downhill stretch of Camden Road heading north just before Holloway Prison – so probably it was quite fast. The Cooper had crashed into a parked car, an Austin Cambridge, and both cars were write-offs. The engine of the mini had come through on the passenger side and would have taken the legs off a passenger.

I was in hospital for weeks. There were two operations on my nose and I refused a third, cosmetic, operation because I couldn't face the horrible unwinding of the tightly-wound little nostril bandage which snakes up into the sinuses to keep open the nasal passage after an operation. Glass, whether from my spectacles – which I wore for night driving – or shards from the car mirror had become embedded in my eye and took weeks to work their way out. This only hurt when I closed my eyes and my eyelid put pressure on the cornea. Sleep thus proved difficult so I was given very strong painkillers and consequently was in a dopey detached haze all that time in hospital. My eyelid had been sliced through, but miraculously not the eye itself.

One evening a constable arrived and stood framed against the corridor light in the door of the large dark ward and sent a nurse to ask me if I'd been drinking before the accident. "Just a couple of lagers," I told her. He looked over and saw my face and left. Yet I must have stunk on the operating table, all that Dubonnet. But I looked worse than I actually was. They wouldn't give me a mirror for a couple of weeks so I buffed up a chrome towel machine in the toilet to catch a glimpse of the monster I'd temporarily become: I didn't recognise the reflection. There were plenty of visitors – my fearful parents, diligent girlfriend Carol, friends galore. Peter Meaden arrived with Jimmy James, who, as Peter later said, "turned white" at the sight of my face. Because I could walk well enough, I would make tea for everyone in the huge circular ward and first thing in the morning I'd open up the ward kitchen, switch on the lights and watch the big black cockroaches scuttle away.

A criminal was given the bed next to me for a week with a policeman guarding him. One night he made a bid for freedom via the fire escape but was caught and taken somewhere more secure. It was a strange twilight existence and I had plenty of food for thought. I read an article about LSD in Life magazine and thought it sounded interesting, never having heard of LSD before, or at least never having paid it any attention. After six weeks I was allowed to leave. The facial swelling had gone down a lot, but I wore dark glasses for a year. The first thing I did was get Bob Bedford to drive me to the breakers' yard in Camden Town to see the wreck of the Cooper. The bloke at the gate told me he couldn't believe anyone had survived in that car. There was dried blood everywhere, a tangled mess of twisted and broken metal, even the steering wheel bent into a fantastic shape. It chilled me but made me elated to be alive. I resolved never to drink and drive again. And I never did…well, not to the same extent as I'd been doing.

I was very happy to get back to work. Earlier, I'd kicked off '66 with an interview with Goldie Zelcowitz, who'd split from the Gingerbreads and was aiming to be a soulful solo artist – which she eventually succeeded at. But in *Goldie Tells What's Wrong With British Record Buyers!* she'd observed, not particularly accurately, that "…the American charts are full of soul records while the British charts aren't". She was sort-of right, but not quite. Nevertheless soul music was increasingly hitting the UK mainstream. Tony Hall then did a very clever thing that February and took one of the best tracks from the new LP "Otis Blue", Otis Redding's version of the Temptations' "My Girl", a US No. 1 but a minor hit in the UK (one week at No.43), and issued it as a UK single, quickly following-up Otis's previous single, a flop, his frantic version of the Stones' "(I Can't Get No) Satisfaction". "My Girl" catapulted Redding into the Top Ten and made him a UK star, and not only a star but the very figurehead of soul personified. Redding was a dynamic, charismatic performer with a heartfelt vocal gift, and although I wrote a long profile on his career in January – *Otis R: The Man Who Sings As Though He Means It* – I was a bit ambivalent about him. "Otis Blue" featured a white blonde model on the sleeve, and his newer recordings, increasingly peppered with self-consciously "soulful" extemporisations and mannerisms, smacked to me of gilding the lily in order to convince white audiences of his soulfulness – something, I felt, he of all people didn't need to do. But commercially it seemed to work a treat, so what did I know? That month I also profiled the complicated saga of Bob And Earl in *Bob And Earl Unmasked!*, the duo whose all-time soul-dance classic "Harlem Shuffle" was nestling at No. 3 in our R&B chart on Guy's Sue label, two years after its US success, and two years before its future UK pop success. George Harrison had famously named it his favourite "disc of the moment": what none of us then knew was that the distinctively hypnotic arrangement was by the then-unknown (in the UK) Barry White

In *'Our Act Is Dangerous – last time something went wrong there was blood everywhere' say Dave Dee etc* I spoke to newcomers Dave Dee, Dozy, Beaky, Mick and Tich, currently scoring a minor hit with "You Make It Move" but about to break nationally via their forthcoming tour slot supporting Gene Pitney and Len Barry, and their forthcoming single "Hold Tight". DD & Co were a Wiltshire beat group ready to split up when they met Ken Howard and Alan Blaikely, the writing/management team responsible for the Honeycombs' hits. Howard and Blaikely recognised that Dave Dee & co were powerful and competent with a good stage act that included comedy and impersonations, and over the next three years would write all their hits, produce their records and manage them. It was a blueprint for the pop group machine of the future. Luckily for all concerned Howard and Blaikely's instincts were right on. Dave Dee & co went on to become one of the biggest pop groups of the late '60s. No "cred", nothing progressive, just a string of catchy and increasingly gimmicky singles.

One of the last interviews I did before the car smash had been with Georgie Fame: *The Sad Tale Of A Smashed Jag And Georgie*. Georgie was a smart guy who always gave a good interview and this was no exception, mainly being a catalogue of minor woes including one that was particularly poignant:

RM w/e 5th February 1966

"...Just when 'Yeah Yeah' reached the top I was still living in North London – Muswell Hill to be exact. I didn't have a motor then and whenever I stayed out too late in the West End I'd have to catch the last tube home. But the nearest tube station to where I lived was miles away. And I'd be walking through the freezing cold streets thinking that I'd got a big hit – a number one – and I was still having to half kill myself walking miles and miles home shivering with cold."

The Georgie Fame story had the ring of truth about it, but many of the pop star stories touted to us smacked of a laboured gimmicky stunt dreamed up by one of the many publicists who were constantly trying to get their client's names in print and were relentless in their feeble and unbelievable fictions. Particularly peeved by publicists was fellow RM hack Richard Green, who reserved his special scorn for their ilk – somewhat unfairly, actually, considering how pathetically reliant we were on their news tit-bits.

Back at Record Mirror I kept a low and considerably battered profile, concentrating on reviews and layouts. But I couldn't resist interviewing soul goddess Irma Thomas that April, and met with her at the Italian House restaurant on Shaftesbury Avenue. Soul guru Dave Godin accompanied me, together with several of his acolytes: soul divas were Dave's special interest, and Irma, with her impeccable New Orleans credentials and warm and wonderful voice fascinated him, and me too. Irma spent most of the interview talking about her home town, regaling us with anecdotes such as the practise in New Orleans of burying bodies in tombs above ground "because about two feet below ground it's water". Irma had written only one of her many hit singles – her biggest, the gorgeous million-seller "Wish Someone Would Care". She wrote it, she said, while she was depressed about her old record label Minit packing up, and her contract being renewed with the Imperial label.

There was major label news in the UK that season. The big four – Decca, EMI, Philips and Pye – had been joined by CBS in 1964 and now a fifth major was emerging. Polydor, the pop arm of the giant German Deutsche Grammaphon group, was flexing its considerable financial and creative muscle steered by its new MD Horst Schmolzi ("...they parachuted him in," said Peter Meaden), whose first coup was wresting the prestigious Atlantic/Atco label group away from Decca. The acquisition was timely: Atlantic was about to expand its roster from jazz and R&B to white rock, with future signings including Vanilla Fudge, Iron Butterfly, Buffalo Springfield, Led Zeppelin and the Rolling Stones. Schmolzi was also in the process of signing Kit Lambert and Chris Stamp's Track label, which also took the Who away from Decca and would shortly sign Jimi Hendrix. Future deals would include Robert Stigwood's protégés Cream and the Bee Gees...

That spring was New Orleans-flavoured because my next interview was with the likeable Lee Dorsey who was on a roll in '66, just off the hit "Get Out Of My Life Woman", currently scoring with "Confusion", and set to notch up two top tenners before the year was out with "Working In The Coalmine" and "Holy Cow". Lee was a fascinating interview: after his debut classics "Ya Ya" and "Do-Re-Mi" hit the US charts in '61, he'd just vanished. What had happened?

RM w/e30th April 1966

THINGS YOU DON'T KNOW ABOUT LEE

"...I had a good reason for quitting," Lee explained, "my record company was stealing so much money from me it wasn't worth sticking around. In fact they even took to stealing from themselves so that when the taxmen wanted their money there was none left. So they had to close down.

"Then I went back to my automobile repair shop which I ran before I discovered singing. Well, this place

started making money for me – and I liked working there anyway. After a few years these guys from the record scene came back and said 'Lee, why dontcha make some more records?' No, never, I said. But they said they had a new record company that was honest, and the guy that ran it – he had a lot of money.

"So I said I still didn't want to, so they gave me two thousand dollars and I said Yes, I would make a record. They said I'd be given a song by Allan Toussaint who'd I worked with before, Allan and I went around together for a few weeks, he was just sizing me up I guess.

"Then he said he'd write me a song. He sat down, looked at me, and in ten minutes out came 'Ride Your Pony'. I didn't know what to make of it. I didn't feel like a jockey even if I looked like one! But it was a big record.

"While it was big I went back to my repair shop and all the kids would come around and say 'That can't be Lee Dorsey, he wouldn't be mending fenders with a big record.' I was amused by that. Money hasn't really changed me – everything that goes up must come down and nobody wants to know you if you were acting big once and you're not big anymore..."

The following week at a Philips' reception for the Walker Brothers – just off their smash hat-trick hit "The Sun Ain't Gonna Shine Anymore" – Richard Green and I spoke to Gary Leeds and Scott Walker, who was clearly miffed at the recent Stones versus Walkers spat which had been gleefully reported by all the music press. "Don't ask me any more about Mick Jagger. I don't want to talk about any of those incidents," snapped Scott, "I just want to forget about it. In fact I don't even know Mick Jagger, and I'm not concerned with replying to any of the allegations he makes. Incidentally, I like the Rolling Stones, in as much as I can like anything of that type of music. I think those stories have been blown out of all proportion by the press." It would be nice to say that we slunk off shamefaced, but in fact we did no such thing: I started talking cars to Gary Leeds who explained he'd bought a red Marcos because E-types were too common. This gave me food for thought as I was currently without wheels and itchy to start zooming – soberly – around Swinging London again.

However, before embarking on a life of serious sobriety, I managed to get completely wasted one last time while wheel-less – on a Fashion Cruise across to France and back, for which Richard and I had been sent complimentaries. With no work to do and stuck on a ship with the "fashion" crowd, our only logical recourse was to drink. Over in Calais we got stuck in a long queue at a perfumier where I hoped to buy a bottle of scent for Carol. Richard, getting impatient, marched straight up to the counter, pocketed a huge sample bottle in full view and pulled me outside, thrust the giant bottle in my hand saying "She'll like this – why waste good drinking time?" I have no memory of the homecoming voyage, but woke up collapsed in a toilet cubicle in the bowels of the ship. Unfortunately the vessel had docked, and Richard – and all other staff and passengers – already disembarked. With the luck of the inebriated I managed to somehow clamber off the ship in darkness and stagger along the wharf towards a light. A kindly customs official directed me to a short-cut to the street where I wouldn't be subjected to the time-consuming formalities of passing through customs, which suited me fine as I still had the big sample bottle of perfume bulging in my pocket. I'd lost my wallet, but a local taxi driver agreed to drive me from Tilbury to North London for payment in kind (i.e. a suit) and back in Wood Green I donated him my very first suit, the dark grey pinstripe. It didn't fit him, but he graciously accepted it. I never got that wasted again.

Despite sensible suggestions that I should next buy a sturdy saloon, I decided I wanted a proper sports car, not some pokey little tin can, however nippy. I liked the idea of a long bonnet, convincing myself that this would minimise what happened in the Mini-Cooper crash, i.e. the engine coming through the passenger side and possibly taking off the mini-skirted legs of whatever dolly I was squiring. As soon as the insurance money came through on the Mini-Cooper I sent off for all the brochures and sat salivating over them for hours. I finally decided that an E-type was out – too expensive; the MGB was pretty, but seemed a bit small; the Austin Healey 3000 was a contender but seemed old-fashioned (what did I know!); the MG Midget and Austin Healey Sprite were fun, but too cheap and small and looked flimsy. That left the Triumph TR4A. I liked the look, liked the spec. I went straight to the nearest local dealership – in Friern Barnet – and placed an order for a white TR4A with soft top and wire wheels. They phoned me back a couple of days later: no idea when they could get a white one, but they'd just been delivered a red one – with soft-top, wire wheels. That was alright with me. Within a week I had wheels again…and how I loved that car.

That April US Columbia Records kindly – and unexpectedly – sent to Record Mirror a sensational batch of 35mm colour transparencies of Bob Dylan, fresh studio poses where he'd finally achieved 'the look'. 'The look' centred on the hair, "as if every individual strand has been carefully groomed to fit in with the overall look of unkempt elegance", together with expensively fashionable clothes. As an excuse to use the best picture, I cobbled together an article: *the new cool-looking Dylan explains the change in his words and music* (I was going through an all-lower-case long headline phase) which cribbed some meagre quotes from an American interview, then padded it out with lists of songs from each Dylan album which were hits for other artists, the conclusion eventually being reached that the more obscure his lyrics got, the less his songs got covered, culminating in the 'sensational' revelation that none of the songs from his last album "Highway 61 Revisited" had been a hit for anyone else at all. The most interesting bits in the article were Bob's own words:

> *"Everything is changed now from before…I was playing a lot of songs I didn't want to play. I was singing words I really didn't want to sing. I didn't mean words like 'God' and 'mother' and 'President' and 'suicide' and 'meat-cleaver'. I mean simple little words like 'if' and 'hope' and 'you'. But 'Like A Rolling Stone' changed it all".*

One major UK group who'd done well with Dylan songs over the last year – and would go on doing well – was Manfred Mann, just off an unprecedented gap of six months between singles. The length of this gap in itself was actual "news" because of the awesome level of current creativity in pop. The musical cross-fertilisation between UK and USA, between black R&B and white pop/rock, was currently producing several masterpieces weekly, and the rate of record releases from the big groups was prodigious: four singles a year were expected, and at least three albums every two years. That rate – imagine the creativity involved! – was maintained by the Beatles, the Stones, Manfred Mann, the Kinks, the Animals, the Who, and in America the Beach Boys, the Byrds, Bob Dylan and now the Lovin' Spoonful and the Mamas and the Papas, not to mention all the Motown and Atlantic artists. This would all change within two years: drugs – and "Sgt. Pepper"– would see to that. But for now, the writing was on the wall – even Tony Hall, staunch champion of jazz, R&B and soul, headed his latest column *Now it's the white groups that are 'where it's at'.*

Manfred spoke to me about "the great gap" between their singles:

RM w/e 7th May 1966
MANFRED AND THOSE DISCARDED SINGLES

"...the only reason we didn't have a single was because nothing we recorded was suitable. We had been into the studios on many occasions thinking we had a good song for a single. But after the session when we heard the playback they were never any good. Did you know that of the four songs on our EP 'Machines', three of them were planned as singles? The only one which was cut specifically for an EP or LP track was 'Tennessee Waltz'. There's still a lot of material at EMI which is unreleased – including one song called 'Driver Man' which was cut as a single. That was by Max Roach and Oscar Brown Jr.

"One peculiar thing about our absence from the scene was that several groups sprung up in the meantime. There were people like Spencer Davis and The Small Faces. I thought we might have been forgotten in that time but evidently we weren't. I remember about three months ago a young boy knocked on my door. When I answered he asked me why we hadn't been seen on television and

*how nobody was talking about us or anything. I thought
it was somewhat insensitive of him!"*

Nothing for Manfred to worry about though – the band were barely
half-way through their remarkable run of Sixties hits. Manfred also
told me that Paul Jones hadn't been confident about their latest single
"Pretty Flamingo": "...I think he would have been pleased at the
time if it hadn't been released". That same week "Pretty Flamingo"
moved comfortably to Number One and stayed there for three weeks.

Their line-up had changed – Mike Vickers had left, and in came
Lyn Dobson, Henry Lowther and Jack Bruce, joining Manfred,
Paul, Tom McGuinness and Mike Hugg. At the end of the interview
Manfred asked me not to build up "the bit about Paul and me, you
know, 'Manfred Slams Paul'. There was a terrible bit about Paul in
one of the pop papers last week, so corny." Manfred didn't seem at
all uptight about Paul, but nevertheless "Pretty Flamingo" would be
Paul's final single with Manfred Mann...

I missed Dylan live in the UK in '65, but wasn't making the same
mistake this year. He was at the Albert Hall that June, and Carol and I
sat there upstairs fascinated, agog at the electric Dylan and even more
agog at the audience antics. I could understand why the American
audience, plus Pete Seeger, et al, got rattled at the 1965 Newport Folk
Festival when Dylan, supposed heir to Woody Guthrie and anthemic
Civil Rights troubadour, appeared onstage with a bunch of amplified
rock'n'roll musicians and kicked up a din. But this, the Albert Hall,
was over a year later and Dylan's folk-era fans had already had plenty
of time to adjust: for starters, one side of last year's LP "Bringing It
All Back Home" was electric; and so were both sides of "Highway
61 Revisited", also from 1965 and undeniably the most artistically
advanced album thus far in rock music.

RM w/e 11th June 1966

*WITH A MIXTURE OF FOLK, ROCK AND COMEDY,
DYLAN SHOWS HE CAN TAKE EVERY INSULT BUT
NOT A COMPLIMENT*

"EQUALITY, I spoke the word, as if a wedding vow, ah but I was so much older than, I'm younger than that now..."

Bob Dylan thus changed. It all began with a song called "My Back Pages" recorded some three years ago on an LP and reached its probable culmination at the Royal Albert Hall the other week when he performed his last British concert.

As always, Dylan is logical and compromising. A full half of his concert is given purely to his "folk" image in which he accompanies himself on guitar and harmonica. He sang songs like "She Belongs To Me" (nothing like the record), "It's All Over Now Baby Blue", "Desolation Row" and "Mr Tambourine Man". No new songs of protest – of course – although a few of the tuning up sounds were suspiciously reminiscent of the intro to "With God On Our Side".

If any of the Beatles were in the audience they may have been embarrassed – or flattered – by Bob's version of "Norwegian Wood" which enlarged and coloured on the original theme by Lennon-McCartney.

He also sang "Visions Of Johanna" which he hasn't yet recorded and another tune, beautiful and nameless, which proves his talent in this field is unblemished and unaffected by his rock exploits. But before he sang one song he had something to say.

"I'm not going to play any more concerts in England." (This was greeted by a loud silence, which was obviously greatly appreciated by Bob Dylan, who crouched even more elf-like over the microphone like some Uriah Heep).

"I'd just like to say that the next song is what your English musical papers would call a 'drug song'. I have never and never will write a 'drug song'. I just don't know how to. It's not a 'drug song'. It's just vulgar."

These brave words were greeted by loud cheers, even though "Rainy Day Women" (he didn't plug that one) is supposedly an American term for Marijuana cigarette. After the interval he returned with his group and launched into an ear-splitting cacophony which he hadn't recorded. The sound, despite being electrical and groupy was still so far removed from conventional group music as to be still strictly Dylan...

Then the old guard started walking out. The people who had been secretly hoping that Dylan would reform and make a full confession of his musical sins realised that Dylan was taunting them as much as ever. Before the end of the concert, about 25 percent of the total audience had walked out. Another 25 percent stayed under sufferance and didn't show overmuch enthusiasm.

"I like all my old songs," he said. "I never said I didn't like my old songs." (his pronunciation when saying this was unbelievably funny). "It's just that things change all the time. Everybody knows I never said they were 'rubbish'. That word isn't in my vocabulary. I wouldn't use the word 'rubbish' if it were lying on the street and I could pick it up."

The hecklers were in full force now and just about everything possible was being hurled at Bob (verbally, no missiles were seen). He coped very well with them, like "The music you are hearing – if you have any suggestions on how it could be played better or the words could be improved?" He ploughed through "I Don't Believe You" which was originally a folk tune and which he's now rocked up. Others included "Everybody's Down" and "I See You've Got Your Leopard Skin Spotted Pill Box Hat".

"This is not English music you're listening to. You haven't really heard American music before. I'm sick of people asking what does it mean. It means NOTHING." He then launched into "Just Like Tom Thumb's Blues" amidst shots of 'Rubbish' and 'Rock and Roll for ever'.

The highlight came when Bob sat down to the piano and did "Ballad Of A Thin Man", which silenced even the folksier elements. He ended up with "Like A Rolling Stone", jumping and yelling all over the stage and looking (as all the girls said) very sweet.

But the only thing he couldn't do was take compliments. When anyone yelled out in favour of him, all he did was give a sheepish embarrassed smile and a little condescending wave.

Several of the songs performed were from his forthcoming double-album "Blonde On Blonde", including the one I described as "beautiful and nameless" – "nameless" because I didn't know the title. I wonder which song that could have been? It wasn't always easy figuring out Dylan titles from new songs you'd never heard before.

Phil Spector was back in the charts…after an upset. His ungrateful protégés the Righteous Brothers, doubtless noting the fate of the Crystals, the Ronettes, Bob B. Soxx & The Blue Jeans, Darlene Love, etc, had a few months earlier parted acrimoniously from Phil following the Spector-produced global chart-topper "You've Lost That Lovin' Feelin'" and three subsequent US Top Ten hits – "Just Once In My Life", "Unchained Melody" and "Ebb Tide". They then signed to MGM's Verve label where Bill Medley had the temerity to persuade Barry Mann and Cynthia Weil, co-writers of "Lovin' Feelin'", to let the Righteous Brothers record their song "(You're My) Soul And Inspiration", described by Cynthia as "'Lovin' Feelin'' sideways." Rubbing salt in Phil's wounded pride, Bill then dressed it up in a production indistinguishable from that of the master himself. It topped the US charts.

Phil bounced back, signing R&B duo Ike & Tina Turner for an album deal, but stipulating he didn't want Ike in the studio, a fact unrevealed till years later. Another of Phil's favourite songwriting teams, Ellie Greenwich and Jeff Barry, who'd written all Phil's biggest girl-group smashes, penned a new song for him – "River Deep, Mountain High". He cut it with Tina and his "wall of sound" studio crew, but credited it to "Ike & Tina Turner".) It was a thunderingly magnificent record and promptly hit No.3 in the UK, kept off the top only by the Kinks and the Beatles. But it flopped in the States. No-one seems to agree exactly why, but whatever the reason or reasons, it damaged Phil's self-esteem to the extent that he would never fully recover.

I profiled him yet again, together with Ike and Tina, for *More Spector Magic Out Of The Hat;* I interviewed Allan Clarke for a Hollies' update in *Home Is Where The Heart Is – For Allan Clarke At Least.* The Hollies, like Manfred Mann, were proving one of the most consistently successful groups of the Sixties – and they'd go on scoring big hits till the mid-Seventies. I'd seen them earlier in the year performing at a May Ball in one of the Oxford colleges which I'd attended in a purely 'civilian' capacity with some student chums. I also profiled Tommy James & The Shondells, destined to be major US hitmakers, who had one of the strangest hits that year with another Ellie Greenwich-Jeff Barry song, "Hanky Panky", a dated-but-exciting three-year old single that charted via plays on a US Oldies-But-Goodies station. I cribbed the article from a US publicity handout which included the dubious info that James & co "...didn't like the British Boom, were against long hair," and were "...against the scruffy look as exemplified by some of the British acts".

At the other extreme of the American spectrum I profiled the Mamas and Papas in *If You Can Believe Your Eyes And Ears,* and their producer, Dunhill Records' chief Lou Adler in *Lou – The Big Back Room Boy.* The info on the latter two articles had arrived courtesy of Dunhill publicist Andy "Wipe Out" Wickham, former EMI and Andrew Oldham press officer/publicist, and whose obsession with the California dream had recently inspired him to emigrate to the West Coast and get a job with Lou Adler – a textbook example of an ambition fulfilled. Now he was feeding us some nice semi-exclusives from Los Angeles, which was beginning to rival London in cutting-edge pop creativity.

As Bob Dylan sings – or sneers – so very chillingly in "Ballad Of A Thin Man": "*...and something is happening, but you don't know what it is, do you Mr Jones?*", and then "*and you know something is happening here, but you don't know what it is, do you Mr Jones?*", I too knew something was happening here, but like Mr Jones I didn't really know what it was. But I did know that much of what was coming out of LA was part of it. Donovan was part of what was happening too, as I became aware when I interviewed him early that June. He'd been making some major career changes: a dispute with original managers Geoff Stephens and Peter Eden had prevented the records he was currently cutting with new producer Mickey Most from being released – among them "Sunshine Superman", recorded back in December '65. Don had just returned from the States with his new manager Ashley Kozac where he'd signed for America with Epic, part of the giant CBS group, and for the next year his records would first be released in the USA. But the big change was in his music. Like Dylan, Donovan was embracing new sounds and concepts, and he was full of it. He was so enthusiastic and had such ambitious plans I couldn't help feeling slightly sceptical – and a bit cynical. Shame on me, because nearly everything he told me in the interview came to pass:

RM w/e 30th June 1966

THE NEW BREED
Donovan talks about the exciting new images in the field of pop

WHEN Donovan becomes enthusiastic about something, an idea, a theory, all other problems are wiped away from the face of his mind. He becomes a dreamer, a visionary, and is carried away by his own enthusiasm.

He sees pop music as something which is capable of tremendous artistic expansion and already feels that pop music on the higher levels is no longer juvenile rubbish.

"My idea," he explained, "is to bring back a kind of vaudeville, using the best in pop music and utilising a small West End theatre. There would be a small, appreciative audience and the performers could really play the kind of music that would bring them out artistically. There would be improvisations, artists getting together for impromptu workouts and in fact a whole new concept for vaudville.

"I think I would have a combination of musicians with me which would enable me to get virtually any sound which I wanted. I've already spoken to people like John Lennon and Brian Jones about this idea and they think it's great.

"It's about time something was done for pop music. Everything else, from women's clothes, to furniture, is being brought up to date. Pop music should be given this treatment too."

Then Don's manager Ashley Kozac began to talk about Don's music.

"Pop music has been so raucous and sexy in the past. Our aim is make the kids like beautiful music – that's what Donovan plays. It's so much more worthwhile. Don is also working on an LP of children's songs and our organisation has complete control over anything to do with the records – from the songs down to the sleeve notes and the cover picture."

Donovan was clutching several acetates of his new single and LP and he played them to me, explaining as he did so when they were recorded, where they were recorded, and what he thought of them.

"These sitar ones were recorded in the States. I've made the sitar sound subtle, as opposed to being brash. I think that George's playing on 'Norwegian Wood' was very delicate and understanding. On 'Paint It, Black" I feel that Brian's use of the sitar is a little brash. But perhaps he will grow more subtle as he uses it more – after all, he hasn't been playing one for very long."

The Donovan gang (Don, Ashley Kozac and Gypsy Dave) don't have any worries about the gap which they left when Donovan was in the States and had no new recordings issued.

"I think that I'll be accepted with my new records," Donovan explained, *"and I may have built up a kind of mystique while I was away,"* (he said this in a very tongue-in-cheek manner).

"The gap I left was partially filled by Bob Lind, although Bob is going to find it hard to keep up the standard of 'Elusive Butterfly' which was a very good song."

"I'm progressing musically all the time. Mind you, I may well revert to any previous style of mine at any time. I've

been studying all types of music and I use them as backings on my new albums. I write the songs with various musical forms in mind. The sitar and the Indian influence was one. I use classical backings and influence, the music of Charlie Mingus, oh, and so many others. Here's one track which I recorded which goes through SEVEN different types of music!"

Donovan then put on the turntable a song which sounded haunting, interesting and nightmare-ish at the same time. Not a single, obviously.

"Well, my single releases wouldn't be as way-out as LP tracks. You have a certain market to aim for and it would be foolish not to. But I'm looking forward to when my records are issued again."

Then Gypsy Dave drove up in a large Jaguar and the Donovan gang leapt inside and drove off, shouting farewells and promising to keep us informed.

Legalities prevented "Sunshine Superman" from release in America for another three months. It would go on to top the US charts and become Donovan's first million-seller. In the UK we would have to wait till December '66 for its release – and a month later it would become his biggest British hit, reaching No. 2.

The day after seeing Donovan, I strolled round to Leicester Square to keep an appointment with Kim Fowley, a 6'5" Californian beanpole with charisma, charm, and a fund of esoteric music business stories.

RM w/e 18th June 1966

KIM – the story of a story-book American

KIM FOWLEY sat in the Angus Steak House munching buttered toast and drinking milk, happily unable to communicate with the waiters. He was wondering – and so was I – how I should describe him to Record Mirror readers.

"You could say I wrote 'Nut Rocker' which was a number one here," Kim said hopefully. When I dared

mention the name of Tchaikovsky, Kim had an answer.

"It's all a question of copyright, I mean, YOU could write something like 'Nut Rocker'. It's all a question of knowing the legal side of it. Actually I did the arrangement and got these coloured session musicians together in a studio about the size of a lavatory, and when it became a hit I found a white group on the streets and we sent them round as B.Bumble and the Stingers. I should have come to England then, but I missed my chance.

"No, 'Nut Rocker' is too old, and so was 'Alley Oop' which I produced too. There was no such group as The Hollywood Argyles. It was me, Gary Paxton (who was half of Skip & Flip, remember 'Cherry Pie'?), Gary's girl, Sandy Nelson and a couple of others. It was written by Dallas Frazier who was also on the record – he's just had a hit with 'Elvira'".

The article went on to chronicle Fowley's chequered West Coast pop history, producing US hits on the Murmaids, and Thee Midniters, jamming with Dylan, but the real point was to plug his new single "The Trip", a "spontaneous song" he'd made up in the studio and now released in the UK on Island Records. Kim was no newcomer to London – he'd been a fixture on the London pop-and-party scene since '64 when he flew in with P.J. Proby – "a California failure", according to Fowley. Fowley was a terrific dancer and relentless womaniser and his extrovert behaviour was undoubtedly captivating, but being a Swinging London "character" was not exactly what Kim had in mind: he wanted to be a star. He'd observed up close his friend Gary Leeds – who'd originally accompanied Proby to the UK as his drummer – bust up with Proby, return to LA and recruit John Maus and Scott Engel to find huge UK and then global success as the Walker Brothers. "After Proby and the Walkers I feel it could be me," said Kim plaintively. It was never to be…but not for lack of trying.

A week later I bumped into Gary Leeds again, who was delighted the Walkers' new single, "Baby You Don't Have You Tell Me" was more upbeat than their previous singles, though it wouldn't sell in the same massive quantities. Gary, the Walker brother who actually enjoyed rock music, was also enjoying modest solo success on the CBS label. Curiously, he wasn't allowed to record with the Walker Brothers as he was contracted elsewhere: not until their reunion and final classic hit "No Regrets" in the mid-70s would Gary cut records with Scott Engel and John Maus as the Walker Brothers. I ungraciously reminded Gary about comments regarding the Walkers' recent appearance at the London Palladium – no complaint about the music, only their static appearance. Gary was ready for it, though:

> *"...we were not too nervous at rehearsals. But when we actually came on to do the real thing, we found that there were a lot of girls in the audience – young girls who were fans of ours.*
>
> *"Now, I have nothing against young girls! In fact I can say for the group that we prefer playing to young people to adults, because we are young ourselves, and we feel closer to the audience. But on the Palladium we were trying to come across to an adult audience – to really appeal to them. Now, we know that our records appeal to adults because of the letters and things that we've had, but we wanted to appeal to them in person.*
>
> *"However, when we got on the stage, and every time we moved an inch there were screams and screams and girls crying and everything, and we were paralysed with kinda fear. Whenever I looked up I could see about ten girls, all personal fans of mine I guess, and they screamed whenever I moved.*
>
> *"So you see, every time we tried to do part of our act it just made the Palladium, which after all isn't a kids' place, into a shambles. Luckily I've been told the sound was OK because they turned down all the house mikes which prevented viewers from hearing the audience noise. As you can guess, we were very brought down by it all."*

I don't suppose Kim Fowley would have minded that at all.

If my ill-advised criticism of the Stones' "19th Nervous Breakdown" back in February had been my first professional faux pas of the year, my second was worse. At least with the Stones' record I had real and immediate reasons for my objections, even though I should probably have kept them to myself. But that July my slightly mean-spirited and luke-warm review of the Beach Boys' "Pet Sounds" LP was one of the worst and most mis-judged things I ever wrote. I had my excuses: I didn't dislike "Pet Sounds" – who could? – but at the time the LP didn't seem to me to merit the avalanche of praise flooding in from all quarters, with everyone everywhere in the music business seemingly trying to out-do each other in superlatives glorifying Brian's masterpiece (which I privately thought sounded like Phil Spector producing the Four Freshmen, though I didn't write that). So, determined to write an "unbiased" review, I ended up publishing a long badly-written piece which ended thus:

> *"The only real complaint is that nothing has been left to the listener's imagination. Every track is terribly complicated and cluttered up with vocals and backings galore, and even Beach Boys' fans must like some simple and uncomplicated forms of music from their idols.*
>
> *"It will probably make their present fans like them even more, but it's doubtful whether it'll make them any new ones."*

My comeuppance for this tetchy tripe was swiftly beamed down on me through the ether one fine evening a few days later while driving through Alexandra Palace in my red TR4A and listening to Kenny Everett on Radio London. He exploded on air at my review, reading out all the worst bits, and finishing up with "...and who is this Norman Jopling anyway!" which at least gave my girlfriend Carol a laugh.

Later I discovered I wasn't the only music writer to be less than enthusiastic about a great album. Richard Green had dismissed the Beatles' "Revolver" a few months previously, and I should have learned from his mistake. And other scribes in future years confessed to me their less-than-appreciative reviews of such gems as Santana's "Abraxas", the first Elvis Costello LP, and the second Oasis album. Shame on us all!

The next big LP release in 1966 was Dylan's double-album "Blonde On Blonde", and I combined an in-depth review, glowing, of course, with the news of Bob's motorcycle accident when he – supposedly – suffered broken neck vertebrae and concussion. But whatever did happen to him, the event in retrospect marked the end of the phenomenal second phase of his career, that giddy 18-month period when he abandoned acoustic-based folk-protest music, embraced rock, and in doing so opened up the genre to new dimensions of lyrical possibilities. "Blonde On Blonde" was released less than a year after "Highway 61 Revisited" which itself had followed hot on the heels of "Bringing It All Back Home". Despite the many fine Dylan albums which would follow, it would be difficult not to see this period as the artistic zenith of Dylan's career, creatively equalled by few other artists in rock music.

That same month marked another major music milestone: the end of the Beatles as a touring band. Fed up with the circus created around their still-unequalled ability to attract, scared of the death threats against them prompted by Lennon's intemperate remark about the Beatles being "bigger than Jesus", they wisely decided to concentrate on studio work. And what studio work it would prove to be.

The Beatles themselves were still the finest example of one of Liverpool's great gifts to the world: the beat group. It was a Liverpool invention and it had conquered the world. And although nobody calls themselves 'beat groups' anymore (at least not at the time of writing), they're as popular in the 21st century as in the latter half of the 20th. It could be argued that a group of young males playing rock'n'roll-based music had been current ever since Bill Haley & The Comets, and Elvis, Scotty and Bill. But the Comets were a hot western swing band who successfully incorporated black rhythms, which nevertheless sounded revolutionary. And Scotty and Bill – essential though their contribution was to the birth of rockabilly – were "simply" the backing group for Elvis Presley, definitively a solo artist. You might even say with more accuracy that the Crickets were the first of the true beat groups, initially comprising the classic line-up of drums, bass, rhythm guitar, lead guitar. But the Liverpool bands took it further. They incorporated their own vocal harmonies, they used electric bass, and they realised and fulfilled the power and potential of the form.

294

It was a simple combination but capable of almost unlimited artistic expression. And it was in Liverpool where it proliferated and where it was understood that the group itself was the solo unit – and a named leader not particularly essential.

But now, towards the end of 1966, four years after the first UK hit from the Beatles and almost three years since their musical conquest of America, many of the first and second wave of British beat groups were breaking up, and not all of our readers were happy about it. Some, indeed, were anguished:

RM w/e 29th October 1966

'Here's why we won – and lost – America.'

A RECENT check showed that 21 records in the British top fifty were American sung and produced. Half the top thirty LPs are American. In the American top fifty there were just eight British records – a bit pathetic isn't it! We are drifting back to pre-Beatle days. It's a British disease, a strain of unrealism that makes British groups think they can rely on popularity when they split up etc. Do they think the public a crowd of nitwits? Groups like the Yardbirds, Hollies, Them, Moody Blues, Pennies, Pretty Things, Manfred Mann, Animals, Searchers, Georgie Fame, Wayne Fontana & Mindbenders, Mojos, Nashville Teens, Ivy League etc. Only a few, a very few, can carry success after splitting and changing members, especially lead singers, they are just not the same group. I was worried about trouble in the Who until I read your article on Roger Daltry. The Who are in the forefront of a new wave of groups – and this wave could re-establish British Pop Supremacy. I can only hope the Who, Troggs, Cream, etc don't catch the "disease" otherwise our achievements spearheaded by the Beatles, Stones, Herman, Kinks, will be eclipsed in this American resurgence. – Gerrard Barron, 19 Singledge Avenue Whitfield, Dover, Kent.

Gerrard's main point was interesting but, with hindsight, invalid. The "American resurgence" was happening because young Americans including many middle-class kids – the sort who previously looked down on rock'n'roll – became inspired by the cleverness, coolness, and general artistic validity of the Beatles and the British groups, and then proceeded to form such unstoppable combinations as the Byrds, the Mamas & Papas, the Lovin' Spoonful, the Left Banke, Love, and hundreds more. Also, American ingenuity was about to launch the Monkees, the most notorious of all the "manufactured" beat groups, in order to successfully exploit the sub-teen void left by the now-musically progressive Beatles and their ilk. But Gerrard was correct in identifying the proliferation of groups splitting up. In fact it was a major theme in many of my interviews at that time. In *Reformed – "We Just Can't Keep On Fighting The Rest Of The World" said Phil May*, the Pretty Things' charismatic singer wondered if the sacking of drummer Viv Prince would "restore confidence". It did, gig-wise, but didn't help chart-wise – the Things would score no more hits, though cred-wise they would soon cut their classic psychedelic albums "S.F.Sorrow" and "Parachute". And in *Then There Were Two*, Tony Crane was happy his old group the Merseybeats had broken up and were now a duo – Tony and Billy Kinsley, the original members. As the Merseys they'd just hit big with the irresistible "Sorrow", but would also score no more hits despite the efforts of new management team Kit Lambert and Chris Stamp who, famously, looked after The Who.

More breaks-ups: Richard Green and I trotted along to a Manfred Mann press reception where Paul Jones announced he was quitting for a solo career, and his replacement Mike d'Abo was introduced. This was big news. Richard spoke to Manfred and I spoke to Paul, but unfortunately over-imbibed and offended him by suggesting he'd split "for the money", then asking him if he'd feel guilty if Manfred Mann got no more hits. "Nasty question, Norman", Paul replied, reasonably enough. But in fact it didn't happen. Manfred Mann carried on churning out hits regardless, whereas Paul, who made (what I believed) was the mistake of going too pop (he was an R&B vocalist at heart), only scored two more major hits. Richard and I wrote up the sorry saga in *At Last – Manfred And Paul Tell The Truth About The Big BreakUp*. Of course they did no such thing. A few weeks later, in *The Dreadful Assassination Of Four Pop Songs By The Manfred Mann Group*, Manfred himself enthused about their new EP (jazzed-up versions of current hits), enthused about new lead singer Mike d'Abo, but admitted he didn't much like their new single "Semi-Detached Suburban Mr James" ("...patronising", he said). Yet despite changing labels, producers, several group members and losing the charismatic Mr Jones, Manfred Mann continued their seamless run of hits barely pausing for breath. Nevertheless, being part of an efficient hit-making machine always seemed ever-so-slightly irksome for Manfred. Luckily for him, progressive rock was just round the corner.

Another major split was the wrenching apart of Manchester's Wayne Fontana from his group the Mindbenders. Together they'd sold millions in 1965 with "Game Of Love" which had topped the US charts, and in summer '66 the Fontana-less Mindbenders did it again with "A Groovy Kind Of Love". Back from their obligatory US tour, Eric Stewart told me an interesting thing in *The Mindbenders Tell Of U.S. Race Rioting, The Girl Who Writes Their Songs, And What Happens When You Hire An Airplane* (my current penchant was for long headlines):

> "...but one thing we didn't like about America was the equipment for the stage shows. Now, America is supposed to be the home of pop music and all that. But you wouldn't think so by the disgusting equipment they provide you with. Any British group will tell you that. They've no idea – it's diabolical."

One of the biggest breakups was the fragmentation of the original Animals. Their ex-producer, the modest yet staggeringly successful Mickie Most, selling himself short in: *Mickie, branching out into films says 'I've never made a classic pop record...'* told me:

> "I feel sorry about the Animals breaking up, even though I don't record them anymore. They were a fantastic group in their hey-day. But the sound can't continue with everyone leaving. In my opinion the Animals were Eric Burden and Alan Price. Now, when Alan and John left, the sound was watered down. I'm not slamming Barry or Dave. But the

Animals were the Animals and you can't put in substitutes for the original members, no matter how good they are."

But it wasn't just the British groups who were splitting up. John Phillips had sacked his errant wife Michelle from the Mamas & Papas that summer and replaced her with another classy blonde, Jill Gibson, long-term girlfriend of Jan & Dean's charismatic Jan Berry – who'd almost died that April in his '66 Stingray and would take years to even partially recover. But substitute Mama didn't last long – when John and Michie were reconciled that autumn, out went Jill and back in came Michelle. A more serious split was the charismatic Gene Clark quitting the Byrds in April '66, leaving the leadership and musical direction of the group entirely to Jim, later Roger McGuinn.

In contrast, on a togetherness note, this was my interview with Roger Daltry – the "we're not breaking up" story which had given comfort to Gerrard:

RM w/e 17th September 1966

'There's no more trouble in the group now – we won't split up...'

"COME up and see the attic," said Roger Daltry, "I decorated it myself last month."

I gingerly climbed the stairs, pushed open a round-topped polished wooden door and sank down on a huge sofa in the attic of Roger's new flat in London's Maida Vale. If ever the Who fold ("I can't see us lasting longer than three years," said Roger) then the lead singer could make a good living doing interior design and decoration. He has covered the ceiling with polished wood, whitewashed the walls and generally converted the attic into an interesting place instead of a dirty musty old room.

Also padding around the room was Mouse, a Saluki, which is a rare and expensive dog which can run at the phenomenal speed of 45mph. Its former name is unpronounceable and Roger was given it as a present some months ago. He was ejected from his last flat becase Mouse wasn't trained properly at the time, when he was just a pup.

"I enjoyed decorating this room. It would have cost me about £300 and I've bought all the bits and pieces from junk shops, markets, etc. I moved into this area because it's so quiet. Pete's got his own flat, he has done for some time now, but John and Keith still live at home.

"You know I'm completely out of the picture as far as our image is concerned. We were out of things for so long because of all these legal troubles that I feel that we're starting all over again. There's no more trouble in the group now – we won't split up or anything. We couldn't though, because we just wouldn't be the Who if any one of us left. We feel we are a group of individuals rather than Roger Daltry and the Who, or Pete Townshend and the Who.

"I can't see how some groups keep going with all the changes they go through. Manfred Mann, for instance. It's hard on Michael d'Abo because Manfred seems to be trying to push him into the Paul Jones slot. It must be terribly hard for him."

At the moment the Who have two records in the charts, and they're still entangled in legal deals and arguments. But the boys are quite happy with the set-up at Polydor.

"We had one row because of the 'My Generation' LP. It was so rushed it was ridiculous. The instrumental parts were really rushed and they put out all those old James Brown things, which weren't intended for it. They're fine for the stage, but not for a record. The same thing applies to some of the songs which will be on our new LP, except for vice versa: they don't go down well on stage but they sound good on the record.

"We've recorded a version of 'Barbara Ann' for the LP and there's also Pete's song 'So Sad About Us' which flopped for the Merseys. For the never-say-die Who fans we've included 'Heat Wave', but the track I like best so

far is Pete's 'Disguises'. There are still a lot more to record and the LP will be ready in about a month."

The Who are shortly to start a tour with the Merseys. But there are still some more big names to come. On stage the Who still smash equipment but there's more to it than meets the eye.

"We do it more for our own sake than the audiences," explained Roger. *"It's a kind of relief, smashing things up. And it's not as bad as you think. Most of the equipment can be repaired again – in fact we've got everything from amplifiers to guitars all covered in patches. They sound exactly the same. And our two road managers are geniuses at putting them back together again. It's only Pete who permanently damages things and that's because some of his guitars are so fragile. It all started when Pete slipped on stage and broke his guitar. The reaction was terrific! No really, he started when he used to play about with amplifiers and pull them and everything for the feedback sounds. It's just developed. It makes us feel much better to do it.*

"The rest of our act is for the audience. But the smashing up bit is for us." Roger explained that it was harder and harder to keep one jump ahead on stage numbers.

"When we were the High Numbers we used to do things like 'Gotta Dance Top Keep From Crying', then when we became the Who it was James Brown. Everyone started on those so now it's all down to originals. But we don't do all that much stage work. We turn down more dates than we accept. Sometimes I think we should have done them...

"It's the money situation that bothers me. I mean, we never used to get any. Things aren't so bad now. But for a top group our money was terrible."

The Who (slogan: "Maximum R&B") had in fact dropped most of the rhythm & blues from their act, but there was no sign of black music's popularity diminishing. Our R&B chart was a year old, and Keith Yershon compiled a survey covering the first year. Top ten artists were: Otis Redding, Wilson Pickett, James Brown, the Four Tops, Lee Dorsey, Stevie Wonder, Junior Walker, the Miracles, Don Covay, and Marvin Gaye. Top ten singles were "In The Midnight Hour" – Wilson Pickett, "My Girl" – Otis Redding, "Ride Your Pony" – Lee Dorsey, "Up Tight" –Steve Wonder, "Rescue Me" – Fontella Bass, "Wooly Bully" – Sam The Sham & Pharaohs, "I Can't Help Myself" – Four Tops, "1-2-3" – Len Barry, "Respect" – Otis Redding", "See Saw" – Don Covay.

I was still writing – and championing – rhythm & blues, but had dropped *The Great Unknowns* column. Many of the artists featured were now no longer unknown. Many of them had become UK hitmakers: Otis Redding, James Brown, Doris Troy, John Lee Hooker, Dionne Warwick, and a host of Motown giants – the Miracles, Mary Wells, the Marvelettes, Marvin Gaye and Martha & the Vandellas. Of course there would always be great unknowns, but I felt that this had been essentially a black music series – and with regard to esoteric knowledge about black artists, the game had caught up and passed me. Others were digging deeper, getting more into it. Besides, I was now equally interested in progressive white music. But I did profile Junior Walker in *Autry (De Walt, not Gene) aids Tamla's British chart invasion…*(Junior's sax-drenched version of Marvin Gaye's original "How Sweet It Is" hits the Top 30); profiled the phenomenal Four Tops in *Here's how a sophisticated night club act became the world's top rhythm & blues group and why it took them 13 years to do it* (the Tops zoom to UK No.1 with "Reach Out I'll Be There"); and on the British black music scene in *'We'd never play Calypso or Ska' says the answer to America's R&B supremacy*, I spoke to Jimmy James, who with the Vagabonds was now arguably Britain's hottest live soul act. Jimmy, an old-school West Indian R&B man, was eloquent on the subject of music:

> *"…when we came over from Jamaica, everyone expected us to play Calypso and something they called Blue Beat, but later we realised was Ska. In Jamaica, the dominating kind of music is American. In fact, throughout the whole of the West Indies and Caribbean it is American rhythm & blues that is the big music. Calypso is big only in Trinidad, but of course when the Mighty Sparrow sings a Calypso it's big everywhere. But that's as often or not because it's blue.*

> *"Ska started out about four years ago. It's by no means a cultural form of music, or any part of the West Indian heritage. It started because of the West Indian beatnik set who used to spend hours playing drums and making them sound like any instrument they wanted to. They used to sit there all day with their beards and long hair and play. A record was made called 'Oh Carolina' which was an enormous hit. It had that Ska sound on, just drums. Then everyone copied it. But it wasn't really big world-wide until Millie's 'My Boy Lollipop'. But we've never played Calypso or Ska."*

Jimmy was a powerful, soulful and distinctive vocalist whose latest single "This Heart Of Mine" on Pye remains a classic. But his fine slew of '60s records was never destined for major chart success. The British record-buying public were only just beginning to regularly buy R&B / soul music in quantity. And America, with Atlantic, Stax, Motown, Chess and many other great labels at the top of their game, could always attract the punter's money over the home-grown product.

On the first night of the big Rolling Stones / Ike & Tina Turner / Yardbirds tour in late September at the Royal Albert Hall, I got back – sort of – with the Stones. Long John Baldry was compere, and Peter Jay and the New Jaywalkers opened the show. Everyone shone. The Yardbirds, always terrific in small clubs, rose impressively to the big venue occasion, better than I'd ever heard them, transmitting real power. And Ike and Tina, with the Ikettes and their band, were everything you hoped they'd be – a hard-edged exciting sexy R&B show, so good I couldn't help but wonder how the Stones would fare following them. But any concern was unmerited. The Rolling Stones were now on another level: The Beatles had retired from live performances a month earlier, and the Stones rocked with the authority that comes with knowing they were the biggest and best live band in the world. The evening was sensational.

Afterwards at the backstage party chatting with my current girlfriend Maggie, I noticed she was stealing the frequent glance – as women tend to do – at Mick Jagger who was standing a few yards away. Mick certainly noticed Maggie with her long hair and long legs and pert face – and then noticed me. Over he came, friendly as anything. Even when I'd been 'in' with the Stones, he'd never been this friendly. But other than a grin and a hello, he didn't attempt to chat up Maggie, and there was a warm and likeable sensitivity about him, a side of him, so I've heard, infrequently revealed. He was on a happy high after the gig and the feeling I got was that he'd made a point of coming over in order to, well, simply as a boost for everyone. And it was.

Outside the Albert Hall there were several policemen surrounding my car who seemed glad to see me. They explained, firmly but not unpleasantly, that the amount of heavy traffic along Kensington Gore had been triggering my car alarm all evening and infuriating everyone in the area. I got the feeling I was being let off lightly, so I apologised profusely, switched off the alarm and never switched it on again.

Another big tour debut I attended with Maggie was the Walker Brothers tour, kicking off rather less salubriously in East Ham. We arrived late, in the middle of the Montanas' act, mainly impressions, but including a brilliant impersonation of P.J.Proby. First of the hit groups was Dave Dee, Dozy, Beaky, Mick and Tich, currently No.2 with "Bend It" (stuck behind the late Jim Reeves' No. 1 "Distant Drums"). Zany and garish with absurd lighting, the group's clowning belied their musical talent. The Troggs followed, still wearing their stripy "Wild Thing" jackets and didn't play their first two hits so impressively, but then made up for it with a powerful and dominating "I Can't Control Myself", their current hit. But most of the audience that night were there for the Walker Brothers, specifically Scott, and after half a dozen more-than-competent beat numbers, mostly with John singing lead, Scott launched into the ballads, beginning with "I Need You" and "Another Tear Falls"...and there was the rush for the stage. He sang beautifully, talked a lot to the audience. He was brilliant. When we came out the theatre I saw to my delight that some girls who'd been waiting at a nearby bus-stop when we went in and who'd very definitely noticed us had written their phone numbers on my TR4A in lipstick, pink on red.

I'd caught Ike and Tina at their hotel a day or so before the Royal Albert Hall concert. Tina, bold and sexy on stage, seemed a lot younger and more girlish in person. But Ike, with his formidable musical reputation and impeccable R&B track record was the one I was interested in, and despite his legendary menace – and Ike certainly knew how to to turn it on – was happy enough to talk about his career to someone who was obviously interested in and not altogether ignorant of his music.

RM w/e 8th October 1966

IKE tells, among other things, why he wants to change the act's name, and why he dislikes 'River Deep'

IKE and Tina Turner aren't just another American rhythm and blues act riding the crest of a British hit wave. They have been making top quality records for six years and until the success of "River Deep Mountain High" they were almost completely ignored by the majority of the British record buying public.

I met them at their hotel a few days before their first concert tour here with the Rolling Stones and the Yardbirds.

"We've been trying to get into Britain for a couple of years now," said Ike, "but I wouldn't come along until I was sure I could bring all the act. It would have been no good just Tina and me coming here. I didn't want to be a letdown act. I don't even know how we all managed to get in this time, but here we are."

The act that Ike was talking about is in fact himself Tina, three girls called the Ikettes, and their band, which includes two lead male singers, Jimmy Thomas and Prince Albert. Which is a lot of American talent to bring into Britain, especially in view of some of the permit troubles which both U.S. and British acts have had recently when trying to cross the Atlantic.

Ike's band is called the Kings Of Rhythm and was formed after Ike had played with several other bands. He met Tina by accident and she became an Ikette and later they cut their first single together "A Fool In Love" for the Sue label. On almost all of their records Tina sings solo, while Ike plays guitar. Only on their best-selling "It's Gonna Work Out Fine" does Ike sing – or talk – and on some obscure LP tracks.

"For years I've been trying to get the name of the act changed on records," explained Ike. "It should just have 'Tina Turner' on the records, but none of the record companies will have this. It's very confusing, especially to somebody who doesn't know the act. They come up to Tina and say 'Hello Ikeantina', thinking that's her name."

Until the first concert at London's Albert Hall, neither Ike nor Tina had met any of the Rolling Stones, although some of the group had been to see the Ike and Tina Revue in the States.

"We don't rehearse very much," confessed Ike, "but we still manage to put on an almost identical sound to the records when we're on stage. I remember once when I told the band to be somewhere, and none of them turned up. So I had to replace them all! Things just work out. We tour nearly all of the States and keep on touring all the time so most people get a chance to see us if they want to.

"I'm not concerned with singing personally. I'm more interested in arranging and guitar work. You ask me what I think of 'River Deep, Mountain High'? Well, I'll tell you.

"I liked the track. And then I liked Tina's voice when it was put over the track. But I didn't like it when Phil put on the 26 voices and all the strings. We met Phil through a film he was doing. It was a musical film and was supposed to have the Rolling Stones in it. But they couldn't get them. They did have some other big names and we were asked to come along. When Phil saw us he liked what he saw and asked me if we would like to make a record with him. Naturally I said yes. Tina hadn't heard of Phil, but I knew of him through the Ronettes.

"Our new LP has five Spector produced tracks on it. The others I produced. Bob Crewe produced our next single,

one side of which is 'Two For Tango'. We were looking for a new record label when we met Phil.

"Our first record label was Sue, and we made some hits with them. But after Juggy Murray signed Inez Foxx and some other artists, he didn't take very much interest in us. So when our contract ran out I signed with an old friend of mine who runs Kent Records. The material recorded there was partly recorded when we were at Sue in my private studio. I had it all at home and we just put it out on Kent. Like 'I Can't Believe What You Say'. Then we had an offer from Warner Brothers. They said they would give us maximum promotion.

So I signed with them. We had one single put out, and an LP which I didn't like. That's all. And we didn't get the promotion we thought we would. So after our contract ran out – it was for a year – we left. Then we moved to Ray Charles' Tangerine label. We cut 'Anything You Wasn't Born With' and Ray produced the disc. Just the one. We were still 'looking for a home', you might say. And then Phil came along.

"We haven't any plans for any more records apart from our new single."

Tina was quite flirty which made me slightly nervous with Ike around but he didn't seem to mind, or even notice. They didn't seem at all like husband and wife together: there was no chemistry between them. As I left she sidled up to me and said coyly, "You know, you remind me of Phil Spector. He's very English, too". I guess it was meant as a compliment, but I just didn't know what to make of it.

Another famed duo, Sonny & Cher, whose global chart-topper "I Got You Babe" a year ago had been an all-time favourite among young couples – as we'd learned from the RM postbag – were still riding high after a string of duo and solo hits. They'd just returned to the States after a week in London for a few concert dates and the

London premiere of their film "Good Times". They'd also managed to squeeze in an RM competition, personally phoning five lucky fans, a job they did with grace and enthusiasm. But now, the release of Cher's version of Bobby Hebb's "Sunny" as a single had provoked substantial criticism from UK record fans, and Sonny called me from LA to explain:

> *"...originally the track was a cut off Cher's new LP,"* said Sonny, *"Now, Bobby Hebb's record was issued a couple of months ago in Britain and it didn't mean a thing. I thought that it was a dead record, and the the single by Cher was put out. Then, about three weeks, ago Bobby's record started to happen.*
>
> *"I don't like making cover records. I never intended this to be a cover record, and I hope that Boby's record gets the success it deserves. I hope that British record buyers will buy what they wanna buy, you know. I hear there's another version of 'Sunny' – by Georgie Fame?*
>
> *"The reason we recorded 'Sunny' in the first place, for Cher's LP, was because it expresses a relationship – it's a fine song, but I never thought it'd be out anywhere for us as a single."*

The "Sunny" result was: Cher's version reached No.32, Georgie's version reached No.13, and Bobby Hebb's original reached No.12.

"Sunny" was a big song, but not really a big record. When it came to big records, the last few months of 1966 had heralded the massive No.1 hit and future pop standard "Reach Out I'll Be There", which effectively launched the Four Tops in the UK. It was one of those records you couldn't get away from, it dominated the airwaves for weeks and it elevated Motown's profile in the UK into the top strata of the pop mainstream. I'd featured the Tops three weeks previously, but when I got a call in November from Brian Epstein's NEMS Enterprises asking if I'd like to interview them, there I was in a flash:

RM w/e 19th November 1966

The Tops talk about the songwriting set-up at Tamla, British R&B, the Beatles, and the Motown Revue

NATURALLY enough, the Four Tops weren't nearly as busy the last time they visited Britain. That was about eighteen months ago when they came over to promote their record of "I Can't Help Myself", which at that time was the biggest-selling record experienced by the Tamla-Motown-Gordy corporation. Even including such previous hits as the Supremes "Where Did Our Love Go" and Miss Mary Wells' "My Guy", both of which almost topped the charts in Britain as well as America. Now let the Four Tops continue.

"This is the most important record of our career. At the time, 'I Can't Help Myself' was important, but this is bigger. We have been aiming for a number one record in Britain, and our writers and producers Holland and Dozier have been aiming for us too."

The Four Tops, who have been on the music scene together for well over ten years have very definite aims and ambitions, and many of them have already been achieved.

"It took Tamla Motown to bring out the Four Tops, as it were. When we joined the label, Holland and Dozier moved around the country with us for a month. They listened to everything we did – and we didn't try to impress them, we just sang what we could, and then they started to write songs for us.

"The first one was 'Baby I Need Your Loving'. That's still the favourite song of three of us. That could have been a standard if we hadn't been a new group. Actually, if it had been the Beatles who had recorded it, then it would have been a standard.

"Talking about the Beatles, they've done a lot for pop music. Before the British sound invaded the American charts, US pop music was very dead-beat. There was no *real tuneful music and the whole thing was stagnant. The British groups, and especially the Beatles, brought a big revival to the scene. Some of the Beatles' tunes featured real chord changes and were genuinely good musical tunes. Good music became accepted. Would 'Michelle' have been a hit before the Beatles? Of course not. It was the Beatles that enabled such music to be accepted in America.*

"The other side of our album is quite interesting, we feel. Side one appeals to the rock fans who know us as a rock group. The other side is completely different, it sets up another mood. We think it may appeal to other types of record buyers".

I asked the Tops about the other type of songs in their style which had been written by Holland-Dozier-Holland, but recorded by other Motown stars, such Smokey and the Miracles, Kim Weston, and the Isley Brothers.

"Well, this was how it was", replied Duke. "They had written 'This Old Heart Of Mine' for us, and then the Isley Brothers joined Tamla. Now, they realised that the song would suit them, but it had been written for us. So they asked us if we would mind if the Isleys could have the song. Of course we said that they could gladly have it. But it's nice that our status at Tamla is such that they do ask our consent before letting someone else record our songs. As for the Miracles recording a Holland-Dozier-Holland song, well, Smokey is a very intelligent fellow. He knows that trends are changing, and when it was time for a new Miracles single he had nothing suitable written. So they recorded 'I'm The One You Need' which had been written for us – of course the Miracles recorded it in a higher key.

"As for 'Helpless' which Kim Weston recorded, well, that was going to be a single for us. But it didn't work out nearly as good as we expected, so when we found a stronger song that was issued instead. We have three songs recorded as future singles, but of course we have to be very careful about a follow-up to 'Reach Out I'll Be There'."

I asked the Tops about their opinion of white British rhythm & blues and received a somewhat unexpected answer.

"Of course your stars can perform it. The Rolling Stones are the perfect example. When English music was getting big in the States, then Negro music had a big upsurge too. They go hand-in-hand. English music is very influenced by R&B.

"But of course the blues forms the basic ingredient of Tamla, blues and gospel. Now, Tamla-Motown is run on feeling. It's run on soul. The Tamla-Motown Revue doesn't go out like before. The acts in America became too big and can go out as stars in their own right. But there may well be another Tamla-Motown Revue coming to Britain soon. But not, we think, in the States. We can go out now and star on our own. We take a rhythm section on the road with us. We do, really, work very hard, and when we're not touring then we're in the studio. But we all enjoy it."

While I was interviewing the Tops, the NEMS house photographer was unobtrusively snapping away and a week later I received a print in the post of me interviewing the Four Tops, with a personal dedication signed by all four Tops on the reverse. I never had that happen before or since, and I treasure that photograph.

That same month we published our 1966 end-of-year Poll results. The top three in each category were: World Male Vocalist: Elvis Presley, Gene Pitney, Bob Dylan. World Female Vocalist: Dusty Springfield, Cher, Brenda Lee. World Male Vocal Group: Beach Boys, Beatles, Walker Brothers. World Female Vocal Group: Supremes, She Trinity, Martha & The Vandellas. World Instrumental Group: Shadows, Herb Albert, Sounds Incorporated. Solo Instrumentalist: Duane Eddy, Hank Marvin, Herb Alpert. Large Band or Orchestra: Joe Loss, Herb Alpert, Henry Mancini. World's Best Disc: "Love Letters" – Elvis Presley, "All Or Nothing" – Small Faces, "You Don't Have To Say You Love Me" – Dusty Springfield. Best Dressed: Elvis Presley, Cliff Richard, Dusty Springfield. Most Disliked Record: "They're Coming To Take Me Away, Ha-Haaa!" – Napoleon XIV, "Yellow Submarine"

– Beatles, "Tears" – Ken Dodd. British Male Vocalist: Cliff Richard, Tom Jones, Billy Fury. British Female Vocalist: Dusty Springfield, Sandie Shaw, Cilla Black. British Vocal Group: Beatles, Small Faces, Rolling Stones. Most Promising: Chris Farlowe, Crispian St Peters, David Garrick. DJ: Jimmy Savile, Simon Dee, Kenny Everett. TV/Radio Show: Top Of The Pops, Ready Steady Go!, Presenting Elvis.

The biggest poll upset was the Beach Boys toppling the Beatles. It was no fluke: NME's poll results showed the same. 1966 was the pinnacle of the creative rivalry between the two groups and both released great records. But the Beach Boys had two advantages. Firstly, they were benefiting from the "catch-up" factor which had proved so sensational for the Beatles when they conquered America, and which had so benefited Bob Dylan in the UK. When an artist suddenly becomes hugely popular and already has a substantial back catalogue, their older albums also chart. And often, all at the same time. The Beatles' tried-and-tested UK LP release schedule had been the same for years: an album mid-year(ish), and an album just before Christmas. In '63 it was "Please Please Me" (April) and "With The Beatles" (November). In '64 "A Hard Day's Night" (July) and "Beatles For Sale" (December). In '65 "Help" (August) and "Rubber Soul" (December). And in 1966 "Revolver" (August)...but in December the weaker "A Collection Of Beatles Oldies" (which only reached No.7 – all the rest hit No. 1). Of course, the Beatles were working on "Sgt. Pepper" – but that wouldn't be released for another six months. The Beach Boys, however, benefited from the "catch-up" factor. They had no LP chart-toppers, but who could argue with what they did have: "Beach Boys Party" (February, No.3), "Beach Boys Today" (April, No.6), "Pet Sounds" (July, No.2), "Summer Days (And Summer Nights!)" (July, No.4), "Best Of The Beach Boys" (November, No.2). And their new single was the soon-to-be chart-topping classic "Good Vibrations". Secondly, the Beach Boys, unlike the Beatles, were still touring, and at the time of the poll were touring the UK – I'd caught them in concert that very month:

...in fact, it's unlikely that anyone who goes to see the Beach Boys will be disappointed with their stage sound. At Finsbury Park Astoria for the second performance last

Saturday, they came up with a shattering succession of their hits. If there was any complex backing sound lost, it was more than made up for by excitement and a professional stage presence, especially by Mike Love. Surprisingly enough, the group excelled on what one might think would be the hardest sounds to reproduce. "Good Vibrations" was sensational, and so was Carl's atmospheric "God Only Knows". Al Jardin led through rockers like "Wouldn't It Be Nice", "Help Me Rhonda" and a "Barbara Ann"/ "Papa-Oom-Mow-Mow" medley, while Mike sang lead on "California Girls" and "I Get Around". If you like their records but think they might not be as good on stage, forget it. Their happy enjoyable act is as good or better than most British bands.

No other real surprises, other than She Trinity – what a fan club they must have had. And the obligatory Elvis block-vote was so stuck for decent product in '66 they had to settle for the King's competent if uninspired copy of Ketty Lester's version of "Love Letters" – best disc of 1966 indeed! The "worst disc" was actually better than Elvis's "Love Letters": a zany thumper that sounded like it came straight from the pages of Mad Magazine. Earlier in the year I'd spoken to its creator:

...but the things he (Napoleon XIV) was saying had no relation to the things which thousands of people are paying seven shillings and fourpence halfpenny to hear, on a record which has been dubbed "tasteless and offensive".

"No, I didn't realise there would be much in the way of allegations of bad taste," said Napoleon, alias New York recording engineer Jerry Samuels.

"I don't think it is in particularly bad taste. Certainly not like 'Rainy Day Women' or 'Let's Go Get Stoned', which I think really are in bad taste. And all those other dope songs that are going around. But most people have taken the record in the spirit in which it was intended.

"I can't tell about the British market though. I don't study your charts so I don't really know whether or not

my record is in bad taste compared to other records which get into your charts."

It wasn't really in bad taste: in the song, Napoleon XIV was becoming mentally ill because his dog had left him – not his girl, which you were intended to presume until the 'surprise' punchline. A month or so later there was an even better "answer" record purportedly by the dog itself, a bitch called 'Josephine' (not historically accurate, but you get the picture) called "They Took You Away, I'm Glad, I'm Glad". The whole mad, sorry saga was so popular that the increasingly desperate-for-a-hit Kim Fowley cut a tardy cover version which proved too late for chart action. But he did invite a whole gang of people, including me, to the session, during which he ad-libbed his next single "Lights The Blind Can See", later less controversially abbreviated to "Lights". Kim was an impressively clever ad-libber, and as a bonus at the session/party I met a girl I liked named Norma and we dated for a few weeks as Norman and Norma till the gimmick wore off and we split. Quite Kim Fowley-esque, actually.

I was becoming increasingly convinced that the elusive "where it was at" factor was somehow currently connected with LSD. Therein lay the key to the seismic changes that were happening socially and musically, so I was beginning to believe, antennae a-twitch, if a bit late off the mark. But Kim Fowley attempted to (partly) disabuse me of this. The latest star he had hitched his wagon to was something called "Freak Out": in fact he was the self-appointed "Prince of Freak Out", and convinced me that the West Coast Freak Out movement was important enough to merit a full-page article in Record Mirror with, naturally, a freaky picture of Kim illustrating the concept, and copious Fowley quotes explaining it all.

RM w/e October 22nd 1966

FREAK OUT! The latest West Coast way of life – rebels with a cause, and their music

313

'FREAKING out' is a term which is being thrown about with gay abandon on the West Coast (California, not Cornwall), and like all successful movements there are plans afoot to introduce the concept on this side of the Atlantic.

Freaking Out is described in detail on the sleeve of the "Freak Out" album from the Mothers Of Invention, one of the leading pioneer groups of the movement. It reads "...on a personal level, FREAKING OUT is a process whereby an individual casts off outmoded and restricting standards of thinking, dress, and social etiquette in order to express CREATIVELY his relationship to his immediate environment and the social structure as a whole. Less perceptive individuals have referred to us who have chosen this way of thinking and FEELING as "Freaks", hence the term 'Freaking Out'. On a collective level, when any number of 'Freaks' gather and express themselves creatively through music or dance, for example, it is generally referred to as FREAK OUT. The participants, already emancipated from our national social SLAVERY dressed in their most inspired apparel, realise as a group whatever potential they have for free expression..."

If you read through that a couple of times, it becomes quite interesting, especially regarding the fact that the whole movement was initially underground (even now Freak Out records are not played on U.S. radio stations), and that the philosophy is one of the few in connection with the pop music field (or rock'n'roll, as the Americans call pop) which was not concocted by Madison Avenue. In fact, U.S. big business is only just beginning to realise that there are dollars to be made from this cult.

Last week's Billboard reports that many record companies are reaching out for "underground" groups – who are getting nearly all their exposure in coffee houses. Three labels – ESP, Atlantic and MGM – are battling to sign the Fugs, whose first LP on ESP has been on the Billboard chart for fourteen weeks without any airplay.

Other groups in this category include the Mothers of Invention, the Blues Project, the Velvet Underground (this group is handled by film-maker Andy Warhol, who is responsible for many major "happenings" in the U.S.) and the Paul Butterfield Blues Band, who although they play a different kind of music, are still regarded as an underground group due to their lack of airplay.

The music itself ranges from rock'n'roll to near-psychedelic free form. In the case of the Mothers Of Invention, their music progresses from one form to the other through intermediate stages, but they send up everything they play – nothing is serious, or sacred to them, and it is impossible to take them seriously.

The connection between Freaking Out and psychedelic music is not as strong as supposed. And the equally tenuous connection between both of them is more of an enigma than a tie-up. The leaders of the Freak Out movement claim to have never taken LSD – Frank Zappa and the omnipresent Kim Fowley.

Kim has a freak-out record issued by EMI next week. It's called "Lights" and you need to hear it to believe it. It was recorded a couple of months back at one of Kim's "happenings" at a recording studio in Bond Street. Kim probably knows more about the movement than anyone else in this country. Here, in his words, are the beginnings, and if you need that pinch of salt go get it now.

"You want me to start from the beginning. Right. Well, back in 1934 or something there was this artist called Clay Vito, who lived in California. He had a Beatle hair cut and all that, and he was the big hippie of the time.

"Time went by and Clay made a solid reputation and he began to get interested in music. Well, when rock'n'roll came along about 1954 him and his crowd began to get interested. There were different stages of rock, you know, the British sound, and Clay had this reputation as a patron.

"Groups started coming to him for guidance. One day, five guys came along and were broke – they asked

315

if they could sleep at his studio. They were the Byrds. He also discovered groups like Love and the Leaves, who made 'Hey Joe'. Nowadays if anyone opens a club on the West Coast they have to invite Vito and his crowd. They all wait there eagerly to see if Clay turns up. If he does, everything's OK. It makes the place. You see, Vito's been with this Freak Out movement for years."

Kim recorded his records "Lights" (formerly titled "Lights The Blind Can See" but toned down for England) at the same session as his version of "They're Coming To Take Me Away, Ha-Haaa!". Like all Fowley songs, he ad-libs as he goes along. EMI's Parlophone label issues this record which is the first Freak Out single issued here. EMI also have the rights to the Mothers Of Invention LP, but as this is a double-album there may be some difficulties about its release.

But whether the whole Sunset Strip happening scene of Freaking Out "creative expression" et al is repeated in Britain, probably depends more on the passing whim of certain susceptible pop group members rather than a revolutionary change in the social pattern of young people...

The year ended with a clutch of modest interviews. In *ANTI-LOVE: You won't find any moon-June romance in songs from the Who*, bassist John Entwistle declared "We're the most unromantic group around... we've never recorded a real love song. And we couldn't do it now. It wouldn't be our image...we do have quite a following of blokes which may have something to do with this anti-love thing...I mean, 'I'm A Boy' is almost a queer song..." In *Dave Dee & Co keep one jump ahead*, the quaintly-named quintet bemoaned other groups 'copying' their zany togs, and promised more sartorial suavity in the future. And former teen queen gymslip pinup Helen Shapiro, still only 20, in *Helen looks back on schoolgirl success, the No.1 record she couldn't stand, and talks about her career now, 6 years later* (I was still hooked on long headlines) told me she was currently working the northern club circuit and was still making records – which didn't sell anymore. She was was also seriously sexy. Or sexily serious. And the chart-topper she couldn't stand (and still hated): "Walking Back To Happiness".

On a different note, an ongoing letters page rhythm & blues/soul controversy regarding white men singing black music (a subject debated in our columns for years, ever since the emergence of the Stones and the Animals, et al) was reaching a climax. The correspondence was becoming interestingly thoughtful, kicking off with this:

THE SOUL MYTH
WHEN is this great "soul" myth going to be exploded? The assumption that the colour of your skin has bearing on whether you can put guts and feeling into a song is ridiculous. Sure, a coloured American, because of his tragic heritage, has every right to sing the blues but he cannot claim that right as his alone. There are thousands of people and individuals, besides Negroes, who have been, and are being, persecuted in this world. Are we to accept that these peoples, because their skin is not a certain colour are unable to give their all when singing a song? Who can say that the back-street orphan of the Glasgow Gorbals, or the hungry, neglected kid from London's East End can't put his soul into a song merely because his skin is white. The American Negro has his own peculiar brand of music which is his and his alone, but the right to sing with soul is definitely not exclusively his. This letter was not inspired by any racial prejudice and I know at least a few coloured people who agree with my views – Doris Troy, for example – Ron Turnball, 57 Paisley Drive, Edinburgh 8.

A week later we had a postbag of replies, including this:

SOUL ANSWER
READER Turnball misses the point about "soul". There is no reason why other persecuted individuals shouldn't put great feeling into their music. He's right when he says that the American Negro has his own peculiar brand of music which is his and his alone...this IS soul music, R&B and

so on, and is his way of expressing himself, stemming from when all he could do to entertain himself was to sing the blues. British soul singers are only copying and imitating, but why do they all put on phoney American accents? – Michael Norman, 28 Elmcroft Avenue, Wanstead, London, E11.

And the lead letter that week came from Dave Godin:

SOUL
The reasons why are explained

IT is way off beam to say that fans of R&B and "Soul" say it is the colour of a star's skin that brings the elusive "soul" quality. Anyone who has seen opera performed with sensitivity and skill will agree that the depth of emotion and feeling doesn't particularly hinge on the singer's past suffering, but on his dramatic ability and acting power. We do maintain, however, that because American Negroes can only enter the musical field, and are denied opportunities to enter other fields, this pent-up power will dominate the one area where they are allowed artistic expression. The analogy with a Glasgow orphan is false. A Glasgow orphan doesn't find doors closed in his face just because he is an orphan but this is what does happen to the American Negro, day in and day out. The same orphan singing with an assumed Negro accent would still be as much of a phoney as any British singer with a less unhappy background singing as if he'd just come out of the cotton fields – and the whole cult of "one accent for the interview and another for the record" won't survive the flimsiest examination. – Dave Godin, Friends Of American Rhythm & Blues Society, 139 Church Road, Bexleyheath, Kent.

Godin was in the vanguard of the new seriousness in pop. A radicalisation was taking place among hard-core soul and rhythm &

blues fans, nurtured through deepening knowledge of, and sympathy with, those who created the music they loved. For Dave Godin – his Tamla Motown Appreciation Society now metamorphosed into The Friends Of American Rhythm & Blues Society – love of soul music could and should lead inexorably to solidarity with and support for the American Negro (as was the term then) and concomitantly active participation in striving for freedom and equal rights. Dave's dedication was mirrored by soul and rhythm & blues enthusiasts throughout the UK, among them our own freelance stalwart Alan Stinton.

Godin had also recently fulfilled his ambition to open a record shop, Soul City in Deptford, now the centre of his enterprises – which would shortly include a record label. And Stinton, the most knowledgeable of Record Mirror's freelance writers on all matters soul and R&B, compiled for us a fearsome end-of-year quiz. The prize? A generous handful of imported LPs from Soul City...

Another high-profile soul aficionado interviewed at the end of 1966 was one Austin Churton Fairman, better known as Mike Raven, the UK's most respected blues/soul/rhythm & blues DJ. Mike had just quit the pirate station Radio 390, an event deemed important enough to be written up in the News Of The World. The importance of the pirate stations in the evolution of UK pop cannot be overstated, and Mike was one of the emerging new breed of DJs who were revolutionising UK pop radio. Many of these would shortly go legit when government legislation forced a mass DJ exodus to BBC Radio One, but in late '66 the pirates still ruled the airwaves.

Before his career with offshore radio, Mike had worked as a photographer, conjuror, ballet dancer, interior decorator and flamenco guitarist – among other things. A cousin of Oliver Smedley, chairman of Radio Atlanta, Mike joined that station from its start in May 1964 and presented a programme called All Systems Go. From there he moved to King Radio where he was Programme Controller. Based on Red Sands Fort off the coast of Kent, this sweet music station suffered from severe under-funding and never put out a strong enough signal to get sufficient listeners. New owners installed a more powerful transmitter, better equipment and relaunched it in September 1965 as Radio 390 which quickly won a huge audience for its middle-of-the-road programmes. On both King and 390 Mike presented programmes with his wife, Mandy, but it was for his evening R&B show that his reputation as the UK's premier black music DJ was established.

Mike often used to visit Record Mirror and DeHems, and I was a regular at his local gig, Bluesville, over the Manor House pub in North London. It was there I first witnessed an interesting phenomenon: Mike would play his records from his turntables set-up at the edge of the stage, and clustered in front of this area were a dozen or so youths clutching boxes of 45s. If one of the 45s in their collection matched the record Mike was playing, it would swiftly be sorted out from the box and brandished triumphantly in the air. This ritual went on all evening. It was a level of record collecting and identification with the music that was beyond anything I could have conceived.

Like Guy Stevens (and most other UK fans), Mike's taste for R&B had developed from rock'n'roll:

FOR many years I was completely uninterested in any kinds of pop music," he explained. "In fact my greatest musical love was for classical music. The pop singers of that era, the Guy Mitchells, Johnnie Rays, etc, just left me cold. For me they had no excitement.

"Then rock and roll came along. It was the very first type of pop music that interested me. It had excitement. This of course led me to similar interests, blues, etc. But at that time rhythm and blues was still race music. Artists like Little Richard couldn't perform before white audiences. And it was Presley that changed all that.

"No matter what else Presley has done before or after, that was his greatest achievement because he sang race music, and because he was so immensely popular , the door was opened for national acceptance of coloured artists.

"And in my opinion those early Presley records were not only the best that he ever made. They were the best pop records ever made".

Mike went on to tell how he had been working for the BBC, and how he eventually turned 'pirate', and started his own shows which featured exclusively his own favourite types of music. Why the specialisation?

320

"Purely for selfish motives. I play the type of music which excites and appeals to me the most. And you only have to look at the charts to see that this music is becoming more and more accepted."

Interviewing Mike must have been good for my karma because two months later I met my future wife Ruth at one of his gigs.

The top ten UK artists – according to the charts point system – for 1966 were:

UK	USA
The Beach Boys	The Beatles
Dave Dee, Dozy, Beaky, Mick & Tich	Gary Lewis & the Playboys
The Kinks	The Rolling Stones
Ken Dodd	The Lovin' Spoonful
Dusty Springfield	The Beach Boys
The Spencer Davis Group	The Supremes
The Small Faces	Simon & Garfunkel
Cliff Richard	The Mamas & the Papas
The Beatles	Herman's Hermits
Cilla Black	Herb Alpert

But, as compiler Richard Green pointed out, if the table was based on sales then the Beatles would obviously finish top. The 1966 chart survey was one of Richard's last features for Record Mirror: tempted by a substantial offer from NME, he quit RM in January '67 – but not before interviewing Jimi Hendrix for us. And my final interview of 1966 was with Scott Walker, serious, sensitive, troubled (though no-one seemed to know quite what these troubles exactly were – only their calamitous manifestations, i.e. heavy boozing, an accidental OD, hanging out with Jonathan King, etc). Being a superstar pin-up didn't sit easily with him – and he hadn't been prepared for it, as John Maus (John 'Walker') had been the group's original lead vocalist. Nevertheless, for all that, I couldn't help thinking that for someone who was currently a globally massive pop star, staggeringly physically attractive (so all the girls said), and was possessed of a wonderful voice which would give him a lifetime career, he certainly did his fair share of griping. Still, I hadn't walked the proverbial mile in his shoes, so really, what did I know?

RM w/e 31st December 1966

THE RELUCTANT AMERICAN
Some interesting opinions from Scott Walker

"I DIDN'T like it in America, and I'm not going back to live there. When I did live there it was terrible – once I got knifed, and I never got on well with the people there. I'm not a big-voiced loud-mouthed Texan and I never was."

The speaker was Scott Walker, formerly Engel, and a very reluctant American.

"As for Viet-Nam, I don't want any part of it. I don't want anything to do with it. I think it's a very bad thing – but then all wars are bad. When I was in the States, everything was so fast. Competition was cut-throat and it wasn't for people like me. Now, I haven't been back since we first arrived and I don't intend to. If we go back to work it will only be after everything has been carefully planned and scheduled. I certainly don't intend to ever go back to live there."

But living in Britain has presented considerable difficulties for Scott. For instance, he has to move house every couple of days or so. The reason is to prevent the invasion of his privacy. When I interviewed him, he was in a Hampstead retreat, armed only with a few clothes and his stereo record player and some records. No pop, beat or R&B records, incidentally.

"I've got nothing against fans," Scott explained. "But there are some girls who won't stop chasing around and pestering me. It drives me mad. Most fans are OK. If I tell them that I don't like them hanging around, and that it makes me go very peculiar and get mad, then they

understand and go away. But there is one group of girls who don't. They always catch up with me. I get ringing at my door all day and they phone me up all night. It really drives me mad. I completely smashed up the last flat I was in, I was so angry.

SETBACKS

"This invasion of privacy – you know, I don't believe in the old thing all about anybody being entitled to knowing about, or intruding in my private life. And I don't get about very much. I have a club where I go to drink, but I'm left alone there. I seldom visit the 'in' clubs – it's completely impossible for me to sit at the Scotch of St James at a table and hold a serious conversation with anybody about pop music and records.

"I've never really liked beat music. When I was younger I grew up on ballads and standards. Therefore if I tried to like pop I'd have to lower my tastes, look down, and I can't do this. There are a couple of pop songs which I like, but not many, not many at all."

What about Scott's image, and the amount of publicity he has received about various things? Were any of them publicity stunts?

"My image, well, I've handled it very badly. I've done everything wrong. I used to go out, get drunk, and when I looked in the paper next morning, I'd see something and think 'Oh God! That's done me no good.' But now I try to be much more careful. I don't have many interviews, but when I do the paper often puts a damaging headline on it. Like this thing about the Monastery.

"I had to leave the Monastery earlier than I planned, but I felt fine. I thought I was in good shape mentally but I'd only been out a couple of days, and I was back out of shape again."

Scott said he hoped the time would come when he wouldn't be pestered by the kind of girls who make his home life intolerable. Also, what kind of plans have the Walkers got for their career?

"We're very brought down at the moment. I'm really angry with Philips over this new single ("Deadlier Than The Male"). Now, the fact is that it isn't supposed to be a new single as such. I was approached about doing the title music for a film and I said it would be OK, but I made Philips promise me that the record wouldn't get any exposure, and wouldn't get played on 'Juke Box Jury'. I just wanted the record to go along with the promotion of the film. But when I was in the Monastery, Philips put it out and it has been played, and seen on 'Juke Box Jury' and all the things I didn't want to happen with it. I'm just about as mad as I can be with Philips.

PRIVACY

"That's the only thing which Philips have done which I've taken exception to. In other ways they've been very good – very fair and all that. I was surprised about this. But it's another obstacle we've got to overcome, a set-back. The kids, the teenagers and the housewives will hear this record and think, well, that's the new Walker Brothers single and it isn't too good. But really you see it ISN'T our new single. We've got some great material for proper singles. And our new LP, that should be great – it's coming out in February.

"The other really big set-back we had was 'Baby You Don't Have To Tell Me'. We put that out after 'Sun Ain't Gonna Shine' and it just wasn't our image. The people who bought our records wanted to hear the slow, dramatic, heartbreak ballads that they could associate themselves with. We mirrored their way of thinking. But that record wasn't like that. I wanted 'In My Room' to be put out, and even 'Another Tear Falls' would have been OK. So we've got a lot of lost ground to make up.

"But where we're going in the future I don't know. I can see us singing the same old songs and see us on stage, exactly the same movements and everything. It's very worrying. But there's not much chance in the foreseeable future of the group splitting up, even though we don't mix socially, and don't agree musically. I do feel responsible to a certain extent for the other two. On the last LP I let John have more solos than me. I try to push him because I think he's good. In fact at one time I didn't used to sing – I was John's bass player!"

What about the old tracks put out by other record companies of Scott's?

"They're awful. They were never meant to be released at all – they were only demos. I cut them in the States when I was working for a music publishing company – I was working with Proby as a matter of fact. We cut demos of the songs in the vague style of the artist we wanted to sell them to, Jim Reeves, etc. The company was owned by Liberty and those discs were never meant for commercial release. Luckily they didn't get played much, but people wouldn't have known that they were recorded so long ago – they just would have thought I'd made a bad record."

But the Walker Brothers never recovered from "Deadlier Than The Male", their poorest-performing single. Six months and two minor hits later they broke up.

1967

What a year 1967 would turn out to be. A legend among years! Yet for all the great group sounds being churned out, and the forthcoming psychedelic revolution waiting eagerly in the wings, the UK's vast MOR audience still bought lorry-loads of records and could still thwart the chart-topping pretensions of even the coolest contender. Just as Ken Dodd's lachrymose "Tears" had prevented Manfred Mann's groovy take on Dylan's "If You Gotta Go, Go Now" from hitting the top in '65, and the Seekers' "The Carnival Is Over" had blocked the Who's magnum opus "My Generation" three months later, so Tom Jones's "The Green Green Grass Of Home" was currently denying Donovan's masterpiece "Sunshine Superman" from repeating its US triumph. And in a few months time, Tom's label-mate Engelbert Humperdinck would even break the mighty Beatles' four-year number one run when "Release Me" held one of the Fab Four's finest singles "Penny Lane" / "Strawberry Fields Forever" from the top spot. But in America the New Year was ushered in to something a lot more life-enhancing – the sound of the Monkees' terrific "I'm A Believer", itself ushering in a (purportedly) new era in pop: the "manufactured" group. Would that all (or any!) of the "manufactured" acts over the coming decades would make records as good as that one.

Record Mirror proved it was still the publication of choice for R&B and soul fans judging by the size of the post bag(s) crammed with entries for Alan Stinton's Soul and R&B Quiz from our 1966 Christmas Eve issue. Interestingly, by the time the answers were published and the prizes presented less than a month later, it was simply referred to as 'The RM Soul Quiz'. It was a devilish quiz and several questions had acceptable alternative answers; there was also a crossword which of course had no alternative answers. Of all the entries, only one contestant got everything right: Trevor Churchill, a trainee label manager at EMI, who later became a good friend. Everyone in the UK who considered themselves a serious R&B and soul fan had entered the competition, several had teamed up, and there'd been a real buzz over Christmas among the soul fraternity. Trevor's prize was a number of imported American LPs to be selected from Dave Godin's Soul City record shop in Deptford.

Trevor Churchill would go on to become prominent in the UK music business, firstly heading Bell Records for EMI, then the Rolling Stones label, and moving effortlessly through several majors including Motown and Polydor before realising his true ambition of running his own small specialist quality record company: Ace Records, with partners Ted Carroll and Roger Armstrong.

The first big interview I did in '67 was with Spencer Davis, increasingly becoming titular head of the highly-successful Spencer Davis Group. Spencer was in the invidious position of knowing that his group's success, and all everybody talked about, was the prodigious talent of keyboardist / lead vocalist Stevie Winwood. The group were about to score their fourth smash hit in a row: the first two, "Keep On Running" and "Somebody Help Me", had been written by Jamaican superstar Jackie Edwards: "Gimme Some Lovin'", currently breaking the group in the USA, was penned by Spencer, Stevie and his brother Muff, while their latest release "I'm A Man" was written by Stevie and producer Jimmy Miller. As a musician, Stevie was terrific. As a singer, well, a bit problematical: Stevie actually sounded black. He wasn't like Jagger, Burden, Van Morrison, who, good and sometimes great though they were, rarely if ever sounded other than young white men imitating older black men. Of course, they also sang 'white' too, particularly Jagger, with things like "Lady Jane" and currently "Ruby Tuesday". But Winwood was a slightly different proposition because he was better at it, as Joe Cocker would be the following year. Even our dedicated soul freelance and black music advocate Alan Stinton had been raving about Stevie Winwood, but that may have been because they were both Brummies. Nowadays – the twenty-first century – white singers imitating a black vocal style causes no comment; in fact, today's vocal blackface is the norm among many, if not most white pop and so-called "R&B" singers. It's considered legitimate, which may be why creative black talent has moved into more extreme areas inaccessible to most whites. Unsurprising, when a white girl singing in a black style is likely to be a lot more successful than a black girl with a better voice. Dave Godin was right. Today, in our highly racist-conscious society, it seems strange that doubts about the artistic validity and integrity of this practise have all but disappeared, whereas in the more racially-naive Sixties, serious misgivings were felt and discussed by serious people.

During the interview, Spencer loyally defended Stevie against some of those doubts – not that I'd done any accusing:

> *"...a lot of people think that Steve is a very inspired copyist. Now I don't. I've been working with him for years and I'm convinced that Steve, as a singer, has a definite individual style of his own. Of course, he is a very talented musician anyway – quite astounding. The idea behind his song was to make the record as exciting as possible."*
>
> *Spencer asked me what I thought of "Gimme Some Lovin'" and seemed a bit surprised when I told him I thought it was exciting but retrogressive – a sort of instant flashback to the rock era.*
>
> *"But we all like rock'n'roll in the group," said Spencer. "I must admit that I was pleased with the sound we captured. Of course, it has been slightly changed for American release. The backing is the same, except with a girl chorus in parts, but Stevie has re-recorded his vocal. It's not very much different though, but you know, after a record has been issued you think of little changes or improvements you could have made. So it was changed for US release. We had nothing to lose, and we've still kept the basic earthy sound..."*

The conversation turned to cars, speeding tickets, and Spencer's record collection. "I'm A Man" turned out to be the last big hit for the Spencer Davis Group: Winwood was already preparing to quit, and two months later in April would form Traffic, the rock-psych-folk supergroup who would go on to score three Top Ten hits during 1967 following their much-imitated (and much-parodied) "getting it together in a cottage in the country". Spencer had known all about it for some time but wasn't giving the game away. The official announcement came two weeks later.

Spencer wasn't the only Davis I interviewed that week. Well, almost. I also spoke to Kinks' leader Ray Davies, whose "Dead End Street" was slowly descending the charts, and for whom, following such other classics as "Sunny Afternoon" and "Dedicated Follower Of Fashion", the not-too-distant future held such awesome delights as "Waterloo Sunset", "Autumn Almanac" and "Days". Truly, a man at his creative peak. As always, Ray was an interesting and down-to-earth interview.

RM w/e 4th February 1967

RAY DAVIES ON HOLLY, & THE ROCKING KINKS

ONE of the nice things about interviewing Ray Davies is that he doesn't come out with all the usual stock phrases that most group members do. You can't predict what he's going to say about anything, which makes a change from most groups who are ultra-predictable and typecast.

Funnily enough whenever I talk to Ray the subject seems to work around to Buddy Holly, who is a mutual favourite of us both. It was eight years ago to this week when Buddy Holly died on February 3rd 1959.

"When Buddy Holly was alive I wonder if anyone used to interview him and write things about him like this," mused Ray. "I remember reading things about him, with the Crickets posing with cricket bats, and all that. But his records – you know they still sound so fresh. The voice is clear, and stands up above the backing, and the guitar

sound is so good. I don't know why they bother to alter the backings, the originals ones were great.

"It must be uncanny when they play about with the master tapes and re-dub backings. Because in between the different vocal takes you would be able to hear Buddy's voice talking to the producer and the Crickets – all this stuff is left on the tape – telling them what went wrong, and what to do and everything. It must be strange hearing someone talking informally like this, someone who has been dead for eight years".

The subject of Hank Williams then came up, and Ray, who has several Hank Williams' records, was interested in the record which Hank's son made using old tapes of his father's and his own voice dubbed on.

"It must have been very strange for him to hear his own father's voice on those tapes. I'm surprised that Hank Williams hasn't become more popular. I thought he could have been the next big thing after Chuck Berry..."

Ray went on to talk about the attitudes of the rest of the group towards the type of songs that they are now recording.

"I think that Pete and Dave are happier playing rock'n'roll. Mick and I seem to prefer the kind of thing we're doing now, but I'd like to make a rock'n'roll record – as a single. Yes! I think we're capable of it, but I'm afraid that everyone would think we were copying the Troggs.

"I can't see us changing the type of song that we're recording at the moment. We've only had a few singles out on those lines, and there's plenty of scope. But I wasn't too keen on the last LP – it was more a collection of songs than an LP, it didn't seem to fit together too well. The Simon and Garfunkel LP 'The Sound Of Silence' was like that – just tracks put on an LP. I'm working on a new LP which I hope will be our best yet.

"Our two biggest mistakes were not putting out 'Well Respected Man' and 'Dandy' as singles. We released 'Dandy' in Germany and it sold tremendously well there – it had been released as a single all over the continent,

but not of course here. I thought it was a bit too much like 'Well Respected Man' at the time to be used as a single".

The Kinks have just returned from a very successful tour of Germany – they have had many many hits there, ever since "You Really Got Me", and Ray obviously enjoyed it.

"Yes, it was great there. I don't usually enjoy touring too much – it's the travelling. I like playing though, and in Germany the audiences were fine. Perhaps a bit older than here. We've always done well there, ever since our first hit in England. Funnily enough, that's the one record I wouldn't want to improve on. I can look back on all the others and think how they could have been better – everyone does this – but 'You Really Got Me' I wouldn't want to change. The reason why we hadn't recorded any of my songs before that as singles was just that I didn't have the confidence. As a matter of fact, I still haven't. I don't know whether 'Sunny Afternoon' would have been a hit if we had been an unknown group. Certainly we were in a far better position then, than when we had 'You Really Got Me'.

"In America our success fluctuates. I didn't think that 'Sunny Afternoon' would be a hit – there were so many summery records out then – like 'Sunny', 'Summer In The City', Sunshine Superman'. But it was a hit, although it took a long time. 'Dead End Street' is doing nothing in the States.

"I don't really think we've ever been promoted too much as a group, visually anyway – there are some artists who I wouldn't want to see performing – Dylan for example, it would ruin the image. But I don't want us to ever get in that position. I'd always like to have this visual thing."

That same week Joe Meek murdered his landlady and killed himself with a shotgun at the same flat-cum-recording studio in Holloway Road where I'd met him on my first RM assignment six years previously. It was on February 3rd, the same date that Buddy Holly, one of Meek's primary inspirations, had also died.

The Saville Theatre in Shaftesbury Avenue had lately been bought by Brian Epstein who was promoting a series of prestigious pop concerts on Sunday evenings and would continue doing so until his untimely death later in the year. The first one I attended was headlined by the Who, and in slightly smaller type the Jimi Hendrix Experience, currently in the Top Ten with their debut smash "Hey, Joe".

As usual I wrote a review, but regrettably I was a writer who did not learn from his mistakes and was thus condemned to repeat them – in my case again and again. I didn't enjoy the gig. The support acts didn't impress me; Hendrix's stage presence seemed to me to verge on overkill distracting from his obviously huge talent, and the Who were the worst I'd ever seen them – in retrospect probably numb at having to follow Hendrix, who was probably unfollowable. So I knocked out a nasty little review:

RM w/e 4th February 1967

GLOOMY SAVILLE

I HAVE seldom seen a less enthusiastic audience than the one at the Saville Theatre last Sunday which turned up to see a bill headed by the Who and the Jimi Hendrix Experience. The bill of fare was a sad faux pas and opened up with a five-piece beat group called the Thoughts, who were followed by the Koobas, and the least said about these two groups, the better for all concerned. The audience seemed to be thinking the same way – there was almost negative response. Compere Mike Quinn was hilarious, especially in acting as though he had to cope with mobs of screaming, exciting girls – he did a sort of Tony Hall gone very wrong and proved embarrassing – but he WAS resplendent in those carpet slippers and dressing gowns which he wore.

Jimi Hendrix received the best reaction – especially the gimmick of having loads of technicians rushing on and off the stage trying to fix the mikes which wouldn't work. Let's have some more of that. Jimi's guitar work was quite incredible but predictable and noisy too. His singing was not too bad but he looked so terrifying that I was scared he would jump down into the stalls and carry away some of the audience. He was supported vocally by his bass guitarist whgo looked like an ersatz Bob Dylan, or was it a Caucasian Jimi Hendrix?

The Who came on and everyone, including me, hoped they would show themselves to be the great group, head-and-shoulders above the others, but they seemed to stand around infected with the gloomy atmosphere and ploughed through their hits. They did "Boris The Spider" well, and "Happy Jack" was OK, but even the frantic, despairing enthusiasm of Mike Quinn couldn't keep the audience from clapping any longer than a few seconds after they departed. The moral of this story is that if the audience's average age is above sixteen, try to use a little imagination to entertain them.

I got what I deserved when Tony Stratton-Smith, then managing the Thoughts and the Koobas, replied in a letter which we published the following week. I'd never met Stratton-Smith, who would later go on to create Charisma Records and was one of the most respected – and apparently nicest– men in the music business. He was an ex-Fleet Street journalist, and nice as he may have been, his ire had been unleashed:

A FINE British poet once told me, "Criticism is of no value to a subject unless the critic has a loving involvement." – and if that be so, is the time not right for Norman Jopling to retire?

His sneering dismissal of a hard working Saville bill topped by The Who belonged to a school of journalism which I thought had long ago expired of its own fatuity and – to keep on quoting – brings to mind the advice of a Daily Express editor for whom I once worked, "It is easy to knock, much harder to say something worthwhile and say it in an interesting way," an exercise which Mr Jopling is clearly unwilling to take.

The Saville Sunday shows are a growth thing with which groups and management alike are trying to get on terms, and perhaps that is also true of the audiences. The limitations of Sunday presentation – no stage wear, no scenery, no special effects – have always given problems, and in this theatre, being newly oriented to pop, there is also the problem of building an atmosphere. I think everyone concerned at the Saville is working very well on this, and getting results – but such criticisms as Mr Jopling's will not help them.

He seemed to find it amusing that Jimi Hendrix had technical problems – without perhaps being aware that in the first house a lead had failed him in his very first number; a mishap which clearly threw him, this, as I understand it, having been his first solo appearance on a theatre stage , and in the West End at that. In my opinion, and that of everyone to whom I spoke on the night, Jimi did very well. Remember he is only 21, and new to the scene here: with a little more experience, a little loosening up of his undoubted personality, can anyone doubt he will develop this year into one of the most exciting pop performers around.

"As to his crack that 'If the audience's average age is above 16, try to use a little imagination to entertain them' – which followed his remarks on The Who's excellent act, well, I simply can't comprehend Mr Jopling's frame of mind. I was accompanied at both houses by a leading book publisher, a well-known fashion model and a well-known photographer – all three a good deal over 16 years of age. Without exception they were thoroughly entertained by The Who's stage presentation. As to his dismissal of The Koobas and The Thoughts – the last, a new group having the difficult task of warming up the audience – well, I won't even bother to comment as I am their personal manager. I will only say that if every professional in this business is to have his efforts evaluated so immaturely then indeed the business already has a knife in its back. Tony

Stratton-Smith, Stratton Smith Music Ltd., 11 Dryden Chambers, 119 Oxford Street, London W1.

I was stung by his letter, but not just because of what he said. As I saw it, rightly or wrongly, my function was that of a critic dispassionately reviewing a show, not a PR person hired to boost the image of the Saville Theatre, or promote any of the acts, or to make excuses for any of their respective shortcomings. What had stung me was that Tony had been so upset by my review that it provoked such a damning reply. I had no desire to upset anybody and felt ashamed at having done so. Yet not ashamed enough apparently, because in a couple of months I would do the same thing again to someone else.

Bloody but unbowed, more or less, I continued to churn out the features, articles and interviews. *Hello Sexy!* featured Dave Dee, recently voted by RM readers "the sexiest personality in pop", eloquently explaining the group's transition from comedy to scream appeal:

> *"Now I don't think that anything we do is disgusting. But when girls pay 15s which after all is quite a lot of cash for a front stall, they expect something for their money. So I lay on my back and wave my legs and they go mad. They enjoy it. Obviously I don't expect blokes to enjoy this kind of thing. I mean, if I were a bloke and I spent money taking a girl to a pop concert I'd be very annoyed if she went beserk over some long-haired git moving around the stage, and she thought he was good. But then we are trying to appeal to girls, after all."*

A fortnight later I interviewed two very different female American singers – Sandy Posey and Maxine Brown. At her hotel Sandy's managers warned me beforehand, "She's very difficult to interview – she's very quiet and she's only interested in music and people concerned with music," and so she proved to be. Nevertheless she was interesting, growing up as she did on the Alabama music scene, which included singing backing vocals on Percy Sledge's massive '66 smash "When A Man Loves A Woman". But there was controversy surrounding meek Sandy. It concerned the lyrics of her two recent global hits "Born A Woman" and "Single Girl", both written by Martha Sharpe, and both depicting women as submissively dismal and downtrodden creatures able only to be redeemed and find happiness through the love of a man: "Not exactly empowering", as Helen Reddy later remarked. The phrase "women's liberation" had first appeared in print only the previous year, but you didn't need to be a feminist to find the lyrics dubious. Not that I even knew what the word "feminist" meant at that time, getting it completely wrong in the last paragraph of the interview:

> *Now, the question that we all want to know is: does Sandy agree with the feminist lyrics of both of her hit records? Yes, she does. And strongly too. So if you like your women to be man-reliant and feminine, then you can safely dig Miss Posey.*

Sandy's career flourished nevertheless. She scored one more big pop hit in America, married an Elvis impersonator in 1968, performed with the real Elvis in 1969, and carried on cutting country hits.

I met Maxine Brown also at her hotel where she was recovering from a back injury sustained from falling down a flight of stairs at a venue on her current UK tour. Maxine was a soul goddess and a fine singer, versatile too. Best known for cutting the original version of the Goffin-King pop standard "Oh No Not My Baby", she'd begun her hit solo career in 1960 with the tortured soul ballad classic "All In My Mind". Her current hits were all duets with Wand label-mate Chuck Jackson, but she was hoping her excellent version of the Beatles' "We Can Work It Out" would be released in the UK. Not that it did much in the States, and she explained why:

> *"It came out about three weeks before John Lennon's quote about the Beatles being bigger than Jesus Christ broke. Of course they stopped playing anything connected with the Beatles then. Including my record! I imagine that Lennon's quotes were taken the wrong way, but it really was an immense national issue at the time."*

The Beatles themselves were, as usual, evolving. Having incorporated the huge influence of both Bob Dylan and marijuana over the past two years, they were presently coming to terms artistically and personally with the vistas opened by LSD. There'd been early psychedelia from them in 1966 on "Revolver", but their new single "Penny Lane" / "Strawberry Fields Forever" was art of a high order, awesome in conception and execution. Not that all their fans agreed with their new direction – we got plenty of letters wishing they were still the Fab Four:

'THOSE DISGUSTING MOUSTACHES'
An RM reader complains about the Beatles

WELL, really. I was utterly ashamed of the Beatles on 'Top Of The Pops' – they looked absolutely disgusting with their moustaches. I used to be an ardent follower of the Beatles, my favourite being Paul. But now he looks... well, I don't know how to explain. Please, Beatles, do something about it before you look even worse. Miss Kim Spanswick, Le Courtil Brousard, La Villiage Lane, St Andrews, Guernsey, Channel Islands.

'SELFISH BEATLES'
An RM reader complains

FOR years now letters have appeared complaining about the fact that Elvis has never visited Britain and that his films are poor. But what many people don't realise is that the Beatles will very soon be in a worse position – they don't even make films. All they do is make records and two-minute films to promote their records on pop TV shows. They have not appeared live on television for nine months (just before the miming ban) and they have not done a concert for ages. I know they put a lot of work into their records but they must realise there is more than one side to the pop music business. The Beatles have developed what could appear a very selfish attitude and unless they

> *re-assess their position quickly they will be submerged*
> *in as much ridicule as Mr Presley. I'm sure if you print*
> *this letter, people will make excuses for the Beatles. But*
> *no honest person can deny that I have written the facts.*
> **Russell Carey, Cirencester, Glos.**

Our regular freelancer David Griffiths was the only RM staffer to have thus far taken LSD, or "dropped acid", as it was becoming colloquially known. David, then a well-known journalist and broadcaster, was thirteen years older than me, a jazz fanatic nevertheless finding the current pop scene greatly interesting. He scored his acid from Michael de Freitas, shortly to become the notorious Michael X, and Michael's acid was the the pharmaceutical "colourless, odourless, tasteless liquid" variety of which, according to David, Michael had an extremely large supply, telling David he preferred taking it in tandem with heroin in order to cool out the more extreme affects. Being a relatively early acid-head, David had recognised the Beatles' LSD use months before the rest of us straight staffers, and his theory regarding their moustaches was that they'd grown them as a sort of acknowledgement of their now-cosmic maturity and wisdom caused by acid-tripping which, according to David, was not only potentially a "born again" experience, but enabled one to live lifetime after lifetime within the eight hours or so of an average trip's duration. Never having taken it, none of the other RM staff could convincingly argue with him, or even discuss this theory. David was also continuously urging me to take acid, telling me on the one hand that it would make me a better person: "Look at me, haven't I changed for the better?" Yes, he had, actually, but then, when I demurred, still being cautious, he would taunt me with the Donovan song "Mellow Yellow", singing the words "...that yellow streak ain't mellow", which annoyed me sufficiently to put me off tripping, whatever it might be like – especially tripping with him.

Michael de Freitas's connection with RM staffers would not end with his association with David Griffiths. Our office boy Marvin Brown had recently quit to form a company called Clean-A-Flat that hired out domestic and office cleaners. In four years time in 1971, after supplying black cleaners to Michael X's "Black House" in

Holloway Road, Marvin would be lured to Black House by Michael X and become the victim of the notorious "slave collar affair", the prosecution of which precipitated Michael's flight from the UK, and thus his later execution for murder.

I still reviewed Brian Epstein's Saville Sunday concerts, but with a slightly more charitable attitude following my come-uppance from Tony Stratton-Smith. Interestingly, as well as cutting-edge pop, the Saville was specialising in vintage rock'n'rollers – among them the Chuckster himself, who'd recently switched labels from Chess to Mercury. I'd met Chuck informally several times, usually in company with Guy Stevens or Pete Meaden, but never interviewed him. In late February '67 there was a modest press reception thrown for Chuck by Philips who controlled Mercury here, so off I trotted. Lots of Fleet Street journalists were there, and judging by their questions didn't seem too clued up on Chuck, who stood facing the reporters and fielded their remarks very politely, all things considered. I asked him a couple of things, nothing special, mainly about his lyrics. When the reception was over Chuck came over and to my surprise told me I was the only one there who'd asked him any intelligent questions. We spoke for a further twenty minutes, and although I showed my ignorance with a remark about Chuck's country influences, he just laughed about it, and altogether showed a warmth and enthusiasm that took me by surprise:

RM w/e 4th March 1967

ROCK LIVES!
Especially it seems, at the Saville. Chuck Berry talks to Norman Jopling for this in-depth interview.

CHUCK BERRY has become a musical institution in the eleven years that he has been making hit records. Since his first American hit single "Maybellene" in 1955 (before Elvis Presley scored HIS first American hit), Chuck has endeared himself to the hearts of all types of pop music admirers – *from never-say-die side-burned drape-jacketed rockers, to trendy mini-skirted young ladies.*

Just how much has Chuck himself changed in that considerable amount of time, musically? (to go back to Presley, think how much HE has changed!)

"Then was then and now is now," Chuck replied. "I re-cut my old tunes for this new Mercury album, but they're different from on the old albums. I doubt if I could play them the same now. When I listen to my old tunes I'm never completely satisfied with them. I won't say I'm unsatisfied – just not completely satisfied. New songs? Well, I've just written seven, no, eight songs in six months. Five of them I've recorded and sent to Mercury – the others are lying there in my briefcase. One was released – 'Club Nitty Gritty'. The other album I have here is just a reissue from Chess."

The Chess LP was a double-album set, containing most of Chuck's biggest hits, ranging from "Maybellene" and the early hits, to "No Particular Place To Go" and "You Never Can Tell", his later hits for Chess. Why did Chuck leave Chess after ten years of recording with them? Was there any ill-feeling?

"Oh, no, there were no bad feelings. We just shook hands and they wished me good luck. The change-over was just a business deal. The first Mercury album will be released in Britain in March or April."

One thing which fascinates most people about Chuck Berry are the lyrics of his songs. All about life – cars, school, real romance. What has Chuck to say about the words of his songs?

"The car songs – I had a phase of about four or five years of writing songs about cars. Because this was a yearning which I had since I was aged seven to drive about in a car. I first started driving at 17 – one year earlier than I should have. It was my fascination for the roads, for driving, motoring, which prompted me to write those songs.

"I have written about my cars, and about my school. I can't write about something which I haven't experienced.

341

I wrote 'Sweet Little Sixteen' at a concert when I saw a little girl running around backstage collecting autographs. She couldn't have seen one act on the show – unless it was mine! When I wrote 'Memphis' I had known couples who had divorced and the tragedies of the children.

"You can associate these songs with life – for instance, when I wrote 'Maybellene' just about every farmer must have been driving about in Ford, station wagons etc. But then Chevrolet got wise and started a big advertising campaign with the farmers!"

I wondered how much notice Chuck took of the charts. How much does he follow them, and consequently how much is his music influenced by current trends and other artists?

"I don't study the charts – I observe them," he replied. "Of course I've been influenced, by everyone from Bing Crosby to the Beatles. I don't let my music be consciously affected by anything. What do I think of the Beatles' versions of two of my songs? Very nice. But they recorded them two, three years ago now. In fact it's only now that I'm beginning to feel the benefits of them. Those songs 'Roll Over Beethoven' and 'Rock And Roll Music' are now on an upward trend.

"Talking about the Beatles, three or four of their songs are among the best ever written in pop music. Especially 'I Want To Hold Your Hand'. I put that one with songs like my 'Sweet Little Sixteen' – and I'm not saying that just because I wrote it. I'll never write another song like that.

"And of course there's the Everly Brothers' 'Wake Up Little Susie'. That's really one of my favourite songs. Those three songs I've named – they have virtue and freshness. It doesn't matter who sings them."

On the personal side there are a couple of popular misconceptions about Chuck. He stated, "When I meet people they say 'Wow, we thought you were a short man'." *(Chuck is well over six feet tall).* "I guess it's because of the name, Chuck, it's small, you know. And another thing, I have this popular image of being quiet, and people wonder *why, because of my stage act I suppose in which I go pretty wild. Well, you can't expect me to be leaping around when I come off stage, and talking extra-fast!"*

Apart from the musical side, Chuck has developed into a very successful businessman. He has his own music corporation, music publishers, amusement park and several other highly-successful money-making projects. Why, I wondered, had Chuck chosen of all things an amusement park (called Berry Park) to make money from?

"It goes a long way back. When I was a child I lived opposite a park but my father forbade me to go there. We moved somewhere else, and the same thing happened. You see, it's a psychological thing. When I bought the land to develop, it was just wheat land. It was winter at the time and of course there was no wheat growing. The first thing I built there was a swimming pool and I charged 25c admission. Now there are many more things to do and I charge more . I have groups there, Western and Rock. That's the music people want to listen to – they don't want jazz. After all who wants to learn and study music when they go to an amusement park – people just want something to entertain them.

"Myself, I feel like dancing when I play rock music. If I'm in a sentimental mood, then Western music. And of course I do play jazz because that's the only music you can learn something from."

I ventured to suggest it was strange that Chuck, hero of the rock'n'roll set, should like Country and Western music. Especially as his own brand of sound was so different.

"Oh no! You're wrong there. 'Maybellene' was very much a country song, with country lyrics. Maybe a little faster, but basically it was country. You ask me if I'd have made money if I hadn't been an entertainer? Yes!"

Finally, just how much work does Chuck do now, and will he be appearing in any more rock films?

"I take about 60 per cent of the work that's offered to me. That means I work about three days a week. I'm

offered work for about four or five days a week. But I won't do the kind of tours that I used to. They were eighty day tours...really something. I like to do different kinds of venues – colleges, concert halls, different avenues of work. The reason I haven't made any films in a long while is because I haven't been offered any. I wouldn't be averse to making films at all."

And as a final point of interest – Chuck reads a lot. He reads books on psychology and science. Nothing else. No fiction. And he says, "I write fiction. I don't read it..."

Chuck headlined twice at the Saville Theatre in February; other rock'n'rollers who topped the Saville bill during that period included Fats Domino, first time in the UK, whose rollicking performance – he pushed his piano around the stage! – was sheer joy, and he was supported by newcomers the Bee Gees, also remarkably good; and twangy guitar king Duane Eddy supported, curiously, by Edwin Starr, Detroit's Ric-Tic label hitmaker about to get snapped up by Motown and always a compelling performer. I wrote a little piece on Fats but as I was away at the printers I couldn't do the interview– that went to lucky David Griffiths. But I did catch Duane, recently signed to Sinatra's Reprise label, for *Duane And The Hitless Years*, and like Chuck he'd been assessing his back catalogue:

"...I enjoyed working with a girl group for the RCA hits – it made a change – then I received so many letters complaining about them...perhaps the fans thought they were being cheated out of the guitar sound. Talking about the sound, there's no reason why the sound now should be different from when I recorded for Jamie. I use the same studios in Phoenix, Arizona, and most of the same backing musicians. The sound IS different somehow, though!

"I haven't any regrets about any of the records I've made except perhaps the 'Dylan' album. I didn't do that one the way I wanted to. You know, I collaborate with Lee Hazelwood on all of my records, and on that one he insisted on having his own way, and I insisted on having

*my own way. Usually we get together, but this time I let
him have his own way – he's usually right. But I don't
think he was there".*

Also in the UK and about to headline a nation-wide tour featuring
the Small Faces, Paul & Barry Ryan and Jeff Beck was Roy Orbison,
who reminisced about his rock'n'roll years:

RM w/e 11th March 1967

ROY – 'MY WILD STAGE ACT!'

*DID you know that once upon a time Roy Orbison had a
stage act? Listen to what he said:*

*"I had a wild act at one time – it was when I used to
record for Sun. It was really wild as opposed to my act
now, not that I really have an act now! I used to wear loud
clothes on stage and play tremendously loud – I think that
Buddy Holly and I used to play the loudest guitar in the
country then!"*

*Roy's recording career with Sun was short-lived, but
he was in the company of such giants as Jerry Lee and
Carl Perkins. Does Roy think he could have ever become
a rock idol like Jerry Lee?*

*"Well, I think I could! Or should I say I like to think
I could – I reckon it's only natural for me to think that.
I could have become a rock star if I had wanted to, but
even then I wanted to sing ballads. I don't know...I was
very young at the time, caught up in things. It was the first
time for everything – recording, meeting disc jockeys, going
on tour. I made records but didn't have very much idea.*

*"I knew 'Only The Lonely' would be a hit – although
I didn't think it would be as big as it was. I wouldn't go
back to that style of backing, it was a phase in my life, my
career, and I couldn't and wouldn't want to reproduce it.*

*"Also, if you listen to my voice you'll find it has changed,
matured perhaps. If you listen to 'Only The Lonely', then*

'Running Scared', and then 'Pretty Woman' you'll see what I mean."

What are Roy's favourites out of his own songs?

"When I look back, and play my records, the only one I wouldn't change would be 'Running Scared' – although just lately I've been having some ideas about that! I guess you could say it's my favourite. It represents to me exactly how I felt at the time, the soft intro, building up, and the idea of the bridge, or the break at the end instead of in the middle.

"Now that record wasn't very big in Britain – I think it just made your Top Twenty. I think the reason why it wasn't bigger was that it was only played on Radio Luxembourg then, and they used to play only half of the record. Now, only playing the first half of 'Running Scared' – it must have sounded a dull record. They should have played the last half – nothing really started happening until about two-thirds of the way through – it was the same with the follow-up 'Crying'. 'Pretty Woman' was a big hit and I never really liked that. Now of course I can see why it was a hit, the construction of the lyric, the beat, and the appeal it had for the market at the time. I wish I could see things like that BEFORE the record is issued!"

Financially Roy has been successful too – his tours and million-selling records ("Pretty Woman" sold FOUR million copies) have made him into a millionaire – a pound sterling millionaire!!! Roy's career is his life, and recently he has made his first full-length feature film "The Fastest Guitar Alive". Any news of release?

"It's being issued in May in the States," answered Roy. "We wanted a spring or summer release because that's the best time for films in the States. Because that's when the drive-in movie season starts – nearly all of the kids in the States have cars – I don't know when the film will be released here. I think I would ultimately like to make more films, to concentrate on films, but that would not stop me making records or touring.

"I enjoy touring very much – I am much more relaxed now on tour than I used to be several years ago. I like touring here in Britain – I've been here enough times! Talking about touring overseas, I remember once when I was at an interview when a reporter was talking to Jerry Lee Lewis. He asked Jerry if he had ever been abroad. 'Have I ever been a Broad!!?!' said Jerry. So Jerry's manager hastily interjected, 'He means have you ever been overseas, Jerry'."

One final note for Roy's fans – he won't be riding any motorbikes or doing any scrambling while he's over here. So you can breathe a sigh of relief about that, anyway...

'Motorbikes' were a not-so-thinly-veiled reference to the death the previous year of Roy's wife Claudette, whose motorcycle was hit by a truck in Texas.

A week before meeting Roy I'd caught up with his tour-mates Paul & Barry Ryan, identical twin sons of sultry '50s songstress Marion Ryan and then-husband Fred Sapherson. Marion was now married to top impresario Harold Davison, and when Paul and Barry wanted to become pop stars those family connections didn't hurt. The twins had scored a string of minor hits over the past year but also come in for plenty of flak, mainly because of the silver spoons lodged so prominently in their handsome gobs – Marion was a looker, and the twins took after her. Soon, all the pressure would get to Paul, the more vulnerable twin, who left the duo to concentrate on songwriting and straightaway came up with a reputation-redeeming slice of unforgettable high pop drama with "Eloise", taken to No. 2 by brother Barry in 1968. In the meantime, articles like my *Mummy's Boys? We're changing THAT image, say Paul and Barry* couldn't have helped much.

Speaking of songwriting, the Hollies had written several of their own big hit A-sides lately ("Stop, Stop, Stop", "On A Carousel"). Did that mean they'd now always use their own songs as A-sides?

"Oh no, we don't intend being greedy," said Allan. "If we record one of our songs and say Graham Gouldman

comes up with something better, then we'll use Graham's songs. Our aim is always to use the best material. Now that's what has been the trouble with several groups, using their own material regardless. Probably the Rolling Stones for instance for always using Jagger-Richard songs – they could have been at No. 1 with every record if they hadn't always used their own songs."

I suggested that the reason for the Rolling Stones chart decline was more likely their public image which had developed from their famous rebellious attitude, to a melee of Nazi uniforms and women's clothes and brooches.

"Could be," replied Tony, "After all. When they started, when the group thing started, the kids could go out and buy clothes and wear their hair like the groups. They can't do that with Nazi uniforms..."

The Stones' dodgy clobber notwithstanding, they were still the number two UK group, and there was nothing wrong with their current hit, the brilliant double-sider "Let's Spend The Night Together" / "Ruby Tuesday". Admittedly its predecessor "Have You Seen Your Mother, Baby" had been a crock – but then "Paperback Writer" hadn't been so great either.

The big news for soul and R&B fans was the forthcoming tour by the Memphis-based Stax/Volt label stable. Headed by soul superstar Otis Redding, the bill would include the legendary Booker T & The MGs (who could be augmented with a brass section to become the Mar-Keys, creating the unique Stax horn sound); Sam & Dave – truly THE dynamic duo – and Eddie Floyd, Carla Thomas and Arthur Conley. Stax/Volt was distributed by Atlantic Records in the USA, and when their distribution deal with Decca had expired in 1966, they signed with the new UK Polydor label who subsequently moved Atlantic on to a new commercial level in the UK and Europe. In charge in the UK was Frank Fenter, a talented, energetic and likeable white South African who'd been a jobbing actor before moving into the music business via agency and publishing. Frank moved fast and got things done: he was heavily into the whole Stax-Volt scene, became friends with Otis's manager Phil Walden with whom he'd later co-found Capricorn Records, and even managed to send his girlfriend, singer Sharon Tandy, to Memphis to cut some sides with the Stax house studio band, alias the Mar-Keys. And it was Frank who conceived and coordinated the tour, known nowadays as The Stax/Volt Revue, but then, among other things, as Hit The Road Stax.

Unfortunately I was about have an in-print spat with Frank because of my review of the show. My problem was Otis Redding, whose act, despite his unique and soulful voice, personal charisma, and terrific pump-'em-up onstage excitement, just didn't move me on this occasion. Nearly every song he sang prominently featured his "gotta, gotta, gotta" interpolations – I guess you either love that kind of thing or, like me, find it irritating – and I felt that it was a mistake for him to try to compete for excitement with Sam & Dave: nobody could beat Sam & Dave in terms of sheer excitement. Since Otis was topping the bill he had to close the show but personally I would have had him come out and sit down at a piano and sing "I've Been Loving You Too Long" slowly and soulfully, and then everyone would have forgotten Sam & Dave. I also thought there was a slightly patronising element in the Stax tour overall. British audiences were hot for black music and more knowledgeable than white American audiences. I guess Stax didn't realise how hip the British audiences were.

I was being 'honest' but it didn't go down well. If you criticise someone "legendary", many people don't like it. I'd seen and heard enough shows by black artists to know that a stage performance needed to be "a show": black R&B artists had to learn to work very hard indeed to please the discriminating black audiences at the Apollo, the Uptown, and all the rest of the black theatres across the States. But, purist that I still was, I somehow disapproved of the way Redding did it here in the UK, just as a year or so earlier I'd disapproved – though not in print – of the white blonde model on the cover of "Otis Blue", which to me smacked the kind of thing American labels were doing in the fifties to make their products acceptable to the white market.

RM w/e 25th March 1967

"THE Otis Redding Show" as the Stax tour has now been mysteriously re-titled commenced at the Finsbury Park Astoria on Friday (first house) with Booker T. & The MG's, who invariably did "Green Onions" – quite a powerful version too, but Booker's organ work was a bit subdued, which was more the fault of the acoustics than the artist. The Mar-Keys arrived to augment the MG's and did the best number on the show, in terms of nearness-to-record, with "Philly Dog". Closer on part one was Arthur Conley... who put on a very good act, his dance routine was clever and entertaining and his version of his American hit "Sweet Soul Music" was professional. Although Arthur does not yet have that magic aura of "soul star from the States" he showed he was better than many with far bigger reputation. But it was a mystery how he received second billing to Redding when chart names Sam and Dave and Eddie Floyd were on the show. Something to do with being Otis's protégé, I suppose.

Eddie Floyd opened the second half and competently sang "Raise Your Hand" and "Knock On Wood", although by this time a certain same-y sound had set in. Somehow the atmosphere of Eddie's records didn't come across – but it would be difficult to pinpoint any reasons. Sam and Dave crashed into "You Don't Know Like I Know" and had immediate impact – their act was exciting and entertaining. A send-up version of "When Something Is Wrong With My Baby" was followed by a spine-tingling "Hold On I'm Coming" in which they created loads of excitement and were called back for an encore – which unfortunately was a disappointing "I Take What I Want". Otis entered after a big build-up and came out with his typical out-of-breath stuttered soul. He sang mainly fast numbers and I lost count of the number of times he said "Lord Have Mercy" – my sentiments entirely. His closer "Try A Little Tenderness" was better, but the encores were

exceptionally corny. His act was well-received by his fans,
but to anyone who isn't a Redding fanatic the whole thing
must have exploded the soul myth. I would rather have
seen him sit at a piano and sing "I've Been Loving You
Too Long" than attempt any number of Rolling Stones,
Temptations or Frank Sinatra numbers.

Frank Fenter didn't take very kindly to this. His rejoinder, which we published in full in the following issue, was over three times longer than my original review, picking apart my every word, with about half of it taken up explaining the intricacies of billing on this particular tour. Here, near the end, is where it really got personal:

RM w/e 1st April 1967

...you talk about hard-bitten R&B fans. I would like you
to take note that the first ten rows were almost completely
filled by what I would term "teeny boppers" and when
you are making this kind of audience go for R&B you are
really saying something. To describe in so short a space the
dynamic atmosphere that existed from the opening act of
Booker T. & The MGs etc, all I can say is that Mr Jopling
you are not ready for this kind of action, and it seems to
my mind that this is one instance where the audience has
advanced far more than the critic. It just seems incredible
to me that a paper as deeply steeped in R&B should offer to
what Mr Jopling terms fanatical fans this kind of review.

Frank then quoted from the rave reviews published in Disc and Melody Maker, and concluded thus:

In closing, Mr Jopling, I can only say that you come over
as a great disappointment not only to myself, because I
feel certain that to this date (including all the people who
have seen the show so far) at least 10,000 other people will
agree with Melody Maker and Disc.

But to everyone's surprise they didn't all agree with Melody Maker and Disc. A big Record Mirror post-bag was generated by the topic, and opinion was split around fifty-fifty, prompting a further follow-up feature – *The Stax Controversy* – in the time-honoured journalistic tradition of wringing every possible column inch from a story. Lots of our readers had thoroughly enjoyed the Stax show and were shocked and felt let down by the review, especially because it had appeared in Record Mirror, champion of R&B, and especially since it had been written by the author of *The Great Unknowns*. But others held different opinions: some agreed almost entirely with my remarks about Redding and his act, others felt Fenter had misconstrued the review, others were glad we had the "courage" to tell it like it is, and still others that Melody Maker and Disc were raving because they felt they "ought to".

I decided it was my prerogative to have the last word as RM was my paper, so I concluded The Stax Controversy in unrepentant and still-waspish mode:

> *...if the fact that I don't appreciate Otis Redding and his 'Satisfaction' means I don't know what soul is all about and should return to pop music, all I can say is that I'll gladly listen to my Nina Simone, Ben E. King, Impressions and Miracles pop records, and forget all about "soul"...*

I also managed to get in another dig at Stax with my review of Fats Domino at the Saville. Domino's act was sensational, but despite Tony Stratton-Smith's severe admonitions to me a few weeks previously on the subject of the Saville concerts, I nevertheless continued to chastise the theatre over its technical shortcomings – which should, in fairness, by now have been remedied:

RM w/e 1st April 1967

FATS TRIUMPH AT SAVILLE

A FIRST-TIME appearance in Britain for the man who has sold 55 million records. Quite an event at the Saville on Monday when Fats Domino not only lived up to any reputation he may have, but completely and utterly enraptured a thrilled audience with his warm, happy brand of New Orleans rock, blues, or whatever you care to call it. His voice was superb, his piano exciting, and his nine-piece band inspired. Unless Brian Epstein brings Elvis Presley here, he will never score such a musical triumph as this again. Fats played through many of his old hits and created a tremendous atmosphere – he made today's Stax-Tamla-Soul stars seem like frantic amateurs. Whether it's nostalgia or artistry, this week at the Saville should not be missed. Only complaint – the Saville microphones wouldn't work properly and the sound was too soft on certain instruments. Surely by now something can be done about this irritating fault.

The show was opened by the Bee Gees, an attractive Australian group with an excellent lead singer. Unfortunately, the rocker minority in the audience spoiled their act completely – whether the group played a rock medley to please or bait the audience I don't know – it was a mistake though. Their new record "New York Mining Disaster 1941" sounds excellent – it was a pity they didn't also play their "Spicks and Specks" number. The other half of the bill was Gerry and the Pacemakers, who were very good indeed. But again a running battle was fought between the audience (or the rockers therein) and the group (namely Gerry). Gerry won with some witty comebacks, but it seems wrong that an artist of his status should be forced to go through these ridiculous ordeals. Anyone who had come to see Gerry would have been disappointed – not with the act but with the audience spoiling it.

Brian Epstein cannot be pleased to see one of his top stars booed and jeered at, but he can have one consolation. No American star he could possibly bring over has as much talent or all-round appeal as his own group, the Beatles. Why not put them on for a week? They can't be busy...

If only I'd written such a review for the Hendrix/Who show at the Saville Theatre or for the Stax Revue instead of the somewhat mean-spirited observations I did make, a lot of controversy would have been saved – but would also have generated many less column inches of juicy copy.

Record Mirror's circulation was consistently ticking over at around sixty-five to seventy thousand copies sold weekly. A big colour photograph of a hot act like the Monkees on the front page could boost it to pushing eighty thousand. But the following week it would always drop again. NME was probably selling three times that amount. It didn't look like we were ever going to get any bigger.

I wasn't bored – that would have been impossible given the vibrancy of the 1967 pop scene – but I was feeling fidgety and anxious to do something new, to move out of the comfortable yet groovy rut I was in. The obvious alternatives, given my limited credentials, were working for a record company, or venturing into PR. Neither option appealed. I had no wish to work for a big, or even moderate-size company, and pop PR had less status – though more money – than pop journalism. More to the point, I was temperamentally no hustler. What else was there?

The answer came in the shape of a frivolous idea that would generate remarkable – and disastrous – ramifications.

Socialising frequently with Peter Meaden, I sometimes accompanied him to Jimmy James & the Vagabonds' gigs, even those far afield. Peter had moulded the Vagabonds into a tight and exciting unit – "Rock'n'Soul", as he'd branded their act (with a nod to Solomon Burke) – and they were an in-demand attraction nationwide. Wallace Wilson was on now on lead guitar, replaced on bass by former lead guitarist Phil Chen who Peter felt was a stronger contender for the rhythm section. It was a good career move for Phil – he later played bass for Rod Stewart. Peter rightly considered that the bass was more important than the lead guitar in a soul outfit like the Vagabonds – and probably in most beat groups too. The Vagabonds' act comprised not only current US soul smashes, but also more obscure titles, often interspersed with Jimmy's own soul ballad offerings. Their debut LP

"The New Religion" released late in 1966 reflected this mixture, as did their contemporaneous live LP "London Swings!" featuring the Vagabonds and, curiously, the Alan Bown Set.

Lots of their material was chosen by Peter via his friendship with music publisher Sandy Roberton, one-time singer-songwriter with Rick & Sandy, an Everly-type duo; and also as "Sandy"; and future highly-successful folk-rock record producer and even more highly-successful producer manager. In 1966-7 Sandy, whose career as an artist wasn't paying the rent, was running Jewel Music in a small office off Bond Street where he received the latest Chess/Checker releases, most published via Jewel, direct from Chicago. This was manna from heaven for Meaden, who would grab handfuls of unreleased Chess/Checker/Argo 45s plus plentiful swigs of Sandy's office Scotch, to check out which suited Jimmy. One glance at the Vagabonds' recorded output from this era testifies to the Jewel connection, which also suited Sandy because he got covers for his company's songs. They included "Ain't Love Good, Ain't Love Proud", "The Entertainer", "Hi Diddley Dee Dum Dum", "I Can't Get Back Home To My Baby", and "No Good To Cry". Meaden didn't write songs, Jimmy only wrote ballads, so this was the next best thing – comparatively obscure "New Wave Rhythm & Blues" songs, as Meaden – and me in Record Mirror – described them, off-the-peg but nevertheless sounding made-to-measure for Jimmy & the Vagabonds.

A half-baked idea occurred to me early that spring which would involve the Vagabonds, so I took Meaden to lunch in what I thought would probably be a futile attempt to persuade him to start a new venture with me. My proposed scheme was to form a co-owned independent record production company which we would finance equally, initially using the Vagabonds to cut some anonymous ska versions of US soul hits which we would license to a major record company. To my delight Peter thought this idea was terrific, and – amazingly – in a matter of days negotiated a deal with Horst Schmolzi whereby Polydor would retain our production services on an exclusive basis, licensing our masters in return for studio time, office space, and a regular retainer. Polydor's hidden agenda was the hope that Meaden could wrench Jimmy James & The Vagabonds away from Pye, the ultimate master plan being to send Jimmy to

Memphis, Tennessee, to record with the legendary Stax session crew. Despite Pye's John Schroeder cutting a succession of fine sides with the Vagabonds over the past two years, Pye couldn't chart them: in fact, Meaden was regularly resorting to the tried-and-tested standard industry hype that entailed paying the man who fixed the NME chart in order to get a small 'hit' for a week or two. A minor NME Top 30 entry costing around a hundred quid a week boosted a group's live earnings considerably.

With startling unoriginality we decided to name our enterprise "New Wave Productions" and at once began recording with frenzied enthusiasm. Dragging the reluctant Vagabonds into the studio, we cut several tracks including ska covers of Little Hank's "Mr Bang Bang Man" and U.S. Bonds' "Dear Lady Twist". The reason for the Vagabonds' reluctance was because in the hierarchy of Jamaican music soul music was at that time still considered superior to raggedy ska. We were also vocal-less as we couldn't use Jimmy's too-distinctive contracted-to-Pye voice. Peter, therefore, resolved to scout for fresh talent for the vocals, and if there was one thing Peter Meaden was extremely good at, it was talent-scouting. He'd already worked his magic on the Who and on Jimmy and the Vagabonds, so naturally I was prepared to follow him to wherever he might lead. He decided to lead first of all to Manchester's notorious Moss Side, persuading me to drive him there in my TR4A, him stretched out in the passenger seat swigging whiskey and empire-building, with his girl-friend Wendy scrunched up on the hard little bench behind the two front black leather seats – a wonder she wasn't permanently maimed.

Jimmy James and the Vagabonds played in lots of black clubs up and down the country, and Peter, as their manager, could always gain an entry to these exclusive and possibly dangerous places. That evening, marching into one such somewhat unfriendly, not to say hostile dive with Wendy and myself in reluctant tow, Peter – who'd checked out the local talent during Jimmy's gigs – grabbed half a dozen black guys, young and not so young, pulled them outside the club and tried to force them to sign artist contracts there and then on the long bonnet of the TR4A under the street lamp, all the while explaining rapid-fire to us his plans for each of them: this one was "the next Otis", these four guys were "a sort of junior Temptations" and so on and so forth. The talent, recognising Peter for the prize hustler he was, wouldn't all sign the dubious documents but neither did they want to miss out on a potential opportunity.

No good could possibly come of these desperate shenanigans, and sure enough when the junior Temptations, who Peter had re-named the Alphabets, eventually reached the Polydor studios in London a few weeks later, their would-be lead singer found his vocal chords had jammed up and he couldn't croak a note. Peter's frantic protestations and ministrations merely resulted in the would-be lead singer pulling out and brandishing a flick knife in order to shut him up. That was the end of the Alphabets. But the solo singer who had also arrived in London from Manchester was far more professional. This was Ossie.

Ossie was destined to be the latest recipient – or victim – of Meaden's svengaliesque fantasies, following in the illustrious footsteps of the Who, for whom Peter's elegant branding of them as mod icons had already ensured his place both in rock and mod history; and Jimmy James & The Vagabonds, moulded from a somewhat motley multicultural ragbag into a tight, successful soul ensemble. But it was never easy, even with the benefit of Peter's highly-descriptive volubility, to ascertain quite what image he was aiming at. In Ossie's case, Peter appeared to visualise him as a stylish, zoot-suited solo soul giant and in a matter of weeks he'd cut a record with him, found him a backing group of four white North London session musicians, and a tailor, who did indeed rustle up a tangerine zoot suit. Ossie could wear a drape with some aplomb, sporting as day wear a sharp midnight-blue fingertip item with unusually-shaped satin lapels.

New Wave's initial 45 release was a cover version of Toussaint McCall's current US soul hit "Nothing Takes The Place Of You" by 'Ossie & The Sweet Boys', featuring prominent country-soul piano from Tom Parker, the talented keyboardist who would later hit the US Top Ten with "Joy" by Apollo 100, as well as provide arrangements for Gerry Rafferty, among others. Ossie turned in a soulful vocal, unfortunately with a pronounced Jamaican accent and vocal mannerisms. Listening to the record now, it cries out for a gentle ska rhythm which would have metamorphosed it from a slightly ludicrous cover version into something altogether more authentic – which, given the premise of New Wave's birth, should have been the initial intention. But this was merely the first of many lost opportunities, both avoidable and unavoidable, that were to plague New Wave in its brief existence. Yet at the time, with offices at Polydor, steady income, use of studio, goodwill from all, New Wave still held promise, and Terry Chappell, becoming bored with laying out pages for Record Mirror, threw in his lot to work full-time alongside Peter Meaden.

Despite the fact that Peter and I were equal partners in New Wave, my contribution felt minuscule, especially as most of my time was still spent working for Record Mirror. So I resolved to be more pro-active and told Meaden I thought we should record a white group. He agreed, and in order to attract one, I placed a classified ad in Record Mirror, which around the same time ran a piece on Ossie in Peter Jones' Names And Faces Column. Featuring an imposing photo of Ossie wearing his dark drape and smoking a cigarette in a long holder, the piece was typical unedited Meaden prose:

> *"The Astonishing Ossie" (pictured above) must be one of the new phenomenons of the pop world. Discovered in Manchester by New Wave Productions, Ossie has declared "There is a premium on good taste". Arriving in London wearing a tangerine-coloured suit, Ossie has a four-piece group, the Sweet Boys. His chauffeur, Junior, who accompanies him everywhere, uses silk handkerchiefs to mop Ossie's brow on stage, and a fly-swatter to keep away over-enthusiastic admirers, most of whom wish to touch the hem of Ossie's garments. Ossie, who is now regarded as one of the top soul singers in this country, has a great record out on Polydor – "Nothing Takes The Place Of You".*

This piece was a follow-up to our previous week's "news story", also couched in deathless Meaden-esque prose, in which Ossie's "arrival" was announced in our news pages:

> ### OSSIE ARRIVES!
> *A sensation was caused by soul singer Ossie arriving at Euston Station this week in a tangerine-coloured suit. His*

> *chauffeur told press and photographers, "He always wears*
> *something conservative for travelling." Ossie's latest disc*
> *is "Nothing Takes The Place Of You" on Polydor.*

Needless to say, Ossie's version of "Nothing Takes The Place Of You" attracted little interest. How could it possibly have been a hit? Ossie & The Sweet Boys performed one gig at the Speakeasy in front of a disinterested in-crowd, and there was little further publicity. Ossie stayed in London for a few weeks, lodging in shabby digs we provided for him in Walthamstow, and knowing nothing of London, Ossie would walk from his digs to the West End. Despite Terry Chappell's efforts to make life slightly more bearable for our would-be star, the whole saga became sorrier and sorrier, and one day Ossie simply vanished, most probably back to the saner and more comfortable pastures of Moss Side. His follow-up, a revival of Earl Grant's ballad "The End" had already been recorded but it was never subsequently released.

Back at Record Mirror, I raved over Polydor's April release of a juicy batch of reissue 45s from the Atlantic archives in *Those Oldies But Goodies*; I caught a be-robed Donovan at the Saville Theatre (performing solo, then with a group), described him as *A Psychedelic Troubador*, but knowing nothing about psychedelia I gave him a luke-warm review using adjectives like "pleasant" (I'd gotten fidgety after about ninety minutes). With *Bo'n'Chess, The Tender Story Of A Love-Hate Relationship*, I interviewed a subdued Diddley in a cheap hotel room lamenting the loss of Jerome (who'd got married), complaining about Chess's slapdash attitude to his LP releases (rightly so), and apologising for missing his last few dates – not his fault, he assured me, showing me the contracts to prove it; he hadn't got paid, so he didn't turn up for the rest of the gigs. I saw the Beach Boys in concert once again, and headlined the review *Happy Beach Boys Sing The Single They Don't Like* ("Then I Kissed Her"). They were just as good as in '66, this time with a bevy of strong supporting acts including a blues-swinging Helen Shapiro, Simon Dupree and The Big Sound – a big sound indeed – and Terry Reid ("showed great promise") with Peter Jay's Jaywalkers.

Manfred Mann, consistent as ever, were currently scoring big with "Ha Ha Said The Clown", and I spoke to Manfred himself, who could usually be relied on to have an ambivalent attitude to his hits. This time, however, he was more mellow:

RM w/e 15th April 1967

"...but often, when I look back on our records I'm more pleased with them than when they were in the charts and when they were being played all the time. Take 'Semi Detached Suburban Mr James' for instance. I didn't particularly like it at the time. Now, I hear it and it seems to have a lovely flowing sound – very nice. I also like 'Just Like A Woman'. My favourite singles we've ever made have been those two and 'If You Gotta Go, Go Now' – that had a good funky sound. When I listen to things we did like '5-4-3-2-1' I'm amazed. That record was just a frantic sort of thing, it didn't have that funky sound we liked. The reason harmonica was included on it wasn't because of any tendency towards the blues, but because Paul played harmonica."

Manfred had also been recently pilloried in the national press for a letter he'd written to The Times.

Manfred spoke about his recent letter to "The Times" concerning drug taking.
"I expected press reaction to the letter. Obviously there wouldn't have been any reaction at all if I'd been someone other than a pop figure, a housewife perhaps. Most of the press just printed it with the tag 'Pop Star Manfred Mann Says Legalise Pot'. But this wasn't the point at all. You might have seen me on '24 Hours' – I had a chance to talk about it properly. You see, my point was this:
"When kids start smoking pot they think they're taking the big step – the step up from being ordinary to being extra hip, a with-it person. But really, that isn't the big step. This

is just a little step. Because pot, unlike alcohol and cigarette smoking, is non addictive. The really big step is what everyone else considers to be a little step. The step when someone starts taking heroin – because it's a drug and so is pot, what's the difference? The difference is that heroin is addictive and a killer. That was the point of the letter."

It made sense to me, not that I'd tried pot, or heroin, or any other drug for that matter. And as for Manfred's basic premise, well, forty-odd years later we're all still arguing about it.

Every music pundit had recently weighed in with his or her theory as to why the Beatles' four-year run of number one singles had been broken by the failure of the double-header "Penny Lane" / "Strawberry Fields Forever" to hit the top. The short answer was "Release Me" by Engelbert Humperdinck, but more interesting than the opining of the pundits were the views of Record Mirror's readers, collected together in *Beatles No.1 Failure – Readers Tell Reasons*. The most popular readers' theories were: that the single was too artistically advanced (though this was generally considered a good thing); that they'd left it too long between singles (over six months since "Yellow Submarine" / "Eleanor Rigby") and record buyers had switched allegiance to the Monkees and the Beach Boys; overplugging on the pirate stations, and, of course, the strength of the opposition. Said Concetta Verga:

"Could it be we're not so swingin', hippy, with-it as we like to think? Could it be that beneath our mini-mocking freakout-flashing, pop-painting exterior we harbour such old-fashioned corny things as "Love, girls, emotion". How many really understood 'Strawberry Fields'?"

Plenty liked it, though. Wrote Ronnie Poole, whose views echoed those of plenty of males who'd formerly scorned the Beatles as a 'girls' group':

"I had never liked the Beatles, but started to change with 'Eleanor Rigby'. I thought 'Penny Lane' / 'Strawberry Fields' their best ever, and I hope the next one is as good."

Mrs Diana Cavaghan's prosaic explanation was, however, the most interesting and probably the most accurate:

> *I'm a shareholder in Northern Songs. I've just been to the office and find 'Penny Lane' has sold over 481,000 to date. This is more than 'Yellow Submarine' which won an award as the best-seller last year. And much more than 'Paperback Writer' – so it shows no drop in sales. If a ballad catches on it sticks – if 'Tears' had just arrived at the top, neither Beatles nor Monkees would have ousted it."*

Not that the Beatles probably minded much. They were currently putting the finishing touches to their masterpiece "Sgt Pepper's Lonely Heart's Club Band" LP and, once again, were about to change the course of pop music.

Also about to change the course of pop music was Jimi Hendrix, enjoying his second top ten single with "Purple Haze", debut release on the new Track label, the independent imprint formed and owned by Who co-managers Kit Lambert and Chris Stamp under the auspices of Polydor. The Who's "Pictures Of Lily" was scheduled as Track's second single, and to celebrate the label's launch Kit and Chris and Polydor threw a press reception at the hip London club Blaises. Wandering around, drink in hand, I ran into Paul Simon and Art Garfunkel, with Paul voluble and opinionated and not minding at all when I asked him for an interview – and much more good-humoured than the quotes in the interview suggest:

RM w/e 22nd April 1967

SIMON AND GARFUNKEL TALK ABOUT THEIR WRONG IMAGE, THEIR MISTAKES IN RECORD RELEASES, BOB DYLAN, THE AMERICAN CHARTS, AND SENSATIONALIST BRITISH JOURNALISM

COMPARISONS are odious – so are certain kinds of association with other artists. At least they are to Paul Simon. At a recent press reception at a London club (for

*Jimi Hendrix and the Who and Track Records) Paul Simon
of Simon and Garfunkel alias Tom and Jerry (there's a
million-dollar lawsuit over THAT) spoke of the kind of
association he has with British stars.*

*"Like the Seekers, and the Bachelors...what kind of
image are we getting with our songs being recorded by
groups like that? Our version of 'Sounds Of Silence' was
far superior to the Bachelors, but we didn't make the charts
here. I can do nothing to make the charts here – I think I
write the wrong material for Britain regarding the singles
which are put out here – take 'The Dangling Conversation',
it just wasn't suitable for the British market, it was above
the kids. Then there was 'A Hazy Shade Of Winter' – as
soon as I released that I knew that the flip ('For Emily,
Whenever I May Find Her') was better. I should have
put strings on it and it could have been another 'Sounds
Of Silence'. It was Art singing on that one – his voice is
really great.*

*"You know we knocked off 'Feelin' Groovy' really
quickly – and I wasn't satisfied with it, I wasn't just not
satisfied with the record, I wasn't satisfied with the title.
I mean, us recording a song called 'Feelin' Groovy'? So
I thought, give it a more intellectual title – I thought of
'59th Street Bridge Song' which was OK. I knew that
record was a hit as soon as I wrote it. The other version is
alright. But then I put our version on the back of 'At The
Zoo'. Another mistake.*

*"I haven't written anything recently. Four songs in
six months. I can't seem to write anything. Sometimes I
think I should write especially for Britain, for the kids.
But I can't. It's a pity because I want to make the charts
in Britain, to have some hits. I did write a song once for
the kids – 'Red Rubber Ball'.*

*"In America things are very different from what people
here think is happening in America. Dylan is dead, he
means nothing – because he just doesn't release any new
material anymore. There are some hot new groups – the*

Buffalo Springfield really have something going for them with that record 'For What It's Worth' – that's a big hit. And Donovan – his last record 'Epistle To Dippy' flopped – yes I know it was big on the charts but it didn't have the sales or the impact of 'Sunshine Superman' or 'Mellow Yellow'. Those two carried the third one."

The second member of the duo, Art Garfunkel, has had his unruly hair slightly cut to make it look less unruly. He seemed bitter at the attitude of the British towards the American music scene.

"It's the music papers that started it all. If you read them you get the idea that everything concerned with pop music in the States is drug-dominated. It's just not true. There is a percentage, a small percentage. But the music papers and some of your nationals need copy, so you make it look like everything in the States is psychedelic and LSD influenced."

Well, shame on us music scribes. I didn't want to interrupt Paul in flow to point out "Homeward Bound" had hit the UK top ten a year ago, and that "I Am A Rock" had made our top twenty last summer. And as for Donovan, Art's sentiments seemed to be shared by Pye Records who announced that "Epistle To Dippy" would not be released as a single in the UK because "...the press might find controversial drug taking implications in the lyric." More likely, I suspected, because it was an artistic (and in the USA commercial) disappointment after "Sunshine Superman" and "Mellow Yellow", neither of which could possibly have been associated with psychedelia or LSD, as they were given prominent release and promotion by Pye.

Not having a decent recent photograph of Simon and Garfunkel, I used a drawing to illustrate the article. A talented young American named Lon Goddard had taken to hanging out at Record Mirror after showing us some caricatures he'd done of current pop stars. These were stylistically sophisticated spot-on likenesses, sometimes exaggerated, sometimes not. What we didn't know was Lon was also a talented acoustic guitarist – and writer. Predictably, he would soon join the RM team full-time. Another new arrival, but full-time from the start, was Terry Chappell's replacement Derek Boltwood. I interviewed dozens of short-list candidates for the job, advertised in our own classified columns. The response was overwhelming, but I hated doing it – some of the hopefuls were both highly qualified and desperate for work. Eventually I chose Derek, a dapper artistic charmer who soon proved to be equally adept at layouts and sub-editing, and an inspired creator of original artwork which was highly useful with psychedelia on the ascendant – and a budding journalist.

"Sgt. Pepper's Lonely Hearts Club Band" was launched at the end of May with a press reception at Brian Epstein's Belgravia home. I was in Banbury putting the paper to bed and couldn't go, so Peter Jones went, later writing a track-by-track review proving as out of his depth with full-on psychedelia as I would have been. Importantly, George Martin kindly wrote an article for us on the making of "their most ambitious LP" which shared the page with Peter's review.

A month earlier I'd missed another key psychedelic happening on my own doorstep, the soon-to-be legendary "14 Hour Technicolor Dream". I had no excuse as it was held on a Saturday evening and my flat was literally a stones-throw from the gates of Alexandra Palace on the Wood Green side. Where was I? Where was I at? The legendary Summer Of Love was looming, the Kinks' masterpiece "Waterloo Sunset" was being held off the top spot only by the Tremeloes' "Silence Is Golden", and both would shortly be shifted downward by Procol Harum's unstoppable "A Whiter Shade Of Pale", which would lodge at No.1 until being displaced by the Beatles' "All You Need Is Love", in its turn to be dislodged by Scott Mackenzie's flower-power anthem "San Francisco (Flowers In Your Hair)". The Byrds' impressive LP "Younger Than Yesterday" would inexplicably fail to make the UK LP charts, but the Mamas & Papas' "Deliver" would be the foursome's biggest LP yet in Britain.

I was back on familiar R&B territory interviewing an amiable Mitch Ryder for *Sock It To Me, Baby!*, who explained why he'd split with the Detroit Wheels, how his inspiration had been Little Richard, and how his only UK hit, the frantically exciting "Jenny Take A Ride" came about by accident. Mitch suggested that after the press reception we go to one of Lionel Bart's celebrated parties, but regrettably I had to decline the invite as deadlines loomed.

Another amiable luminary whom I'd met at various parties and subsequently encountered strolling around Soho was Mark Feld, a star-in-waiting who'd shot to fame aged 14 in 1961 in an Evening Standard photofeature on modernists, and then a year later had his reputation as a "top face" consolidated with a an atmospheric photoshoot by Donald McCullin spotlighting Hackney's top modernists in Michael Heseltine's About Town magazine. Mark and I got on well, the subject of conversation generally being a mutual admiration of each other's clothes and a mutual interest in the strange life of Beau Brummel. But Mark, inspired by Bob Dylan, had now chosen a career in music and was reincarnated as Marc Bolan, following a brief spell as Toby Tyler. Following several interesting solo singles, Marc was now a member of the South London foursome John's Children's, whose latest single was "Desdemona" on Track, penned by Bolan:

RM w/e 10th June 1967

JOHN'S CHILDREN – A TURN-ON SEANCE FOR A STAGE ACT

"THE REASON we're succeeding is 'cos we do everything for ourselves...we don't sit around waiting for publicity people to do all our promotional work for us. Yeah, and the money we make from playing we invest in other things. We've got our own club in Leatherhead and a big old house in the country which we're converting into a sort of group home. We're going to have a recording studio there and we're building a swimming pool. And we've got a lot of blokes who look after us...and they come round to gigs with us on their bikes...act as an escort and make sure we get our money all right."

John's Children don't wait for questions, nor do they stop talking; nor does their enthusiasm ever drop for a second.

Chris explained about the group: "Andy's the lead singer and he jumps off the stage and things, and does somersaults and belts John when he feels like it, and he's got a gong to hit as well. And Marc, he usually sits in a trance in the middle of the stage, except when he's jumping about like a flea." "Bunny," interrupted John, "Kit Lambert says we should have been called the Electric Bunnies". I asked Chris what he did. "Oh, I just play the drums". "Just play drums," echoes Andy, "How can he say that? He's the best pop drummer ever, he's sensational, he's fantastic." What about John, I wanted to know. "Oh, he's the best seducer ever," said Chris, "if we want something from someone and everything else has failed we send John along. He won't tell us what he does but it always works. His eyes, I think."

"People who see us play often think we're out of our heads," commented John. "It's true," Andy confirmed, "from the minute we get on the stage we lose our minds completely, it's like we're in a trance." "Marc's songs are part of it," John explained, "they're super dimensitive (sic)...not just double meanings but millions of meanings. Take 'Desdemona'. A lot of people say that 'Lift up your skirt and fly' is dirty. But it's not. Marc wrote those words because they gave him a buzz...they weren't meant to mean anything. One American DJ picked up on the line 'naked in the nude. We showed him some well-known songs with the words 'naked' and 'nude' in them. That's all right, he said, but when you put them together then it's pornographic.'"

Marc explained about their stage act: "We don't just do a musical performance...it's a 45-minute happening... sometimes we're barely conscious of what we're doing. It's like a big turn-on séance between us and ther audience. I've seen Andy go quite mad like a witch doctor in a tribal dance. He leaps off stage and runs round the audience or sometimes attacks one of us. In Dusseldorf he got into a fight with John, and they both fell 15 feet off the stage onto Andy's head." "Which was lying at the bottom," Chris explained helpfully.

The BBC wouldn't play "Desdemona" because of the "skirt" line so the group re-cut it for airplay with "why do you have to lie" substituted, but to little avail. It failed to chart. The amphetamine-fuelled foursome had also annoyed headliner labelmates the Who on their European tour in April by attempting to upstage them with their destructive antics – in Frankfurt the promoters stopped the show and the Who never got to perform. Marc, foreseeing the inevitable (and obvious), quit John's Children to form the duo Tyrannosaurus Rex with Steve Peregrine-Took, their image as far from John's Children as it was possible to get. John's Children broke up before the end of the year but like other interesting groups from that period maintained a cult following for decades.

The era of the "supergroup" had begun in 1966 when three exemplary musicians – Ginger Baker, Eric Clapton and Jack Bruce – formed Cream, originally intended to be a purist blues trio. After a hesitant start, Cream was swiftly influenced musically and visually by psychedelia and metamorphosed into a dynamic rock-blues power band, with the debut LP "Fresh Cream" and the singles "I Feel Free" and "Witches Brew". I caught up with Ginger in a pub just after they'd got back from an exhausting US package tour:

RM w/e 24th June 1967

GINGER TELLS OF CREAM'S STRANGE AMERICAN TRIP

GINGER Baker talks about as interesting as he looks – which is something special. That is, if you find a purple cape (with candy-stripe horizontal lining), green trousers with gold braid at the place where most people either do or don't have turn-ups, and various scarves, cummerbunds, shirt, etc, in every colour of the rainbow, interesting.

I talked to Ginger in a pub in Carnaby Street and even there some eyebrows were raised. But Ginger didn't care – especially as he was drinking a double-vodka to each one of my lagers.

Cream, as you may know already, have recently returned from an exciting tour of the States, where they

368

underwent some interesting experiences. Before you start jumping to conclusions, the most interesting one was their stint on the Murray The K Show. Murray, as you may know, is that well-known US dee jay who tends to put on enormous package shows comprising a great multitude of talent, and to make them play as many shows as physically possible in a given number of hours. He also hung around the Beatles when they first visited America.

"I forget who else was on the show," said Ginger, "I remember the Rascals and Wilson Pickett among others. At the end of every show Murray used to call everyone together and say how dreadful we had been - all except Wilson Pickett who he said was OK. Mind you, the American groups used to play him up far worse than the British groups. For the very last show on the last day, everyone bought flour and pies and eggs. Murray found out about it and threatened to stop payment if any of this 'food' found its way on to the stage. So we had to be content with throwing it at the stage door police. I never want to do that many shows again."

Believe it or not, Ginger used to be a cyclist - a sporting cyclist that is, and a good one too. "Those were the days," he laughed. "I had this bike, worth a fortune it was, and I sold it at some enormous loss to buy a drum kit. You have to be fit to play drums, and I'm fit.

"In the States the recording techniques are great. I don't want to record anywhere else. The guy who wrote 'Witches Brew' - it was incredible. We just knocked off a backing track ad lib and he took it home. Next day he came in with this song he'd written with his wife. When we finished the record there was a certain part which needed to be accentuated every time it was played, instead of only once. The engineer cut the tape, measuring it with his thumb - and it was completely accurate! They don't do that here. There, everyone sits around for ages chatting."

Cream's new LP has already been completed - all of it recorded in the States - and it should be out here reasonably soon. Ginger talked about the formation of the group.

> *"I'd heard all about Eric Clapton for a long time and thought, 'Who is he?' When I saw him I thought he was alright, but not spectacular. But after hearing him a few times and seeing him improve, I began to like his style. Eventually I approached him about forming a group – he agreed and suggested Jack. I agreed – I'd been playing with Jack years before. So that's it. People ask me about Eric and Jimi Hendrix – well, I don't just think that Eric's better than Jimi Hendrix – I think he's in a different class altogether. Jimi is first of all a showman and then a musician. But Eric is a musician first".*

I thought that was a very loyal thing to say, considering the awesome reputation Jimi had gained here in less than a year. Mind you, what else could Ginger say? He had to work with Eric.

One of the media's favourite catch-words sprouting from the current psychedelic revolution was that short-lived but forever-memorable phrase that sums up the 1967 Summer of Love – "Flower Power". So in June, Record Mirror started reporting directly from California via our new column "West Coast USA", groovily penned in situ by recently relocated ex-EMI record producer David Gooch ("Reporting Boss Angeles, world centre Flower Power...") The column lasted about as long as flower-power did – a few magic months – but we did get first-class chatty info on the music, the philosophy, the artists, the fans and the happenings, including a report from the Monterey International Pop Festival – the soon-to-be-legendary 'Monterey Pop', the first real rock festival (and maybe the most influential). Well, it certainly was for me, a month later, albeit indirectly.

Meanwhile, I supervised a three-part series *Legends In Their Time*, focussing on the rumours of titles of as yet-unreleased recordings by Buddy Holly and Eddie Cochran, whose fans were still writing to us in droves. These same faithful fans were then roundly condemned by rockabilly purist "Breathless" Dan Coffey, who contributed an article in July on his recent Memphis trip with wife Fay in *A Memphis Snapshot*. Thundered Dan: "...if people who go to great pains to get substandard recordings by Eddie Cochran, Buddy Holly, and even the Johnny Burnette Trio would only direct their attention to the

LIVING rock'n'roll artists like Charlie Feathers and Mickey Gilley and Sonny Burgess and so on, I'm sure they'd find some of these 'Great Unknowns' have as much or more talent than their idols ever had." Then he added, diplomatically, "A personal opinion, that last bit."

Another bona fide original Teddy Boy who had taken to hassling me big-time at the Record Mirror office was Max Needham ("Waxie Maxie"), self-styled 'helmsman' of the "Quest For Merrill Moore", a one-man fan club and promo machine for an obscure San Diego-based rock-a-boogie pianist. Maxie had persuaded Ember to issue an LP of Moore's material, "Bellyful Of Blue Thunder", and to oblige Waxie (and get some peace) we featured a photo and short blurb on Merrill in Peter Jones' Names And Faces column. Max was also a vivid writer: in the LP's sleevenotes he wrote: "...after years of electronically overloaded Mickey Mouse music that makes me think of bonewhite stones against the bottlefly green gravegrass, Merrill's sledgehammer 'Blue Thunder' music is like a fresh stalk of celery in a field of dung!"

In *A Hit – After Six Years Of Soul* I profiled, not for the first time, Gladys Knight & The Pips, whose joyous "Take Me In Your Arms And Love Me" was at last providing them with their first UK hit a full six years after their debut US smash "Every Beat Of My Heart". Another fine singer, one of the best new vocalists I'd seen and heard lately, was Terry Reid, the 17-year old singer with Peter Jay & The Jaywalkers who'd recently supported the Beach Boys. When I spoke to Terry in *Terry – 'Why I Didn't Join Spencer Davis'*, he explained, "... following a man of Stevie's talent wouldn't be easy to begin with, and my style is nothing like his anyway". That was true enough. But turning down plum offers would become a habit of Reid's. Jimmy Page later offered him the job as vocalist in the New Yardbirds – shortly to become Led Zeppelin – and when Terry declined, Page recruited Robert Plant. Reid also refused an offer as lead singer of Deep Purple, which then went to Ian Gillan. He turned down both offers to concentrate on his solo career.

Dave Davies was about to score a solo smash that month with "Death Of A Clown" and I interviewed him at Pye's tiny No. 2 studio straight after a Kinks' recording session: "tiny, but it's got atmosphere," said Ray. Dave's message to our readers was that he was happy making solo discs but wasn't leaving the Kinks. That evening I met up again with Ray for a drink at one of his local pubs in Muswell Hill. "I don't go out a lot," said Ray mysteriously, "Blokes always want to fight me." I thought he was being dramatic, but ten minutes later, as if on cue, for no reason at all a semi-drunk started getting aggressive with him, so we left.

It was my turn again this year to cover the annual European Singing Cup Contest at Knokke-Le Zoute. The British team was sponsored by Brian Epstein, and included several artists with whom I'd previously enjoyed Euro-jaunts:

RM w/e 15th July 1967

IN A contest noted for surprises, this year has been surprisingly...dull. Only when a strong British team (sponsored by NEMS Enterprises) beat the equally good home Belgian team was there any sign of spontaneous enthusiasm from the sophisticated Casino audience.

As for the other four teams, Germany beat Holland, and France beat Italy but for any of these to come within shouting distance of Britain or Belguim it would really require something spectacular to be pulled out of their hats.

The British team, led by Gerry Marsden, is in good spirits (Scotch, gin etc) and the surprise triumph of their Saturday night victory was the astonishingly mature and swinging performance by unknown quantity Oscar, whose previous claim to fame was his "All Coppers Are Nanas" disc. Dodie West, Rog Whittaker and Oscar received the most applause and these three have already been heavily booked for Dutch TV appearances, while other offers are coming in.

Gerry was disappointed with his own performance, and Lois Lane suffered through lack of suitable arrangements for her songs. But if these faults can be ironed out there is no real reason why Britain shouldn't win this festival for the second year running.

Gerry made up for the disappointment with his next performance, which was sensational. But everyone in the team shone, and big-voiced folk whistler Rog Whittaker not only won the press prize, but garnered the most audience applause. The British team won.

It had been two years since Gerry's last UK hit, and almost a year since his last American hit. He'd changed labels, moving from EMI to CBS, ditching the Pacemakers and becoming the solo 'Gerry Marsden'. But he would never have another hit, and his career would now require a different, broader, strategy. Yet with a back catalogue that included his now-definitive version of the standard "You'll Never Walk Alone" and his self-penned Liverpool anthem "Ferry 'Cross The Mersey", he would remain a big star.

Brian Epstein himself arrived a few days into the contest, jovial and smiling as usual, but edgy. I'd only encountered Brian in a professional situation, svelte and confidently in control, but at Knokke he made little or no attempt to disguise his condition, if indeed he cared. He was pilled-up, drinking heavily, florid, and clubbing all night. I was a bit shocked to see him like this. Brian's Liverpool buddy Peter Brown, NEMS executive second-in-command, appeared to be acting as Brian's unofficial minder, staying relatively sober and watching over his friend and boss with trepidation. Brian was also giving his proverbial generosity full rein. He hired a small fleet of huge '50s American cars, all fins and chrome with dashboards like juke boxes, for each of the team members and for me and for NME scribe Norrie Drummond. When the contest was won, he had the entire team plus me and Norrie driven over the border into Holland where there was a world-famous seafood restaurant specialising in lobster that he wanted us to experience.

Brian was scheduled to hold an international press conference at the Casino after the contest, and he decided to use the occasion to take some heat out of the ongoing controversy stirred up the previous month when Paul McCartney had admitted taking LSD and was swiftly pilloried by the entire UK media as well as church and state, a situation that was still making news weeks later. "It's not fair on Paul that he should be subjected to this when we've all taken it," Brian told us, "I'm going to admit to taking it too. I think it's only right." Peter Brown was unhappy about this, but Epstein was adamant. At the press conference, after answering routine questions about the team's performances and whether or not he'd consider returning to Knokke another year with a new team, Brian turned the subject to Paul's LSD confession, admitting that he too had taken it, and subsequently launching into the now-becoming-familiar litany of acid proselytisation with phrases such as "know myself better", "a new mood in this country", etc. This was manna for the journalists, and the next day the European headlines were all along the lines of "Brian Epstein and LSD", and over the next week Brian was to repeat his confessional performance back in the UK to various publications, much to the chagrin of NEMS and many of its straighter artists.

But I respected Brian, and at the press conference listened carefully to what he was saying. Seated next to Peter Brown, I asked him, "What's it like, LSD?" Peter paused for a moment and then – unexpectedly – said quietly, "I think everyone should take it."

What Peter said, and the way he said it, allowed me to give myself permission to take it too. For despite the current proliferation of visual psychedelia, the strains of "Sgt. Pepper" dominating the airwaves, the evident burgeoning of some inexplicable kind of acid-induced spirituality, the explosion of the flower-power scene, the freaky US West Coast / San Francisco psychedelic mecca, the influential celebrities spouting message of love, peace and liberty, until now I'd never seriously considered taking LSD. This stance had little to do with David Griffiths' "...that yellow streak ain't mellow," jibe, nor the fact that Guy Stevens had recently come up to Record Mirror bedecked with beads and bells, his hair "half-a-Hendrix", in order to specifically warn me off LSD. Despite his psych get-up, Guy was no LSD evangelist. He had recently taken acid and had a bad trip, which he recounted in lurid detail. But Guy – unlike me – was nevertheless now "into drugs". Keith Moon had turned him on to speed in 1966, and like our mutual friend Peter Meaden, Guy took to it like a fish to water. As any amphetamine user knows, speed allows you to drink more alcohol and still function. So you drink more. Many other friends and colleagues had fallen into that lifestyle and most – eventually – came out the other side, damaged but alive. Guy would not. He had already been busted and jailed for pot, and worse was to follow.

My curiosity about LSD was becoming so overwhelming I was bursting to know what it was all about, regardless of what had happened to Guy. The effects of it were all around me – but what was this mysterious experience that generated such effects? The only analogy I can make is from when I was a child in the late '40s and early '50s and the grown-ups were still talking about "the war". Everything related to "the war". Every recollection was either "before the war", "during the war", or "just after the war". Bombsites were everywhere, militarism and rationing were still a part of daily life. There were regular radio programmes broadcast to our forces overseas, and people were still talking and newspapers writing about the Germans and Japanese and what they did. And yet there was no war. It had gone. It was all over, I missed it, I was too young. This cataclysmic event that had so shaped the world in which I lived was something I would never directly experience.

But the LSD revolution was happening now, and here I was with this unshakeable inner conviction that I must experience it for myself. Nobody I knew who'd already taken LSD seemed able to describe the experience with any kind of effectiveness, at least not in any terms that I could understand. Yet its evident cultural effects, even to someone like me whose sole experience of change of consciousness was alcohol, were enormous. And if that's how it seemed to someone who hadn't taken LSD, then how would things seem if one actually had taken it, had experienced this whatever-it-was?

Returning from Knokke, I reasoned that the person who could most likely lay his hands on some LSD would be Peter Meaden. So somewhat manipulatively I decided that in order to convince Peter to join me in a "trip", I should sell him the idea of taking LSD as being essential for the furtherance of our ambitions with New Wave Productions – something along the lines of our having to know "what was happening" in order to make some hit records.

The day I returned from Belgium was a beautiful sunny July day, so donning a raffish white trilby and tying on a coloured scarf or two, I drove round to Peter's big house in Offord Road, Islington, where he lived with Wendy and most of the Vagabonds. Peter and Wendy were strangely and uncharacteristically passive, muted, and laid-back, lying a-bed and agreeing at once with everything I said. Peter said he

knew where he could probably score some acid, and so we made a
plan to take it at my flat in Wood Green next to Alexandra Palace, a
spacious ground-floor pad with big French windows and a generally
groovy demeanour.

As luck would have it, Peter visited the Speakeasy that evening and
bumped into Keith Moon. Peter's relationships with the Who had
always stayed friendly notwithstanding their change of management,
and Moon just happened to be carrying a bag of LSD tablets he'd
brought back from California, remnants of the special Monterey Pop
batch made by the San Francisco chemist Augustus Owsley Stanley
III. Unfortunately the police were raiding the Speakeasy that night
and burst in team-handed – fortunately not before Meaden had
persuaded Moon to slip him some of this premium product. The rest
of Moon's stash, regrettably, was swiftly flushed down the toilet upon
the arrival of Mr Plod.

As this trip was ostensibly a New Wave occasion, Terry Chappell was
invited along and duly turned up on the Friday evening. Peter arrived,
dished out the acid and we all swallowed it. Peter then confessed that
this was not his first acid trip. In fact he'd been at the tail end of his
first trip when I'd turned up at Offord Road the previous day, and
had been so convinced by my get-up and acid spiel that he thought I
too had taken it – till he realised I hadn't but wanted to.

The effects of the LSD took several hours to come on, and in the
meantime David Griffiths arrived to check out what was happening.
As nothing was happening, he stayed an hour or so and then split,
disappointed we were not more amusing. Peter mentioned that on his
first trip he'd had an overnight musical conversion – he revealed that
none of his precious soul music LPs sounded any good, but when, in
desperation, he'd played "Sgt. Pepper" – which I'd recommended to
him but which he hadn't yet bothered to play – the penny dropped.
"...Garnett Mimms didn't quite cut it," he said ruefully.

When the acid finally kicked in, it did it for me in a big way. Other
people's psychedelic experiences are seldom interesting (except to the
participant), so I shall draw a veil over this trip and simply say that
it was the full-blown born-again beyond-the-white-light experience
and that the visual effects stayed with me for the next three weeks. I
was changed. When I came back to earth next morning, renewed, I

felt like I'd landed on another Earth in a parallel universe – which is where I've been ever since.

In 1966 the Beach Boys had consistently beaten the Beatles into second place in popularity polls, and – in the UK anyway – probably total record sales. Nice for EMI, who recorded both groups, although the next few years would see the Beach Boys embroiled in various lawsuits against EMI's Capitol label in the USA for purported unpaid royalties. But 1967 was proving a very different story. The Beach Boys' creative '66 double-whammy of the introspectively beautiful "Pet Sounds" LP and the awesomely joyous "Good Vibrations" single had not been repeated in 1967. The Beatles, on the contrary, were unstoppably perched at No. 1 globally with their acid-drenched masterpiece "Sgt. Pepper" and anthemic flower-power single "All You Need Is Love". Years later, we would learn of maestro Brian Wilson's creative desperation upon hearing "Sgt. Pepper" and every heartbreaking detail of the collapse of his monumental "Smile" LP project, rumours of which had been unhelpfully emanating all year from LA. But in August 1967, at the very peak of artistic creativity of rock-based pop music, the world was still eagerly waiting for Brian's response to "Sgt. Pepper", knowing little of his precarious mental and emotional condition.

Brian's first nervous breakdown had been at the end of 1964, after which he decided to retire from live performances to concentrate on writing and producing. Glen Campbell temporarily replaced him until April 1965 when Bruce Johnston joined and became a permanent Beach Boy. Bruce was a perfect fit, a classically-trained pianist who played bass on tour, a fine singer whose voice blended perfectly with the high-level vocal demands of the Beach Boys, a songwriter of talent and originality, and an experienced stalwart of the LA music scene, having worked with such local luminaries as Eddie Cochran, Kim Fowley, Sandy Nelson, and most successfully with Terry Melcher during their mid-'60s stint as producers at Columbia.

Finally scheduled for release was the "Good Vibrations" follow-up "Heroes And Villains", a single with one of the longest gestation periods and biggest budgets in history, and a lyric incomprehensible outside the already-aborted (though we didn't know it yet) "Smile" concept – and maybe incomprehensible even within the concept. The Beach Boys had toured the UK in late '66 and earlier in '67, but this summer they'd dropped out of Monterey Pop, a disastrous career move that in a stroke rendered them, to US rock fans at least, as "unhip". They weren't ready to tour the UK again, least of all to promote a single as complex as "Heroes And Villians", so it was left to Bruce Johnston to visit London and talk up the group's new single:

RM w/e 12th August 1967

BRUCE HELPS TO SOLVE THE BEACH BOYS DISC MYSTERIES

BRUCE JOHNSTON is the youngest Beach Boy – meaning that he was the last of the Beach Boys to join the group. He joined in 1965 when Brian Wilson was ill and has stayed with the group ever since. He has no wish to do anything but be a Beach Boy. And his enthusiasm is shown in the fact that he has now visited Britain by himself to do what he can to plug the new Beach Boys' single "Heroes And Villians". I talked to him at the Waldorf Hotel in the Aldwych, where he is staying for the few weeks he is here.

The first thing I asked him was about the Beach Boys' records – the new single and the anticipated new LP.

Why the nine month wait for a single?

"I guess it's the combination of the legal tangles with Capitol about one thing and another and the fact that Brian wasn't quite satisfied with it. He was worried about the legal thing hanging over his head – therefore he couldn't work properly on the record. Now it's finished and we're pleased with it. But of course it is different from the original idea because so much has had to be cut away, trimmed down. There is still so much happening but it isn't a dance record – still, there are plenty of Beach Boy LPs about with danceable tracks on them.

NO INNER SIGNIFICANCE

"Brian wrote the song with a friend of his. The flipside ("You're Welcome")? Yes, it's different. But I hope no one tried to look for any kind of significance in it. It's just a pleasant nothing. You know, the kind of song we would sing when the audience is coming to see us.

"The LP is finished – at least I've heard it on acetate, so presumably it just needs mastering. I like it – it's different to 'Pet Sounds', gentler, quieter. But there's just as much happening."

No release date yet for the album, but Bruce was confident there would be no more long gaps between Beach Boy releases. About "Good Vibrations", Bruce said that when he first joined the Beach Boys Brian had explained to him that he wanted to do a song made up of many different sounds and styles. That was two years ago.

Brian Wilson, guiding light behind the Beach Boys, no longer plays on stage with the group, as most people know – but Bruce said that if Carl had gone into the US Army, then in all probability Brian would have returned.

"It takes a long time for Brian to accept you," said Bruce. "He distrusts you, then he likes you, he's suspicious of you, until you finally become accepted by him."

Brian works out every part of every Beach Boys' number beforehand, and then tells the boys what he wants. Bruce said that communication between the group and Brian was perfect, but only because the group was so musical. Ideas bounce back and forth between Brian and the boys, and things are improved and polished. The reason why so many old rock and roll techniques are employed by Brian was explained by Bruce.

SINATRA THE FAVOURITE

"Brian grew up with Elvis Presley, the Drifters, Gene Vincent. He was influenced by all this – and of course the

Four Freshmen. In the Beach Boys you hear the finished product. When I joined the group I found that Brian and I both had the same favourite album. It was Sinatra's "Only The Lonely". And we both admired immensely Nelson Riddle, who arranged it."

If the Beach Boys admired Sinatra, then could Sinatra fans dig the Beach Boys? And what kind of fans were the newer, more sophisticated Beach Boys getting?

"Oh yes, I see no reason why Sinatra fans couldn't dig the Beach Boys. And our fans are growing up with us, and of course younger kids are becoming much more aware than we used to be when we were their age. People are becoming more enlightened, but we have to keep on changing our records. We couldn't ever record 'Heroes And Villians' again and again. That is why the new LP is different from the others. But doubtless people will criticise it on the grounds that it is different."

On stage the Beach Boys put over a very happy image. Bruce explained that as such the Beach Boys have no real act – perhaps it would be better if they did, he said, but a lot of amusement was created by Mike. And although Brian sings on every beach Boys' record, the harmony system which the Beach Boys employ sees to it that on stage the vocals are not far different to the record. They also use a small four-piece outfit to augment the group on the more complex numbers – "Good Vibrations especially – but they haven't been allowed to bring them into Britain yet because of union restrictions.

What do the Beach Boys think of the other top groups around the world?

"This may sound surprising coming from a Beach Boy," said Bruce, "but I always thought the Byrds could be America's equivalent to the Beatles. I dig the Byrds, and although I'm glad that it seems it's us in America and the Beatles in Britain, the Byrds could have been there. I've seen the Byrds several times on stage and they're not consistent. Sometimes they're really great, other times

they're not. The other top groups, the ones that will last, are the Lovin' Spoonful, the Stones, and of course the Beatles. But I don't think we compete with the Beatles in any way whatsoever. I've met the Beatles but I don't know any of them.

CLEAN CUT

And finally, how does Bruce, from the inside, see the Beach Boys?

"I see them as a group of young men who have made a lot of money, but who have to earn that money, who have had to work hard, and have known hardships. I don't know if we'll keep the money, you just don't know what's going to happen. I see them as a sensible, efficient clean-cut group, without being the male equivalents of Doris Day, if you see what I mean – no offence to Doris Day.

"I don't think you'll get anywhere in this business if you only think about the money. But you won't get anywhere if you don't think about it at all..."

The LP Bruce spoke of was "Smiley Smile", half of which would consist of tracks from the aborted "Smile" project – "Heroes And Villians", "Wonderful", "Vegetables", "Wind Chimes", "Fall Breaks And Back To Winter" and "Good Vibrations – plus the new Brian Wilson/Mike Love A-side "Gettin' Hungry", plus some terrific newer tracks: "She's Goin' Bald", "Little Pad", "With Me Tonight" and "Whistle In". "Smiley Smile" might have disappointed those unrealistic enough to expect a Brian Wilson masterpiece to top "Sgt. Pepper" – how could it? – but it didn't disappoint me. I loved it, and gave it an in-depth rave review on its release that October. It may have been the poorest-performing Beach Boys' album for six years in America, but it hit the top ten here. Not long after meeting Bruce I ran into his former musical partner Terry Melcher at a deserted press reception in Mayfair one Saturday morning for the Mamas and the Papas. Only half the group were there, Papa John (a charmer) and Mama Cass (not a charmer). No Denny, and regrettably no Michelle. But Terry

Melcher was there and we spoke at length about his producing career, of which I remember nothing except thinking "You lucky sod, your mum's Doris Day!" – Melcher had her freckles.

Another serious and thoughtful guy I interviewed in August was Peter Green, who'd famously replaced Eric Clapton in John Mayall's Bluesbreakers and had now quit Mayall to form his own group which, a little unkindly, seemed like it had originally been planned as John Mayall's Bluesbreakers minus John Mayall, featuring ex-Bluesbreakers Mick Fleetwood on drums, John McVie on bass, and Peter on lead guitar. But it didn't quite work out that way. McVie, who needed a regular paycheck, wouldn't quit Mayall for an unknown group, so Green – with gigs already booked – hired Bob Brunning on bass, with the proviso that if McVie joined, then Brunning would leave, and slide guitarist/vocalist Jeremy Spencer.

RM w/e 19th August 1967

PETER GREEN – THE GUITARIST WHO WON'T FORSAKE THE BLUES

ANYONE who in a year has built up the reputation of being Britain's best blues guitarist, must have some interesting things to say, and therefore be interesting to write about and read about. That's what I figured and indeed Peter Green is very interesting.

He made his reputation as John Mayall's lead guitarist when he replaced Eric (then "Slowhand") Clapton. It is necessary to know that Peter Green really and truly lives for the blues and with the blues, and everything from his East End upbringing (he was a shy and reticent child) to his natural talent has contributed to his present reputation.

When he replaced Clapton after a series of auditions by John Mayall in which Peter won hands down, he was taunted on nearly every date by cries of "We want Clapton" from some of the audience.

"They weren't the kind of things which made me play better," said Peter, "they would just bring me down. For

a long time with John I wasn't playing at my best, as good as I was able. Only in the last few months with him could I really feel uninhibited."

Peter first became interested in the blues when he heard a Muddy Waters record when he was fourteen. At that time he was playing bass, but after hearing more and more blues he felt he could play blues guitar and switched instruments. From playing Shadows material he has changed to playing real blues – he is on the new Eddie Boyd LP and in a private letter to a record producer Eddie said that Peter could play blues guitar better than anyone else he had heard – a truly fine compliment.

Peter's guitar playing has made him into one of the most highly-rated musicians in the country, but does Peter think that his very specialist form of music can be truly appreciated by the audience?

"No, no, only by a few. I think this is demonstrated by the applause I get when I play very fast – it's something I used to do with John when things weren't going very well. But it isn't any good. I like to play slowly, and feel every note – it comes from every part of my body and my heart and into my fingers. I have to really feel it, I make the guitar sing the blues – if you don't have a vocalist then the guitar must sing.

"Only a few people in this country can really do this. Clapton could. I would watch him and think how great he was. But he sat in with us the other week and he isn't the same, he's lost the feeling. Mind you he could, I think, get it back – but he's so easily influenced. He sees Hendrix and thinks 'I can do that, why don't I?'. But I'll always play the blues."

A while ago Peter wanted to go to Chicago because he thought that the blues scene in Britain wasn't wide enough. But he has abandoned the project now and formed his own group, Peter Green's Fleetwood Mac. Why did he leave John Mayall's band, which has the reputation of being the country's most successful blues outfit?

"Various reasons. But the most important was that I didn't agree with the kind of material which was being played. It was becoming, for me, less and less of the blues. And we'd do the same thing, night after night. John would say something to the audience and count us in, and I'd groan inwardly."

Peter's group will record for the Blue Horizon label, a specialist label which will soon be distributed nationally.

If you appreciate blues, and real blues guitar, don't miss them.

The following month I spoke to John Mayall, who told me:

"...I can usually tell when someone – the lead guitarist especially – is unhappy with the group and wants to leave. You see guitarists reach a peak within the group, and then they start to slacken off, become discontent and generally want to do their own individual thing. I've never been unhappy about anyone leaving though – but it is a task to find new members."

Fleetwood Mac made their debut appearance on August 13th at the Windsor Jazz And Blues Festival and their first single – their only record in 1967 – would be "I Believe My Time Ain't Long", a showcase for Jeremy Spencer's slavish yet impressive imitation of Elmore James' "Dust My Broom". Not until the following year and Green's original "Black Magic Woman" would their chart run commence, featuring Green himself on vocals, unsurprisingly proving to be a convincingly honest singer.

Another fine white blues vocalist, albeit one whose music was temporarily straying into psychedelic pastures, was Mick Jagger, and 1967 wasn't Mick's best year. The well-documented Stones' drug busts were still being resolved: Keith's conviction had just been overturned and Mick's sentence recently reduced to a conditional discharge, but Brian's trial wasn't due till November. And the expectation on the Stones, as with Brian Wilson and the Beach Boys, to musically out-do "Sgt. Pepper" was a career pressure the group could have done without. They'd also split from Andrew Oldham, with Allen Klein now well-ensconced as manager and money-man, and the group themselves supervising the sessions resulting in their new single "We Love You" / "Dandelion" and the forthcoming LP "Their Satanic Majesties Request".

A short telephone interview was arranged with Mick, who seemed relatively unfazed by recent developments:

RM w/e 26th August 1967

AFTERMATH
Mick Jagger answers some questions

WHEN I spoke to Mick Jagger everything was "nice" and "groovy" with him, so don't believe everything you read in the papers. And he's happy with the new record "We Love You" which you'll be hearing a lot of...here's a question-and-answer interview with Mick.
Do you think the recent convictions will make any difference to the career of the Rolling Stones?
"No."
Do you think it will make any difference to your own private life?
"Not fundamentally, only superficially. Everything that happened just confirmed beliefs which I had held before it all happened."
How do you feel about the support which you received during the period of the trial — some of it from presumably unexpected quarters?
"Everyone was nice. We had a lot of support from our friends, and they were all very nice. Lots of people were nice, and there certainly was support from people we didn't expect any from."
Do you, or any of your friends and supporters, consider you or Keith to be martyrs to a particular cause?
"No. How can we be martyrs when we're not dead..."
How relevant in the career of the Rolling Stones is "We Love You"?
"That depends on what you mean by 'relevant'. I think it's a nice direction where the record is going. The structure

is more complicated than on most of our other singles, but when it was written – which was about four months ago – it was far simpler. It was originally recorded then, and since that time we have put more voices on, added sounds, changed things around. But you see it's quite an old thing really. I'm very happy with it, but then I'm happy with all the singles, or else they wouldn't BE singles."

What are your recording plans?

"We're recording next week and the week after and the week after and so on. We've loads of work to be done in the studio, and the reason is our new LP. Everything will be out of the ordinary on it, and Bill has written a couple of the songs. They're good. But I don't want to talk about the LP until it's finished."

You still seem to be discriminated against – and the incidents are widely reported in national newspapers. How do you feel about this?

"I don't expect it to keep happening, but I really don't feel it. I'm oblivious to this kind of treatment, and if anything I find it amusing. It's something for the newspapers to write about and they can write about what they like. I don't mind what they write."

Why are the "gaol" noises on "We Love You"?

"I just thought it'd be nice. I mentioned it and the next day someone brought them along, so we used them.

Do you think these noises put down the record to a certain phase in your career, to put a date on the record?

"All our records are dated anyway, like that at least. This one is just summer 1967. There's a date written on the record I think anyway, it doesn't matter if the sound puts a date on the record."

What's happening about your live appearances and will you be able, if you ever appear on stage to perform "We Love You"?

"Well, if we did go on stage, we'd find a way to do it. But as there are no plans for a tour or anything why worry? About a tour, well, we've done a tour already this year. I feel that everybody who wants or wanted to see the Rolling Stones has done so already. They've had ample

chance because we've done an awful lot of touring and shows. But we can't go on doing it forever, we've done it all before. And there are lots of other groovy people for the kids to watch. You see, we have a lot of other groovy things going for us and not just concerning music."

Any chance of any films, ever – and what about the scheduled film?

"I don't know anything about that. I've been offered an awful lot of nice films, but I haven't found a script I like yet."

When "Satanic Majesties" was released that December, their record company Decca, who still co-owned Record Mirror together with John Junor, did something they'd never done before: they specifically asked editor Peter Jones to make sure the LP was given a good review. Presumably the contract was up for renewal, and Decca trusted Klein even less than they trusted Oldham. They needn't have worried, at least not on RM's account. As with the Beach Boys' "Smiley Smile", I went against the prevailing tide of criticism. I liked "Satanic Majesties" a lot and said so, even going as far as writing "...the best album the Stones had ever recorded." A bone of exaggeration thrown to Decca, but I always felt that the critical panning the album received elsewhere on the grounds that it was a sub-"Pepper", didn't sound like the Stones, missed the point.

As everything was going psychedelic, even (briefly) the Rolling Stones, Peter Meaden decided a psychedelic record from New Wave Productions would be just the ticket for chart success. A few months earlier, pre-acid trip, I'd placed an ad in RM's classified columns: "WANTED – Folk or folk rock male group or solo artist for management and recording. Replies Box 0078". We got lots of replies, photos, demos, but nothing grabbed us. Then we received a rough acetate demo from a Midlands-based foursome who'd met on a graphics course at Wolverhampton Art College. Their music was acoustic (including banjo) and quirky, with distinctive vocals, attractive harmonies and very good songs, slightly Beatle-esque. It had the magic. So we signed them, and during the next twelve months got into the routine of arranging for them to come to London to record, while I would regularly take the train to Wolverhampton for their rehearsals. The name I came up with for the foursome was the Peep Show: Stephen Morris, Dave Cartwright, Patrick Burston and Stephen Stringer. Peter soon decided he wanted them to be a beat group, and utilising some of Ossie's Sweet Boys, put together a New Wave studio band to beef up their sound, including such fine musicians as guitarist Brian Parker (later of Consortium), pianist Tom Parker (the multi-instrumentalist later responsible for many hit arrangements on the Young Blood label), keyboardist Pete Dello (about to form Honeybus), and arranger Tony King (shortly to write Amen Corner's smash hit "High In The Sky"). The Peep Show were prolific songwriters and we initially decided that their own records should be recorded at Polydor's own studios, but that we'd also cut quality demos of their surplus songs at the Pan Music studio in Denmark Street using the same musicians, with a view to selling them on to other artists.

The first single was scheduled to be two Stephen Morris songs – "Your Servant Stephen" and "Goodbye Child". "Your Servant Stephen" was lyrically couched in the form of a letter written by the singer to the father of his presumably pregnant girlfriend. We all loved it, both sides were cut, everyone was pleased with the results, and a release date scheduled.

Then we took the acid.

The LSD affected Peter and me quite differently. I was so blown away I knew it would take me a long time to come to terms with the experience. I had no desire to take any more in the foreseeable future. Peter, on the other hand, couldn't get enough of it: I could write a book about Peter and LSD, and he was determined to immediately cut a psychedelic record. So he did.

We got the Peep Show back down to London, and fortuitously Stephen Morris had written a flower-power song titled "Mazy". Peter decided this would be the ideal candidate for his psychedelic masterpiece, but Stephen had also just written a far darker song titled "Morning" and Peter and Stephen figured that the first verse of "Morning" could be effectively tagged on to the end of "Mazy". The studio was booked, arrangements written, extra session musicians hired, and "Mazy" was recorded. I was in Banbury putting RM to bed and so wasn't directly involved with the production – it was all Peter, with Terry Chappell assisting. I got a namecheck on the record nevertheless. Panting with enthusiasm we played "Mazy" to our contact at Polydor, Frank Fenter, with whom I was now back on good terms following the Otis debacle. Frank raved about it, calling us "the new Phil Spector", but nevertheless Polydor refused to release it as an A-side. So "Mazy" was issued as the B-side of "Your Servant Stephen", which, thanks to publisher Sandy Roberton's promotional skills, got some big plugs including "Juke Box Jury". It sold well and just missed a chart placing.

We'll never know whether Polydor made a big mistake, because "Mazy" went on to become a cult psychedelic classic, listed in the all-time Top 40 psychedelic records chart. The original Polydor single would later fetch many hundreds of pounds, and decades later when I re-issued the Peep Show material on LP and CD, both would be titled "Mazy". More profoundly, Peter Meaden – who never received his dues as a record producer – died in 1978, never to see the later rave reviews of the material he produced on the Peep Show. Said Record Collector: "The Peep Show were purveyors of very decent psych fare indeed...Mazy is now rightly regarded as a classic...satirical, pessimistic and peculiarly English, the Peep Show are in a fine tradition that stretches from the Kinks to the Smiths." And from Mojo: "Former West Midlands art students make Syd-styled psych meets Fairport folk meets Beatlesy pop. By 1967 they'd perfected the mix on their mesmeric single Your Servant Stephen." RIP, dear Peter.

Back at Record Mirror, in *Spencer In The USA*, Spencer Davis called me from New York during his current American tour on the back of his group's latest US hit "Somebody Help Me", a former UK No.1. All their hits had thus far been dominated by vocalist/keyboardist Stevie Winwood, now with Traffic:

"...one thing I'm finding is that American audiences are more attentive. I half expected this, but it makes a pleasant change to have the audiences sitting down and listening to what's happening"

I guess they were probably wondering why the group didn't sound like they did on the hit records, or – more charitably – were interested in how the Spencer Davis Group sounded without Stevie Winwood and his brother Muff, who'd also quit to work behind-the-scenes at Island Records with Chris Blackwell. But Spencer hadn't lost his knack of finding fine musicians. He'd recruited organist Eddie Hardin and guitarist Phil Sawyer and had already cut the psychedelic-tinged single "Time Seller", shortly to scrape into the top 30. A year later Hardin and York would split from Spencer to form the duo Hardin York, and their replacements, future Elton John sidemen Dee Murray (bass) and Nigel Olsson (drums) would stay for only six months before Spencer finally broke up the band in '69.

When Record Mirror reader B. Splink contributed to our letters' page that September by suggesting that rock'n'roll fans should shut up about their "out-dated dredged-up rock singers", the return barrage of hate mail was so extreme that I chronicled the furious avalanche in *Rockrockrockrock: Here's What Happens When An RM Reader Writes Knocking The Rock*, proving that our core readership was still quiveringly sensitive to slights to their heroes, although the names named by Mr. Splinks – Helen Shapiro, Gene Vincent, Buddy Holly and Billy Fury – seemed a bit of a broad church to everyone involved.

In contrast to the succinctness of rock'n'roll, at the latest musical extremities of pop-rock during the Summer Of Love was the sound of the current Vanilla Fudge UK hit "You Keep Me Hanging On", a bombastically psychedelic deconstruction produced by Shangri-Las svengali Shadow Morton of the Supremes '66 smash, but which wouldn't hit big in the States till the following year. I must have liked Vanilla Fudge a lot, because I wrote three articles in quick succession: *All About A Group Called Vanilla Fudge, Who Specialise in Re-moulding Other People's Hit Songs*, then *Vanilla Fudge LP – Even More Dramatic Than The Hit Single*, and finally *Distortion – The Vanilla Fudge And Their Fantastic Sound*, an interview with bassist Tim Bogert at the Fudge's press reception at the Speakeasy where their LP was continuously blasted out so loudly that I staggered into the street never wanting to hear them again – but not before New Yorker Tim had told me:

"...there aren't many human beings in New York. There are more in San Francisco, but there are things I don't like about the West Coast scene. You don't have to wear bells and beads to play well – there are so many phonies out there too."

That same week at EMI's press reception for first-cousin Southern soul duo James & Bobby Purify, I spoke to James P. for *The Soul Difference In The USA – by James Purify*, who told me he didn't much like their signature hit "I'm Your Puppet":

"... because we spent so long recording it I got a bad throat. But it was big. This just shows that the thing to do when you're recording is not to try to please yourself – you should try to please an audience, try to give them something different all the time".

James also delivered some complicated theories about soul ballads, uptempo numbers, the generation gap, and British and American audiences. The Purifys were enjoying a three-year run of pop and R&B chart success in the USA, but wouldn't chart here till their Mercury re-recording of "I'm Your Puppet" hit the UK Top Ten in 1976. Another soul legend who EMI generously threw a press reception for that month was Lou Rawls:

RM w/e 14th October 1967

'SPOTLIGHT ON LOU RAWLS, Y'ALL'!

"SPOTLIGHT on Lou Rawls, y'all" yells Arthur Conley on his "Sweet Soul Music" hit single. All of the other names on the single are well-known here – James Brown, Otis Redding, Sam & Dave. Just who is the mysterious Lou Rawls? And what has he done to be included among the greatest R&B names? Here's the answers.
I spoke to Lou Rawls at a press reception given for him at EMI House. Lou was looking confident and relaxed.

In fact he was the only person at his own reception who wasn't drinking, smoking, or eating.

"Yeah, that was quite good," he laughed when we talked about Arthur Conley's tribute. "Of course you know that Sam Cooke wrote that song years ago and called it 'Yeah Man'? I grew up with Sam. We used to sing in church together. Now, this thing about church... well, I started singing in the gospel choir when I was seven. I had no choice. If I didn't go to church, then I couldn't go out during the week. I couldn't go out after dark or go to the movies on Saturday. That was for several years...so of course I went to church regularly on Sundays and I sang in the choir. That's how Sam and I grew up together. We sang together and formed groups together.

"I parted company from Sam – in the gospel field, that is, in 1958 when we were involved in a car smash. We were both seriously injured and nearly died together. I was in a coma for weeks. I didn't work at all during 1959 because I had to recover from brain injuries I received".

Lou went on to say how he was the "second voice" on many later hits by the late Sam Cooke. Hits like "Bring It On Home To Me", "Having A Party" and "That's Where It's At". For Lou, it was a great tragedy when Sam was killed four years ago during a shooting incident.

"Sam was a wonderful guy," said Lou, "It really shook me when he was killed."

It was about the time of Sam Cooke's huge solo disc success that Lou first made the acquaintance of some names which were then not too big, but which are now enormous. Lou Adler, Herb Alpert and Lou Rawls were buddies, together with Sam Cooke...and Adler, Alpert and Cooke began writing songs under the name of "Barbara Campbell" that included "Only Sixteen" and "Wonderful World". The cars they drove at the time, according to Lou, were a '54 Ford for Herb Alpert, a '49 Pontiac for Lou Rawls, and a '56 Chevy for Lou Adler.

> *Lou made solo discs from 1960. He signed with Capitol*
> *in 1961 and made an album called "Stormy Monday" with*
> *jazz pianist Les McCann. After that he progressed to the*
> *heights he has reached now – being acclaimed as one of*
> *America's most popular R&B singers. Yet Lou cannot fit*
> *himself into any category.*
>
> *"I've been called folk, pop, R&B and soul. Yet I've*
> *always been singing the same thing, the same style. I make*
> *the song fit my style, rather than make me fit the song.*
> *Up until a year ago I preferred the older songs, because*
> *the lyrics are that much more expressive. But now, well,*
> *better songs are coming along, with cats like Lennon and*
> *McCartney, etc. I've been told that in Britain I'm more*
> *of an 'in-crowd singer'. Maybe so. I hope I can break out*
> *here more, as I've been able to do in the States."*
>
> *Lou's new single is "Hard To Get Thing Called Love"*
> *and with any luck it'll show the record buyers why he is*
> *included in the list of America's greatest soul/folk/pop/*
> *blues/R&B singers.*

But like James & Bobby Purify, Lou Rawls would also have to wait another nine years until 1976 before scaling the UK charts – with the memorable "You'll Never Find Another Love Like Mine".

Conspicuous by his absence from the Summer Of Love was Bob Dylan, whose motorcycle accident in July '66 resulted in eighteen months without a new album release. But, as we later learned, it was not eighteen months of inactivity. Following his traumatic 1966 world tour accompanied the Hawks, the frazzled Dylan moved to Woodstock in upstate New York where he worked with Hawks' Rick Danko and Richard Manuel on a documentary film of the tour. In nearby West Saugerties, Dylan and the Hawks found a vast pink-painted house ("Big Pink") where they commenced a series of experimental recordings, some of which would form the basis of the first high profile rock bootleg "The Great White Wonder", and, eight years later in 1975, the official (and unconscionably belated and somehow anticlimactic)

"The Basement Tapes" LP. These recordings were so revered by the Hawks' Robbie Robertson that they would inspire him to write the songs on "Music From Big Pink", the impressive debut LP by The Band, formerly the Hawks. And, prolific as ever, in October '67 Dylan secretly returned to Nashville with a completely new batch of songs to cut a new studio album.

We knew none of this in the UK. But the demand for Dylan information from his fans was still feverish, so I cobbled together an article *Dylan – His Songs You Haven't Heard – His Film – And A DYLAN poem Competition*, illustrated by another of those sensational 35mm colour transparencies sent to us by US Columbia in April '66. I dug up up a few recent Dylan quotes such as "...I've stopped composing and singing anything that has either a reason to be written or a motive to be sung...the word 'message' strikes me as having a hernia-like sound.", and made up some flannel about his manager Albert Grossman's relationship with US Columbia, and, for the 'Songs You Haven't Heard' section, bought every Bob Dylan sheet music songbook I could lay my hands on, mostly published by Duchess Music or CBS's own Blossom Music, and listed all the songs Bob had written but never recorded...or if he had recorded them, had never been released. There were plenty of them too, and plenty of big artists had picked up on them, from Joan Baez to Elvis Presley to Dion DiMucci. The final part of the article was the poem competition: US Columbia had also just mailed me a big Dylan psychedelic poster and I put that up as the prize for the "best original poem in the Dylan style".

We got so many entries that after two weeks we had to tell our readers the competition was closed. It took us two months to sift through the seven hundred entries already received, by which time Nick Jones at Melody Maker had wised me up to an article he'd written on some bona fide new Dylan material. Nick suggested I call music publisher Ronnie Beck at Feldmans, which I did, and was invited to come and listen. According to Ronnie, Albert Grossman had sent over a batch of demos of new Dylan songs for the express purpose of selling them to other artists. These were strictly demos, insisted Ronnie, and would not be released in LP form, or any other form for that matter. I was taken into a room with a sound system, ten songs were played, and I made some notes. I wrote the notes up for *New Dylan – Reviews Of Ten New Songs, Plus The Results Of The Recent Dylan Poem' Competition*, an article again illustrated by a fabulous colour shot – the last of the batch we'd been sent, which was timely, because Dylan's "look" was about to dramatically change. The songs I heard – nowhere near all the tracks recorded at Big Pink – were "Million Dollar Bash", "Yea! Heavy And A Bottle Of Bread", "Please Mrs Henry", "Down In The Flood", "Lo And Behold", "Tiny Montgomery", "This Wheel's On Fire", "I Shall Be Released" and "Too Much Of Nothing", the latter already a US hit for Peter, Paul & Mary, conveniently also managed by Albert Grossman. Maybe Manfred Mann were hanging on to the demo of "Quinn The Eskimo", a future chart-topper for them, because they were in the studio that month recording it. Other British artists who would subsequently score big hits with versions of those demos included the Tremeloes with "I Shall Be Released", and the Brian Auger Trinity featuring Julie Driscoll with "This Wheel's On Fire".

Another big hit, but not so welcome for Dylan, CBS and US Columbia, or Albert Grossman, was "The Great White Wonder", the scrappy yet desirable double LP bootleg containing mostly rough-ish transcriptions of many of the basement tapes, plus lots of Bob's own versions of songs never previously released, many of which I'd mentioned in the recent Dylan article. Thereafter, the recording industry purportedly became considerably more careful with demos and unissued tapes but, as Dylan himself once said, the die had been cast: many would be tempted and many would fall. The bootlegging industry was up and running. It would take the record business decades to even partially understand the mentality of bootleggers, who, although making a quick and often shoddy buck, did cater to and understand the outer limits of fan fervour, something the established record companies with all their collective experience singularly and consistently failed to do.

Our Dylan poem competition was won by reader Mick Johnson with his inventively whimsical "Romance Of A Faded Bookworm" – but none of the seven hundred entries remotely threatened Dylan. A month later the basement tapes would become old news when CBS launched the first major album of 1968, Dylan's "John Wesley Hardin", his genius demonstrably unabated.

It was back to the oldies that autumn with a phone interview titled *1958 Flashback!* with hot RCA producer Bob Cullen, over from New York, who'd just produced the hippy classic "Get Together" by the Youngbloods, a minor hit that'd go US top ten in two years time when re-popularised as the theme for the US National Council Of Christians & Jews. The song would also hit the UK top ten, courtesy of a cover version by the Dave Clark Five. The thrust of the article was Bob's early career with Danny & The Juniors, which he described in fascinating detail. Yet afterwards I could find no record of him ever having been in the group, and neither could anyone else.

Another mystery was why Del Shannon's recent LP produced by Andrew Oldham hadn't been released by his current label Liberty: in *Del – His Revived 'Runaway' And His Study Of Creative Pop*, Del lamented that he and Oldham were so busy flitting around the world that they never had time to meet and discuss Del's career. Though Stone-less, Oldham was now riding high again with his Immediate label and had just signed the Small Faces. But Del, alas, would have no more hits. Our end-of-year 1967 Readers' Poll results came in that November, with the top three names in each category as follows: World Male Vocalist – Elvis Presley, Tom Jones, Cliff Richard. World Female Vocalist – Dusty Springfield, Lulu, Cilla Black. World Male Vocal Group –Beatles, Beach Boys, Monkees. World Female Vocal Group – Supremes, Martha & The Vandellas, Marvelettes. Instrumental World Solo Artist – Hank Marvin, Jeff Beck, Jimi Hendrix. Instrumental World Group –Shadows, Booker T & The MGs, Herb Alpert. World Mixed Group – Mamas & Papas, Seekers, Gladys Knight & The Pips. Most Liked Disc – Whiter Shade Of Pale, All You Need Is Love, San Francisco. Most Disliked Disc – Release Me, All You Need Is Love, Whiter Shade Of Pale.

"All You Need Is Love" might have been the second most liked and disliked record simultaneously, but – record-wise, at least – the Beatles seemed unstoppable. Their new single "Hello Goodbye" shot to No. 1 in December, and the cute "Magical Mystery Tour" double-EP artefact followed it to No.2 in the singles charts, the EP chart having been abandoned by Record Retailer just six days before its release, and its success led to great anticipation for the forthcoming TV film of the same title. Anyone buying both releases would have

"I Am The Walrus" twice, but there few complaints as one version was in mono, the other in stereo. Both the single and EP featured that same acid-drenched psychedelic sound that the Beatles had so perfected with their other 1967 releases. I reviewed the EPs in *Magical Mystery Beatles* on a front page of Record Mirror decorated by some preview film stills and psychedelic artwork from Derek Boltwood.

My final interviews of 1967 were with writer-producer Phil Margo of the Tokens, who were currently hot as producers with oldies revivalists the Happenings *(Suddenly It's Happening For The Tokens)*,and, bizarrely, with Murry Wilson, famous father of Beach Boys Brian, Carl and Dennis. Murry was here to promote his solo album:

RM w/e 2nd December 1967

'If The Beach Boys Realise Their Dad Is On The Ball, They'll Work Harder!'

ARRIVING at the Hilton Hotel to talk to Murry Wilson, I phoned his room to enquire as to whether I could go up and start the interview there and then. A voice, seemingly that of a young American girl, answered me saying it would be a pleasure if I would come up. "Thank you," I said. "You're welcome," the voice replied.

At the tenth floor I wandered into the suite and was met by a pipe-smoking amiable-looking middle-aged man closely followed by a slim attractively dressed lady who was obviously his wife.

"I'm Norman Jopling," I said.

"Well, that's a strange name for England – is it English?" said the lady with the voice.

"Might be French," I replied on the spur of the moment.

"I'm Murry Wilson," said the man, "And this is my wife Audrey. Won't you take a seat, let me take your coat."

The interview commenced. Murry is here to promote his record which is an instrumental LP that he produced which features his own songs and other original compositions given a beautiful orchestral treatment. Some of the best session men in America were being used on the record, which is being marketed by Capitol with a coloured sleeve depicting many photographs of a variety of beautiful young women. (The album is called "The Many Moods Of Murry Wilson" and is on Capitol T 2819.)

TALENT INHERITED FROM PARENTS

Why has Murry, at his age, started making records?

"I've always written beautiful tunes," he answered. "And this seemed to me to be the right time to put some of them on record. I've seen the success of my boys – you know, the Beach Boys – and I figured that maybe I should give them a little competition! Well, maybe not quite like that! But I want them to realise that their Dad is on the ball – it will encourage them to work harder – they'll say 'If Dad can do it'..."

My interest in Murry Wilson – a fascinating person – was greatly aroused. How did he think the Beach Boy talent – or more specifically Brian's talent – was inherited from his father?

"We were always a musical family," said Murry. "When Audrey and I were first married and when the kids were young, we'd sit around the piano. Brian's talent was a combination of the genes of Audrey and myself."

Murry said that originally the Beach Boys were managed by him. For a period of four and a half years in fact. When they had declared their intention to be a pop group, he had been adamant that they were not to fall into the clutches of the sharks of the industry. So Murry became their manager to protect them.

In the ensuing years they all made money. Lots and lots of money.

"We've been very lucky and we're very thankful," Murry said. "Brian is the richest – he has about a million dollars. I guess I have about the same." Murry runs the Beach Boys' music publishing company Sea Of Tunes, handled by Immediate here.

Murry talked to me about a variety of subjects – they included his views on communism, his views on the LP covers – he has a habit of talking in man-to-man asides, and also his LP.

FOR WOULD-BE LYRICISTS

One of the tracks on the album is "The Plumber's Song". Murry likes this song very much and up till now no lyrics have been written for it. What Murry wants are lyrics for this tune, and if any readers who have bought this LP feel they can write an appropriate set of lyrics (all about a merry plumber) then they should send them to Sea Of Tunes. According to Murry, the lyricist stands to make anything up to fifty thousand dollars. The address to write to is: Sea Of Tunes Inc., c/o Immediate Music Ltd., 63-69 New Oxford Street, W.C.1

Murry professed to be proud of Brian, proud especially of "Pet Sounds", yet was evidently extremely competitive. The dark side of the Wilson brothers' upbringing had not yet been publicly revealed, but Murry, even on his best behaviour here in an interview situation in London, was not a comfortable guy to be around. He was physically powerful, loud and pushy, and it was plain there was colossal insecurity beneath the bluster. Nevertheless he was a music lover. The genius and beauty of the Beach Boys music, their timeless songs and exquisite harmonies that seem somehow to magically contain so much warmth and sunshine, would not have have developed without his encouragement.

A week or two later I bumped in to Murry's son Carl, he of the beautiful voice ("God Only Knows"), at an EMI press reception where he was being interviewed by David Griffiths for Record Mirror. Carl had been telling David about his recent studies with his holiness the Maharishi Mahesh Yogi, and in fact had only started actually meditating the previous day. Eyes shining with fervour, Carl turned to me and advised me to take up the study of Transcendental Meditation: "If you do you'll never forget it – and it's bound to help you. The Maharishi is on a divine mission. Everything the Beatles have said about his greatness is true. Enormous numbers of young Americans are sure to listen to what he says – and benefit from him. When I get back, I shall be able to tell Brian and my parents all about it so that they can practise Transcendental Meditation too." I didn't mention to Carl I'd recently spoke with his dad, but I couldn't help wondering what Murry would make of this new development.

The year ended badly for some. The Beatles' "Magical Mystery Tour" was screened on BBC-1 on Boxing Day in black-and-white, which was a big mistake, and a few days later on the new colour channel BBC-2. It was savaged by critics who seemed only too eager to grab an opportunity to lay into the Beatles, whose flower-power garb, public revelations of LSD use, and highly-publicised association with Maharishi Mahesh Yogi were beginning to alienate them from a bemused establishment. It was their first real flop. After the critical and commercial success and stunning professionalism of "A Hard Day's Night" and "Help!", "Magical Mystery Tour" simply looked amateurish. Everyone still agreed the pictures and concepts the Beatles were painting in sound were unbeatable, but movies – even psychedelic movies – were an entirely different discipline. The general consensus was that had Brian Epstein lived, he never would have allowed this to happen.

But the worse news of all that December was that Otis Redding, four of his group the Bar-Kays, his valet and the pilot had been killed when their plane crashed into Lake Monona in Wisconsin. I wrote a full-page tribute, *To Otis*, wishing once again I'd never written that review earlier in the year. In the subsequent decades since Otis's death, no-one seems to have come along who sounded remotely like him.

Back at New Wave Productions, Polydor Records were anxious for a quick follow-up to the Peep Show's "Your Servant Stephen"/ "Mazy", and so we decided to doctor up a promising demo recently recorded at Pan Studios – "Esprit De Corps", another Stephen Morris song. Unlike "Mazy", this record was almost wilfully uncommercial, a plaintively folksy piece of poetic lyrical introspection with Stephen, as a somewhat unrepresentative representative of the younger generation, unfavourably comparing himself to a World War II pilot with blood on his hands.

The track opens with an air raid warning siren, and closes with the siren sounding the all-clear. Towards the end of the song pianist Tom Parker cleverly segued into "White Cliffs Of Dover", and we all rushed into the studio from the sound booth to sing en masse in a hearty fashion, clinking glasses and sounding reasonably convincingly like a bunch of doomed-yet-merry RAF pilots ready for the Battle Of Britain on the morrow.

We all loved this song so much and had so much faith in it, that Peter and Terry arranged an ambitious promotional photoshoot featuring a genuine Spitfire at the Shuttleworth Collection in Biggleswade, Beds, with the group standing round the legendary fighter plane in an English field kitted up in full World War II flying ace regalia. The pictures were modestly sensational and formed the basis of the promotion for the single. Unfortunately – as with "Your Servant Stephen", another song with distinctly un-trendy lyrics – several DJs took against it and said so, particularly Johnny Moran at Radio London. Nevertheless it sold almost as well as its predecessor, prompting Polydor to indicate that a Peep Show LP should be their next release.

During one of the group's visits to London, they stayed at Peter Meaden's flat in Cricklewood. Peter, now a zealous LSD propagandist, did a bad thing and unilaterally decided it was time to chemically enlighten them. He told them he'd spiked their coffee with LSD. When none of the group complained, Peter, who had thus far done no such thing, did indeed spike their next cup. Three of the Peeps enjoyed the trip, but one ended up in hospital and they never touched acid again. They did, however, keep on writing marvellous songs.

The only other New Wave Productions release in 1967 was "Baby You've Been On My Mind", a cover of Dion and the Belmont's version of Dylan's "Mama You've Been On My Mind", sung by Lucien Alexander, alias our music publisher Sandy Roberton. Despite unforeseen enthusiasm from our house musicians ("If this is a hit, can we tour with him?" they begged), it flopped. We'd also made friends with maverick US soul singer Donnie Elbert who'd been recording at Polydor studios, and Donnie indicated he wanted New Wave Productions to handle his next record.

In a separate development, Peter's lysergic frolics had lately compassed him in the direction of the New York-based Kama Sutra / Buddah Records stable, run by the enigmatic Artie Ripp. Peter had become an obsessive collector of psychedelic LPs and was currently enthralled with Captain Beefheart's Buddah album "Safe As Milk", and its sister label Kama Sutra's studio groups the Tradewinds and the Innocence, both of which were brainchildren of the multi-talented writing / production / performing duo Peter Andreoli and Vincente Poncia Jr, alias Anders & Poncia. Peter was determined to get himself, and by extension New Wave Productions, somehow involved with Buddah, and after several lengthy phone calls to New York, he announced to us and to the world that he would shortly be promoting the Buddah stable of artists in the UK. He'd discovered Buddah were fortuitously bringing their artists to Europe on a promotional jaunt to the second Midem music business festival in Cannes in January 1968 and reasoned it would be relatively easy to organise the Buddah contingent to afterwards visit the UK, where he would already have the gigs and the promotion arranged.

That was the theory, anyway. Peter gave me the details and I duly printed a news story in Record Mirror:

RM w/e 30th December 1967

CAPTAIN BEEFHEART TO TOUR IN JANUARY

THE sensational Captain Beefheart & his Magic Band are coming to Britain on January 13th. They will be joined by several other acts to make up the Buddah Package, which will include the Lemon Pipers, who have America's fastest-rising hit "Green Tambourine". Other stars on the bill will be Anders & Poncia, who form the Tradewinds, and new Buddah signing Penny Nichols. The 22-piece package is being handled by agent Peter Meaden, who also runs New Wave Productions. Although Beefheart's "Safe As Milk" album has not yet been issued, he has been described by DJ John Peel as "...incredible – the most fantastic West Coast act I've seen." Negotiations are taking place for the package to play the Middle Earth, the Roundhouse, and a major central London Theatre. Also a nation-wide major promotional campaign is being lined up.

Peter had bought himself three copies of "Safe As Milk": one copy for carrying around everywhere and playing at every opportunity, another for playing at home, and the third copy strictly for listening to on LSD: he was good business for import specialists One Stop Records in South Molton Street. He sometimes called himself, partly in jest, "the black tripper", wearing a black velvet cloak beneath which – to be revealed when the acid kicked in – was his beautiful peacock silk Nehru jacket and a dazzling array of beads, scarves and dazzling acid paraphernalia.

I couldn't figure out how Buddah – though I agreed with Peter how good their artists were – could benefit us. But there was no stopping him in his pursuit of them. It would not end well.

1968-9

The music business was going through changes (as we were starting to say). The biggest change was the advent of the LP, as opposed to the single, not only as the prime and most profitable pop music carrier, but also as the vehicle of artistic progress.

Thusly, at the beginning of 1968, we Record Mirror scribes named not our favourite singles from 1967 as we did in previous years, but instead listed our fave LPs. Though in fact, only David Griffiths and I participated, Peter Jones and Derek Boltwood abstaining from the exercise. David weighed in straightaway with "Sgt. Pepper" and "Smiley Smile", thwarting me somewhat, but I managed to mention more of my favourites.

RM w/e 6th January 1968

LPs OF THE YEAR
Norman Jopling

UNLIKE David Griffiths, I have no really clear-cut LP choices of last year. I've narrowed the field down to three records...but there are many others which have afforded me an almost equal amount of pleasure. Among those are re-issues, which obviously cannot be counted among the new albums of 1967. They include...Dinah Washington (the three LP releases on the Mercury Value label), the early Sinatra double-album from CBS, and the Coasters' reissue of "Greatest Hits" from Atlantic which featured an excellent new cover by RM's own Lon Goddard.

I've also discounted "Greatest Hits" albums and although these rate among my "Most Played" LPs of last year, the content does not merit inclusion. My favourite in this section was by the Temptations.

On to LPs "proper". Before I come to my three favourites, sifted out of mounds of albums, these were the ones which very nearly made it. "Tim Hardin 2", "Like It Is" – Aaron Neville, "Electric Music For The Mind And Body" – Country Joe & the Fish, "Gorilla" by the Bonzo Dog Doo Dah Band and of course "Sgt. Pepper" which David has already mentioned.

In no particular order, here are the three.

"Up, Up And Away" by the Fifth Dimension (Liberty LBS 83038 STEREO)

The label "psychedelic soul" has been applied to this group, but I don't see them as being particularly psychedelic or particularly soulful. If you imagine the Mamas And The Papas sounding more coloured, with imaginative, beautifully arranged backings and a collection of varied and poignant songs, then that is the sound of this LP. The intricate harmonies are always effective, and they often surprise by unexpected vocal simplicity. Songs range from the tortured "Never Gonna Be The Same", "Learn How To Fly", "Another Day, Another Heartache", through to ther lighthearted title track which despite the drug connotations can be taken at face value as a happy, beautifully performed and inspired ditty.

Sad optimism creeps through on Johnny Rivers' "Poor Side Of Town" (Johnny produced this LP incidentally) and "Pattern People" is a disturbing piece of emotional analysis. Most soulful track is "Rosecrans Boulevard", that curiously whimsical, haunting song. Credits to co-producer Marc Gordon and Jim Webb for writing so many good songs.

"Together Again" by Dion And Belmonts (HMV CLP 3618)

As far as old-time rock or pop fans are concerned, this should be THE record of 1967. This LP has had no commercial success as far as I can ascertain on either side of the Atlantic but it is one of the best recent albums to come from the States. Dion's poignant vocals on "Come To My Side" and "For Bobbie" are overwhelming, and the simple mellow guitar and drumwork hauntingly pervade nearly every track. Even Dylan would have a hard time to better Dion's version of Bob's "Baby You've Been On My Mind" – incidentally, this LP goes down very well with Dylan fans – and in view of Bob's lack of record releases should be given a hearing by his fans. The two styles are not incompatible, and the fact that the two singers worked in the same studio for several years is reflected in Dion's "My Girl The Month Of May" with its intricate arrangement and interesting lyric.

Dion sends up the scene on "New York Town" and "Jump Back Baby"and his wordless scat vocals on "Berimbau" are stunningly different. "Movin' Man" was one of the best hard-rock singles of last year, and "But Not For Me" takes you back to his "Where Or When" days – nevertheless not even Dion can sing "...and get that way" quite like Ketty Lester. The LP is typified by "All I Wanna Do Is Live My Life", the cynical Mort Shuman item. Produced by Dimont Music.

"Younger Than Yesterday" by the Byrds (CBS 62888)
Possibly the most-played LP in my collection to be issued last year. I'd never been a Byrds' fan or even interested in the group until this album, which really stunned me when I first heard it. Vocals are not their strong point (although their soft voices can and do achieve either harshness or subtlety when required), and consequently the accent is on the instrumentation. And strangely enough, only guitars, drums and bass are used throughout...

I've heard that the Byrds' technique used to obtain their hypnotic guitar sound is to play everything very carefully very slowly and then speed up the tape for the record. The result, as all Byrds' fans will know, is overpowering. From the first bar of "Rock And Roll Star" to the end of "Why", that guitar sound, in one form or another, dominates the album. The recording technique on the gimmicky space-age "CTA 102" is incredible and funny, while David Crosby's "Mind Gardens" can send you reeling with the impact of the harsh compelling backing. There are the usual pleasant songs here, like "Have You Seen Her Face", "Renaissance Fair" and "The Girl With No Name", but certainly the most reflective track is "Everybody's Been Burned", another David Crosby song. It is hard to imagine how the Byrds will efficiently survive now that Dave has been sacked. He was responsible for some of the best songs on the album...the group cannot be as good without him. This is a fantastic, incredible album on which a great deal of care has been lavished and it achieves with simple instruments, rather ordinary songs and vocals which could not be called overpowering or ambitious, an effect which most other groups could never get – certainly no group in the world could gain this type of effect without being much more complex and ambitious, as are the Beatles and the Beach Boys. Produced by Gary Usher.

Can't think why I didn't mention the masterful "Forever Changes" by Love, and "Deliver" by the Mamas and the Papas – maybe one vocal group choice seemed enough.

Another reason for the popularity of LPs was the advent of stereophonic sound, which had been around for a very long time but didn't kick in on disc till 1958. Singles still weren't manufactured in stereo, and were always mixed down into mono with the accent on sufficient direct presence to create maximum impact via transistor radios, car radio speakers and cheap wirelesses, all of which were the favoured listening mediums of singles buyers – young people. All recording studios featured a cheap transistor radio wired up on the console in order to hear how a particular mix would sound to the average punter.

I'd bought a stereo system in 1967 and so was naturally still infatuated with stereo and thus with LPs. In the January 13th issue, I profiled a major LP release on the Tamla Motown label that included such gems as "Motown Memories", "Four Tops' Greatest Hits", "Diana Ross And The Supremes' Greatest Hits", "Everybody Needs Love" from Gladys Knight And The Pips, "I Was Made To Love Her" from Steve Wonder, "United" by Marvin Gaye And Tammi Terrell, and finally "The Detroit Spinners". What a batch! And the following week I penned a front page news story celebrating the UK chart breakthrough of Smokey Robinson and the Miracles with "I Second That Emotion" – five years after featuring them as the first of my *The Great Unknowns* column.

My LP fixation continued later that month with Bob Dylan's "John Wesley Harding":

RM w/e 27th January 1968

A DIFFERENT BRAND OF DYLAN

After the initial shock received upon hearing the first few tracks of Dylan's "John Wesley Harding" LP, the bafflement wears off and the newest aspect of the Dylan phenomena begins to seep through.

This time, Bob has moved away from his previous musical and lyrical styles. No direct link is present to connect this album with the "Blonde On Blonde" collection recorded some two years ago.

The musical frame (or style) upon which most of the songs and the overall sound of the album is built is simply good ole country and western music. Logically enough, the sound of the Dylan harmonica remains unchanged and still fits in ideally with the cowboy rhythms. The instruments he plays on this LP are his acoustic guitar and occasional piano (on two tracks). Charles McCoy plays a slapping bass, Kenny Buttrey is on drums and Pete Drake plays steel guitar on two tracks. The various electric guitars and organ, so prominent on his last couple of albums, are conspicuously absent.

Superficially, the lyrics are far more straightforward, lacking the imagery we are used to. But the simple, sometimes childishly funny words and phrases have been cleverly and subtly used and strung together. All of Dylan's complexity and musical cleverness seems to have been channelled into making these songs basic and simple, rather than obviously full of double-entendre veiled references and imagery. The general effect of the LP is doomy – much more so than on his early folk-based LPs but despite certain similarities, this collection is as far removed from that period as was the rock-based "Highway 61 Revisited" album. But after listening to "John Wesley Harding" the superficialities that strike you the first time you hear it – the considerable change of voice, altered lyrical conception, and absence of the organ-based backing are not noticed.

Instead the more raw, but just as potent Dylan steps out and reveals himself, wearing yet another costume but unmistakably the man who has and is proving himself the greatest figure on the current music scene.

The article went on to describe each song in superficial and unedifying detail – my primitive analysis of Dylan's lyrics were never going to make it into any compendium of great Dylan literature – but the point was made. This was a different Dylan.

My extracurricular activities at New Wave Productions were in full swing. The Peep Show's current single "Esprit De Corps" had been labelled "the most nauseating record of the week" by Johnny Moran on Saturday's influential Radio One show Scene and Heard – he'd not listened properly to the lyric and, frothing at the mouth, branded the song "anti-war": it was neither pro nor anti-war – and the group were, no pun intended, up in arms about the misinterpretation. Despite our protests, letters, phone calls, plus several decent reviews from the pop press, we were given no right of reply and Polydor were not best pleased when "Esprit De Corps" sank out of sight, nevertheless still selling several thousand copies.

Less immediately dismal but with eventual catastrophic consequences was Peter Meaden's adventure with the Buddah package, which arrived in the UK immediately preceding their trip to Cannes for the Midem festival. For anyone who wants to know how good Captain Beefheart and the Magic Band were at this relatively early stage in their career, there exists a film of the group on the beach at Cannes performing "Sure 'Nuff 'N Yes I Do", the first track from "Safe As Milk". Pure dynamite.

Crazily, Pye Records, who handled Kama Sutra/Buddah in the UK, had neglected to release "Safe As Milk" and now, at Meaden's instigation – he had a certain amount of clout with them via Jimmy and the Vagabonds – they had finally scheduled it for release, albeit reluctantly, and inexplicably minus two of the tracks on the US album version, one of which – "I'm Glad" – had recently been recorded by Peter with Jimmy James And The Vagabonds for New Wave. A fine version it was too but which, as New Wave was contracted exclusively to Polydor, and Jimmy was contracted exclusively to Pye, would remain unreleased for forty years.

Under my Wesley Laine nom-de-plume I penned a profile piece on Beefheart, his first UK write-up:

RM w/e 3rd February 1968

THE MAGIC MUSIC FROM THE DESERT

Captain Beefheart (real name Don Van Vliet) and his Magic Band are a group of 'progressive blues' musicians, whose unusual rock-blues format is starting to take off in Britain – as you may have noticed.

The Captain possesses an incredible voice, throatily gutsy, and it is often used more as an instrumental factor with the rest of the sound, rather than as a vehicle for putting over lyrics.

There is certainly something very magic about this band when it comes to creating an impact in group-sodden

411

Britain. The group's LP "Safe As Milk" has been issued in America for nine months – and has sold over five thousand imported copies here at nearly three pounds each. Their single "Yellow Brick Road", which has been taken from the LP, was bubbling under in last week's top fifty.

Yet until this splurge of interest in Britain, nothing happened commercially for for the band either in Britain or the States. The music is not blatantly commercial, nor is it catchy. But record producer Peter Meaden who runs New Wave Productions heard the LP early last summer and began to take an interest in the Captain. The interest culminated in Meaden organising Beefheart's visit here, and two vastly successful dates in London clubs, several radio dates, plus the release of the single, and the release of the first album – both on Pye. A second LP, the double-album set "Censored" is on the way to US release via Buddah records.

All was not smooth sailing getting the Magic Band into the country. No trouble occurred when fellow Buddah stars Anders and Poncia and Penny Nichols arrived, but at the appearance of the Magic Band, all confusion broke loose at London Airport. The officials were put off by the bizarre appearance of the band (see pic above) and the fact that the group only had about ten dollars between them, and called themselves the 25th Century Quakers, didn't help much. Also there were work permit difficulties. But these things were cleared up, Customs officials were pacified and the Captain entered Britain.

The Captain and two original members of the Magic Band had left their homes some two years ago to live in the California desert. They lived with their music and created "Safe As Milk". It was recorded a year ago and was released shortly afterwards by Buddah, a US subsidiary of Kama Sutra. Before, Beefheart had been living in suburban California and had known Frank Zappa from eight years back when the two of them would experiment with unusual music sounds, reverse tape effects, and other advanced ideas. Beefheart had previously been brought up on a diet of classical music and even now has not heard of many other pop groups.

But the psychological side of the music of Captain Beefheart and the Magic Band must not be underestimated. Their power and drive, comparable to early rock'n'roll records, is matched by insidious and subtle cross-rhythms and complicated vocal patterns, making the records incredibly interesting and able to be heard over and over again, always with new nuances coming through..

For a group with no compromise towards pop trends or commerciality to come through so strongly is some achievement – but it remains to be seen whether the public will accept them as a unique musicians, or merely a passing fad.

Much of this puff-piece had been dictated to me by Meaden. But the two sentences "Also there were work permit difficulties. But these things were cleared up..." covered a strange sequence of events. Peter was a man of irrepressible enthusiasms, and being clever and funny and with a great ear and eye for talent, his enthusiasms were infectious. He was not subtle about his enthusings, being unafraid to spike a suitable initiant's coffee with the LSD 'sacrament', nor, as in the case of turning Giorgio Gomelsky on to Captain Beeheart, playing him "Safe As Milk" for "...six hours straight", according to Giorgio, whose swish office – he was currently masterminding the Polydor-financed Paragon Publicity with its art nouveau/psychedelic decor – was adjacent to New Wave's humble room at Polydor in Stratford Place.

According to a report by Duncan Campbell in a 1986 edition of City Limits, some documents from the immigration department had recently been found on a Hounslow rubbish dump, and one of them dealt with the complex background to one of the key phrases in the above article: "Also there were work permit difficulties..." On January 18th, when the Buddah package arrived, the immigration official concerned compiled a report which concluded that the Magic Band didn't have work permits for the UK, had indeed been booked into gigs, and that Peter Meaden was to blame.

Apart from the curiously subjective tone of this 'official' report ("dejected man", "cigarette dangling from his lower lip", "long unkempt hair" – Meaden's hair wasn't long and seldom unkempt, but maybe customs officials saw things differently), it does add up, apart from its final paragraph: "...Mr. Meaden, on whose shoulders the blame for the whole incident must rest, was told by Mr. Ripp that his association with Kama Sutra ceased forthwith." Well, not quite yet, as it happened. The work permit situation was in fact speedily resolved: the Magic Band returned to the UK and fulfilled the dates set up by Peter at the Middle Earth and the Speakeasy. Together with Anders & Poncia and Penny Nichols, Captain Beefheart and his Magic Band stayed in London for a week prior to flying to Midem, giving radio and press interviews, all of which Peter had set up in his inimitable manner, as reported by Record Mirror's David Griffiths:

RM w/e 10th February 1968

FROM LULU TO BEEFHEART
A Little More In The Exciting Informative Life Of RM's Beautiful David Griffiths

...next day at the Record Mirror, Peter Meaden rang up. Now Peter is what you might call a pop entrepreneur – former road manager, former associate of Andrew Oldham, now a record producer and a singer of the praises of Captain Beefheart. Peter wanted to know if I'd care to meet the Captain right away. Well, I'd heard the Magic Band's record and enjoyed it but had been unable to discern the spark of genius that the band apparently possesses. Even Norman Jopling had turned unusually enigmatic when pressed for details about the Captain's finer musical points.

Being curious to meet the Captain the flesh I readily nipped round to Peter's office. He was in a feverish state of excitement, his usual self in fact, and as we strolled to a nearby building to get a pretty American photographer Reanne to come to Beefheart's hotel, Peter filled me in about the personalities about to be seen: "They're fantastic,

414

*not an ordinary pop group, these men are on a higher level
of consciousness. They hold simultaneous conversations
with each other, and with you, using their own codes and
key words. The vibrations in the room are uncanny – Nick
Jones was really quite scared," Peter added darkly. Just as
I was considering running for it, Peter offered reassurance:
"Don't worry – it may sometimes seem like they're taking
the mickey but they're nice guys. The Captain is very
helpful and straight."*

Griffiths went on to describe his encounter with Penny Nichols,
and then Captain Beefheart. The Kama Sutra/Buddah crowd were a
talented, successful and worldly bunch of New York-based hipsters
who knew every trick in the music business book and had been riding
high for years. According to Meaden, keeping up with them required
him to be constantly on this higher level of consciousness, and the
only way he knew how to do that was with acid. So he did.

Although Beefheart and his crew were the focus of Peter's initial
crusade, meeting Peter Anders and Vinnie Poncia proved an even
bigger revelation to him. Meaden loved sophisticated talent, and
both Anders and Poncia were charismatic, talented, and friendly in
a way that the somewhat distant, strange and self-consciously weird
Beefheart – charismatic though he certainly was – was not. It now
seemed that Peter's eternal quest to seek out the great undiscovered
talent – the new Elvis, the next Who – was beginning to crystallise not
around Captain Beefheart and his Magic Band, but towards Anders
& Poncia. I did ask Peter if he'd taken acid with Beefheart, but he
evaded the question, muttering something about Beefheart tripping
on belladonna. Insofar as an opportunity for New Wave Productions
was concerned, Peter's personal Kama Sutra/Buddah initiative went
nowhere – but five years later he did get to work with Peter Anders.

Post-"Pepper", a musical bifurcation of sorts seemed to be emerging.
Groups whose profile relied solely on hit singles remained 'pop
groups' (the phrase 'beat groups', with its Mersey connotations, was
rapidly falling into disuse), while groups whose reputation rested on

415

the quality of their LPs were becoming 'bands'. Certain groups like the Beatles and Stones managed both arenas very successfully, while others, whose artistry elevated them above 'pop group' status, never really managed to make it as an 'album band' – a prime example being the Kinks.

It was all part of a new musical snobbery which would eventually make it impossible for the fan-based pop press to continue its traditional all-round coverage of popular music. But the fact was that people who liked Jefferson Airplane and Cream and the Byrds and Fleetwood Mac really didn't much like Love Affair or Lulu or the Bee Gees and particularly didn't like Engelbert Humperdinck or even Tom Jones. And not only did they not want to read about them, they didn't even want to be seen buying pop newspapers in which those artists were featured.

Unlike the early-mid '60s when pop music seemed to be cross-fertilising and evolving into a universally enjoyable art form, the late '60s demonstrated increasing diversion. Pure pop was becoming poppier (1968 was the year of bubble gum), while rock was getting heavier and more experimental. Drugs had a lot to do with it. And none of this bothered soul music fans one way or the other – singles were still where soul was at, and another two years would elapse until the progressive soul LPs of pioneers such as Sly Stone, Marvin Gaye and Stevie Wonder would sell in their millions.

The complexities and pretensions of psychedelia had also led to a surprising backlash – a revival of '50s rock'n'roll. Elvis was already plotting his TV comeback special, and in spring '68 got two decent hits with "Guitar Man" and "US Male". The Beatles shook off the magic dust and emerged with the rip-roaring Fats Domino-ish "Lady Madonna", and UK promoters began booking various oldies-but-goodies for nationwide tours, including Bill Haley and his Comets whose seminal "Rock Around The Clock" had re-charted. Fleetwood Mac were mixing blues with rock'n'roll in their increasingly-popular act, and in *Rock'n'Blues Via Peter Green*, Peter told me over a pint of Mackeson: "I've always liked rock'n'roll, and it's a pity in a way that everyone is going on about it because it seems as though we're just being 'in'. Actually, I've always wanted to do this kind of thing on stage – but it doesn't mean we'll be neglecting the blues." The revival also gave me an excuse to please Waxie Maxie by publishing a colour pic and long descriptive caption somewhat erroneously titled *Merrill Moore Plays Rock*. This 1968 rock'n'roll revival would reach its apogee later in the year with the emergence of a true neo-rock'n'roll supergroup: Creedence Clearwater Revival. But in less than two years the R&R bubble would have burst and rock'n'roll seldom re-emerge into the pop mainstream.

The Tremeloes were definitely in the 'pop group' category, and very successful they were too. When their string of early-mid '60s hits with Brian Poole dried up in 1966, they left Decca and became a foursome fronted by new bassist Len "Chip" Hawkes – and scored three million-sellers in a row in '67 and broke through in America. Now they were back in the top ten with "Suddenly You Love Me", so we decided to interview them individually in depth for the series *A Tremeloe A Week*. I interviewed lead guitarist Ricky West – *Ricky Started With Skiffle!* and drummer Dave Munden – *Choir Boy Makes Good*, while Derek Boltwood did Alan Blaikley – *My Incredible Legs* and Chip Hawkes – *I Almost Joined The Navy*, while Lon Goddard drew some terrific caricatures. Their new label CBS was on a roll in '68 thanks largely to UK A&R wizard Mike Smith, who'd also absconded from Decca and was responsible for producing the Tremeloes, Love Affair and Marmalade – all featuring an ultra-professional mainstream pop group sound that was currently popular with such other hitmakers as the Herd, Honeybus, Amen Corner and most of the MacLeod-Macauley productions for Pye.

Trevor Churchill, winner of RM's "R&B-Soul Quiz" was now heading up the newly-formed Bell label, which not only handled the US Amy-Mala-Bell catalogues but also recorded home-grown product. Trevor immediately did a clever thing and worked hard on two of Bell's American flops he believed had hit potential, which they did, and became big UK hits: "Keep On" by Bruce Channel, and, the last gasp of the great girl-group hits, the classic "Captain Of Your Ship" by Reperata & the Delrons. Bell brought over the quaintly-named trio to London and they were a refreshing interview:

RM w/e 13th April 1968

REPERATA AND THE DELRONS: 'WE HAD TO SHORTEN OUR SKIRTS!'

INTERVIEWING girl singers is always a pleasure. In the same way that girls are essentially different from boys to talk to, so are girl singers essentially different from boy singers. Reperata and the Delrons have a weird-sounding hit record in the nautical "Captain Of Your Ship". Said Reperata, nee Mary Aiese: "Yes, you COULD say we like 'Captain Of Your Ship'. Who wouldn't like a hit...but it isn't really the kind of material that we always want to be associated with. We should like to perform more meaningful material – rather like the songs the Bee Gees write and sing."

The group then collapsed into a welter of praise for the Bee Gees. The emotion and sentimentality of the Bee Gees obviously appeals greatly to the girls, which is somewhat surprising, because their other big rave is the Mothers Of Invention.

MORE OBSCENE

"We like to do some of the Mothers' songs on stage," said Delron Nanette, "but there are obviously some we cannot do!" The interview room then became a hotbed of discussion on the Mothers and the Fugs, who have no records released here but who the girls say are much more obscene.

Reperata and the Delrons had a big hit in the States some four years back with "Whenever A Teenager Cried", but didn't score here. Now, through an inverted stroke of fate, their latest record has struck in big in Britain but not in the States. Did the girls have any theories as to why this happened?

"I think that as girls constitute the majority of the record buyers in the States, this had something to do with it. "They

prefer records by groups of boys, someone they like the look of. Maybe that's why our record didn't happen here.

Surely the same theory would apply here too, I suggested.

"Yeah, it's just a freak," said Lorraine, the third member of the attractive trio. "There were other songs we cut at the session which we preferred."

As I was asking the girls all the usual questions, I wondered if they had much spare time.

"Oh NO!" they replied in charming unison. "As we're all still studying at college, we just don't get any spare time. We have to fit in boyfriends between recording sessions, exams, dates for hops, etc".

Hops, incidentally, in American terminology are not things which go in beer, but what we call dance-halls or ballrooms.

The group are all about 21 years old, and they all dig artists like Otis Redding, Aretha Franklin and the Four Tops. And although they have a rhythm and blues sound (their record was actually in our R&B chart last week) they have never consciously tried to sound coloured.

Biographically their full names are Lorraine Mazzola, Nannette Licari, and Mary Aiese. "When we came to England," said Mary, "we found that your mini skirts were even shorter than we had imagined. We felt like old fuddy duddies! So we had to shorten all of our skirts!"

Regrettably I was still somewhat hung-over during that interview thanks to spending time the previous day with Tim Buckley. Clive Selwood at Elektra had called to say Tim was available to be interviewed and I jumped at the chance. Buckley's current LP was "Goodbye And Hello", an adventurous record that contained, among other gems, the beautiful and mysterious "Morning Glory" – one of Peter Meaden's favourite records.

Tim wasn't just a superb singer, performer and songwriter, he was also friendly, and a laugh. Small, finely-boned, good looking, he also liked a drink. Clive produced an unopened bottle of whiskey and Tim and I rapidly finished it between us, the interview mainly taking place with Tim and I stretched out head-to-head collapsed on the floor, laughing and drinking.

In all my interviews, I only ever got seriously drunk twice: with Tim, and a few years later with Jerry Lee Lewis. Unfortunately, as a result of inebriation, the Buckley interview suffered because I couldn't read my writing and had forgotten some of the best bits. Nevertheless, here's some quotes from the article, which shared a headline with a Lon Goddard piece on Arlo Guthrie:

RM w/e 13th April 1968

IN BRITAIN – BUCKEY AND GUTHRIE, TWO OF AMERICA'S NEW BREED OF YOUNG FOLKSINGERS

"...I think my main message is breaking down – or trying to break down – prejudice between black and white. Everywhere I go in America I meet prejudice. This is often aimed towards me, prejudice towards my hair, my clothes, the fact that my conga player is a negro, every possible kind of prejudice.

"You live in England and you cannot possibly know this kind of prejudice. I should like to live in England. Everything seems cleaner here and beautiful. I've met some beautiful people here, all the time. Maybe you think London is dirty though, yet compared with New York...

"But living in America makes me feel as though I'm alive. It's something happening, this continual state of prejudice."

But surely, I said, better things could happen to you if all this prejudice was not there.

"Perhaps so, but I would have to live elsewhere for a long time, a year maybe, to see. I'd like to live in England and see the beautiful things here."

I said there were certainly some beautiful things to see if you looked for them.

"Yes, yes, I can tell, just through being here in London," replied Tim. "But I'm going back to New York to play after I leave Britain. Then I can go home for a while after that.

"At least there's no prejudice at home..."

Tim Buckley was born in Washington DC on February 14th 1947, but now lives in Southern California. He moved in the circles of Los Angeles poets and met Larry Beckett, a young poet whose lyrics Tim put to music.

"The reason why the record business is more aware nowadays," said Tim, "is because of people like Dylan and Donovan. Chiefly Dylan, of course. I think that Donovan's flowers and beauty are nice, but when Dylan told it, it hurt. I like his new album. The American scene is more advanced, compared with the British at the moment, and the West Coast doesn't really mean very much. There are much more aware groups and sounds operating from the East Coast, New York.

"My most important songs – or those which are most important to me – will be on my next album. I'm not bothered about what I've already done – only what I am doing or what I am going to do. The LP will be different from the others in that it will be an extension, a progression of their sound. But I will probably change that after a while. There are more jazz-influenced things that I'm doing now, and on stage we do completely different things from on the albums.

Tim always spoke of his live appearances as "we" – including his conga player Carter C.C.Collins, Lee Underwood on guitar, and bassist Jim Fielder.

"You'd be surpised if you saw us on stage. It's the material we perform on stage that's likely to be representative of the next album. More Afro-Cuban sounds..."

You may also be interested to know that one of Tim's favourite British acts are the Incredible String Band, his Elektra labelmates, who are scoring with their new LP "The Hangman's Beautiful Daughter".

This being the psychedelic hey-day, much psychic bonding was happening with acid-heads. It was very much 'them-and-us', though not aggressively so. The LSD experience ("Are You Experienced?")

undoubtedly changed you, made you different – for a while, anyway. It was impossible for anyone who hadn't taken LSD to even imagine this experience, despite the ongoing proliferation of LSD-inspired visual affects, popular art, psychedelic music, cannabis usage, alternative spirituality, the mushrooming of the feminist and ecology movements, and everything else that trailed in the wake of acid-induced enlightenment. Tim had taken LSD; so had I, so we bonded. Clive phoned me a week or so later because he thought I'd like to know that Tim told him how much he'd enjoyed our meeting and that he'd had more fun than at any of his other London interviews. I appreciated Clive telling me that. I never met Tim again, but I could still cry when I hear "Morning Glory", "Once I Was", "Song For A Siren", or for that matter almost anything else he sings. What a loss.

The big Tamla Motown LP release early in '68 was swiftly followed by a similarly yummy batch by soul rivals Atlantic, now highly pro-active in the UK under the auspices of Polydor and riding high with their Stax/Volt subsidiary. This package of soul and R&B goodies included new offerings from Solomon Burke, Aretha Franklin, and Joe Tex, several "Various" collections including the magisterial "History Of Rhythm & Blues" Vols 1-4, as well as reissues from Otis Redding and Sam & Dave. Cleverly, Atlantic had also released a budget (12/6d) compilation featuring hit tracks from such as Aretha, Otis, Ben E. King, Wilson Pickett, Sam & Dave, Percy Sledge, Eddie Floyd, and Arthur Conley. This was the groundbreaking "This Is Soul" LP.

Otis's posthumous single "(Sittin' On) The Dock Of The Bay" had become his biggest hit, peaking at No. 1 in the USA and No. 3 here. We had mark this achievement, and we managed to acquire a wonderful close-up colour transparency, showcased on the front page for what became a sell-out issue. I also wrote yet another feature on Otis, conveniently ignoring my contentious 1967 review of the Stax/Volt tour, but mentioning one of my earlier more fawning articles. It was also an excuse to print an almost unnecessarily atmospheric description of Otis's funeral:

RM w/e 13th April 1968

OTIS' AMBITION WAS TO REPLACE SAM COOKE...

ABOUT three years ago I wrote a feature on Otis Redding as part of a series called "Great Unknowns". It was based on four records, and some information on Otis, which had then been issued. The records were "Pain In My Heart", "Come To Me" and "Mr Pitiful" on London, and "Shout Bamalama" on the Sue label.

A month later I received a letter from Otis' manager, Phil Walden. Here are some quotes from it:

"Both Otis and myself were elated over your column in the May 1st edition of the Record Mirror! Please accept our thanks for a wonderful and factual feature on Otis.

"Needless to say we are hoping his popularity and success will be widespread in your country. Otis has attained a vast following in the United States as well as several South American countries. I sincerely believe his "Redding Feeling" will become an important element in the British music world."

A prophetic letter indeed.

And when Otis DID become a big star here in Britain, several biographies were issued on him by his record company which gave some facts which were not generally known. Here are some of them:

Otis's personal ambition was to fill the vacuum created when Sam Cooke was killed. In fact, Otis's favourite singer was Sam Cooke – followed by Bob Dylan. Among British acts, Otis liked the Rolling Stones (they helped to popularise Otis by recording "Pain In My Heart" – Otis reciprocated by later cutting his version of the Stones' "Satisfaction"), the Beatles, the Animals, and the Troggs.

Otis formed his own record company in America called Jotis Records, Inc. The first disc on this label was "Same Thing All Over" / "The Sloopy Sloop" – this was written, produced, arranged by Otis, who also played piano on the session, and the artist was Billy Young.

Otis's posthumous LP "The Dock Of The Bay" is on Volt 419 and may be issued here shortly. The tracks on it are as follows: (Sittin' On) The Dock Of The Bay; Let Me Come On Home; I Love You More Than Words Can Say; Open The Door; Don't Mess With Cupid; The Glory Of Love; Nobody Knows (When You're Down And Out); I'm Coming Home; Tramp; The Hucklebuck; Ole Man Trouble.

"Tramp", of course, is with Carla Thomas.

Finally, a section from an article in a Canadian newspaper about Redding's funeral. The heading reads: "Wild Funeral for 'King Of Soul'."

"The body of Otis Redding, 'King Of Soul', was carried away to his farm yesterday for burial while his widow wailed and thousands of teenagers mobbed a rock'n'roll singer and his cortege.

"Funeral services for the 26-year old 'Big O', whose records earned nearly a million dollars this year before he died in a plane crash, were held in Macon City's small municipal auditorium. An estimated 45,000 people jammed the auditorium, and dignitaries on the stage behind Redding's coffin were dwarfed by banks of flowers. Outside, thousands more waited under gloomy skies. When the flower-covered coffin was rolled out, followed by Redding's screaming widow Thelma, the crowd tensed.

"When rock'n'roller James Brown, one of several famous recording stars at the funeral, emerged, pandemonium broke out. Brown dived into his car which began to follow the hearse. But howling youths flung themselves on to the vehicle, holding it back. Its efforts to move up produced only spinning tyres and clouds of blue smoke. Police rushed in to remove the youths from the car.

"Office workers leaned out windows cheering on the frenzied teenagers.

"Halfway through the ceremony, while Joe Simon was singing an impassioned 'Jesus Keep Me Near The Cross', Mrs Redding broke down. Her wails punctuated the

amplified sobs of Simon, and her heels beat a drumlike tattoo on the hard basketball floor of the auditorium.

"White clad nurses who were sprinkled through the crowd rushed to her aid.

"Following the services, Redding's body was taken to his Big O Ranch at Round Oak, Georgia, about 20 miles from Macon, for private burial. There were reports that Redding recently recorded 40 songs which had not been released when his chartered plane carrying him and his group to bookings crashed into an icy lake near Madison, Wisc."

Not a very pleasant or dignified event. But Redding will be remembered, not because of his funeral, but through his records, his style, and his voice.

However, proving the adage 'When you're hot you're hot and when you're not you're not', Atlantic may have lost Otis, but they now had a brand-new bona fide superstar. Aretha Franklin, six years at US Columbia, hundreds of songs recorded for them and hardly a hit among them, had signed to Atlantic in 1967. Jerry Wexler sent her down to Memphis to record her first single at Stax and she was now experiencing unprecedented artistic and commercial success:

RM w/e 18th May 1968

LADY SOUL

Aretha Franklin talks to RM's Norman Jopling

SOME people are going around saying that Aretha Franklin is the Queen Of Soul, many people are buying her records, and one person (show compere Johnnie Walker) even said that she was the best coloured girl singer ever to make records.

Now it isn't every girl singer who is fortunate enough to have these things said about her or happen to her, whether you go along with them or not. After chasing around and

425

about the metropolis, I tracked Aretha down to her hotel (in the Penthouse Suite) and asked her a few questions, some of which she answered in length and detail, others which received a mere smile of reply.

As her voice is her fortune, does she do anything to protect it?

"I do vocalistics, if that's what you mean. I was afraid that when I came to Europe I'd end up with laryngitis for the whole trip but I've been lucky this time. My voice changes as I change climate – it goes down about two octaves when I come to a climate like this" (Aretha had been not too happy about our weather, in fact she was welcoming quitting our shores to go back to the USA).

How did she feel when her first record for Atlantic, "I Never Loved A Man" began to shoot up the US charts, after she had been singing so long without a hit?

'RESPECT' POTENTIAL

"To tell the truth, I never expected that song to be a hit. I was surprised. I could see more potential in 'Respect', in fact I can say I knew that would be a hit song. Sometimes I can't get a song right in the recording studio though. We usually work things out beforehand, not like the Memphis studio where they don't plan things like that, but can end up with a master. We usually know what we're going to do. I sing and the musicians kind of fit things around me. Two of my favourite songs incidentally are 'Rock-A-Bye' which was on Columbia, and 'Chain Of Fools'."

Accompanying Aretha was Ted White, her manager and husband. I asked Aretha if it helped to have Ted as a manager.

"Oh yes. I don't have to worry about the business side. As he's my husband I know I can trust him! I just worry about the singing."

Ted explained that although Aretha had no hits when she was on Columbia (CBS here), there was no question of Aretha's style being "suppressed" by that label.

426

"I'd call it more of an exploration by Columbia. They gave Aretha the chance to sing all sorts of things", he explained.

"But it was more kind of 'easy listening' as they say in 'Cash Box'," said Aretha. "I started off there with more powerful material – very similar to the kind of thing I'm recording now with Atlantic – and went on to slower music. But I can say that my big records and my success has been due to the backing which Atlantic have put behind me. I can say that I wouldn't have had these hit records if it wasn't for Atlantic, and their organisation."

Aretha reads a lot of newspapers, not too many books, and likes mostly simple things and straightforward people. What did she think about British audiences and how do they compare with their US counterparts?

"I thought maybe they'd like me," she smiled. "But I never expected this, truly. It was so wonderful. My American audiences are pretty mixed. I get all sorts of people, old and young. It's nice. I don't record with my band though, we use Atlantic musicians."

Did Aretha look back much on old times when she wasn't so successful? Did she enjoy them?

"Oh, we had good times right enough. I was in a group, a gospel group with my sisters Irma and Carol. Carol is with me here as part of my backing group. We split up and went our separate ways, to do different things. My big ambition later on when I was with Columbia was to have a big record. Ted and I have written quite a few songs – but the name on the label credits would be 'White' – we write under my married name. I like writing, and don't confine myself to just the words, or just the music. But I don't particularly write songs with myself in mind."

Ted White explained that they had recently founded the Aretha Franklin Foundation, which gave to charity, and this was an activity Aretha had long been interested in. Aretha's father still sings gospel and has recorded over thirty gospel albums for the Chess label. Aretha's favourite female vocalists are Judy Garland, Shirley Bassey and

Clara Ward. And she digs Charles Aznavour – she even wants to cut an album of his songs when she gets the chance.

I asked Aretha that as she'll undoubtedly be singing in many years time, would she still be doing numbers like "Respect" and "Think" (her latest single)?

"No, I shouldn't think so," she laughed. "Music changes, and I'm gonna change right along with it."

"Think" became Aretha's seventh million-seller in a row. In the US, she charted no less than sixteen titles in '67 and '68.

Another great soul singer was also back in London. Lou Rawls had just won Billboard's Best Male Singer poll, beating Sinatra, but he wasn't happy and unlike his visit here last October he didn't talk much about music.

"...if there's any more tax taken off my money, I guess I might as well stop working. Now I wouldn't mind if this money was going to improve things in my own country but it's not. It's being spent on escalating the Vietnam war.

"You ask me what I would say if I had a few minutes alone with President Johnson, I'd tell him to get out, move over to let another man get on with the job.

"At the moment the majority of the American people just don't respect any of the Presidential candidates. There's no respect for Nixon, and a lot of the support for Bobby is just nostalgia, after JFK.

"I was in the Army before singing professionally. I didn't go to Korea, the war just ended. But I went overseas – to North Carolina – we call that overseas!"

That same month the Rolling Stones, minus any musical psychedelic trappings, returning with new producer Jimmy Miller (who'd supervised the Spencer Davis hits) and the chart-topping single "Jumping Jack Flash", an inspired return to their roots. It would be their final single to feature Brian Jones.

In May there was a high-profile press bash for Johnny Cash. Still virtually hitless here, Cash nevertheless toured regularly, was viewed as a star and treated accordingly. He was a big impressive-looking man, exactly as you'd expect, and by his side was new wife June Carter. I managed to get a few words with him:

RM w/e 11th May 1968

"...I think my only hit in this country was with 'It Ain't Me Babe'," Johnny told me at his reception thrown by CBS. "I know Bob Dylan well – you might say that him and me are going in the same way. He's certainly written some good songs – I'd say he was about the best songwriter around at this time.

"There isn't a definite reason why I sang country music when I started recording for Sun, and Elvis Presley and everyone else was singing rock. I just sing what I feel, there wasn't much difference between us at the time."

Johnny talked about his recent marriage to June Carter, with whom he has cut an LP.

"We've been touring together now for about six years or so. It wasn't a question of romance suddenly blossoming – I was just waiting for my divorce from my first wife to come through," he laughed.

Johnny was asked what he thought about the current generation of young people.

"I like 'em," he replied, "I've got to like them because they buy my records and come to see my shows. There are more people coming to see this tour than the last one, so I guess we must be more popular than last time, making new audiences. I can understand why young people rebel, although I never did it myself. If there was something I didn't like now, I guess I'd rebel in some way against it."

Johnny was impressively dressed in a long black drape jacket with black silk edging and a white shirt. The thirty-six year old singer is touring here with Carl Perkins, June Carter, Johnny's backing group the Tennessee Three, and James Royal.

Another long-standing CBS act with strong Dylan connections – even more so than Cash – were the Byrds, also touring the UK. And their new album, "The Notorious Byrd Brothers" was currently in the LP Top 20:

RM w/e 18th May 1968

HIGH FLYING BYRDS TRIUMPH WITH A BRITISH AUDIENCE

...they were here over the weekend and appeared at the Middle Earth club where they proved conclusively that their days of onstage ineffectuality were over – they were called back countless times by a mainly hippie audience, and DJ Jeff Dexter nearly ran out of nauseous hippie jargon with which to praise them. There were five Byrds – lead vocalist and guitarist Roger McGuinn (who had three guitars which were all used frequently), bass guitarist and supporting vocalist Chris Hillman, drummer Kevin Kelley, vocalist and acoustic guitarist Gram Parsons, and an un-named electric banjo player.

Many of the numbers were in a plaintive country style including their "Old John Robertson" from their hit LP, and their new single "I Ain't Goin' Nowhere". Gram Parsons was the leading country vocalist and he performed many poignant numbers including "Excuse Me", "I Like The Christian Life" and "Under Your Spell Again". Their version of "Foggy Mountain Breakdown" was well-received but the numbers which brought the house down were the big single hits, for which Roger McGuinn used his famous twelve string guitar. They included a scintillating version of "Eight Miles High" and others like "5D", "I'd Feel A Whole Lot Better", "Turn Turn Turn", "Going Back", "So You Want To be A Rock 'n' Roll Star", "My Back Pages", "Mr Tambourine Man". The group's sound was very similar to their records,

*except, surprisingly, on the items from their new LP
which were more country-based, and the Byrds' first
set was finished with a version of Vera Lynn's "We'll
Meet Again". Other numbers they performed included
"Tribal Gathering", "Baby What You Want Me To Do"
and "Bells Of Rhymney".*

There's nothing like seeing a good band in a small club and
the Byrds were superb. The "un-named electric banjo player" was
Doug Dillard. And in my rush writing the review to include it into
the next issue, I forgot to mention they had a steel guitar player
– Sneaky Pete Kleinow. Gram Parsons was a revelation. He sang
country music with the gift of re-contemporising the genre while
retaining its intrinsic sincerity. I'd never heard country music sound
so relevant, and neither had plenty more in the audience including
Keith Richards, who latched on to Gram with interesting (though
some might say devastating) musical and personal consequences.
Gram was effectively inventing country-rock, but what no-one here
knew was that his massive vocal contribution to the next Byrds'
album "Sweetheart Of The Rodeo" – already recorded – had been
stripped off and replaced by vocals from McGuinn and Hillmann.
Parsons had neglected to mention that he was still contracted to
Lee Hazelwood's LHI label, and upon hearing Gram was recording
with the Byrds, Hazelwood got miffed to the point of threatening a
lawsuit. US Columbia backed down, unsure anyway of the potential
of the Parsons-inspired "Rodeo" project, and thus a masterpiece
was compromised. Parsons' refusal to to tour South Africa with
the Byrds the following month – he cited an aversion to playing in
front of segregated audiences, but less charitable sources blamed
his increasing desire to hang out with the Stones – would lead to
his sacking from the Byrds.

In contrast to the good vibes generated at the Byrds' hippy-ish
happening, Bill Haley's concert at the Albert Hall the previous week
had startled me. Not everyone, it seemed, was enamoured by the
seemingly inexorable artistic progress of '60s pop music. A lot of
people wanted to turn the clock back:

RM w/e 11th May 1968

THE GREAT LEAP BACKWARDS!

BILL HALEY and his Comets did not perform an encore at the Royal Albert Hall because they were chased off stage by a group of rockers. Earlier in the show, Duane Eddy's drummer had been hit on the head by a carefully-aimed bottle, stopping the rock for some minutes. And one of the girl go-go dancers employed to writhe on stage to the twangy guitar had been the victim of a scratch-and-claw attack by a rocker girl.

Not only is this 1968, a year after the Beatles' "Sgt. Pepper", and 17 years after "Rock Around The Clock" was written, but the artists who provoked this frenzy were mostly un-sexy American musicians. If you were not there, be assured that the sight of Bill Haley and his Comets being chased off stage by a group of people who at best looked like 1954 hippies was quite amusing. And these kids weren't the original beat generation being nostalgic, who grew up with James Dean and the Suez Crisis, but a strange breed of throwbacks dedicated (or so it seems) to preserving the more ridiculous aspects of rock'n'roll.

Most of the audience, though, had arrived at the Albert Hall because of a mix of curiosity and nostalgia. Like me. And even the Quotations (who backed Duane Eddy) were given more applause than boos when they attempted – not too solidly – to reproduce those dear dead rock sounds. Another group called the Wild Angels obviously had their hearts more in rock'n'roll, as could be seen from their attire and hair, a fact which was appreciatively reflected by the hot, excited multitude around the stage.

During Duane Eddy's rendition of the monotonous, primitive, concrete jungle tune "Peter Gunn" the rockers around the stage were so frenzied that I imagined the whole stage, noise, and writhing multitude, sinking into the fires of iniquity below, the floor of the Albert Hall being split asunder by an unseen, righteous and wrathful hand.

Duane's fine guitar work has never been truly showcased on his hit singles and he only had time to perform a few of them, all of which followed the same twangy guitar, sax and percussion format. Duane looked as though he was waiting at a bus stop, not playing to a hotbed of rock revivalism, and his coolness carried him through well.

Haley, of course, was excellent. His sound is much stronger than on those early records, and his showmanship, sheer professionalism and ability to lay down a real beat created a tremendous atmosphere with everybody.

"I want to tell you, said Bill, "How very happy you've made me tonight."

Bill made everybody else very happy too.

But he did insist before he came on that no-one gets on to the stage. "I knew rock'n'roll would come back, it's gone the full cycle," he said.

Even to the riots, it seems.

There was plenty of music being released which I enjoyed and even loved – I was a music lover, after all – but the business of being in the day-to-day thick of it year after year was palling. I didn't feel so involved anymore. I didn't want to interview any more beat groups. And I'd had enough of pure pop, especially 1968 pop. Contemporary music that I did like – mostly sophisticated white pop-rock and mainstream soul – was attracting writers far better than me. My stock-in-trade fan-based prose felt distinctly creaky and superficial: the music pieces currently being published by the UK underground newspaper International Times by such writers of the calibre of Barry Miles and, particularly, the 6-month old American music magazine Rolling Stone, had changed the face of popular music writing. It wasn't pop reportage anymore: it had become rock journalism and in the UK was now attracting quality writers like Richard Williams and Charlie Gillett, and I felt out of my depth. I resolved to take some time out to pursue my various new interests – and to try to learn to write better. Besides, I'd been working non-stop at Record Mirror for over seven years, writing, reviewing, interviewing, supervising the production, putting the paper to bed, a full-time full-on job and then some and I needed a break.

I decided to drop out for a while.

My final scribblings for Record Mirror as a full-time staffer included a rave review of the new Small Faces LP "Ogden's Nut Gone Flake": *Cockney-Rock LP Puts Small Faces in West Coast Bracket.* I admired the Small Faces rather than liked them, but there was no denying their all-round artistry on this album – or the commerciality of the round tin gimmick. In a pot-boiler titled *The Emancipation Of Country Music* various UK country pundits told me their reasons why country wasn't bigger here, the feature closing with the timeless line "It could happen!" Yet still it hasn't, forty-odd years on.

Focus On 2 Giant LPs was my last in-depth review – of Simon & Garfunkel's soon-to-be-classic "Bookends" and Dave Dee, Dozy, Beaky, Mick & Tich's surprisingly good effort to crack the album market "If No One Sang". The former hit number one, the latter didn't trouble the chart. I raved about Cilla Black in cabaret in *Saucy Cilla Shocks Savoy*, and, appropriately, my final interview was with Captain Beefheart who'd been on a nationwide tour with his Magic Band, mostly clubs and colleges. It was the tail end of the tour and the band was zonked – they cancelled out their forthcoming Amsterdam gigs – and Don had to be woken up for the mid-afternoon interview which, all things considered, he conducted with reasonable grace. He also made a point of complimenting me on my shoes, a pair of formal mid-brown Oxfords, though I wasn't sure whether or not he was mocking me. I felt guarded, but I did remember Peter Meaden to him, which elicited Don asking me why Peter hadn't been to see him. I evaded the question. Peter was slipping further into withdrawal and lately appeared to have only a passing interest in Captain Beefheart. There would have been little point in sharing that information. Here are Don's quotes extracted from the article:

RM w/e 1st June 1968

"...we try to tell the kids to watch out" said Don. "It's something that started years ago when I was sixteen and I was stopped and searched by a cop because he didn't

434

like the way I looked. This is a free country. It's getting closer to '1984' when a television set in your room will register a change in your facial expression. The kids have to watch out for the men in grey flannels, and this generation of young people is completely different to any other generation. They are more aware, and this has been caused by their attitudes, mind-expanding drugs, and most important of all the music they listen to. Music is the most important medium of all the art forms because for the kids it is the easiest to understand – it gets through to them.

"You can write a poem, and use the word 'yellow'. OK. But if you put music to it, you add another depth to the word yellow, and this conjurs up pictures in the mind – and that's where it's all at, in the mind. This is why Dylan puts his poems to music, and very successfully too. I can admire Dylan – he's a God in the States.

"The important thing to the group is to communicate. There's really only one song on 'Safe As Milk' that starts to put across this message, and that's 'Electricity'. If you asked the guy downstairs what I meant by electricity he'd think about the plug in the wall. Our next LP will be full of these type of songs. Next to telepathy, music is the best form of communication. We get kids in Britain who stand and watch our act and afterwards say to us 'Don't change a bit.' We want to have ears that will listen to us. I can't express these ideas properly in words, I'll have to play you our new LP when it comes through, that's better, and points towards the aim, the ideal. There aren't many other groups trying to do this, putting across this type of message. The Byrds? No, they only hinted at it when they reflect Dylan. Not the Beatles, though they have certainly brought some fresh air on the scene. And done a lot of good. But 'she loves you yeah yeah?' They're better now – a bit better. The Mothers Of Invention. Yes, they're nearer to it than anyone else, but as I say, I haven't heard many other groups.

'ANYONE OVER THIRTY...'

"Anyone over thirty isn't capable of understanding what this is all about, and this is the big gap between the generations. The kids of thirteen nowadays – the ones who see us – they're the kids who are really going to get this message. George Orwell who wrote 1984 knew what was going to happen, and now this is nearer, but it was pretty near even when he wrote that book. People are brought up in a completely protected atmosphere, but it isn't for their good, it confines them, they're restricted by these conventions. Like if a guy wears grey flannel and those square gold-rimmed glasses, then he's OK for President. Also, he'll have a few million so everyone'll say 'He must know what it's about if he's got that money'. As for actor Ronald Reagan...I can just see his wife – she's the real governor – saying to him 'Comb your hair THIS way, dear'."

As I got up to leave, Don reiterated his point by treating me acapella to a couple of lines from "Electricity":

"...high-voltage man kisses night, to bring the light to those who need to hide their shadow deeds."

The hotel room where I'd interviewed him, where the Magic Band were sleeping crashed out on sofas and on the floor (Don had the bed), was dark and dismal. I walked out into the sunlight and thought about Peter Meaden.

I quit Record Mirror at the end of June. Earlier that month Peter Meaden had attended the Yoko Ono exhibition at the Arts Lab and had to be restrained from donating all his remaining money to Yoko's charities. Lately we were hanging out more with our new New Wave Productions artist Donnie Elbert, who'd been in London for two years and liked it here. One day Peter and Donnie were smoking and drinking at Donnie's girlfriend's house in Edgware when there was a police raid – the girlfriend's brother was on the run and the police thought he was holed up there. For some reason Peter and Donnie were both packing heat. Without getting up, Peter opened the bay window and dropped his piece in the dustbin outside – and, with awesome timing, the dustmen came along at that very moment and emptied the bin. But Donnie got busted with his piece, a gas gun he'd brought over from NY. By the time the case eventually came to court, Peter had been sectioned and I had to testify as character witness for Donnie. I wore a beautiful suit and told the judge Donnie was set to earn £50,000 over the next year. He got cautioned – but never earned a penny from us.

As usual with New Wave, our grand plans for Donnie came to very little. Peter's problems resulted in secure hospitalisation that autumn, I was on my own at New Wave (Terry Chappell had quit when the Polydor retainer dried up), so I resolved a new course – our own record label. Donnie presented me with a single: "Baby Please Come Home"/"Without You", two competent sides featuring his distinctive vocals over an authentic rock-steady track ("version") supplied from an existing master tape from which he'd wiped the original vocal and substituted his own voice and song. Donnie insisted that "Baby Please Come" was the A-side, but I disagreed: I found his continuous falsetto on it overwhelming and preferred the catchier, more mellow "Without You". But it was Donnie's record, he owned it, he had the say-so. Our plan was to follow up the single with an LP, and so I slipped a plug article into the ever-helpful Record Mirror *(Soul Singer In The Suburbs)* that December which included the information: "Donnie is planning an album for New Wave, which will contain some old and some new material, plus his original unreleased version of 'Open The Door To Your Heart' which Donnie wrote and Darrell Banks took into the US charts".

This new New Wave label was manufactured and distributed by Melodisc Records, from whom Donnie had obtained the backing tracks. Siggy Jackson was amiable enough, loved the single, and liked our plans for New Wave. I was also planning to license some indie soul singles which Trevor Churchill was advising me on, and we were soon in discussions with RCA to release the first batch.

Our activities somehow caught the attention of future American record business mogul Seymour Stein, currently in London looking for promising British groups to release on his new Sire label. Seymour was interested in what we were doing with New Wave. He knew and liked Donnie from when they were both at King Records in the late '50s – Donnie had recorded for the King subsidiary DeLuxe – and Seymour was a big fan of his voice and music. He also loved the Peep Show, particularly the single "Esprit De Corps" – but with a caveat: "It's a demo! You released a demo!" (He was right; it was a spruced-up demo). "Re-cut it and I'll release it on Sire."

In the event, Donnie's single did not prove to be airwave friendly and flopped – I doubt it sold more than a couple of boxes on New Wave – and he quickly resold the master to Decca's Deram label, this time wisely promoting "Without You" as the A-side: it went on to top the Jamaican charts. The LP failed to materialise. Donnie used to jump labels very quickly, but he did leave us with an acetate of a good falsetto-filled production titled "So Soon". Years later when the Joe Boy label released it, Motorcity supremo and Northern Soul authority Ian Levine got cross with me and said it wasn't Donnie at all. No surprise there, then!

The Peep Show had already more or less given up hope of anything positive happening once the Polydor deal fell through, but early the following year I booked them into Regent Sound Studios together with some of our old studio crew to re-cut "Esprit De Corps" for Sire. We finished the backing tracks, but then I ran out of money. RCA was stalling on the licensed singles deal and, more importantly, without Peter Meaden around I ran out of enthusiasm. The re-recorded "Esprit De Corps" remained unfinished...and that was the end of New Wave Productions.

Seymour Stein did eventually take something from us: our name. When he signed the Ramones and the Talking Heads for Sire in 1976, he considered the UK term "punk" derogative. So he coined the term "New Wave" for the genre and it stuck.

Pursuing my new literary pretensions and spiritual aspirations meant spending more time at home in my flat in Alexandra Park. A regular visitor was an old acquaintance, Martin Anthony, the man who for years had been fixing the NME chart. Anthony lived in nearby Muswell Hill, wore shades summer and winter, day and night, and made his dubious living as a minor crook and con man. One day he arrived at my front door complaining his phone had been cut off and he was unable to conduct his business. He asked if he could use my phone for a few days and I agreed, especially when he proffered a little cash. After a busy two or three days Anthony told me that he'd done all he needed to do here, as his own phone was now reconnected. That was that, or so I thought.

A couple of weeks later I got a call from Rik Gunnell, with whom I'd always been on good terms. Rik was a successful and colourful music business entrepreneur who'd run a string of London clubs since the early '50s including Studio 51, the Flamingo, and currently the Bag O'Nails. Gunnell Enterprises – Rik and his brother Johnny – was a management and agency company which handled, among others, Georgie Fame, Chris Farlowe, Zoot Money and Geno Washington. Rik was now far from friendly: "Why the fuck isn't the Cliff Bennett in the charts?" he demanded. I didn't know what he was talking about, or even if he knew the person he was talking to. Then I realised he meant Cliff Bennett's new single, a cover version of "Back In The USSR". I explained to Rik that he was talking to me, Norman Jopling, that his beef was with Anthony who'd simply been using my phone. Gunnell was having none of it.

"He told me you were in business with him, this was the new number for his business, this was the number we did business on. You've had eight hundred quid of my money...if the record isn't in the charts next week we'll be round there and break both your legs".

I was shaking. I tried Martin Anthony's phone number but unsurprisingly it was dead. Trembling, I ran to Wood Green tube station and went straight to Gunnell's office: I knew I had to explain him in person what had happened and look him in the eye while I told him. Fortunately he was there, fortunately he believed me. Gunnell could be charm personified, but few would consider crossing him. I never saw Martin Anthony again and never heard another word about him. I guess the NME scam had recently been blown and he'd had been gathering some final hype money before word got out. Luckily no-one else had been conned using my name – or if they had I never found out about it.

By the middle of 1969, a year after I'd left Record Mirror, I may have been a lot better-read, and a lot more educated in matters spiritual, but I'd also made the discovery that the more you know, the more you know you don't know. I was flat broke, and despite valiantly toiling at some desperate and poorly-paid temporary jobs ranging from driving for Manpower to a stint as Press Officer for John Curd's Head Records, the only area where I was still in any demand was back in music journalism.

I decided to go free-lance and concentrate on layouts and production. Luckily Peter Jones was glad to get me back to part-time production work which at least paid the rent. Nevertheless I knew I had to return to writing sooner or later. That summer I penned some soul articles for Peter Burns' fanzine Earshot, and then someone introduced me to Richard Branson who was running a magazine called Student. There was already a buzz about Branson, primarily because he'd plastered little stickers all over the West End for his Help Advisory Centre which offered young people counselling on birth control and sexually transmitted diseases.

I went to see Branson in the basement where he was working and discovered that the only counsellor seemed to be Richard, who was spending most of his time talking earnestly to droves of young girls constantly phoning for sexual advice. I thought this was a bit strange considering Richard was himself still only in his late teens – although he was a big chap with a certain charisma and serious beyond his years. I went on to spend quite a few hours sitting in Richard's basement office being entertained and impressed listening to him doing his counselling routine, and despite my antennae being slightly a-quiver for any sign of deviant vicarious kicks (I couldn't help wondering: it was definitely an incongruous situation) there was never any indication that his concern was anything other than genuine. He seemed sincere, matter-of-fact, and efficient. But that particular facet of his Student Advisory Centre charity ground to a halt very soon afterwards when his little stickers were deemed illegal and he had to take them all down.

Richard was cautiously dipping his toe into rock music and he asked me to write an article on the current fashion for free concerts, in particular the forthcoming Stones In The Park gig at nearby Hyde Park. He had a press pass, so on the day off we went, together with a Student photographer. Richard, for all his public school confidence, wasn't at all confident going to this event. He wasn't used to being

440

in a rock milieu. I had to lead the way through the throng, flash the press card, do the introductions, and all the rest of it. Richard was happy to tag along: the pop music world, the rock world, wasn't his world – yet.

I wrote the article *Free Pop* for him – around two-and-a-half thousand words – but he didn't publish it. He didn't pay me, either, which rankled. The article was a curate's egg, only good in parts, and with writers of the calibre of Jean Paul Sartre, James Baldwin, Robert Graves and R.D.Laing jostling for column space in Student, I guessed he could afford to be fussy. Nevertheless, some of the observations in Free Pop did convey a flavour of the event:

> *Everything was relaxed and noisy in a warm, stoned way, and we arrived at the press enclosure situated by a mountainous pile of stage and scaffolding swarming with photographers, groups and groupies. Inside were the elite, looking indistinguishable from the audience pressed fearfully up against the barriers behind them. Climbing the barriers we were stopped by apologetic young officials who asked for passes. One between four didn't seem enough. "You know man, I mean, I really hate to do this to you but you can't all come in, I'm sorry..." Two entered, two fell back. Clambering over pressmen and freeloaders whose faces impassively betrayed a kind of detached tolerance at being constantly kicked and trod on, we flopped down, our photographer immediately playing his role with enthusiasm, crouching and squatting, standing and snapping.*
>
> *The most impressive thing about the event was the audience; and the most professional act was compere Sam Cutler. Order was purportedly kept by the Hell's Angels, a bunch of ugly swaggering rockers richly ornamented in leather, Nazi insignia and helmets, chrome, vicious pieces of metal, grease, boots and winklepickers. In this inner sanctum interesting people abounded; apart from the groups and their trains of hangers-on, there was a photographer with a Dali-esque moustache, girls with*

nipples protruding through string vests, debs squatting in the dried mud, fat sweaty journalists cursing their editors and cursing the Stones – and a huge array of posers of every description. The Stones ran on to cheers and then silence as Mick read Shelley's poem, a tribute to Brian, but while he did so people lounged against the blown-up photograph of the dead hero obscuring his face from public view. The music began; thousands of butterflies were released...

"It was great from where I was," said Keith Richard. "After two years it was hard to believe we were doing a live show again and it took me a while to get back into it, but when I did, I really enjoyed it. In England we've never had that size concert. I'm surprised so many people showed up. It must have been very hot out there and it was nice of them to sit out there all that time."

The concert was a social phenomenon, but in terms of generating column inches it paled into insignificance compared with the Stones-related events that sandwiched it: Brian's death, and the collapse and illness of Marianne Faithfull. I delivered the article to Student and never heard from Branson again. I guess I'd done my bit for him: at least he hadn't been Dickie No-Mates at the historic event – and I'd got to sit next to Jane Fonda.

The US trade magazine Billboard must still have been labouring under the misapprehension that I was still an expert on UK soul because they commissioned an article in August 1969 on the current state of the British soul scene. As I'd barely glanced at the charts since leaving Record Mirror in June '68, I was forced to submit a flannel job which painted the picture in the broadest possible strokes:

Billboard, w/e 16th August 1969

OLDIES, JAMAICA, INFLUENCE BRITISH SOUL SCENE

442

THE soul scene in Britain is going through a lot of changes. A personification of it would look like a very thin sick man speaking in a Detroit accent and leaning heavily on a stick made of Jamaican wood.

Very few current US soul hits are making it here and American soul music is mainly reflected by the massive resurrection policy kicked off by EMI with "This Old Heart Of Mine" which led to a backwash of dozens of hits from hundreds of revived oldies.

Most of the obvious golden goodies have been scraped from the barrels, but very few of the follow-ups are making it: "Get Ready" was the Temptations' biggest hit here a few months back, but the follow-up "Ain't Too Proud To Beg" (which made it first time around) flopped dismally.

Other stars with the same problem include Jackie Wilson, Martha & the Vandellas, the Righteous Brothers, Jr Walker, Ike & Tina, and many many more. Only the Isley Brothers, after three solid top ten hits are scoring consistently, but their new hit "It's Your Thing" seems too progressive for the British market and barely scraped the top thirty. None of the other US items in this New Beat bag – James Brown, Tyrone Davis – mean very much here despite their popularity with in-crowd soul fanatics and Jamaicans.

The more sophisticated American soul stars like the Impressions, the Delfonics and Jerry Butler have never made it here, and the Dells' current hit "I Can Sing A Rainbow/Love Is Blue" is unlikely to be the thin end of any wedge. The principal reason for this is lack of exposure – the BBC has only one R&B show (hosted by Mike Raven) on its one pop channel. But current black music which can make the charts without heavy exposure (surprisingly enough the BBC plugs the reissues heavily) are the Jamaican reggae items.

Reggae has two advantages over US soul: firstly there is a large Jamaican record buying public in the UK who spend proportionately more on records, mainly singles, than whites do, and also a large new cult of whites in their early teens who have taken Jamaican music as their own. This social group, mainly from working class areas reacts against the hippy values (in the widest sense) by wearing cropped hair, jeans and suspenders, heavy boots and getting involved with violence and speed drugs. Spearheading the reggae craze are Desmond Dekker and Johnny Nash and the movement is still growing. With no superstar to replace Otis and no Holland-Dozier-Holland, it seems unlikely that the black music scene will shift yet from its basic foundations of reissues and reggae.

In America reggae was – and maybe still is – categorised as a sub-genre of soul music: definitely not the case in the more-nuanced UK.

The Stones In The Park concert had coincided with the final day of the Woodstock Festival in upstate New York, but Woodstock's most famous current resident neither performed nor attended that soon-to-be-legendary happening. Not that those "three days of peace & music" took place in the town of Woodstock or even nearby: the festival merely borrowed the groovy name. But Bob Dylan did headline a big festival of his own that summer: at the Isle Of Wight on August 31st. Bob topped the bill on the second day of the festival, with the first evening headlined by the Who, just back from their Woodstock triumph and still plugging "Tommy" in its entirety.

Though I wasn't officially writing for Record Mirror, Dylan at the IOW was one gig I had to see. Lon Goddard and I managed to persuade RM to pay for a cosy junket including hovercraft transportation and hotel accommodation – but, alas, only for the Dylan evening. I wrote the review using my old RM alias; Lon wrote up the press conference. On the Dylan day, leaving the hotel and being driven to the site by taxi, stepping over and around the thousands of people lying and squatting on the brown ground looking like they'd had a less than comfortable night and then being ushered into the press enclosure made me feel slightly uncomfortable, isolated from the "authentic festival experience". But I dare say most of the audience would have changed places with me in an instant. And we all, press and public, had to wait hours and hours for Dylan to finally show up after his appointed time to appear:

444

RM w/e 6th September 1969

'LOVE IS ALL THERE IS...'

Wesley Laine & Lon Goddard report from the Isle of Wight

BOB DYLAN – your friend and mine – did what was expected of him (his new thing and less than he was purportedly paid for) and left the Isle of Wight in a privately hired hovercraft which took him to a fleet of privately hired limousines: Rolls-Royce for the Dylan family and Daimlers and Austin Princesses for the Band.

The night before he delighted lots of people with his new versions of old songs done in his new marshmellow voice with gutsy blues backings, sparse and effective, by the Band, who also tendered strong vocal support.

After the event different sections of the press saw the event from opposing sides of the fence. "Dylan Cuts It Short After Midnight Flop" screamed the Sketch with appropriately derogatory story, while the Telegraph claimed "150,000 Go Wild As Dylan Rocks Isle" with appropriate love'n'peace copy to follow.

Neither was accurate, but both were picturesque, as were the faces of Sketch reporters when compere Rikki Farr on the previous day had said: "You people from the press, some of you are doing a good job writing about the music, but you people from the Sketch and Mirror, and the People, you should be ashamed of yourselves, you write a lot of shit." So some got offended and the others got smug.

The crowd became impatient after waiting a couple of unscheduled hours for Bob. When he appeared after the Band's spot someone sent a rocket up, a gesture of joy rather than analogy. We all cheered and we were all happy especially when he broke into "She Belongs To Me", which was the same song he started his last concert here with at the Albert Hall three years ago. That time he sang it very differently to the record, no less this time. His new

"Nashville Skyline" voice was used throughout the show, and combined with his well-scrubbed clean wholesome physical appearance (comfortable white suit, open-neck pea soup-coloured shirt, trim beard) he seemed the very essence of the ungimmicky entertainer. He was as different from the wild, brightly-dressed, freaky-haired and tortuous poet of three years ago as the new post-Army Presley was as different from the sensual stuttering rocker.

Bluesy "heavy" (is that the right word?) guitar punctuated the first song and Dylan glided smoothly through the lyrics. The song was smooth on record – this time it was smoother, last time it was drawn out.

From behind a forest of microphones Dylan became more solemn and sang "I Threw It All Away", putting even more feeling into it than on the LP. It was beautiful. "Love is all there is, it makes the world go 'round," he sang, and I naively believed he meant it.

The Band came in vocally for "Maggie's Farm" which had earlier been folk-bluesed by Richie Havens: Dylan rocked it up and shouted the crushing lyrics while the Band echoed "no more" again and again, thrusting their faces towards Dylan's at the barrage of mikes, and the three vocalists exchange grins and contractions of facial muscles towards each other. Dylan seems to evolve a close relationship with his backing groups: at the Albert Hall during the electric half of the performance he strutted around with his his group's lead guitarist thrusting their guitars at each other and doing some kind of primeval war dance.

"Wild Mountain Thyme" is a beautiful tune that Dylan didn't write but surprisingly sang as he launched into the unaccompanied section. It was followed by "It Ain't Me Babe" which wasn't suited to his new vocal phrasing and voice. The song can only be bitter and cutting and doesn't suit his latest image.

"To Ramona" was the closest he came to the original Bob Dylan version. He tried to change bits but couldn't help

446

falling back into the phrasing, if not the poignant cadences that marked the song as it appeared on "Another Side..."

Claps, shrieks, cheers, whistles, greeted the first bars of "Mr Tambourine Man". The song was probably the first hippy anthem, sung when the word 'hippy' hadn't even been coined, and would have brought the house down had there been a house. Bob kept near the original feeling of the song – a loving wistfulness pervaded the atmosphere and we all felt, here is Bob Dylan, in front of us, flesh and blood, really here, singing his most famous song, the one that told us before anything else that something was in the air, and it was happening to us all.

After that came "I Dreamed I Saw St Augustine" – it made the "John Wesley Harding" version seem dated – and the Band came back on and someone played a nice guitar solo on the middle. The audience and the press were in a state of rapt attention, only the photographers externally buzzing down and around and up weren't quiet.

Faces were still alight when he sang "Lay Lady Lay" without the subtle, beautiful backup that the record has, and it didn't particularly inspire or excite. Nevertheless the atmosphere kept up, people high and low were digging everything and somehow the vibrations from the stage brought through memories that not even the re-playing of his record manage to evoke.

The next number was for me the best. Dylan rocked his way through "Highway 61 Revisited". Grins and smiles and laughs of delight pervaded the starry faces in the press stands as the Band provided a sensationally rocking country backdrop, loudly yelled "down Highway Sixty One", and the fingers of the bass player flapped frantically like no other bassist I've ever seen. They even threw in a Saturday morning Granada organ solo which lay nicely behind the pounding cowboy rock. It was all too much.

After that, "One Too Many Mornings" was an anticlimax. Dylan set it to the beat of "It Takes A Lot To Laugh, It Takes A Train To Cry" and freaky guitar

447

stuttered throughout but nothing really fell together. The next song "I Pity The Poor Immigrant" was also disappointing – but mainly because the backing drowned out the vocals, at least from where I was squatting. There was an amusing break for a piano accordion, however, which one of the Band sported.

"Like A Rolling Stone" was given a jerky vocal treatment. The Band yelled out "how does it feel!" but it had shades of the single hit all over it. It was good and the words sounded as good as ever.

"I'll Be Your Baby Tonight" followed, given a less mellow treatment than the single, with considerable beat added. The charm remained, even for a bubbly version of "Mighty Quinn".

"This is a song that was a big hit in England for Manfred Mann. A great group, great group," said Bob.

He went off and was called back.

But he didn't return for a couple of minutes. The people behind me, who had partly succeeded in getting me contact high said "Dylan's too big to do an encore, man", profoundly seriously.

The next song I didn't know. "Who's gonna throw that minstrel a coin," he started. It was a gospel-tinged number with good lyrics that sounded like Bob's. Rolling beat backed it up and the Band featured heavily.

The last number was "Rainy Day Women Nos. 12 & 35" without the rollicking stoned beat of the original. Bob removed the stoned atmosphere and gave it to us straight. In country-rock, well-sung, straight-faced.

There were no new songs as such, and the event was predictable and it was a big success. Dylan had appeared, he had been there, and he had entertained. The show had been a good one and Dylan's act had been thoroughly professional and musically near-perfect.

"I think I prefer the new Dylan, you know" someone said on the way out as we passed a portable record player playing "Masters Of War".

Also on the bill were Richie Havens, the Pentangle, Julie Felix, Indo-Jazz Fusion, the Liverpool Scene – and Tom Paxton. It was a boho-folk line-up with everybody turning in fine performances, Paxton especially good, communicating his warm intimacy with his many memorable songs to the huge audience who forgot their impatience for Dylan. This single concert would earn Paxton a new audience and major career boost for a long time. I thought Dylan slightly disappointing. Interesting, certainly, but this slightly square reinvention seemed a bit cautious, a tad lacklustre. I enjoyed Paxton more. But in fairness it had been Bob's comeback gig, just as Hyde Park had been the Stones. Neither had performed in public for years. Both had returned to a rock scene that was now more overblown and hyped-up than ever.

At the end of 1969 Record Mirror changed hands. John Junor and Sir Edward Lewis finally let go, selling out to US Billboard who now published the UK trade paper Record Retailer. The RM office in Shaftesbury Avenue closed down and some of the staff decamped to Billboard's HQ in Carnaby Street. Record Retailer, which seemed grossly overstaffed to us, already had plenty of receptionists, advertising, and accounts personnel, so Roy Burden and Pat Farnham were made redundant; Dezo Hoffmann negotiated sole ownership of the photographic studio; on the editorial side Derek Boltwood and David Griffiths quit, but Peter Jones and his team of writers – Lon Goddard, Ian Middleton and Val Mabbs – moved seamlessly into a more corporate world.

1970-1972

Having little desire for working at corporate Record Mirror, and also experiencing some personal ups and downs with Ruth, I figured a long holiday abroad for us might help the situation. So at the beginning of 1970 we encamped to Tunisia accompanied by several tabs of mescaline. Soon after arrival, we palled up with a couple of German guys, Joachim and Nick, who owned record shops in Germany and appeared to do little except roam the world dropping acid and having fun. We joined in.

A few months later we were back in the UK and broke – but rescue was at hand. I was contacted by my old Record Mirror editor Jimmy Watson who was now editing a new paper titled Music Now, formerly Top Pops. Music Now was a groovy little independent weekly situated out of a couple of rooms in Park Road off Regents Park, directly beneath the Famepushers agency, of Brinsley Schwarz-in-NY fame (or infamy). Not only was Jimmy working there, but so was ex-RM scribe Derek Boltwood plus a talented team that included deputy editor Tony Norman and writer/reviewer Karen De Groot. It was selling well: a circulation survey commissioned by Melody Maker gave current pop paper readership figures as: Melody Maker – 1,216,000 / NME – 1,079,000 / Music Now – 585,000 / Disc & Music Echo – 544,000 / Record Mirror – 434,000. Nice for Music Now, but a nasty downturn for Record Mirror, which usually sold more than Disc.

When I told Jimmy I was on my uppers he straightaway hired me as production editor to do all the layouts and picture research and to put the paper to bed every week at the printers, in Bristol – which I didn't mind at all. The ambience at Music Now was a bit "underground", pot was smoked in the office, and everyone working there seemed happy. The money was especially useful as Ruth and I had now moved into a flat in Belsize Park and things were starting to get serious again between us.

I wrote no more than half-a-dozen features for Music Now: the first a light-hearted front page spoof early in 1970 on the break-up of the Beatles: *Yeah, Yeah Yeah – selections from the Lennon-McCartney Laugh-In*, provoked by Paul's testily-worded press release for his first solo LP. Nobody seemed aware of the momentous import of the death of the Beatles, mainly because everyone was waiting to hear what they'd do next as solo artists. Music Now was heavily into in-depth album reviews and gave me Ringo's first solo album, which took six days to record, and George's Phil Spector-produced "All Things Must Pass", which took six months to record, to write about at length. "All Things Must Pass" itself took quite a long time to pass, being a bloated three-LP set, but it did contain many fine songs and its huge global success was said to have worried McCartney, who purportedly phoned Lennon to tell him that it was topping the LP charts. "Yes," replied John, "...but will he be able to follow it up!"

If "All Things Must Pass" was top of the 1970 spiritual LP hit parade and "My Sweet Lord" top spiritual single, hot on its heels was Norman Greenbaum's "Spirit In The Sky". Eager to meet and interview the creator of this brilliant record and also being a fan of his quirky earlier sides with Dr West's Medicine Show And Junk Band, I lolloped along to Pye's press reception to interview the global chart-topper. But when I got there I couldn't find Greenbaum anywhere. Finally I spotted him, a small nondescript lank-haired hippy squatting on the floor giggling uncontrollably, completely ignored by all and sundry. I kind of dug it; I could see where he was coming from.

The most memorable feature I wrote for Music Now came about when our advertising manager, Doug Collins, took a call late one morning in September:

"Hendrix is at the Londonderry Hotel, doing interviews," shouted Doug, "can anyone go now?"

I was alone in the editorial office poring over layouts, but in a jiffy I was in a cab and off. This plum job would normally have fallen to Tony Norman or new writer Dai Davies, but both were out on assignments. It would be the first time I'd seen Jimi in person since Epstein's Apollo gig back in '67 when the Experience was new, hot, flamboyant. What with that and Jimi's subsequent gargantuan sex & drugs reputation – mythology or not – and the fact he'd vanished from the UK for ages, I was a mite trepidatious about my ability to get a decent interview. Arriving at the Londonderry I was the last reporter scheduled – or more accurately, one of the last two; there were so many demands on Jimi that the journalists were doing the interviews in pairs. My co-interviewer was Rob Partridge from Record Mirror, which was alright because Rob was alright, and not alright because Music Now was in competition with Record Mirror, making us a funny sort of double-act.

We were ushered in. Jimi looked really good. In these kinds of situations – meeting a hugely-talented bona-fide superstar which Jimi always very much was – one registers and imprints the occasion as deeply as possible, for these are encounters, even for seasoned journalists, which one already knows are destined to become unforgettable experiences.

Jimi must have been talking for hours to dozens of reporters and posing for myriad photographers, yet he was relaxed, energetic, seeming like he was having a good time. When we suggested he might be stressed out with all the interviews, he was adamant he was fine with it all: "But a few months ago, no way," he said, "you know, if I even thought anyone was coming into the room I'd go and hide in the cupboard. Now I'm OK again..." Indeed, he seemed extremely together, and there was no residual drugginess about him, up, down, or anyways-else. He was thoughtful, intelligent, and he was warm. But most strikingly, he was also incredibly attractive to look at, with a panther-like grace in his movements. I was at ease immediately, and Rob also, and so we just started in gung-ho with the questions.

Music Now w/e 12th September 1970

MAN, MYTH OR MAGIC?
Jimi Hendrix is back, and happy, and talking...

JIMI HENDRIX is staying at a West End hotel prior to his appearance at the Isle Of Wight Festival and his forthcoming European tour. Black-clad, Jimi sprawled incongruously amidst the penthouse splendour...wild thing Hendrix and all that tasteless luxury ("...not even kitsch," said Rob Partridge, doing the stint for Record Mirror). Jimi poured out chilled white wine to the strings of reporters and photographers who kept trooping in, and occasionally used the hotel telephone to order various bits of food to munch while he answered questions, talked, laughed and gestured.

"I'm so nervous about the Isle Of Wight, you know, so nervous. I can't believe it. I really hate waiting around like this and that's what makes me so nervous. I think it would be better if I'd gone to the Isle Of Wight and mingled... took a sleeping bag with me and mixed with the crowds, to identify with it all. It would be so much better than all this, but there are the usual problems. If I do things like that the people keep coming up to me and saying 'look it's him' and 'c'mon, c'cmon' and all that, prodding me.

"I dug the Woodstock Festival – especially Sly and Richie Havens. And the guy from Ten Years After, yeah I was just a little bit jealous when I saw him play. Have you heard the record? I don't know why they used those tracks of mine, I really don't."

Jimi was relaxed enough to treat the interviews as a floorshow and he seemed particularly happy to be back in England.

"We'd been touring a lot in the States and we didn't think there would be the demand for us here after so long away. I wanted to come back but the people said, well you're playing in Boston on so and so day, and all that.

454

So...there it was, but here we are now. I'd like to get an English tour going soon."

I told Jimi that I'd read in Cashbox about his own recording studio, 'Electric Ladyland'.

"Yeah, yeah, and this is a different kind of studio. Chuck Berry and Sly have been down there doing a few things. It's a very relaxing studio, and it doesn't have that typical studio atmosphere. There are lots of cushions and pillows, thick carpets and soft lights. You can have any kind of light combination you like...just what you feel like. I think this is very important. There are many capable engineers around now, the problem is this atmosphere thing. And we have the best equipment too...

"I was saying earlier about the light and sound thing. I'm into this combination of music and colour – it's an extra area of awareness. I'm thinking about a film using those techniques."

Jimi has some tentative recording plans which include an album sometime in October and a double album following that. The double album, he says, will be mainly instrumental.

The 'super-star' aura that has always surrounded Jimi isn't at all apparent in an interview, or a conversation. How much of it is hype? How much is it a part that Jimi plays?

"I wouldn't know how to play that part. But I get a lot of people trying to make me play it. I'm here to communicate, that's my reason for being around, it's what it's all about. I want to turn people on and let them know what's happening. Even if they have nine to five jobs and come back to the family and TV, that's what counts, to keep turned on."

Isn't it a responsibility to communicate – especially at such an open-minded level?

"Yeah, sure, but I keep doing fresh things. Kids listen with open minds but I don't want to give them the same things all the time. Different things visually, different songs."

Where do those songs come from?

"Oh, they come from anywhere. I spend a lot of time daydreaming, they come from there. And from the people, all around. From the traffic too. They all give me ideas for songs, everything out there.

"But I really want to play England again. Do about eight cities or so. I'd like to go to Stonehenge, for the vibes. They're cooler heads in England compared to America.

"Sometimes I think we should do a free concert. I see the prices that the kids pay to see us and it's just ridiculous...I have a bad habit of talking too much."

How does Jimi feel about the pirate tapes and records that are circulating?

"I haven't had many records out for a while. Those pirate tapes, you know, some cat went to a private practise session with a tiny tape recorder and made a pirate LP. The quality must be terrible. There are pirate tapes of the Woodstock thing around too. The only reason we put out 'Band Of Gypsies' was that Capitol was pressing us for an LP - we didn't have anything ready at the time - so they got that."

Jimi will be backed by Billy Cox (an old friend of his from the USAF) and Mitch Mitchell on the European tour. And if he comes to doing an English tour, that's probably what we'll see.

How did he see himself with regard to working with a group in the future?

"Well, when it was the Experience there was more room for ego-tripping. You know? All I had to blast off stage were a drummer and a bass! But now I want to step back and let other things come forward. This is the idea of my getting a band together...a big band to develop new ideas. I don't know what my music will be like, I don't know if I'm playing differently now.

"No, I haven't been playing with the old Experience, certainly no official gigs or anything anyway. Mitch will be playing with me - he's never been better than he is now.

*And Noel, when I first picked them for the Experience, I
picked Noel because he could play ANYTHING on that
bass."*

*Jimi's head is full of ideas, some half-baked and some
matured. He may take some time getting them together, but
it's likely that the outcome will be no less spectacular than
the experiences he's delivered to us over the past three years*

We finished the interview and got up to go, Rob to a deadline,
me to get a train to Bristol. Jimi, realising he'd run out of company,
asked if we'd like to hang around for a while: we'd all been enjoying
ourselves a lot. But no, Rob and I departed all the same, rushing back
to work, like everyone else unable to see just around the corner – and
forever after wishing we'd stayed. It's one of my biggest regrets that
I didn't just say fuck it and hang around that day. Less than a month
later Jimi was dead. Because my impressions of him were so fresh, I
was chosen to write the obituary for Music Now:

Music Now w/e 26th September 1970

A MAN OF OUR TIMES

HENDRIX was unique.

*He was a young American Negro (and all that implies)
who was caught up in an environment and culture that
was rapidly becoming more hysterical and more paranoid
every year.*

*He transcended it by reflecting it. He became the greatest
rock guitarist of all time in addition to being an outrageous
entertainer, and it was all because he was young and black
and freaked out and an absolute virtuoso.*

*The combination of his background, his psychology,
and his power to play music so it smashed into your nerve
ends made him into the Black Elvis. The pre-Army Elvis
that is, whose raw self-confidence and sexual aggression
shook up the kids of the fifties. Hendrix used his guitar
like Presley used his voice with one difference. Presley*

would never have dared sing directly of what Hendrix spoke of with his guitar.

It would be sweet agony to listen to the intensity of the experiences that Hendrix could communicate. His own emotions, fears, dreams and triumphs. Everything from psychotic aggression, gentle pleading, sexual excitement, orgasm, and finally that white hot soaring psychedelic nirvana that Hendrix could return to and reflect with his beautiful guitar.

Jimi was born in Seattle, Washington – James Marshall Hendrix. His mother died when he was 10 and his father, a gardener, couldn't afford to keep him at school. At 15 he left home and found his way to New York where he hung around the Village. He was around just after another Village singer – Bob Dylan – found nationwide fame, and to the end of Jimi's life, Dylan remained the strongest influence on him.

He served some time with the United States Air Force as a paratrooper: it was during this time that he first met Billy Cox, later to join him on 'Band Of Gypsies' and play with him at the Isle Of Wight Festival. "We used to steal parachutes together," said Jimi.

It was while playing in a Greenwich Village night club that Jimi was seen by an English girl who told ex-Animal Chas Chandler and Mike Jeffery, who were visiting New York, to see Jimi. They were impressed – and saw at least some of the potential that Hendrix since fulfilled. Although Jimi had played with many big bands in America, including the Ike & Tina Turner Revue, he didn't have a steady group. Chas and Mike brought him to England, nurtured him for three months before launching him in December 1966 at the Bag O'Nails Club to an audience of pressmen and would-be bookers. In the meantime Jimi had picked up his sidemen from auditions that had been arranged. They were Mitch Mitchell on drums and Noel Redding on bass – the Experience.

They were both great rock musicians and were both in near-perfect empathy with Hendrix as he carved his way through the British music scene in 1967 with hit records like "Hey Joe", "Purple Haze", "The Wind Cries Mary" and "The Burning Of The Midnight Lamp". Together with the Beatles and the Cream, the Experience were at the front of the psychedelic movement that shook Britain in that year. The jams were being kicked out and the most savage trip was Jimi's, with his voice, a combination of blues and Dylan, and that unique guitar. He was one of the great figures of the head culture.

As far as Britain was concerned there had been no gestation period. Like the 'children' in Shaw's "Back To Methusalah", Jimi had been born at the age of twenty – he had emerged from an egg, a frightful chicken with his beautiful bizarre clothes, his sex and his drugs, and his weapon, the guitar. Other bluesmen were Back Door Men. Hendrix was a Voodoo Child.

There were a lot of obituaries written about Jimi, and to my astonishment and pride it was mine that was read out on Radio One.

Unfortunately the Music Now job lasted barely more than a year before the postal strike early in 1971 put paid to the 16-page shilling-a-week sheet forever: always hand-to-mouth, the weekly balance between print bills and incoming advertising cheques was delicate, easily upset, and credit from the printers available only for so long.

The last piece I wrote for Music Now was an interview with one of the most influential figures in British rock'n'roll history: Jack Good. Following the massive success of "Hair!" rock musicals were thriving, and Jack was appearing in "Catch My Soul", his musical adaptation of "Othello", at the Roundhouse in Camden Town. Jack played Othello – and "blacked up" to do it:

The interview took place in Jack Good's dressing room at the Roundhouse prior to the show last Saturday. Jack's make-up takes several hours to put on, and during the interview his head (with a two-day growth of hair) was shaved by Emil Dean Zoghby. Emil plays Montano and the Priest, and has also written many songs for the show. Jack was transformed, firstly with a fibreglass nose glued to his face ("I'm worried about the postal strike," he said, "the noses are changed for each performance"), and then with dye dextrously applied by his dresser. The result – at the end of the interview – a black Jack Good.

I asked him about the make-up:

WHEN YOU'RE WEARING THIS MAKE-UP, DO YOU FIND YOURSELF THINKING AND FEELING BLACK?

It's true of any part, but especially when the change is so dramatic. I mean, if you took off all the clothes you're wearing put on a tail suit, you might be wildly out of tune with what you're wearing but it would have its effect. Of course, everybody said 'What will the black people think', as far as I know they loved it. Anyway, the ones in the cast did. It was a big celebration the night I first wore this. I think everybody should be black for a time, and the blacks should be white. In fact there should be big blacking and whiting parties.

The make-up took a long time to put on, giving me a chance to talk to him in detail about his astonishing career. And his answer to my final question hinted at his future direction in life:

DO YOU SEE YOUR OWN LIFE AS A SERIES OF INCIDENTS, OR AS A CONTINUOUS FLOW?

I'd never really thought about it until 'This Is Your Life'. You see your life popularised and encapsulated, and when it's all over you feel you might as well go away and die. Then of course you realise that's not right. I'm really looking forward to having time to get myself together, but one needs quiet.

What one does, one is. You can't change the quality of what you do until you change what you are. When

*everything's taken away, all that's left is being, and if the
quality of that isn't much good...*

Jack Good later went to live in New Mexico for many years before
returning to Oxfordshire. He left show business, converted to Roman
Catholicism and became an icon painter.

Jimmy Watson, my dear friend, editor and mentor, took the demise
of Music Now badly. Always a heavy smoker – 80 a day – he came
to see me and Ruth at Belsize Park a year after Music Now went
down. He was chain-smoking, one lit from another. He was ill and
we begged him to stop, but he laughed. A tumour on his lung was
already strangulating his heart and a few months later he died.

Now married and with a baby on the way, I had to pick up the pieces
again quickly. Freelancing was the answer. Terry Chappell was back
at Record Mirror as production editor, Peter Jones was still editor, so
I soon got myself a regular retainer there for a couple of days a week
production work under Record Retailer's layout chief Bob Houston,
the larger-than-life Scot who had visually revitalised Melody Maker in
the late Sixties. Houston was an interesting bloke, a big, bearded rabid
left-winger who also edited the National Union of Miner's publication
The Miner, and whose visual style was an eye-grabbing tabloid format
with huge punchy headlines: the look was innovative and became much-
copied. He worked closely with Peter Jones and editorial director Mike
Hennessey, the writer and jazz musician, and over the next few months
they also commissioned a good deal of reportage from me. Bob also
encouraged me to contribute to his new rock magazine Cream, which
was convenient for delivering copy and attending editorial meetings
because Bob and I lived in the same street in Belsize Park. I also
managed, through the good graces of Waxie Maxie, to pick up the
editorship of the specialist magazine Rock'n'Roll Scene, plus, under
the alias of "Rockin' Henry", a new weekly column in the NME called
Roll, specialising in the UK R&R scene and which would include gig
info for the surprisingly large number of R&R revival bands currently
on the circuit. *Roll* proved especially useful because it opened the door
for me to contribute bona fide features to NME.

Ever since Bob Dylan's more lyrically obtuse LPs had emerged side-by-side with the general rise in pot smoking and acid tripping, it was open season on lyric interpretation, and nowhere was this more evident than among the new breed of rock scribes. Though not a new breed of rock scribe myself, I was as guilty as anyone of this trait, my currently oft-stoned and frequently tripped-out brain sometimes seizing on the most imaginative and far-out interpretation of what was often a very straightforward lyric. Of course, plenty of rock musicians who happened to be clever lyric writers were then creating deliberately multi-level lyrics: this era produced some extraordinary rock poetry – but at the same time I'm well aware that any insight revealed whilst tripping might well be breathtakingly subjective and utterly alien to its composer.

The classy and currently hot US folk-rock duo Brewer & Shipley were frequently subjected to this type of interpretation – not least by myself – and when I interviewed them in mid-'71 for both Record Mirror and Cream I questioned them about lyrics and meaning. To an extent, Mike Brewer and Tom Shipley had asked for it; no-one outside Kansas City knew what a 'toke' was until Brewer and Shipley popularised the word in their hit song "One Toke Over The Line", giving them an instant 'head' constituency. In fairness to Brewer & Shipley, they intended the song merely as a filler album track – but it got released as a single by Buddah Records who knew a hit when they heard, or smelled, one:

Cream, July 1971

...what about their lyrics? Do people read much into them?
"Oh, we get this all time. We get people coming up to us and saying how deep and meaningful some song or the other is, and how much it gets through to them. And we just didn't write it that way. One of our songs is called 'Pig's Head' and we wrote it about one of those riots – a friend of ours had been around at the time and got involved. These demonstrators were throwing real pigs' heads – you know, the ones you buy at the butchers – at the police! Now, we're really anti-violence, and that's an anti-violence song. But

462

people come up to us when we're playing and say "G'on man, sing that song about killing the Pigs"!

"Some of our songs are just straight literal things. Like 'Can't Go Home'. We had to write that one quickly to complete 'Tarkio Road' – and that's something we don't like doing – 'cos we couldn't go home at the time. And one of the lines said 'singing songs I never sung before.' Well, that's exactly what we'd been doing. Singing songs for the new album."

But a lot of their songs have real depth, I countered. What about 'The Light'...religious imagery...? Brewer and Shipley gave each other a look I still haven't figured out.

"That's another example of reading things into our songs. We wrote that when we were in a car, we wrote it in about an hour, using the basic riff for 'Mary had A Little Lamb'. In fact, that was another of the rush songs for 'Tarkio Road', and I think it's my least favourite song on either album." That was Mike talking.

"A lot of singers must just make those lyrics up in the studio," said Tom, 'like some of those lyrics on Dylan's 'Blonde On Blonde'. I'm sure he must have created that imagery in the studio. But whatever you write, whether you write it fast or slow, deliberately or spontaneously, it's still you that's coming out. You just can't help it. In fact, the easier it flows, the more representative of you it's likely to be. I like to keep writing as free as possible."

Serious literary critics explain all this quite nicely by making a distinction between the 'verbal meaning' of a text (what the author intends) and its 'significance' (what that text means to an individual reader – which will depend upon his or her individual circumstances). The same applies to rock lyrics, and although plenty of rock fans were barely listening to lyrics, plenty of others were currently placing the most fantastic interpretation on them. A famous example was Charles Manson and the twisted Armageddon scenario he'd recently and murderously constructed from his readings of songs from recent Beatles' LPs, which included presumably deluding himself regarding the Beatles' intention and connivance.

463

But what also got rock fans listening to Brewer and Shipley, apart from the dope song, were the other musicians involved. Producer Nick Gravenites, who'd earlier exported the white Chicago blues scene – Paul Butterfield, Elvin Bishop, Mike Bloomfield et al – to San Francisco, then worked with Janis Joplin and Quicksilver Messenger Service, had recruited such stalwarts as Bloomfield, Nicky Hopkins, Red Rhodes, Mark Naftalin and Jerry Garcia for Brewer and Shipley's first two Buddah albums "Weeds" and "Tarkio Road". Unfortunately for B&S, they dispensed with Gravenites for their next album "Shake Off The Demon", produced it themselves, and lost some of the subtlety and balance Gravenites had brought to their music.

Brewer & Shipley's lyrics, whatever they might mean, were nevertheless straightforward compared with those of their ex-Buddah labelmate Captain Beefheart. In giant artistic strides, Beefheart had progressed from "Safe As Milk" in '67 to the psychedelically overloaded "Strictly Personal" a year later, and thence to old pal Frank Zappa's Straight label for the avant-garde masterpiece "Trout Mask Replica" in '69. Beefheart followed it with the similarly breathtaking "Lick My Decals Off Baby" in 1970, and at the beginning of 1972, following Straight's collapse, emerged on Reprise for "The Spotlight Kid", a growling work of swamp-blues genius that managed to be both highly accessible yet still crammed with his trademark cross-rhythms, fanciful time signatures, superlative musicianship and – once you figured out what you thought they meant – awe-inspiring lyrics.

Captain Beefheart and the Magic Band were back touring the UK in spring '72. He was more popular here and in Europe than America, and in London filled the Albert Hall: the gig there was stunning in its power and virtuosity. Reprise was using ace publicist Tony Brainsby for Beefheart during the tour, and when I arrived at his office to interview Beefheart, Tony seemed uncharacteristically nervous. Highly-strung though he was, Brainsby was usually jovial and super-confident; tall, skinny, red hair, suit with skinny tie, glasses, quite unique actually, and most likeable.

He sat hunched in his chair. "Are you high?" he demanded.

"No!" I replied indignantly.

"Smoke this quick, then," he said, thrusting a US-style reefer of extra-potent grass into my hand, exhorting me to take ever-deeper tokes.

"You'll need it in there!" he explained in deadly seriousness, indicating the room where Beefheart was presumably ensconced. I'd only half-finished the joint before Tony ushered me in: it was a large-ish room and Don was sitting behind a desk and to my astonishment I could see his aura. He looked a lot different to when I'd last met him, back in 1968 in the dingy hotel room in Kensington. In addition to the aura, he seemed considerably larger – stouter. This wasn't unexpected as I'd already caught his stage act. The interview, such as it was – I'd never previously interviewed anyone when this stoned – couldn't be published in the next issue of Record Mirror because of time and space constraints, although Peter Jones persuaded me to extract a few paragraphs concerning Beefheart and Paul McCartney for his Keeping Up With Jones diary, with the hippy-ish article/interview proper published the following week.

RM w/e 1st April 1972

COME OUT PAUL...BEEFHEART'S HERE!

UNDERGROUND hero Captain Beefheart surfaced in London with a plea: "Where are you, Paul McCartney?" and being a helpful sort of diary page, we echo: "Come out, Paul, wherever you are".

Point is that Paul is the Captain's favourite Beatle. He said: "They could have come to see me anytime, because I couldn't very well go and see them. But only Paul came to see me...in Cannes, in 1968. But I haven't been hiding!"

Beef really laments their break-up. "What do they think they're doing? They did so much...you know what they did. And now, throwing all those rocks at each other – specially at McCartney.

"He was right all along. It was a shame their music got so complicated. When they were doing 'I Wanna Hold Your Hand', that was it. No, I wanna meet Paul Again. But where is he? How do I get to him?"

A final cryptic message from the Captain, "There are big-eyed beings from Venus and they're right here among us.". His next album, appropriately, "Brown Star".

I guess I must have mis-heard the Captain, because a major track on his forthcoming album "Clear Spot" (not "Brown Star") would be "Big-Eyed Beans From Venus". Close enough, though.

RM w/e 8th April 1972

LOVE OVER GOLD

CAPTAIN BEEFHEART talks to RM readers

FIVE years ago the magic name of Captain Beefheart was no more than an imported LP in the window-display of clique-ee One-Stop Records. There it caught the eye of Peter Meaden, entrepreneur extraordinaire and ex-protege of Andrew Oldham.

So fascinated was Peter with the LP (simply titled 'Safe As Milk') that he purchased it and upon listening, realised that the Captain was, to quote a recent Warner Bros. Press handout, 'a cosmic genius'. The rest is history, of sorts. Peter hustled himself almost out of business to bring 'The Buddah Package Show' to London in 1968 from Cannes' Midem festival – it included Captain Beefheart and his Magic Band, Penny Nichols, and the sadly under-rated Anders & Poncia (remember the Tradewinds...the Videls... the Innocence?).

Beefheart was already known to John Peel (for John had met Beef in the USA) and 'Safe As Milk' received regular airings on John's radio shows. But Beefheart's course of reality didn't run smooth. Pye (who leased Buddah) declined to issue 'Safe As Milk' until pressure became so strong that they put it out...in mono! It made the charts... and its producer Richard Perry (of 'Nilsson Schmilsson' fame) is quoted as declaring 'Safe As Milk' his best job of work.

Other records followed, charting the Captain's progress through the stormy seas of more and more reality: 'Strictly Personal', 'Trout Mask Replica', 'Mirror Man', 'Lick My

Decals Off Baby' and now 'Beefheart's most accessible recording to date' – 'The Spotlight Kid'.

Beefheart, alias Don Van Vliet, is currently engaged in a sell-out tour of the UK – at the Albert Hall there were queues of fans being turned away from a full house – a far cry from the days of '67. But is all this as far as Beef can go? Can he ever be another T. Rex? Is his popularity strictly limited to the long-haired freaky underground set? The Captain thinks not. He is, as he insists, a real artist. But can he be accepted as such with his...full figure?

"I'm working on this," he told me, pointing at his ample frame. "People find it difficult to accept me as an artist like this." But he proved his point at the Albert Hall, when he strode around the stage, looking powerful and sounding penetrating. It's only one of the many jams that the Captain is always engaged in kicking out – on behalf of himself and Spaceship Earth. We talked about women.

"I'd known my wife for years before I..."

"Before you met her," he explained.

"Right," I said.

"Everywhere you go, it's all cock," said Beef. "Penis buildings sticking up everywhere. I want to build some cunt buildings. For women."

Somehow we talked about Zappa.

"Ringo...getting mixed up with Zappa in that movie..." His vibe was disapproving.

"But you were involved with Zappa," I said.

"Don't talk to me about that. How can I answer you?" said Don,

"Zappa was putting it around that I was a freak. That I conceived all my music, wrote it, sung it, all on acid. LSD-25. Twenty-five...I'd TELL everyone if that was true. I did it all without acid. I did it all on reality. But Zappa put me in a box."

He gesticulated to show me how he felt.

"But you'd KNOWN Zappa already!" I whined.

"Yes, yes! But don't you see. I thought that the consciousness of myself and my band could get to him. I thought we could. But I couldn't. He's so uptight. Always trying to prove to everyone that he's a MAN."

If all this gives the impression that Beefheart bears grudges or is a negative person, then I've given the wrong impression. Beefheart is incapable of negativity – but unlike most artists he's capable of telling the truth, as anyone familiar with his records will know. He has the supreme artistic gift of TOUCHING a reality inside anyone who cares to listen to him. He's intense...and truthful.

"How's Record Mirror?" he asked.

"Oh...they've been taken over by Billboard," I replied.

"Billboard! Not Billboard! The Mirror...taken over by Billboard!"

He was so astonished he got up from his chair and walked around, and sat down again.

"And there's a new policy," I added. "Appealing to the young...the thirteen year-olds".

"Do you know thirteen year olds? They're BEAUTIFUL," said Don. "And we're another generation."

"Maybe you could give me a message for the young readers", I asked.

"Tell them 'I'LL LOVE THEM IF THEY LOVE THEMSELVES.'"

"And tell then 'LOVE OVER GOLD'", he added.

The Captain then rapped at some length about the Beatles (see last week's Record Mirror, Peter Jones' column).

We talked about lots more things (including Don's ecology warnings on his early albums) but, sadly, Record Mirror has no more space for any more of Don's reality.

Just remember that he's a man who loves us all. If you don't believe it – go and buy 'The Spotlight Kid' and by the time you've played it a few times you'll have a new friend.

The article reads like I was still stoned when I wrote it, as did much what I wrote at the time: my head was wide-open, I was trippy as anything and stayed that way for ages. Appropriately, I caught the archetypal trip band the Grateful Dead at the cavernous and still-chilly Wembley Empire Pool early in April '72, and the following month caught them again – and Beefheart, too – when I covered the Bickershaw Festival in Lancashire near Wigan. But my all-too-brief marriage with Ruth was falling apart, and taking her with me to Bickershaw proved a bad idea: my negativity coloured the review. Nevertheless it truly was one of those festivals where the music was terrific and everything else terrible:

RM w/e 13th May, 1972

BICKERSHAW

DID JONI Mitchell REALLY write "we are stardust, we are golden?" Well, maybe she did, but then she never went to Woodstock anyway.

And sure as hell she never went to Bickershaw where 40,000 candidates for the Aquarian Age, deceived by false promises of "proper facilities" and spellbound by Design Centre typefaces, grovelled in the mud hoping to be hypnotised by rich rock musicians doing their thing – making even more money.

The organisers, to give them maximum credit, did lay on some good music and must have paid for it in advance. To be sure, lots of groups didn't turn up. Maybe they didn't get any deposit – therefore no return. I dunno what happened to Spirit, Roy Harper, Memphis Slim, Third Ear Band, Maynard Ferguson Big Band, Dion, or Stackridge. I didn't see them.

The festival area was heavily, but inefficiently guarded (I made about seventeen in-and-out sorties without any aggro, so any enterprising punter would have had no trouble). There was a good high stage ("...after being elevated to this lofty position" – Ray Davies) with fine lighting and some imaginative backcloth work by Joe's Lights throughout.

The between-act facilities were generally good, especially on Saturday night when the "History Of Rock'n'Roll" movie was jerkily screened. At least I'll always remember Bickershaw for seeing Carl Perkins sing "Glad All Over."

BUMMERS

The announcements were the usual pot-pourri of "Do-this-do-that" warnings to the punters, and Woodstockian announcements, some of which were real bummers – "there has been a three year old boy missing since yesterday afternoon", "will so-and-so come to the Release tent urgently for her fix of insulin", delivered in that studied John Peelian English doper voice.

If you were prepared to camp for two days at the front of the area in a makeshift city of disposable sleeping bags, plastic corrugated roofs, unbelievably pervasive mud and an atmosphere of bad food, discomfort and dope (they sure needed that dope down there) then you got some fine music.

You saw Dr John put out a bit of New Orleans, complete with night-tripping tinsel-and-saxophone glory ("a bit of Louisiana corn-ass music") and a beautiful vibe.

You saw Hawkwind's magnificent visual effects and heard their equally unmagnificent music; you could groove to Donovan, trade licks with Wishbone Ash, be affronted with Ray Davies, rock with the Flamin' Groovies, and boogie with Beefheart. You could get stoned with Brinsley Shwarz, sing-along with Country Joe or trip with the Grateful Dead and New Riders Of The Purple Sage.

The audience feedback problem must have hit the musicians. Only Hawkwind and Beefheart were "wanted" and the Flamin' Groovies had a tough time getting the compulsory encore. Ray Davies worked out his personal psychosis on the audience, pissed off his own group, and should have paid the crowd for the therapy.

If you didn't get near enough to see the performances, then the salvation bridgade on the outskirts really launched into you with brands of potential paradise.

Krishnaburgers, loaves-and-fishes, hashmescalineacidspeed, and hundred of mimeographed documents published the Untarnished Truth, all of which found their way into the incinerator together with the multitude of beer cans, fag packets, plastic cups, bottles ad nauseum that carpeted the festival area.

One bit of paper reads: "Yes folks, Bickershaw is undoubtedly a Grade A catastrophe. It's got the lot – over population, high technology, a disposable philosophy to match a philosophy of disposability, plastic food, and underneath it all, right up Bickershaw's arse: Kapitalism.

"And the people? They spend the days in an unreal, irrelevant world of distorted rock music, failing to make contact with their neighbours in Instant City and ignoring the garbage which this modular system produced. Something's wrong." Maybe THAT was the Untarnished Truth, or maybe it was just another leftie blurb.

Sitting near the stage watching the Kinks, someone trod on my hand and punched my neighbour's head and pushed their way through to the front. A while later my companion advised splitting, declaring that there's trouble. I didn't see any. But he smelt it. Five minutes later, the Hell's Angels – those sick adolescent products of a ignorant society – were thoroughly (and deservedly) beaten up by local heavies.

Later we gave a lift to some 16 or 17-year olds whose belongings (tent, money, CLOTHES – except for what they were wearing) had been ripped off by the Angels. "Go to the police and get them back," we said. "No," they replied. They were too disheartened, and their philosophy was that anything's better than a knife in the ribs.

Maybe if you're young enough, from a dreary home environment with nothing but a soul-destroying future, then maybe you could enjoy a festival like Bickershaw.

471

> *Maybe you could ignore the mud and the discomfort
> and the rotten stinking chemical food, the loos swimming
> with shit, vomit and urine, the people wandering around
> who should have been locked away, the sellers of instant
> paradise, and worse, all the other people like you.*
>
> *Maybe you saw rock as a banner for the future, an
> alternative vibration, a place to go and a place to stay. But
> unless someone or something gets it together to run a festival
> without the mammon motive, and unless they extend that
> vibe into everything they do, there'll be no hope for the
> "festival" goer today, tomorrow, or for the rest of their lives.*

How wrong could I be! In future years, Glastonbury would prove
a triumph of capitalist festival organisation. Maybe I'd have have felt
differently if I'd got down and dirty in the mud with the punters
instead of resting in comfort at a nearby hotel, thereby being insulated
yet again from the "authentic festival experience". Or maybe I'd have
hated it even more.

At the "new look" Record Mirror, Mike Hennessey was fond of the
bombastic concept series, and his first foray into this four-page pull-
out supplement-style genre was titled *The Great Ones*, which kicked off
with his own interview with John Lennon, a particularly useful piece
of work because he managed to get John to discuss the entire Beatles'
repertoire, identifying which songs John wrote by himself, which songs
Paul wrote by himself, and which songs they actually wrote together.
John evidently enjoyed this exercise, as the four ex-Beatles were still,
in Beefheart's words, "throwing rocks at each other". Hennessey
commissioned me to write *The Great Ones* piece on McCartney – merely
number eight in the series – but as the combined forces of Billboard,
Music Week and Record Mirror failed to secure me an interview with
Paul, I simply wrote a fairly preposterous and pompous profile piece
which included such breathtaking assumptions as:

> *...McCartney was also the unsure one. Unsure of his own
> ability as a writer even after many years of acclaim and*

472

success ("I was worried stiff when 'Hey Jude' came out in case it wasn't any good. I wasn't sure if it was any good. I can never tell.") Unsure of the Beatles early appeal ("When we played outside Liverpool, as often as not we would hire a couple of coaches and take our audience with us.") Unsure of where his head was at ("I was the last one to take LSD")...

Another of Hennessey's bombastic concepts was *The Immortals*, and I kicked this series off with a centre-spread on Buddy Holly (*The Day The Music Died* – a title not yet over-used: "American Pie" was still a current hit), and churned out further episodes on Gene Vincent and Johnny Kidd. I was beginning to feel I'd been relegated to the back numbers department as I seemed to be getting lots of work writing about rock'n'roll. Not only was I the mainstay of *The Immortals*, but my *Roll* column was proving so popular at NME that they were loading more and more R&R-related stuff on me: I profiled Chuck Berry, did features on British R&& acts the Wild Angels and the Houseshakers, did in-depth reviews on the superb "Cruisin'" series of US LP, and a lot more else besides. I guess their own journalists figured it might blow their cred to cover R&R – but I needed the money. I also got to interview Jerry Lee Lewis again, at a press reception where several journalists were sitting on both sides of a long table with Jerry at the head. Luckily I was seated next to Jerry and was able to talk to him easily. Unluckily this meant matching him drink-for-drink, and during the course of an extended lunch break Jerry proceeded to try to drink everyone under the table. Being the last man standing (or sitting upright), I was the one who got the full interview:

RM w/e 6th May 1972

WIFE TROUBLE FOR THE ROCKIN' CHRIST

LIFE CAN be tough for an ageing rock'n'roll star.
*   Not too many of them survive, but those that weren't cut down, countrified, retired, Las Vegased or depraved are just starting to feel the benefits of the camped-up fifties revival.*

The killer – alias Jerry Lee Lewis – has survived the obstacle race so far, and despite the sticky hurdles he's currently trundling over, he looks like making it to the end of the track – wherever or whatever that might be.

In the States Jerry has been riding the crest of a country wave for five years, and even allowing for his natural hyperbole (that means boasting), he's still clicked up an impressive list of big-selling country hits.

Jerry is expanding his range of activities into movies. He's even growing a beard for his next movie.

"It's about Christ. It's really a musical on the life of Christ, with about twenty-five songs, like the stage show 'Jesus Christ Superstar'. It's gonna be called 'The Carpenter'. It's all happening – they're putting up a lot of money on it."

"It's a long way from 'High School Confidential'," I said.

"Well, I just sang the one song on the truck. But I made more money out of that than all the actors did. It was good, but it was bad, too. I play my piano, sing, cut my records, do my shows. I don't know if I'm a great actor. But I've thought and thought about this movie.

"There never has been, and you mark my words, anybody who has ever played the role of Christ and made a success out of it. This film has got the most beautiful song I have ever heard in my life. At the Last Supper when Christ is sitting there with his Disciples. It's like I'm sitting here and talking to you, but it's a song.

"I'm not worried about it hurting my image, or my record sales. I just have a feeling to do this movie and I'm gonna do it. Basically I'm a religious person – I don't live it, I know what I am. But this movie is gonna be the biggest."

Jerry is a media manipulator. He's lost count of the number of times he's sung his rock hits like "Great Balls Of Fire", "Breathless", "High School Confidential" and "Whole Lotta Shakin' Going' On". In his interviews he gives the same answers to the same question. Every intonation is sincere, every one is identical.

Just like we all buy the same record, we all get the same answer told in the same way. And if Jerry drinks to forget all the repetition, he can't forget about his trouble with women. He jokes about it on stage, sings about it in his country weepies and gut blues, and confides to reporters about it.

In 1958 he came here with his second wife who just happened to be his 13-year old cousin. How did Jerry take it at the time, especially when his tour was cancelled and he was virtually hounded out of the country?

"I didn't care, I just laughed. I've been married five times now, but twice to Myra. I wanted to make it legal 'cos they said it wasn't legal, and I thought it WAS legal."

"Do you still believe in marriage?" I asked him.

"I believe in marriage if it's really a genuine marriage, if a man and a woman are joined together and really love each other. Not mixed-up kids – or mixed-up people – who don't know what they're doing. A genuine marriage is something I believe in. I don't think I've ever really found it yet. At least I married them – I've taken them and lived with them and shacked up with them, but at least I married them. I did right."

"Why did you marry them?" someone asked.

"That's a question. I shacked up with a flock of them. I could never count the number of women that I have been with. Does this make me the worst person in the world? Maybe it does, but I've been with some of the finest women in the world. My wife caught me with twelve women..."

Whatever motivates Jerry Lee Lewis into being the great artist and consummate entertainer that he is, it's apparent that he goes through a lot of pain. The process hasn't yet fully rewarded him for the joy he's given others. Here are his last words:

"But what is my situation? Love or what? I mean, I'd like to figure it out myself. It's like this movie we were talking about. I search for everlasting love. God is love. But I haven't made it. I don't believe I'm a no-good person,

I've always taken care of my family – I've given them everything I've ever made in my life.
"Yet look what happens in life. What are we struggling for?"

I guess all the R&R stuff was my karma coming back to me for all those articles I'd penned on Buddy, Chuck, Elvis, Johnny Burnette, Little Richard, Fats Domino et al. I even got work as a DJ – using my "Rockin' Henry" persona – at several Wild Angels, Houseshakers and R&R All-Stars gigs, turning up my shirt collar a la "Vince Everett" and brylcreeming my hippy hair into a semblance of authenticity. This wasn't difficult as I was be-quiffed for several teenage years until my conversion to bohemian modernism in 1960, and the skill of fashioning a decent quiff was forever deeply imprinted (I now like to think I must have looked like a Roxy Music prototype). DJ-ing was fun, and impetuously I sold the VW Beetle so kindly bought for us by my mother-in-law, investing in a specially-converted Bedford Dormabile to transport a state-of-the-art twin-deck DJ system purchased in partnership with Terry Chappell, intending to pursue a parallel career as a platter spinner. But the whole thing fizzled out after doing a wedding or two – in fact I was useless at self-publicity – and a few months later the entire kit and caboodle was "lost" in suspicious circumstances after lending it to a fellow-DJ.

However, the DJ thing would have fallen through anyway because in mid-'72 graphic designer pal Peter Burns, who ran the soul fanzine Earshot and had just sold his house, invited me to accompany him to America for a four-month coast-to-coast trip. How could I refuse?

We figured this trip would be an opportunity to indulge in some seriously interesting music journalism and straightaway I managed to acquire letters from the editors of Record Mirror, NME, and Melody Maker stating I was their accredited representative and appreciating any cooperation, allowing me to proceed without let or hindrance etc.

Everyone's first trip to New York is an event and it certainly was for me. Emerging from JFK in early September into the blazing sunlight, air charged with energy and pollutant particles, sucking on a coarse cigarette, standing watching the general hurly burly and organised pandemonium, ears assaulted by the clatter of yellow cabs, whistles, and all the yelling and the shouting, I almost burst with excitement at the sheer vibrancy of it all, at actually being here, now, in the New World. And then the cab to the city, and that first glimpse of the Manhattan skyline.

Our plan was to stay in New York for a month or so, then buy a car and drive across America, visiting Philadelphia, Chicago, Nashville, Memphis, Las Vegas, LA, San Francisco, up to Tacoma, then fly home. And that's what we did: staying with friends and acquaintances old and new, staying at various YMCAs and at cheap motels, writing articles and selling them in the UK and USA. Because we were English we were a novelty – very few UK music writers had done this, and so almost everyone we desired to meet marvellously and graciously made themselves available.

The news when we landed in New York was all Olympics. The day we arrived was the day the aptly-named Palestinian terrorist group Black September had kidnapped (and would murder) nine members of the Israeli Olympic team in Munich. And the German hosts didn't even stop the show.

The month we spent in New York was busy. We were privileged to be able to use Atlantic Records' office as a base, courtesy of head of promotion Pat Mulligan, a wonderful lady who set us up with interviews and contacts throughout the length and breadth of the NY music scene. But my first interview never got sold: it was with John Prine, about to have his second LP "Diamonds In The Rough" released on Atlantic, and currently appearing in Greenwich Village at the Bitter End. Prine was a hot "new" talent, and the interview was refreshingly candid:

> *"When I was in the military, I really thought it was worthless, and the only good thing about it was that it gave me a lot of time to just think, because there was nothing else to do...although you are supposed to look busy all the time. A lot of people when I started out thought I was singing protest songs, only because I was singing about social issues, but it just so happened that was what was*

going on. At the time, things around were very political. It's not that I was trying to be political – but that was what people were talking about and that's what the songs were about. It turned me off when people labelled me a protest singer. As a matter of fact I thought there were very human things which people could relate to regardless of how they felt politically – I had a feller from the Young Conservatives Party (sic) come up to me after a show (this was one of the nicest compliments I ever got) – he said 'I really wish you were on our side.' I said 'I am, I am!' He didn't understand. He missed the whole show!"

These USA interviews were all done using a cassette recorder, which I'd never bothered with in the UK. Back home it was churn-'em-out and forget 'em, and besides, my note-taking ability and memory, despite periodic assaults on my brain cells, were still good. But Peter bought a Panasonic cassette recorder in New York for the interviewing, citing "authenticity", and I concurred. It was certainly better at catching speech verbatim, but it was tedious transcribing the tapes: it took longer to transcribe the interview than ever it took to write the article. We were also lugging around a fancy Valentine design-winning portable typewriter, so together with the vast amount of free LPs being accumulated, we were toting a considerable stack of gear, especially cumbersome as we were continually moving in and out of this and that apartment, in and out of various Y's – including, in our naivety, the notoriously gay Central Park YMCA, a real eye-opener for me when I went to take a shower one evening.

We caught dozens of gigs: the reorganised Isley Brothers at the Bitter End with Ernie Isley on biting guitar sounding like their old friend Hendrix. They were dynamite, but the blacks in the audience booed their version of Neil Young's "Ohio", and myself, I didn't much care for their "Lay Lady Lay". Nearby at the Village Gate we saw the great LaBelle, and Jimmy & Vella – both WB promo gigs; Rod Stewart and the Faces triumphed at Madison Square Gardens where the audience threw fireworks – mainly bangers – in the air which was kind of worrying; Loudon Wainwright III, Hamilton Camp, both terrific at Max's Kansas City; Slade at the NY Academy

478

of Music. In the UK Slade were huge; "Mama Weer All Crazee Now" was currently top of the UK pops and they were slugging it out with fellow-glamsters T. Rex and Gary Glitter for the top spot on a regular basis. Not in America, though. Backstage I talked to them, but with one ear cocked at bill-toppers J.Geils jamming on "You're So Fine" with Hank Ballard who'd dropped in:

RM w/e 30 September 1972

SLADE START FROM SCRATCH

WHAT'S big in England ain't necessarily big in America. Not yet, anyhow. But Slade are having a lot of fun starting from the bottom again – this time without that sensationalist publicity that clad them in Brutus shirts, braces, and bovver boots. How fashions change!

"This tour is really to get experience," said Noddy, "it's like a feeler for us, learning how American audiences are different to British audiences, learning how to cope on the road, learning which numbers to do. And learning about sound..."

"We've always been considered loud in England," said Jimmy, "but over here we've been lost. We've had to stick mikes in front of everything and the gear's been so battered about it's dropping to bits."

Noddy was delighted the band was getting such a good reaction, especially from audiences that had never heard of them: "We know that when we go down a storm over here it's purely because of the act we do on stage, not any records we have.

"We're learning so much, we started from scratch here again. In England we go down well anywhere, but now in America we we have to work our knackers off to get to those audiences. It's going great!

"One of the problems is that being bottom of the bill we only get about half an hour. You only just get going, and then you're off. And if you've got a possible encore – forget

it. The lights are being turned on and they're getting ready for the next band.

"Yet we've had this incredible reaction – promoters saying they've never had the first band on a bill go down like us – usually the first band on is a warm-up, and that's it. But the promoters have been saying, 'If you can get off like that starting the show you'll have to do your own tour."

Slade interrupted their US tour to open the new Sundown rock venue in the Mile End Road and Noddy enthused.

"It was fantastic, probably one of the best gigs we've ever played. That place is going to be a fantastic gig and it was really worth the trip to go back and work it. We weren't too happy about it at first but we knew we had an obligation to do it because it had sold out. I suppose we could have blown if we'd wanted to, but we thought, well, we'll go back and do it."

"It's only the same as we'd do here," interrupted Dave, "I mean, from England to America if we had something special."

"When we first went to the Rainbow," explained Jimmy, "we played there and filled the hall – we were used to small clubs and we thought '...all these people come to see us!' Then we got to Long Beach and saw 18,000 people! Going back to the Sundown didn't bother us, it seemed so small, like playing in a bog"

GROUPIES

"Every gig's got better here," explained Noddy, "and at the end of the tour we'll know what to do here next time. We needed this tour to find out what it's all about. Every band has to find out the same way about America"

"There another thing you get over here," said Jimmy, "and that's people trying to get into our hotel rooms. There was a feller who said he was a reporter from Rolling Stone. So we phoned Polydor to check him out and they'd never heard of him. And the groupies..."

"The best in the world," said Don.

"The hotel we stayed at in LA, that's known as the groupie hotel," said Nod. "They all sit around waiting in the foyer, waiting for the groups to arrive. They know the whole schedule...the flight, the itinerary. They know who they're gonna pull. It's ridiculous, they know everything. When we were in Chicago two nights ago...you wouldn't believe it. Home movie cameras and all!"

"I woke up in the morning and there were these two birds," said Jimmy in his inimitable way, "and one of them came into my bedroom and pulled the sheets off me and screamed, 'Hey, he's in the nude! Let's get him!'"

Earlier in the day Polydor held a press conference for Slade. The interest in the music was minimal but Noddy aptly described the questions – and answers.

"They asked us nothing about the band or the music – only sex, groupies, drugs, what cream we used on our haemorrhoids. That's all they asked us, nothing else.

"I don't think they're interested in the music, not seriously or anything. They even asked us about politics! They were into everything – everything but the music. It was great though, it was a great laugh.

Slade went on to talk at length about plans for forthcoming American tours, but as for their or their managers' obsession with "breaking America" – it would never happen. In America they were perceived as part of the UK Glam Rock movement, and Glam would never dominate mainstream pop in the States like it did in Britain. Slade would have stood a much better chance in the States without their Glam threads. Purely on the music they were sensational: at the Academy gig, J.Geils sounded feeble following them.

There were plenty of old friends and acquaintances from the UK working, visiting, or just bumming around in Manhattan and this was especially pleasing when funds ran out, which was frequently. My first Record Mirror mentor Ian Dove was now editing Billboard in New

York and paid me in cash for the features I was currently writing which he'd select to use either in Billboard or its sister consumer magazine Hit Parade. Neil Bogart at Buddah also forked out handsomely for a short biography Peter Burns had written on current US LP chart-topper ("Superfly") Curtis Mayfield, thanks to an introduction from ex-UK PR Nancy Lewis, now at Buddah and who would shortly – after sterling efforts – introduce America to Monty Python's Flying Circus. And Jimi Hendrix's much-maligned co-manager Mike Jeffery, known to me from the UK R&B scene, proudly showed us around his plushly innovative Electric Ladyland studio and then, discovering we were broke (again), laid some hefty bills on us. Mike would die a year later in a mid-air collision over France – and decades later the Hendrix estate is still in contention.

Still churning out the rock'n'roll for NME (the UK gig lists were being handled for me in London by Terry Chappell) a mutated *Roll* – temporarily retitled *Rockin' Henry Cruisin' In The US of A* – reported back a bunch of current NY R&R exclusives including the Broadway premier of future phenomenon "Grease" – grittier than subsequent versions – at the Broadhurst Theatre. I was surprised and somewhat strangely gratified to discover that oldies were such big business in New York: Richard Nader's Original Rock 'n'Roll Revival Spectacular (Volume 10) package tour hit Madison Square Gardens on October 13th and featured Chuck, Bo, the Coasters, the Crystals, the Dovells, Gary U.S. Bonds, Chubby Checker, the Five Satins and Bobby Comstock (I'd interviewed several of these acts first time around!) There were also several 24-hour oldies radio stations on the air, including the powerful WCBS-FM, a revelation to Brits acclimatised to the BBC airwaves monopoly and dodgy AM waveband.

One of the best press receptions I ever attended anywhere was for The First Fabulous Fifties Flick Festival ("six movies for the price of one": "Blackboard Jungle", "Jailhouse Rock", "The Wild One", "Rock, Rock, Rock", "The Thing", plus a Bill Haley short) at the Ziegfeld Theatre, where the pre-movie press reception boasted the biggest and best buffet I'd ever laid into, and also featured an impressive motorcade of famed fifties' wheels including an Edsel and a custom '56 Chevy, plus a well-publicised dress-up '50s competition. The organisers had supplied some decent prizes like tape machines, radios, stacks of

LPs, and hired a gang of resting actors to dress like rockers in case no genuine contestants turned up. But turn up they did – real rockers too, a scary bunch from the depths of Brooklyn, who chased away the phoney '50s actors and grabbed the goodies; their ponytailed "Peggy Sue" was especially awesome and justly walked away with the first prize. The whole thing was so perfect that it couldn't but remind me in no uncertain terms that America was the homeland and birthplace of original rock'n'roll and was still doing it better than anyone else.

There also were gigs galore which I reported back for the *Roll* column: the re-formed Ben E. King and the Drifters (the classic "There Goes My Baby" line-up); Len Barry and the Dovells, Johnny Maestro and the Crests, Jay & the Americans, R&R revivalists Flash Cadillac & the Continental Kids, and Sha Na Na (these latter two always vying with each for the "50s Rock Championship", whatever that was), the latest incarnation of the Platters, and the amazing Wayne Cochran: "...he looks like a sweaty Conway Twitty with a platinum-blond candy-floss wig that stands a full six-inches above his head. Or maybe it's his hair, I dunno..." On the oldies trail we met with Florence Greenberg at Scepter where I literally bumped into the burly shoulder of the legendary Morris Levy of Roulette Records – one of those Americans who registered a surly frown of contempt at my shoulder-length hair and hippy-ish attire.

But oldies were still oldies, and it was the contemporary NY scene that was where it was at, certainly in terms of selling features. I interviewed ex-Fug Ed Sanders whose book on Charles Manson "The Family" was published in 1971. Ed was likeable, smart, funny, and told me insider stuff about Manson and his mad family that made my long hair nearly stand on end. He also told me all about his and his publishers' current litigation with The Process, a post-LSD religious group with an interesting God-Lucifer-Satan belief system that Ed had claimed – wrongly, it seemed – was linked to Manson and his grim antics. The Process would win the case but unfortunately for them several hundred thousand first editions of "The Family" had already been sold containing the libellous chapter, which was removed in later editions.

Another interesting interview was with Danny O'Keefe, a singer-songwriter currently in the US top ten with his third recording of his soon-to-be-a-standard "Good Time Charlie's Got The Blues", and was also high on the album chart with "O'Keefe". Atlantic Records distributed O'Keefe's label Signpost and were anxious I interviewed him while he was in town as he was touring nationwide on the back of his hit. We caught up with him in a mid-town hotel where he was staying with his roadie. O'Keefe was a terrific talent and a highly intelligent individual: he also turned us on to cocaine, which I'd never tried before and was still then known as "the millionaire's drug" on account of its exorbitant price and its popularity among celebrities and gangsters.

O'Keefe would never achieve greater success as an individual artist than he was having at that moment, but he would go on to create some memorable albums. His next, "Breezy Stories", would manage to get itself astonishingly a full-page rave review in the columns of The Sun in the UK, thanks to their music writer Mike Nevard's appreciative ear. Nevertheless, O'Keefe would triumph big-time as a writer: "Good Time Charlie's Got The Blues" was cut by, among others, Elvis, Willie Nelson, Charlie Rich, Waylon Jennings, Jerry Lee and Mel Tormé. "The Road", another fine song from the same album, was cut by Jackson Browne for his 1975 masterpiece "Running On Empty". It was a shame that O'Keefe, with his beautiful evocative voice, couldn't have been heard by more people.

Singer-songwriters were currently popular and fashionable and the latest rave for discerning pop connoisseurs, and we caught the mesmerising Jackson Browne at a promo gig thrown by Atlantic, who seemed like a stand-alone company but nowadays were part of the WEA group – Warner-Reprise/Elektra/Atlantic – which distributed Asylum, Browne's label. Asylum had been set up by David Geffen and Elliot Roberts primarily to showcase Browne's talent, but then they discovered – and nurtured – the Eagles, who'd kicked off their career with Browne's "Take It Easy". Wandering around the Browne press party munching canapés and quaffing champagne, I bumped into Andrew Loog Oldham and his business partner Tony Calder, Andrew looking and seeming quite hippy-ish, and being very friendly. He was vague about what he was up to, but seemed a lot more relaxed than when he was masterminding the Stones. Mind you, he said the same thing about me.

The most memorable gig we saw in New York was James Brown at the Apollo in Harlem. This had been a must. I'd phoned the Apollo theatre one morning, reeled off my credentials, and was told to come along at a certain time later that day, which we did, by cab: "I don't wanna frighten you guys, but stay as innocuous as possible" warned our driver. Outside the Apollo a hefty queue snaked around the block with not a single white face among the multitude. As requested, we made our way to the box office and to my horror were instructed to go directly into the still-empty theatre and sit wherever we liked, two white long-hairs given special privileges. This did not seem to me like "staying innocuous" and a certain amount of trepidation set in. Frankie Crocker was the dynamic MC, and very entertaining he was too, but the legend himself, the Godfather Of Soul, exceeded all expectations:

RM w/e 30th September 1972

"...it was James Brown's last appearance in his current season and, together with the great Bobby Byrd, his band the JBs ("Another big hand for the JBs") and Lyn Collins the Female Preacher ("I want every woman whose man don't do her right to stand up!"), he put on an ultra-tight, ultra-funky review.

He stills draws capacity crowds, two-hour queues, and he still leaves the stage in a state of near-collapse, with an aide throwing a robe over his sweating body. And he still staggers off, and just before reaching the edge of the stage (and inspired by the funky music the JBs are putting down) throws off the robe and leaps back to the mike for another chorus or two."

Here on his home turf James indulged himself and his doting audience with an uncomfortable (for us) amount of lengthy, preachy and virulent between-song platter extolling the virtues of Black Power and all that went with it, causing us to shrink down into our seats even deeper. But it was all show business. All eyes weren't riveted on to us even if felt like they were: we were barely noticed. The revue gave

485

excellent value, and when we finally got outside it was two o'clock in the morning. We didn't know which direction to walk in and couldn't see any cabs. Bunches of guys in pimp hats were jiving us at every corner, and the general Harlem ambience began to feel threatening. I suddenly became nervous. Then, just as a four or five mean-looking dudes began to make a move on us, a local yellow cab zoomed out of nowhere, screeched to a halt, flung open his door and rescued us: "Bin to see James Brown, fellers..." he crooned, driving us back through a Central Park heaving with illegal nocturnal activity.

The only time on this trip we were directly threatened with violence – and this in the crime-ridden New York of the early '70s – was when walking with Linda Solomon of Chess Records (who also wrote a US column for the NME) and a couple of other new friends down a dark street in Greenwich Village leading on to Washington Square when we were jumped by a white guy with a blade. We all took off like a shot except one of our number, a big Canadian, who stayed to face up the knifeman... who turned and fled. Brave, but a tad foolish, I thought. Linda was a generous person who knew the US music scene inside out – we spent a lot of time with her; she laid loads of Chess goodies on us, and gave us some invaluable contacts for the next part of our trip, to Chicago.

Peter Burns was writing a book on the Drifters and to please him I phoned, purely on the offchance, the offices of legendary writer-producers Jerry Leiber and Mike Stoller to request an interview. I held no real hopes for this, but amazingly got straight through to Stoller, told him who we were and what we doing and asked for an interview with him and Jerry. "Why not," he said.

Next day we spent several hours with the urbane pair who, at that time, had seldom been interviewed in any depth. I suppose we were a novelty for them, a diversion from their considerable musical and business interests, and the interview proved very entertaining: Mike and Jerry were passionate, serious, funny and – to an extent – frank about their career. The interview was published in UK Cream and US Pop Monthly, and to my chagrin, wherever I'd written the words 'rock'n'roll' or 'rock'n'roller', some patronising would-be-hip Cream sub-editor had altered it to the new rock journalism spelling 'rockanroll' and 'rockanroller'(thankfully soon obsolete), making me cringe and very cross.

I found it interesting that Leiber and Stoller were enthusiastic fans of the Beatles and their producer George Martin, though they were predictably dismissive about their former protégé Phil Spector's efforts on "Let It Be".

Pop Monthly, December 1972 / Cream, January 1973

MIKE AND JERRY'S LOONEY TUNES

"...we didn't TRY to do everything. Nobody can do everything, unless you're the Beatles."
This led to a heated discussion about whether or not the Beatles could, or did, do everything. But Jerry stuck out that they did, and gave his reasons.
"There was the fact that they all played and sang. One of OUR biggest problems was translating the work from the page on to the tape. Mike played piano, but the minute you're the producer of the record, you're the guiding board, the shaping board, you're not doing it, and so there is a link broken in that creative chain that maintains control over the work until it reaches its final result. So there's quite a difference between an organic group that sings, and writes and plays its own stuff, and writer-producers who must give their work to other people to, in some degree, translate all the time, and then to other musicians who are outside the realm of the initial creative situation to play things for you. Sometimes marvellous things happen because you DON'T control them. Sometimes you control things and they get very fucked-up because they're OVER-controlling the situation – and I'm referring to the Beatles' situation – I'd say that was the IDEAL situation for the best work to happen. The work maintained its integrity from the inception of the idea to the completion of the record."

Mike and Jerry had just returned from London after producing the debut LP by Stealer's Wheel, which I wouldn't get to hear till its UK release the following year. One evening several months later back in London, I was driving to the Speakeasy and "You Put Something Better Inside Me" came on the radio. I thought how uncannily similar it was to the Beatles and not until later discovering it was Stealers Wheel. Then I remembered Leiber and Stoller saying how much they liked the Beatles. But they'd hated the slow pace of producing Stealers Wheel: despite their stated appreciation of the talents of Joe Egan and Gerry Rafferty, Leiber and Stoller were appalled at a situation where half-written songs were brought into the studio and finished off in studio time. That didn't stop them producing the group's second LP, the gorgeous "Ferguslie Park", a year later after "Stuck In The Middle" had charted globally. But for that LP they used session musicians.

Next stop was Chicago, via Philadelphia, in a VW Beetle ('Bug' in USA-speak) bought cheap in Harlem. For the first few days in Chicago, thanks to Linda Solomon, we stayed with Steve Goodman and his wife Nancy Pruter. We couldn't stay long because Nancy just had their first daughter, but the couple's hospitality was warm and generous. Goodman was one third of "the trinity of the Chicago folk scene", the other two thirds being John Prine and Bonnie Koloc. Steve and Nancy lived on Chicago's North Side where a flourishing folk scene was centred on the Earl Of Old Town pub and where we caught gigs not only from Steve (a riveting performer), but other local folk luminaries including Koloc, Ed Holstein, Jim Post, and Ramblin' Jack Elliott.

Arlo Guthrie was currently chugging down the national charts from a high point in the top twenty with Steve's song "City Of New Orleans" ("...the best damn' train song I ever heard" – Kris Kristofferson) which would become an American standard, cut by – among dozens of others – Willie Nelson, John Denver, Johnny Cash, and Judy Collins. The word generally applied to Steve Goodman's songs is "bittersweet", a word which also applied to his short life: a few years previously he'd been diagnosed with leukaemia – not that you'd know it from his bright demeanour, devoid of self-pity – and he would die from the disease twelve years later in 1984.

The Chicago music scene was rich and vibrant. Folk, country, blues and soul music flourished. Nancy Pruter arranged for us to stay with their friend Bill Redhed, a university lecturer in English, who was also a folk musician. Bill lived in a house of historical architectural importance which was always being admired by groups of students from all over the world. But however big the Chicago folk scene was, it was dwarfed by the Chicago soul scene, and several local soul luminaries were in high-profile residence. Curtis Mayfield and his red-hot Curtom label, distributed by Buddah, had just moved into new premises on Lincoln Avenue, and while I was beavering away transcribing tapes and dashing off articles and newsletters at Redhed's classy pad, Peter Burns interviewed Mayfield, returning with a fistful of unreleased demos Curtis laid on him. Meanwhile, Mayfield's friend and erstwhile partner in the Impressions, Jerry Butler, was still performing but nearing the end of his hitmaking solo career, and was moving in a new direction – one which would eventually lead him into the political arena in which he now resides:

NME w/e 23rd December 1972

THE ICEMAN COMETH

CHICAGO's BLACK population – now 50 percent of the city's souls – has a hero in Jerry Butler. The Iceman, as he's known to his friends and fans, had an idea back in '68 for a music workshop in Chicago which would service and finance writing and performing talent, especially black talent.

Necessity forced Butler to realise the project after he split with Gamble and Huff, the production-and-writing team responsible for his string of hits in the late sixties.

His ideas must have sounded like a good business investment because finance came from the publishing giant Chappell's, and now – two years after its inception – the Workshop has a past, a present and a future.

Butler and his team, half a dozen young black writers and artists, have smashed into the charts with material performed by themselves and other artists: the Dells, Wilson Pickett, Aretha Franklin and Jerry himself.

We met Butler, an impressive and formidable character, at the Butler Music Workshop where he was in company with his old friend and mentor Calvin Carter, co-founder and A&R genius of Vee-Jay Records. Carter, who also participated in the interview, told me I looked like Mick Jagger: "I wish I had his money," I said. "I wish I had his broads!" retorted Calvin. After the interview we relaxed over a glass of wine with house writer Larry Wade, who'd co-penned with Terry Callier the previous year's Dells' smash "The Love We Had (Stays On My Mind)", as fine a soul record as has ever been recorded but which I rarely play because it makes me cry. Larry laid a slim spliff on us for our return journey to the North Side, containing some of the finest grass I've ever smoked, making the Beetle feel like it was floating, with a gorgeous sunny autumn afternoon in Chicago helping everything along nicely.

There was so much happening in New York and Chicago, and later in Nashville, Memphis, and Los Angeles, that in addition to sending single-artist features back to the UK, I was also able to churn out 'USA newsletters' from those musical cities for the UK pop press, all crammed with info, gossip, reviews and opinion. It was turning into a productive trip.

The road from Chicago to Nashville is straight but long, and after negotiating Chicago's interminable and jaw-droppingly decrepit South Side – into which it seemed to me you could drop Harlem and lose it – we at last hit the fabled mid-west. Our plan was to drive to Nashville in a single stretch, which we didn't quite manage: even with copious handfuls of No-Doz, pathetically, the only stimulant I could lay my hands on. We ground to a halt at a big empty all-night diner a couple of miles outside Nashville at four in the morning. Peter slept in the car; I was so wired I wandered into the diner and further poisoned myself with more caffeine while the waitress, the only other person there and intrigued at a long-hair Englishman arriving in the middle of the night, kept playing me her current favourite hit on the juke-box – Chi Coltrane's "Thunder And Lightning".

At dawn's early light we drove to Nashville's bus station for breakfast, where we shared a table with a young hippy woman who called herself Ramona, after the Dylan song, who'd hitchhiked from San Fransico with her baby, Ocean, heading across country to a famous commune, a vast acreage a hundred miles or so south of Nashville. This sounded interesting, so after breakfast we drove her there, the last leg of her long journey. But when we finally arrived after many a mishap (I'd got ill with all the caffeine), the snotty hippy crew at the gated entrance astonishingly refused entry to Ramona and Ocean, accusing her of "speeding" (taking amphetamines rather than driving too fast), therefore rendering her unable "to telepath" – apparently a commune requirement. So we drove her back to Nashville and dropped her off at the Salvation Army hostel, but not before sliding into a ditch and having to be hauled out by a middle-aged local farmer with tractor who, gallantly though unsuccessfully, offered to take on both Ramona and Ocean, a possibility she seriously considered for a while, stating fiercely and with some justification that he was a better man than all the smug hippies up the road.

Back in Nashville we walked gawping down Music Row. A smiling Carl Perkins look-alike, fingering us as long-hair rubes, cadged a dollar to "get a jug together" but, unlike Carl, looked like he might be hiding a mean Southern streak (rather like Carl's Dan the razor man – "born and raised in a butcher's shop") which would instantly emerge if we refused. Nashville proved to be a gas, but unfortunately by the time Cream got round to publishing my Nashville newsletter it was six months or more out of date. Nevertheless it covered the spectrum, a snapshot of Nashville in late '72:

Cream, May 1973

COMPUTER AMONG THE COWBOYS

Cute signs embellished with guitars (what else!) indicate the outer limits of Music City USA: Nashville. On Broadway, Nashville-style, a paradise for country fans exists. At the Country Music Automobile Museum you can see 'The Cadillac Hank Williams Died In!' Or take the WSM-sponsored Grand Ole Opry tour past Music Row and all the big record company studios (set appropriately in ranch-style suburban residences), past the Grand Ole Opry house itself (due for demolition this year) and – as a thrilling climax – to view the estate of Johnny Cash.

491

If you want to see your idols in the flesh you won't be so lucky. But you can see them in the wax! The Country Music Wax Museum features effigies of Kity Wells, Marty Robbins, Johnny Cash and many others, and if they don't turn you off your food, then try a tasty Twittyburger nearby, or snack in style at Tex Ritter's Chuck Wagon. Record shops present mainly country fare (with soul usually segregated in an unlit corner), Ernest Tubb's Record Store sends sounds all over the world, while loudspeakers on the street blare Hank Williams and Merle Haggard.

But dig a little deeper and a more interesting Nashville emerges. Studios are opening everywhere – the demand for Nashville's session pickers is getting heavier and heavier as the feedback between country and rock grows and grows. At Ray Stevens' Sound Laboratory, engineer Ben Tallon built his own 32-track studio with some of the most devious electronic aides available. He's presently waiting for a computer (not quite invented, but not long to go...) to take away the grind of going back and hand-mixing the mix eventually required – in future the computer will store the information on each mix and produce the desired product at the push of a button or two.

Ben, who previously worked with Jack Clement, Owen Bradley and Monument, claims the studio is almost fully booked for the next year or so. Bob Johnson has already booked 50 per cent of studio time for this year, and artists' schedules include B.B.King and Andy Williams: "Now, Ray calls in for a session and I tell him we're fully booked," said Ben drily.

Just down the road is Troy Seals, just signed as the first artist-producer for Atlantic Records' new country venture. Troy was on the road for almost 12 years with a tight R&B band that often backed James Brown and included Troy's wife Jo-Ann Campbell: "When the Beatles came along we just couldn't get into it," says Troy. "We were into short hair and mohair suits – we dug the music but we couldn't see ourselves changing." Troy, who often worked with

492

his friends Jerry Lee Lewis, Wilson Pickett and Conway Twitty, is producing an album on Dobie Gray, the "In Crowd" man for MCA. He has some exciting ideas for the Atlantic deal and his band will include a girl fiddle player – Lisa Silvers.

Dig even deeper and some decidedly un-Nashvillian activities emerge. At the Exit-In club, a double-movie programme Reefer Madness (a 1936 government-sponsored movie to get the then-legal weed outlawed) is showing, together with the Firesign Theatre's Martian Space Party, plus the Kossi Gardner Group – a great jazz team. At the nearby Calamity Jane's some of the worst excesses of acid-rock are realised in the personalities of George And The Arizona Star. George (a lady) has short hair, a velvet dress (also short), long legs, boots, a real sword and a dragon tattooed on her rump. The Arizona Star is a Monroe archetype who never stops acting. Their songs include "Do It To Me", "Latin Movie Star", "Tattoo Man", "Garbage Head", "Boogie Man", "Let's Hook It", and "Tony The Gangster".

"It was real rednecksville when we came," said George, whose ambition is to leave Nashville. Their act recently slid to a halt because of undue violence directed towards their backing group by locals. They weren't sure whether or not their projected happening would come off. "Probably not," says George, "someone would get killed".

This last comment was no exaggeration, as the current talk of the town was of recent drive-by random shootings of harmless hippies. What I didn't mention in the newsletter was the awesomely-big sackful of grass stashed in full view in the corner of Ray's studio. And, of course, Troy Seals' productions on Dobie Gray were about to launch "Drift Away" on to the world.

It was another of Linda Solomon's contacts who provided us hospitality in Nashville: Travis Rivers, then managing the hot country rock outfit Mother Earth featuring Tracy Nelson. Rivers was an interesting character: originally from Austin, Texas, where he'd hung out with such local luminaries as Janis Joplin, Sir Douglas Quintet, and psychedelic pioneers the 13th Floor Elevators, he moved to the SF Bay area where he founded and edited the famed alternative paper Oracle, then decamped to Nashville with Austin originals Mother Earth. A couple of days after we arrived, Travis suggested we might just want to talk to a friend of his who lived opposite. "Who might that be?" I enquired. "Scotty Moore, he used to play with Elvis," replied Travis. Struck dumb at the opportunity I nodded frantically and less than twenty minutes later was sitting opposite the legend himself. One of the things I asked him was what was his favourite guitar break of all the Elvis records he played on:

"I guess I'll have to say a thing called 'Too Much, and that's simply because I was lost. And that was the take they used – the one where I can't duplicate myself. If you ever get the chance to listen to it you'll hear what I mean. It came out OK though. I went into a thing and got all balled up but it kinda works itself out...I was lost, absolutely lost."

We Elvis fans know what he means. And we can replay that terrific solo – at least in our head – note for note...

The road from Nashville to Memphis is also straight, but not too long, and en route we picked up a hitchhiker, Memphis resident James W. Anderson, who offered us hospitality. James was a sweet guy invalided out the US Army after being badly hurt in Vietnam and who – like so many other wounded veterans (including John Prine's "Sam Stone") – had emerged with a heavy drug habit. Plenty of his friends had similar problems. They weren't hippies, they were pretty much all-American guys, but they'd got so fixated on injecting themselves they'd cook up and inject any drug, from aspirin to LSD. "What happens when you shoot acid?" I had to ask. "It comes on quicker – but not as quick as you might think," replied one of James' ex-army buddies while fixing an acid trip for Halloween. I decided this was an experience I could forgo.

The three best-known recording studios in Memphis were Sun Records, closed down at that time; Hi Records, riding high with quality talent like Al Green and Ann Peebles; and likewise the famed Stax studio. I did no interviews in Memphis: soul man Peter Burns went along and covered Stax, interviewing Isaac Hayes and Steve Cropper and then partying at Hi Records. I sat in James Anderson's house all day catching up with tape transcriptions and writing articles to send back to New York and London, my only excursions a stroll along Beale Street and a half hour hanging out by the gates of Gracelands hoping Elvis, then on tour, might return in some swish motorcade. No such luck.

Driving across America "from sea to shining sea" has the quality of a rite of passage. From Memphis we caught Route 66, following it for the next few hundred miles, then diverting via the awesome Hoover Dam to Las Vegas where I was briefly arrested: my doppleganger, it seems, was an English con man. Leaving Las Vegas we drove to Los Angeles, discovering, as most first-time drivers do in LA, what a bewildering and scary place it is to motor to and through. There we looked up an old colleague, Allen McDougall, former NME staffer and now chief publicist at A&M Records' HQ situated in the quaintly historic (for Hollywood) Charlie Chaplin Studio. Allen, charming and enthusiastic, was liberal with the coke and grass, and advised us to check out the newly-opened E (short for 'English') Club on Sunset Boulevard, run by Rodney Bingenheimer who, according to Allen, was a big fan of English music.

Rodney, who later became a famous DJ, was singularly obsessed with glam rock and with its stars and their groupies, who were also stars, according to Rodney, but most of all with David Bowie, who he insisted would be arriving at the club any moment. Although the club was empty, Rodney decided that as I was English it was appropriate I man the turntables. This I did till Bowie arrived with a small entourage. They looked exhausted: Bowie was currently promoting "Ziggy Stardust" and though he was the hottest thing globally in pop music, that afternoon seemed a bit of a drained old Ziggy.

Once Bowie was seated, Rodney elbowed me from the turntables so he could showcase his own DJ routine, but to his disappointment nothing he played had any effect on the slumped superstar. Rodney was near to tears that his esoteric glam selection was failing to move Bowie, who appeared too zonked and distant ("coming down" was how I would have characterised it) to enjoy himself. Nevertheless, pity for Rodney overcame me, and though I hesitated to exhaust Bowie any further, I whispered to Rodney that if he played "Brown Sugar" by the Rolling Stones, David would get up and dance. Though sceptical and slightly hostile, the desperate Bingenheimer dug out a copy of the Stones' disc. Sure enough, the irresistible intro to "Brown Sugar" jerked Bowie to his feet and he began dancing like a weary marionette manipulated by a merciless puppetmaster. Curiously, none of his entourage joined him. Everyone just gazed at him as he reluctantly christened the E Club dance floor with his undoubted glam-and-glitter magic. When the record finished and he sat down, we went over and introduced ourselves, us being the only other people in the club apart from Rodney. But Bowie was so tired and disinterested he could barely focus, let alone speak. We crept out, leaving Rodney with his triumph.

I was still contracted to feed my *Roll* column, so a visit to Art Laboe at Original Sound Records – the first "Oldies-But-Goodies" label – plus a Ron Holden gig at Laboe's Sunset Boulevard club replacing a no-show Rosie, of Rosie & The Originals, and an interesting conversation with the ebullient Rockin' Ronny Weiser of the Hollywood Rock'n'Roll Club managed to fill a few more columns. But I was getting tired of writing about oldies. More to the point, I had come to realise I had become terminally tired of pop music reporting altogether.

Travelling north from Los Angeles we left the music business behind, staying with friends near San Francisco and then Tacoma, astonishingly selling the VW there at a profit, and then jetting back to London from Seattle via Chicago. The four-month trip was over – and also, I decided, was my career as a music reporter.

From '61 until '72 I'd been writing about pop music, firstly as an active participant at the heart of the zeitgeist – the seminal '60s UK R&B scene – but now, as the music of the '70s was getting into its stride, I was little more than a barely-interested observer. The music had changed and so had I: contemporary pop, the glam and the glitter, didn't much grab me. Yet my love for music was as strong as ever, and on returning to London in 1973 I was able to discover other musical and journalistic arenas to explore, arenas that would rekindle my original exuberance and enthusiasm. But never again would I experience that strange, vivid, and curiously satisfying sensation I had during those first magic years at Record Mirror – the feeling I was a character in a play which was being acted out in the real world... because, for a while, I guess I was.

INDEX

Hollies 100-1, 121, 122, 123, 124, 207, 287, 295, 347-8
Holloway, Brenda 191
Holly, Buddy 29, 31, 34, 50, 57, 66, 79, 88, 91, 103-9, 114-5, 124, 137, 199, 261, 330, 332, 345, 370, 390, 473
Hollywood Argyles 291
Hollywood Flames 78
Holstein, Ed 488
Honeybus 388, 417
Honeycombs 202, 237, 276
Hooker, John Lee 89, 109, 124, 175, 202, 301
Hopkins, Nicky 103, 464
Houseshakers 473, 476
Houston, Bob 461
Howard, Ken 276
Howes, Arthur 205
Howlin' Wolf 28, 67, 89, 98, 109, 164, 200, 201
Hugg, Mike 153, 168, 283
Humperdinck, Engelbert 327, 361, 416
Huston, Chris 102

I

Ian Campbell Folk Group 230-1
Ideals 28
Ifield, Frank 49, 122, 137,
Ikettes 301

Impalas 26
Impressions 137, 164, 208, 248, 352,443, 489
Incredible String Band 421
Indo-Jazz Fusion 449
Innocence 402, 466
Iron Butterfly 278
Irwin, Big Dee 135, 175
Irwin, Colin 73
Isen, Ben 157, 168, 229
Isen, Rita 168, 229
Isis 223
Isley Brothers 110, 309, 443, 478
Isley, Ernie 478
Ivy League 258, 295

J

J.Geils Band 479-81
Jackson, Chuck 199, 268-9, 337
Jackson, Mahalia 173
Jackson, Siggy 154-6, 437
Jackson, Tony 154, 185
Jackson, Wanda 258
Jacobs, David 180, 194, 227, 253
Jagger, Mick 69, 70, 74, 117, 135, 142, 180, 190, 253, 279, 303, 328, 348, 384-7, 490
James, Elmore 384
James, Etta 164, 191
James, Jimmy (& The Vagabonds) 258-9, 275, 301-2, 354-7, 375, 411
James, Stu 270

James, Tommy (& The Shondells) 287
Jan & Dean 41, 110, 208, 298
Jardin, Al 312
Jay & the Americans 483
Jay, Peter (and the Jaywalkers) 51, 113, 302, 359, 371
Jaynetts 137
Jeffery, Mike 220, 458, 481
Jennings, Waylon 484
Jimmy & Vella 478
Jive Five 26
Jivetones 26
John Barry Seven 31, 90
John, Elton 390
John, Little Willie 248
John's Children 366-8
Johnny & the Hurricanes 8, 62
Johnson, Bob 492
Johnson, Langley 51
Johnson, Marv 191
Johnson, Mick 395
Johnston, Bruce 377-81
Jones, Brian 69, 74, 99, 117, 135, 142, 206, 270, 288, 428
Jones, Casey (and the Engineers) 79, 170
Jones, Davy 57
Jones, Ken 261
Jones, Nick 394, 415
Jones, Paul 151-3, 168, 201, 283, 296, 299
Jones, Peggy 'Lady Bo' 116
Jones, Peter 15-16, 19, 20, 21, 22, 30, 31, 32,

Lewis, Jerry Lee 78, 89,
90-7, 118, 124, 143,
181, 210, 243, 244,
268, 345-7, 420, 473-
6, 484, 493
Lewis, Nancy 482
Lewis, Rudy 148, 195
Lewis, Sir Edward 17,
128, 148-9, 262, 449
Leyton, John 29, 34,
41
Licari, Nannette 419
Lightfoot, Terry 41
Lightnin' Slim 80
Lind, Bob 289
Little Caesar and the
Romans 27
Little Eva 45, 136, 197
Little Hank 356
Little Richard 6, 41,
46-7, 52, 83, 87, 102,
113, 117, 118, 120,
121, 134, 169, 171-3,
202, 232, 237, 246,
320, 365, 476
Liverpool Scene 449
Locking, Brian
'Licorice' 135
Lockwood, Sir Joseph
200
Lomax, Jackie 102
Lopez, Trini 121-2
Lord, Jon 245
Loss, Joe 180, 253, 310
Love 296
Love Affair 416, 417
Love, Darlene 137, 160,
197, 286
Love, Mike 312, 381
Lovin' Spoonful 188,
282, 296, 321, 381
Lowther, Henry 283
Lukas, Feri 1, 238

Lulu 180, 270, 396, 414,
416
Lymon, Frankie (and
the Teenagers) 6,
26, 55, 63
Lynn, Vera 258
Lyon, Ben 209

M

Mabbs, Val 449
Mackenzie, Scott 365
Mad Mike and the
Maniacs 26
Maestro, Johnny (and
the Crests) 483
Magnus, David 91, 94-
5, 100
Maharishi Mahesh Yogi
399-400
Majors 103
Mama Cass 381
Mamas and the Papas
282, 321, 381, 396,
406, 408
Mancini, Henry 310,
312
Manfred Mann 142,
151-3, 168, 185, 200-
1, 207, 220, 260, 281,
282-3, 287, 295, 296-
7, 299, 327, 360-1,
395, 448
Mann, Barry 286
Manson, Charles 463,
483
Manuel, Richard 393
Marathons 27
Marauders 137
Marcels 23, 33, 62
March, Peggy 110, 197
Margo, Phil 387

Mar-Keys 348, 350
Marmalade 417
Marsden, Gerry (and
the Pacemakers) 42,
81, 82, 102, 113, 118,
120, 126, 137, 185,
196, 198, 204, 212
224-229, 353, 357,
372-3
Marsh, Jimmy 91
Marshall, Joy 255-6
Martin, George 196,
365, 487
Marvelettes 64, 88, 89,
164, 188-9, 301, 396
Marvin, Hank 118, 180,
252, 258, 310, 396
Massereene and
Ferrard, Lord 138
Maus, John 291-2, 303,
321, 325
May, Barry 72, 162,
195, 217
May, Phil 396
Mayall, John (& the
Bluesbreakers) 144,
237, 382-4
Mayfield, Curtis 238,
248, 482, 489
Mazzola, Lorraine 419
McCann, Les 393
McCartney, Paul 2-4,
52-3, 111, 125, 143,
213-4, 219, 239-241,
270, 284, 373, 393,
452, 465, 472-3
McCoy, Charles 409
McCullin, Donald 366
McDaniels, Gene 23,
41
McDevitt, Chas 28, 31
McDougall, Allen 495
McGowan, Cathy 270

S

Sainte-Marie, Buffy 236, 260
Sakamoto, Kyu 91
Sam & Dave 348, 349, 350
Sam The Sham & The Pharaohs 270, 301
Sampson, Dave (and the Hunters) 31
Samuels, Jerry 312
Sanders, Ed 483
Sanderson, Tommy 100
Sandon, Johnny (and the Remo Four) 109
Santana 293
Sapherson, Fred 347
Sartre, Jean Paul 441
Savile, Jimmy 180, 227-8, 253, 311
Sawyer, Phil 390
Schmolzi, Horst 278, 355
Schroeder, John 259, 356
Scott, Jack 46
Scott, Linda 41
Scott, Simon 175
Seals, Troy 492-3
Searchers 42, 102, 110,118-9, 121, 122, 154, 169, 180, 185-6, 197-8, 206, 295
Seekers 270, 327, 363, 396
Selwood, Clive 419, 422
Sha Na Na 483
Shadows 33, 58, 89, 118, 137, 153, 180, 252, 258, 310, 383, 396
Shafto, Bobby 210

Shallit, Emil 154
Shangri-Las 252, 390
Shannon, Del 23, 34, 41, 66, 88, 126, 145, 218-9, 396
Shapiro, Helen 31, 34, 41, 121, 270, 316-7, 359, 390
Sharp, Dee Dee 39, 58, 88, 120
Sharpe, Martha 337
Shaw, Sandie 252, 253, 270, 311
She Trinity 310
Shep and the Limelites 26
Sheridan, Tony 89
Shipley, Tom 462
Shirelles 23, 28, 33, 34, 52, 57, 62, 83, 121, 134, 164, 180, 194
Shouters 26
Showmen 57
Shuman, Mort 139-40, 407
Silvers, Lisa 493
Silvester, Victor 121, 261
Simon & Garfunkel 321, 331, 362-4, 434
Simon, Paul 362-4
Simone, Nina 266, 352
Sinatra, Frank 351, 380, 406, 428
Sinatra, Nancy 272
Sinks, Earl 106
Sir Douglas Quintet 494
Six Teens 26
Skip & Flip 291
Skyliners 42
Slade 479-81
Sledge, Percy 336, 422

Small Faces 282, 310, 311, 321, 345, 396, 434
Smedley, Oliver 319
Smith, Ethel 5
Smith, Huey 'Piano' 232
Smith, Jimmy 78
Smith, Mike 417
Smiths 389
Smythe, Frank 218
Softones 26
Solohettes 42
Solomon, Linda 486, 488, 493
Sommerville, Brian 233
Sonny & Cher 270, 306-7
Soul Sisters 167, 251
Sounds Incorporated 172, 180, 252, 253, 310
Sounds Orchestral 252
Spanswick, Kim 338
Spector, Phil 52, 62, 135, 142, 146-50, 158, 168, 198, 219, 220, 286, 287, 293, 305-6, 389, 452, 487
Spencer Davis Group 184, 282, 321, 328-30, 371, 389-90, 428
Spencer, Jeremy 382, 384
Sperling, Deedee 205-6
Spidermen 42
Spirit 469
Springfield, Dusty 66, 180, 206, 252, 253, 270, 310-1, 321, 396
Springfields 66, 137
St. John, Barry 247
St. John, Dick 205-6, 224

Lightning Source UK Ltd.
Milton Keynes UK
UKOW02f0218091114

241324UK00001B/5/P